Black Americans and Organized Labor

Black Americans and Organized Labor

A New History

Paul D. Moreno

Louisiana State University Press ✷ Baton Rouge

Designer: Amanda McDonald Scallan
Typeface: Minion
Typesetter: G&S Typesetters, Inc.
Printer and binder: Edwards Brothers, Inc.

Library of Congress Cataloging-in-Publication Data
Moreno, Paul D., 1965–
   Black Americans and organized labor : a new history /
Paul D. Moreno.
      p.   cm.
   Includes bibliographical references and index.
   ISBN: 0-8071-3094-x (cloth : alk. paper)
   1. Labor unions—Social aspects—United States—History.   2. African American labor union members—History.   3. African Americans—Civil rights—History.
4. Discrimination in employment—United States—History.   5. United States—Race relations.   6. African Americans—Employment—History.   7. Labor movement—Political aspects—United States—History.
8. United States—Politics and government—1865–1900.
9. United States—Politics and government—20th century.
I. Title.
HD6490.R22U649 2005
331.88′089′96073—dc22

                                        2005001806

This book is dedicated to Lisa:

the good, the true, and the beautiful.

Contents

Acknowledgments

I am grateful for the help of many individuals and organizations in the preparation of this book. I benefited from the encouragement of scholarship from administrators and colleagues at Hillsdale College on a daily basis and am especially grateful for my good friends and colleagues in the Department of History and Political Science. The John M. Olin Foundation awarded me a junior faculty fellowship that enabled me to spend a year in research and writing. The Hayek Fund for Scholars also provided assistance. The help of the library at Hillsdale, especially Judy Leising, was indispensable. I am also grateful to the staffs at the University of Michigan and Michigan State libraries, the Library of Congress, the Wayne State University/Reuther Library, the library of the University of Wisconsin, and the George Meany Memorial Library. I am most obliged to the individuals who read and commented on all or parts of the manuscript: Jonathan Bean, Andrew Kersten, Burt Folsom, Mel McKiven, Ray Wolters, and Kevin Murphy (Murph—we're even). I'm fortunate to have had the staff and anonymous readers of LSU, especially Sylvia Frank Rodrigue and MaryKatherine Callaway, guiding the editorial and publication process. I am most grateful to my wife, Lisa, who also read the manuscript, and to whom the work is dedicated.

Abbreviations

The following abbreviations are used for commonly cited sources. Roman numerals are used for volume (print), reel (microfilm), or group/series (archival) numbers; Arabic numerals for page (print), frame (microfilm or fiche), or box (archival) numbers.

ANB   John A. Garraty and Mark C. Carnes, eds., *American National Biography,* 24 vols. (New York, 1999).

BND   John B. Kirby, ed., *New Deal Agencies and Black America in the 1930s,* 25 reels (Frederick, MD, 1983).

BTWP   Louis R. Harlan, ed., *The Booker T. Washington Papers,* 14 vols. (Urbana, 1972–89).

BWGM   James R. Grossman, ed., *Black Workers in the Era of the Great Migration, 1916–29,* 25 reels (Frederick, MD, 1985).

CBP   *The Claude A. Barnett Papers: The Associated Negro Press, 1918–67,* Part 3: Subject Files on Black Americans, Series C: Economic Conditions, 1918–66, 13 reels (Frederick, MD, 1984).

DH   Philip S. Foner and Ronald L. Lewis, eds., *The Black Worker: A Documentary History from Colonial Times to the Present,* 8 vols. (Philadelphia, 1978–84).

DHIS   John R. Commons et al., eds., *A Documentary History of American Industrial Society,* 11 vols. (Cleveland, 1910).

DuBP   *The Papers of W. E. B. Du Bois,* 89 reels (Sanford, NC, 1980–81).

FEPC   Bruce I. Friend, and Charles Zaid, eds., *Selected Documents from Records of the Committee on Fair Employment Practice,* 213 reels (Glen Rock, NJ, 1970).

HNCF   Hampton University Newspaper Clipping File, microfiche.

LC   Library of Congress.

LCCR   Papers Leadership Conference on Civil Rights Papers, Library of Congress.

NAACP 1   *Papers of the NAACP,* Microfilm edition, Part 1: Meetings of the Board of Directors, Records of Annual Conferences, Major

Speeches, and Special Reports, 1909–50, 28 Reels (Frederick, MD 1981).

NAACP 10   *Papers of the NAACP,* Microfilm edition, Part 10: Peonage, Labor, and the New Deal, 1913–39, 23 reels (Frederick, MD, 1981).

NAACP 13A   *Papers of the NAACP,* Microfilm edition, Part 13, Series A: Subject Files on Labor Conditions and Employment Discrimination, 1940–55, 21 reels (Frederick, MD, 1981).

NAACP 13B   *Papers of the NAACP,* Microfilm edition, Part 13, Series B: Cooperation with Organized Labor, 1940–55, 25 reels (Frederick, MD, 1981).

NAACP 13C   *Papers of the NAACP,* Microfilm edition, Part 13, Series C: Legal Department Files on Labor, 1940–55, 12 reels (Frederick, MD, 1981).

NAACP 13S   *Papers of the NAACP,* Microfilm edition, Part 13, Supplement, 1956–65, 16 reels (Frederick, MD, 1981).

NAACP   Papers of the NAACP, Library of Congress.

NNBL   Kenneth M. Hamilton and Robert Lester, eds., *Records of the National Negro Business League,* 14 reels (Bethesda, MD, 1994).

NUL   National Urban League Papers, Library of Congress.

RG   National Archives Record Group.

SCCF   Schomburg Center for Research in Black Culture, Schomburg Center Clipping File, microfiche (New York, 1974–).

SGP   Stuart B. Kaufman et al., eds., *The Samuel Gompers Papers,* 9 vols. to date (Urbana, 1986–).

UNIA   Robert A. Hill, ed., *The Marcus Garvey and Universal Negro Improvement Association Papers,* 9 vols. (Berkeley, 1983–95).

Black Americans and Organized Labor

Introduction

Today, black Americans are the demographic group most likely to belong to a labor union: 17 percent of black wage earners are union members compared to 13 percent of the population as a whole.[1] Blacks and organized labor are also close political allies in the Democratic Party. These facts are the mirror image of the case a century ago, and indeed throughout most of American history, when black workers and organized labor were bitter antagonists. Union exclusion and job competition figured prominently in several American race riots. Frederick Douglass wrote of the "folly, tyranny, and wickedness of labor unions"; American Federation of Labor president Samuel Gompers warned that "Caucasians are not going to let their standard of living be destroyed by Negroes, Chinamen, Japs, or any other"; communist leader William Z. Foster complained that blacks were becoming a "race of strikebreakers"; and A. Philip Randolph, who would eventually become the principal figure in uniting blacks and organized labor, in 1919 called the AFL "the most wicked machine for the propagation of race prejudices in the country."[2]

Similarly bitter has been the controversy among historians who explain the problem of racial discrimination in the American labor movement. Predominantly hostile to business, American historians have depicted organized labor as a heroic, progressive force.[3] But as the civil rights movement brought the issue of racial equality into focus, the discriminatory role of labor unions became more apparent. The first generations of labor historians generally ignored it. The "new labor historians" of the 1960s, in their effort to tell the story "from the bottom up," were embarrassed to find that the rank and file were usually more racist than the union leaders on whom the first generation of labor historians had focused. Many

---

1. U.S. Department of Labor, Bureau of Labor Statistics, *News*, 25 Feb. 2003.

2. Frederick Douglass, "The Folly, Tyranny, and Wickedness of Labor Unions," *New National Era*, 7 May 1874 [DH II: 178]; Samuel Gompers, "Talks on Labor," *American Federationist* 12 (Sep. 1905), 636, 638 [DH V: 124]; William Z. Foster, *The Great Steel Strike and Its Lessons* (New York, 1920), 208; *The Messenger* 2 (May-Jun. 1919), 7, quoted in Sterling D. Spero and Abram L. Harris, *The Black Worker: The Negro and the Labor Movement* (New York, 1968 [1931]), 390.

3. Louis M. Hacker, "The Anticapitalist Bias of American Historians," in Freidrich Hayek, ed., *Capitalism and the Historians* (Chicago, 1954), 64–92.

of the new labor historians attempted to vindicate labor unions' racial practices.[4] Others, more influenced by the black civil rights movement, undermined the rosy depiction of black-union relations.[5] Their followers have been locked in battle ever since.

No problem better illustrates "the liberal-center versus radical-left argumentation that dominates American historical thinking."[6] The liberals defend organized labor and emphasize "class." The radicals attack white unions and emphasize "race." The controversy reflects the crisis of the New Deal order in the 1960s and historians' appraisal of the labor movement at the center of that regime. Liberals were most likely to blame employers for working-class racism, using the Marxist "divide-and-conquer" thesis: capitalists deliberately foment racial antagonism to keep the proletariat divided and weak. Radicals, on the other hand, regarded race-consciousness as overwhelming class identification, so pervasive that it was as much a part of working class as employer psyches.

The "divide-and-conquer" explanation of racial conflict in the labor movement is a very weak one.[7] Left-wing economists began to recognize its limitations in the 1970s and devised an alternative explanation, the "split labor market" theory, in which employers respond to, but do not create, competition among groups of workers. "In sum," sociologist Edna Bonacich writes, "the prejudices of business do not determine the price of labor, darker skinned or culturally different persons being paid less because of them. Rather, business tries to pay as little as possible for labor, regardless of ethnicity, and is held in check by the resources and motives of labor groups. Since these often vary by ethnicity, it is common to find ethnically split labor markets."[8]

Though split labor market theorists tried to preserve a kernel of Marxian analysis, they actually came close to various neoclassical, public choice, and "eco-

---

4. Herbert Gutman, "The Negro and the United Mine Workers of America: The Career and Letters of Richard L. Davis and Something of Their Meaning, 1890–1900," in Julius Jacobson, ed., *The Negro and the American Labor Movement* (Garden City, NY, 1968), 49–127.

5. Herbert Hill, "Myth-Making as Labor History: Herbert Gutman and the United Mine Workers of America," *International Journal of Politics, Culture, and Society* 2 (1988), 132–200.

6. Alonzo Hamby, *Liberalism and Its Challengers: FDR to Bush* (New York: Oxford University Press, 1990), 10.

7. See appendix.

8. Edna Bonacich, "A Theory of Ethnic Antagonism: The Split Labor Market," *American Sociological Review* 37 (1972), 553.

nomics of discrimination" theories, which have received almost no attention from historians.[9] Thus, many historians, perhaps unhappily recognizing the similarity of split labor market and neoclassical theories, have abandoned economic analysis of the problem altogether and taken up the "cultural studies" mode that describes the "construction of whiteness."[10] Whatever value these studies have in describing the cultural sources of racism, they flee from useful analyses of the economic motives and, most especially, of the costs and benefits of racial discrimination.[11] Other historians have taken up the challenge of defending the class-based divide-and-conquer interpretation, fearing that "the current rage to demonstrate the social construction of race and white workers' agency in creating their own racism has left capital largely off the hook, with workers dividing themselves and capital merely walking away with the proverbial shop."[12] Labor historians have illustrated cases in which white unionists did act in racially egalitarian ways, and there certainly were cases in which employers used "divide-and-conquer" tactics. Most of these were in southern (particularly Alabama) or declining, "sick" industries, or during times of heightened racial tension, such as that following the Supreme Court's 1954 school desegregation decision. These were exceptional cases that do not explain the phenomenon.[13]

9. Michael L. Wachter, "Primary and Secondary Labor Markets: A Critique of the Dual Approach," *Brookings Papers on Economic Activity* 3 (1974), 666; Robert E. Hall, "Comment," ibid., 688; Thomas D. Boston, *Race, Class, and Conservatism* (Boston, 1988), 93; Patrick L. Mason, "The Divide-and-Conquer and Employer/Employee Models of Discrimination: Neoclassical Competition as a Familial Defect," *Review of Black Political Economy* 20 (1992), 73–89.

10. Bonacich noted that her theory explained the paradox of the conflict between economic and ethnic democracy, "without having to resort to psychological constructs like 'authoritarianism.'" "A Theory of Ethnic Antagonism," 558.

11. For critiques of "whiteness" theory, see Eric Arnesen, "Up from Exclusion: Black and White Workers, Race, and the State of Labor History," *Reviews in American History* 26 (1998), 164; Arnesen, "Whiteness and the Historians' Imagination," *International Labor and Working-Class History* 60 (2001), 3–32; Peter Kolchin, "Whiteness Studies: The New History of Race in America," *Journal of American History* 89 (2002), 154.

12. Arnesen, "Up from Exclusion," 156.

13. Daniel Letwin, *The Challenge of Interracial Unionism: Alabama Coal Miners, 1878–1921* (Chapel Hill, 1998), is a mild defense of Gutman that actually shows employer manipulation of racial antagonism but also shows how all parties could play the race card. Mining the same sources is Brian Kelly, *Race, Class, and Power in the Alabama Coalfields, 1908–21* (Urbana, 2001), who makes a more forceful argument than the evidence permits. Demonstrating that even Alabama was variegated, see Henry M.

The history of racial discrimination in the American labor movement better supports the neoclassical and public choice models of the "economics of discrimination."[14] Though often strident and partisan, the race-based analysis of racism in American labor history is more accurate.[15] Its advocates have not gone far enough, however. While grasping that unions have usually acted as "white job trusts," they fail to see that this is because unions are, first of all, job trusts.[16]

Like the split labor market theory, the "economics of discrimination" interpretation assumes that "business tries to pay as little as possible for labor, regardless of ethnicity." If employers are racially prejudiced, they may favor workers of one race over those of a disfavored race who are equally or more efficient. If they do so, they will pay for it in terms of a less productive work force. In a competitive labor market, another employer will recognize that he can profit by employing members of the disfavored race, and eventually this will make it more costly for employers to indulge in their taste for discrimination.[17]

It is important to recognize what this theory does not claim. It cannot be reduced to the simple idea that "market forces eliminate discrimination." There are many reasons why an efficient market will not eliminate discrimination, or even reduce it very much. Most important, if there are more than enough workers of the favored race who are roughly as efficient as workers of the disfavored race, employers will be able to indulge in discrimination without cost.[18] Workers of the favored race often are, on average, more efficient than workers of the disfavored race and so discrimination against the latter is "rational." When it is more costly to

---

McKiven Jr., *Coal and Iron: Class, Race, and Community in Birmingham, Alabama, 1875–1920* (Chapel Hill, 1995).

14. For a good overview of the various liberal theories, see William A. Darity Jr., "What's Left of the Economic Theory of Discrimination," in Darity and Steven Shulman, eds., *The Question of Discrimination: Racial Inequality in the U.S. Labor Market* (Middletown, CT, 1989).

15. Nelson Lichtenstein, "Walter Reuther in Black and White: A Rejoinder to Herbert Hill," *New Politics* 7 (1999), 133–47. For Hill's views on advocacy history, see *International Journal of Politics, Culture, and Society* 2 (1989), 591–93, and Ronald Radosh, *Commies: A Journey through the Old Left, the New Left, and the Leftover Left* (San Francisco, 2001), 86–88.

16. Herbert Hill, "Lichtenstein's Fictions Revisited: Race and the New Labor History," *New Politics* 7 (1999), 157.

17. Gary Becker, *The Economics of Discrimination*, 2d ed. (Chicago, 1971). W. H. Hutt provided an argument along similar lines for South Africa in *The Economics of the Colour Bar: A Study of the Economic Origins and Consequences of Racial Segregation in South Africa* (London, 1964).

18. Paul H. Norgren and Samuel E. Hill, *Toward Fair Employment* (New York, 1964), 87.

identify the more efficient individuals among the generally less efficient group, it makes economic sense to use race as a proxy for merit. Employers also may favor a one-race work force because the introduction of workers of another race would lead to complaints by the incumbent group—this is known as "employee discrimination."[19] Finally, employers respond to the discriminatory tastes of their customers.

The "economics of discrimination" analysis is not a "monocausal explanation of racial discrimination."[20] It is not a causal explanation at all. It does maintain that there are *costs* associated with discrimination—that, most of the time, discrimination is not free. It is a better explanation of discrimination by labor unions than it is of discrimination by employers.[21] It will not suffice to say that white employers and white workers alike discriminate, as if both act against their economic interests when they discriminate but do so nevertheless because they are consumed by racism.[22] Such an argument fails to recognize that while employers usually paid for discrimination, union members usually benefited from it.[23] As a cartel or trust, a union's goal is to "control the labor supply," to reduce competition among workers and thus to acquire the power to raise their wages.[24] Since exclusion in general is in their interest, it is not surprising that labor unions have a long history of racial discrimination.[25] Chief Justice Warren Burger noted in a 1979 opinion that

19. This was the most common excuse that employers gave for refusing to hire blacks. It is also another reason why employers would eschew "divide-and-conquer" tactics.

20. Thomas J. Sugrue, *The Origins of the Urban Crisis: Race and Inequality in Postwar Detroit* (Princeton, 1996), 6, 284.

21. Wachter, "Primary and Secondary Labor Markets," 660; Glen G. Cain, "The Challenge of Segmented Labor Market Theories to Orthodox Theory: A Survey," *Journal of Economic Literature* 14 (1976), 1234.

22. Herbert Hill, "Black Labor and Affirmative Action: An Historical Perspective," in Shulman and Darity, eds., *The Question of Discrimination,* 190.

23. Becker, *Economics of Discrimination,* 62–74; Barbara R. Bergmann, "The Effect on White Incomes of Discrimination in Employment," *Journal of Political Economy* 79 (1971), 311. For a contrary view, see Albert Szymanski, "Racial Discrimination and White Gain," *American Sociological Review* 41 (1976), 403–14.

24. G. Warren Nutter, "The Limits of Union Power," in Philip D. Bradley, ed., *The Public Stake in Union Power* (Charlottesville, 1959), 284–300; Morgan O. Reynolds, *Power and Privilege: Labor Unions in America* (New York, 1984); Richard A. Posner, "Some Economics of Labor Law," *University of Chicago Law Review* 51 (1984), 988–1011.

25. Some of the early works in sociology and economics recognized this point, but in a tangential way. Herbert Northrup, "Organized Labor and Negro Workers," in Bernard Sternsher, ed., *The Negro*

"The gross discrimination against minorities to which the Court adverts—particularly against Negroes in the building trades and craft unions—is one of the dark chapters in the otherwise great history of the American labor movement."[26] In fact, racial discrimination was part and parcel of that history.

In the largest sense, everyone loses by discrimination—it is unproductive and inefficient. It is easy to see that white capitalists and black workers lost, and organized white workers gained, by discrimination. The other gainers in the process were black capitalists, who enjoyed a monopoly in a segregated market. In particular instances, however, even these assumptions do not hold: some white capitalists were able to take advantage of discrimination and some black workers also did, though all would have been better off without it. Monopolies hurt everyone but the monopolists. Everyone, or the aggregate economy, suffers from labor unionization, but unions do benefit their members—in the short run.[27]

No economic model can account for the great variety of individual employer and worker responses in a complex and largely free economy. There were a great variety of practices by employers, unions, workers, of different races in different parts of the country at different times. Novelist Chester Himes put it well when he described how his protagonist "came to believe that more dissimilarities existed among Negro people than among the people of any other race on earth . . . Each one's reaction to an interracial union was an individual emotional process, each reaction requiring an entire organizational campaign to itself."[28] The "economics of discrimination" theory is not perfect, but it is a better model than rival theories that have dominated the historical literature.

This work seeks to integrate black and labor history with business and economic history, and to "bring back in" both employers and the state.[29] But it does

in *Depression and War: Prelude to Revolution, 1930–45* (Chicago. 1969), 131; Sterling D. Spero and Abram L. Harris, *The Black Worker: The Negro and the Labor Movement* (New York, 1966 [1931]), 55–56; Horace R. Cayton and George S. Mitchell, *Black Workers and the New Unions* (Chapel Hill, 1939), x.

26. *United Steelworkers v. Weber*, 443 U.S. 193 (1979), 218.

27. Richard Vedder and Lowell Gallaway, "The Economic Effects of Labor Unions Revisited," *Journal of Labor Research* 23 (2002), 105; Charles L. Flynn Jr., *White Land, Black Labor: Caste and Class in Late-Nineteenth-Century Georgia* (Baton Rouge, 1983), 5, 74, 82, 150.

28. Chester Himes, *Lonely Crusade* (New York, 1947), 60–61.

29. Arnesen, "Up from Exclusion," 156; Peter B. Evans, Dietrich Rueschemeyer, and Theda Skocpol, eds., *Bringing the State Back In* (Cambridge, 1985); Melvyn Dubofsky, *The State and Labor in Modern America* (Chapel Hill, 1994); Dubofsky, "The Federal Judiciary, Free Labor, and Equal Rights," in

not regard capital as hegemonic, or the state and the law as instruments of class domination. Employers acted within the constraints set by a variety of economic, social, and political factors; the various state actors also responded to a host of interests, including their own. Race is a central concept but not the metaphysical key to history. This study explores the interaction of race, economics, and law from a liberal or neoclassical perspective. The employment-at-will principle has been largely excluded from historiographical analyses, but it was the dominant view of the period before the New Deal and, while the New Deal permanently altered it, the principle remained an important part of American thinking about labor relations to the present day.[30]

The economics-of-discrimination theory has been elaborated and augmented by the "public choice" school of political economy, which accounts for the role of the state in the process of market competition.[31] Like most cartels, labor unions were only effective when they had legal privileges. In an unregulated labor market, labor organizations would only succeed when their members possessed special skills or if they occupied particularly vulnerable points in a business where stopping work would be very costly to employers—in effect, the kinds of workers who did not need unions because they had bargaining power in the market. The ensuing narrative traces the relationship of black Americans and organized labor through four principal periods: the late-nineteenth-century liberal or laissez-faire phase (chapters 1–2); the transitional progressive era (chapters 3–4); the New Deal period (chapters 4–5); and the civil rights and affirmative action era (chapters 6–7).

Richard Schneirov, Shelton Stromquist, and Nick Salvatore, eds., *The Pullman Strike and the Crisis of the 1890s: Essays on Labor and Politics* (Urbana, 1999), 159–78.

30. Robert H. Zieger, *American Workers, American Unions, 1920–85* (Baltimore, 1986), ix; Friedrich A. Hayek, *The Constitution of Liberty* (Chicago, 1960), 291.

31. Jennifer Roback, "Racism as Rent-Seeking," *Economic Inquiry* 27 (1989), 661–81.

1 / Free Labor

The relationship between black workers and organized labor began to take shape during the Civil War and Reconstruction. The war transformed millions of slaves into free laborers and also caused a great revival of union activity, dormant since the depression of 1837. But it was not until after the war that the nation completed abolition and defined civil rights. By the late 1860s the politically established principles of "free labor" faced the challenge of the first nationwide labor organization.

BLACKS AND THE ANTEBELLUM LABOR MOVEMENT

Given the anomalous status of free blacks before the war, it is not surprising that they played almost no part in the antebellum labor movement. Free blacks in the North and the South faced habitual discrimination by white laborers, and organization often sharpened that discrimination. As early as the first decade of the eighteenth century, Pennsylvania mechanics petitioned for action against the hiring out of Negro mechanics.[1] Henry Boyd, a Kentucky slave carpenter who bought his freedom, could not find work in Ohio due to journeymen prejudice. An English master who hired him found that his white journeymen threatened to quit if he employed Boyd, even if he set him to work in a separate shop. Boyd later became the owner of a bedstead factory that employed about two dozen men, black and white.[2] White workers north and south often petitioned legislatures to forbid the teaching of skilled labor to blacks.[3] In 1831 a workers association asked the legislature to forbid slaves to learn trades as a way to increase the number of white mechanics, and in 1849 a Petersburg group pledged to refuse to work for any employer who hired blacks.[4] English geologist Sir Charles Lyell noted that "the jealousy of an unscrupulous democracy invested with political power" was curtailing the eco-

---

1. W. E. B. Du Bois, *The Negro Artisan* (Atlanta, 1902), 15.

2. William C. Nell, *The Colored Patriots of the American Revolution* (Boston, 1855), 265–70 [DH I: 63]; Charles H. Wesley, *Negro Labor in the United States: A Study in American Economic History* (New York, 1967 [1927]), 53; David A. Gerber, *Black Ohio and the Color Line, 1860–1915* (Urbana, 1976), 5.

3. Lorenzo Greene and Carter G. Woodson, *The Negro Wage Earner* (New York, 1930), 16; Petition, c. 1831 [DH I: 85]; Williston H. Lofton, "Abolition and Labor," *Journal of Negro History* 33 (1948), 274; Sterling Spero and Abram L. Harris, *The Black Worker: The Negro and the Labor Movement* (New York, 1931), 8; Leon F. Litwack, *North of Slavery: The Negro in the Free States, 1790–1860* (Chicago, 1961), 161.

4. Wesley, *Negro Labor in the United States,* 71; *North Star,* 2 Nov. 1849 [DH I: 86].

nomic success of free blacks, reflected in a state prohibition of black labor in construction work.[5] Atlanta laborers petitioned for protection against black mechanics in 1858, and the city council passed an ordinance requiring free blacks to post a $200 bond.[6] An Ohio mechanics association tried one of its members in 1835 for assisting a Negro to learn a trade.[7] The city of New York kept blacks from working as cartmen by requiring that all cartmen secure licenses from the city, which never granted them to blacks.[8]

The organization of artisans in American cities in the 1830s also showed the tensions that would characterize the history of black-labor relations. Columbia, Pennsylvania, workingmen resolved to boycott employers of blacks in 1834, and job competition helped spark the Philadelphia riot of that year. As a subsequent public investigation noted, "An opinion prevails, especially among white laborers, that certain portions of our community prefer to employ colored people, whenever they can be had, to the employing of white people; and that, in consequence of this preference, many whites, who are able and willing to work, are left without employment, while colored people are provided with work and enabled comfortably to maintain their families; and thus many white laborers, anxious for employment, are kept idle and indigent."[9] John Campbell, an English Chartist and head of the Philadelphia Typographical Union, published a racist book, *Negro-Mania,* in 1851. Abolitionists did not sympathize with the white laborer in the North, Campbell claimed; instead they "encourage the negro to rob his master, but will not lift a finger in behalf of the oppressed and degraded of their own race."[10]

A similar mood characterized the radical workingmen's movement in New York City. "Most craft workers and white laborers . . . retained a deep distrust of the small, unskilled black community as a class of supposedly abject dependents," one historian notes. "Outright racism, a fact of lower-class life even in good

5. Charles Lyell, *A Second Visit to the United States,* 2 vols. (New York, 1849), II: 78–82 [DHIS II: 361]. Also in W. E. B. Du Bois, *The Negro American Artisan* (Atlanta, 1912), 31–37.

6. DHIS II: 367–68.

7. Wesley, *Negro Labor in the United States,* 71; Du Bois, *The Negro Artisan,* 16.

8. *Colored American,* 16 Sep. 1837 [DH I: 137].

9. DH I: 175; Committee Report on the Causes of the Philadelphia Race Riots, *Hazard's Register* 27 Sep. 1834 [DH I: 170].

10. John Campbell, *Negro-Mania: Being an Examination of the Falsely Assumed Equality of the Various Races of Men. . . .* (Philadelphia, 1969 [1851]), 469–70.

times," was exacerbated by immigration and job competition in the 1830s.[11] An English socialist observed in 1844, "It is a curious fact that the democratic party, and particularly the poorer class of Irish emigrants in America, are greater enemies to the Negro population, and greater advocates for the continuance of Negro slavery, than any portion of the population in the free states."[12]

Abolitionist Frederick Douglass experienced antebellum labor discrimination. In 1836 Douglass went to work in a Baltimore shipyard, earning money to purchase his freedom while being "hired out" by his owner. Douglass worked as a caulker, a trade dominated by blacks, but met resentment and severe assault from the white carpenters. The slaveholders, Douglass noted, had manipulated poor white animosity against blacks in order to plunder both groups. White race consciousness prevented them from realizing that they were robbed by being forced to compete with slave labor. Douglass predicted, along the lines of Hinton Helper, that eventually poor whites would understand how slavery harmed them and would join the abolition movement. Northern antislavery leaders often made a similar argument.[13]

When Douglass escaped to New Bedford, Massachusetts, he worked as a caulker for Rodney French, but French's white caulkers demanded that he relegate Douglass to unskilled labor.[14] Back in Baltimore, lower-paid white workers broke the black monopoly on caulking and then sought to exclude blacks entirely. After appeals to the legislature failed, the whites resorted to violence. A local court ordered the dissolution of the rival caulker unions, the Association of Black Caulkers and the white Society of Employing Shipwrights. The black group disbanded, but the white organization continued to press for the replacement of black with white labor.[15] The Baltimore business community argued that "Every employer should

11. Herman D. Bloch, "The New York City Negro and Occupational Eviction, 1860–1910," *International Review of Social History* 5 (1960), 26–38; Sean Wilentz, *Chants Democratic: New York City and the Rise of the American Working Class, 1788–1850* (New York, 1984), 263; Litwack, *North of Slavery*, 159.

12. John Finch, "Notes of Travel in the United States," *New Moral World*, 29 Jun. 1844 [DHIS VII: 60].

13. Frederick Douglass, *My Bondage and My Freedom* (New York, 1968 [1855]), 309–10. Helper's argument was expressed in *The Impending Crisis of the South* (New York, 1857). Douglass's argument was not aimed at "the racist component of the capitalistic labor system" but at the *slave* labor system. Cf. William S. McFeely, *Frederick Douglass* (New York, 1990), 62; Robert L. Factor, *The Black Response to America: Men, Ideals, and Organization from Frederick Douglass to the NAACP* (Reading, 1970), 9.

14. Douglass, *My Bondage and My Freedom*, 349; Douglass, "My Escape to Freedom," *Century Magazine* 23 (Nov. 1881), 125–31 [DH I: 136]; McFeely, *Frederick Douglass*, 79.

15. M. Ray Della Jr., "The Problems of Negro Labor in the 1850s," *Maryland Historical Magazine* 66 (1971), 14–32.

FREE LABOR / 11

be allowed, without let or hindrance, to employ black or white men, as he may think proper, and if the white caulkers have, as is alleged, resolved that no black caulkers should work on the South side of the basin . . . they should be taught that such resolve cannot be carried into execution." [16] But soon after the Civil War, whites had completed their exclusion of black workers. [17] Douglass's experience left him with the impression, he told Harriet Beecher Stowe in 1853, that "Prejudice against the free colored people in the United States has shown itself nowhere so invincible as among the mechanics." [18]

REPUBLICAN FREE LABOR PHILOSOPHY AND THE CIVIL WAR

When the Civil War erupted, national policymakers had not given much thought to the question of free black labor. None expected the rapid abolition of slavery—what Lincoln called the conflict's "fundamental and astounding" result—that the war brought on. But once Republicans decided on a standard of civil equality, they easily incorporated blacks into their established "free labor" philosophy.

Historians have discerned an inherent tension in the "free labor" philosophy of the antebellum Republicans. One strand of the philosophy derived from an older, traditional, communal, and republican understanding of free labor as economic independence, best expressed in the artisan's ownership and control of his tools and workshop. The antebellum labor movement championed this view. The other strand embraced a modern, market-oriented, individualistic, and liberal view of free labor as "self-ownership," the right to buy and sell labor freely. The Anglo-American antislavery movement emphasized this principle. [19] As a legal historian puts it, "It was the abolitionists who first lent moral sanction and rhetorical energy to the notion that the northern worker's freedom rested simply in self-ownership and the right to sell his own labor." [20]

The antislavery principle grew stronger during the antebellum period and through the war. Antislavery men emphasized voluntarism as the essence of the

16. *Baltimore American and Commercial Advertiser,* 8 and 9 Jul. 1858 [DH I: 237–39].

17. Bettye C. Thomas, "A Nineteenth Century Black Operated Shipyard, 1866–84," *Journal of Negro History* 59 (1974), 2; Philip S. Foner, *Organized Labor and the Black Worker, 1619–1981* (New York, 1982), 11.

18. Factor, *Black Response to America,* 13.

19. William E. Forbath, "The Ambiguities of Free Labor: Labor and the Law in the Gilded Age," *Wisconsin Law Review* (1985), 767–817; Eric Foner, *Politics and Ideology in the Age of the Civil War* (New York, 1980).

20. Forbath, "Ambiguities of Free Labor," 770.

"self-ownership" view of free labor. Put simply, labor was free when coercion was absent.[21] This belief led many antebellum liberals to oppose slavery as well as other coercive economic arrangements like tariffs, legal monopolies, and labor unions. Denouncing trade unionists for rioting against an alleged flour monopoly in New York in 1837, Jacksonian Democrat William Leggett argued, "What, let us ask, is the very first and cardinal object of the Trades Union? To enable *labor,* by the means of combination, and of extensive mutual countenance and cooperation, to command its own price."[22]

To the "labor" advocates of free labor thinking, the "self-ownership" view of liberalism masked "wage slavery."[23] They condemned liberals for failing to see that compulsion characterized even formally "free" labor relations.[24] While employers could no longer physically compel workers to provide labor, they retained effective coercive power by being able to deny them the means of making a living.[25] In this view, compulsion inhered in wage-labor capitalism.[26]

The frequent hostility of the antebellum labor reformers to the antislavery movement demonstrated the tension between the two theories. In the early Philadelphia labor movement, cordwainers denounced the undemocratic application of English common law to workers. "At the very time when the state of the negro was about to be improved, attempts were being made to reduce the whites to slavery," the *Philadelphia Aurora* complained.[27] Similarly, the New York General Trades Union saw abolitionism as a conspiracy to depress white wages.[28] Labor editor

21. Robert J. Steinfeld, *The Invention of Free Labor: The Employment Relation in English and American Law and Culture, 1350–1870* (Chapel Hill, 1991), 99–100.

22. Lawrence H. White, ed., *Democratick Editorials: Essays in Jacksonian Political Economy* (Indianapolis, 1984), 110; Dorfman, *Economic Mind in American Civilization,* II:658; Paul K. Conkin, *Prophets of Prosperity: America's First Political Economists* (Bloomington, 1980), 132.

23. Bernard Mandel, *Labor, Free and Slave: Workingmen and the Anti-Slavery Movement in the United States* (New York, 1955), 76–81.

24. Jonathan A. Glicksetein, "Poverty Is Not Slavery: American Abolitionists and the Competitive Labor Market," in Lewis Perry and Michael Fellman, eds., *Antislavery Reconsidered: New Perspectives on the Abolitionists* (Baton Rouge, 1979), 204; Forbath, "Ambiguities of Free Labor," 812.

25. Steinfeld, *Invention of Free Labor,* 157.

26. Christopher Tomlins, *The State and the Unions: Labor Relations, Law, and the Organized Labor Movement in America, 1880–1960* (Cambridge, 1985), 51; Robert L. Hale, "Coercion and Distribution in a Supposedly Non-Coercive State," *Political Science Quarterly* 38 (1923), 470–94.

27. Foster Rhea Dulles, *Labor in America: A History,* 3d ed. (New York, 1966), 30.

28. Alexander Saxton, "Race and the House of Labor," in Gary B. Nash, ed., *The Great Fear: Race in the Mind of America* (New York, 1970), 100.

George Henry Evans claimed that the abolitionists' goal was to reduce "both Northern workers and Southern slaves to the lowest level of wage dependence, and to anarchical competition with each other, for the privilege of doing the drudgery of capital."[29] When Orestes Brownson came to address the problem of poverty in the North, he argued that slave labor was less oppressive than wage labor. The slave's "sufferings are less than those of the free laborer at wages" who "has all the disadvantages of freedom and none of the blessings," Brownson claimed.[30]

Some antislavery activists shared the labor view and attempted to unite the antislavery and labor movements. The New York City Workingmen's Party sought the abolition of both chattel and wage slavery in its 1829 platform. While the evangelical individualism of most abolitionists led them to embrace market competition, some evinced a collectivist view of Christian brotherhood that made them suspicious of the free market. But such critics were few, and though there was some shift from liberal to labor views over time, the liberal version of free labor was the dominant one by and through the Civil War.[31] Most abolitionists belittled the "wage slavery" view and regarded the differences between southern slavery and northern (or English) free labor as obvious, "as far apart as the poles," due to the absence of coercion and availability of legal protection.[32] Real slavery was distinguished by physical coercion, most abolitionists argued. "All these distinctions may be resolved into this fundamental difference," the abolitionist *National Era* noted, "the free working man owns himself; the slave is owned by another."[33] Free labor might bring distress and dependency, but it was not equal to slavery. "Grant that he is obliged to labor hard, labor long; still, he labors to provide himself a subsistence, to rear a family," another antislavery paper noted. "He is under no *physical* coercion, and thus escapes essential and perpetual degradation."[34]

29. Joseph G. Rayback, "The American Workingman and the Antislavery Crusade," *Journal of Economic History* 3 (1943), 153.

30. Orestes Brownson, "The Laboring Classes," *Boston Quarterly Review* (Jul. 1840), 368–71, in Philip S. Foner and Herbert Shapiro, eds., *Northern Labor and Antislavery: A Documentary History* (Westport, 1994), 2; Marcus Cunliffe, *Chattel Slavery and Wage Slavery: The Anglo-American Context, 1830–60* (Athens, GA, 1979), 21.

31. Lofton, "Abolition and Labor," 251; Rayback, "American Workingman and the Antislavery Crusade," 158; Glickstein, "Poverty Is Not Slavery," 197, 213.

32. William Powell, letter from Liverpool, *National Antislavery Standard*, 23 Mar. 1851 [DH I: 84].

33. *National Era*, 25 Mar. 1847, in Foner and Shapiro, *Northern Labor and Antislavery*, 48.

34. *Cincinnati Morning Herald*, 12 Jun. 1845, in Foner and Shapiro, *Northern Labor and Antislavery*, 131.

Some labor leaders pressed the "wage slavery" argument so far that they sounded like apologists for chattel slavery.[35] However much John C. Calhoun, as the "Marx of the Master Class," may have envisioned an alliance between southern planters and northern capitalists to hold down black slaves and white workers, he actually got more support from northern labor activists than from northern businessmen. Calhoun was "one of the visionaries of the southern slavocracy who conceptualized the possibility of an alliance between the pro-slavery South and the burgeoning union movement in the North," an AFL-CIO official said recently; he "repeatedly attempted to convince southern plantation owners to make common cause with the burgeoning union movement of the North against the industrial capitalists."[36] Abolitionists tried to distance themselves from the early labor movement. William Lloyd Garrison denounced class resentment in the inaugural issue of the *Liberator,* excoriating the effort "to inflame the minds of our working classes against the more opulent, and to persuade men that they are contemned and oppressed by a wealthy aristocracy."[37] Attributing class resentments to envy, he concluded that workers suffered more injustice from other workers than from their employers.[38] The abolitionist editor relegated "wage slavery" arguments to the "Refuge of Oppression" column, the section of the paper set aside for pro-slavery opinion.[39] Frederick Douglass also refused to let a wider labor agenda absorb the antislavery movement. He dissented vehemently from Fourierist John A. Collins's equation of property with slavery and "accused Collins, not without plausibility, of 'imposing an additional burden of unpopularity on our cause' when Collins attempted to introduce socialist ideas at abolitionist meetings," a biographer notes.[40]

35. Lofton, "Abolition and Labor," 266; Joseph Dorfman, *The Economic Mind in American Civilization,* 5 vols. (New York, 1946–59), 2:693; Cunliffe, *Chattel Slavery and Wage Slavery,* 23. For arguments that the antebellum labor movement was sympathetic to abolition, see David Montgomery, *Beyond Equality: Labor and the Radical Republicans, 1862–72* (Urbana, 1967), 123–24, and Michael Goldfield, *The Color of Politics: Race, Class, and the Mainsprings of American Politics* (New York, 1997), 104.

36. Richard Hofstadter, *The American Political Tradition and the Men Who Made It* (New York, 1948), 98–117; Richard N. Current, "John C. Calhoun, Philosopher of Reaction," *Antioch Review* 3 (1943), 223–34; Bill Fletcher Jr., "Seizing the Time Because the Time Is Now: Welfare Repeal and Labor Reconstruction," in Steven Fraser and Joshua B. Freeman, eds., *Audacious Democracy: Labor, Intellectuals, and the Social Reconstruction of America* (Boston, 1997).

37. *Liberator,* 1 Jan. 1831, in Foner and Shapiro,*Northern Labor and Antislavery,* 108.

38. *Liberator,* 29 Jan. 1831, in Foner and Shapiro, *Northern Labor and Antislavery,* 109.

39. Foner, *Politics and Ideology,* 63, 69.

40. McFeely, *Frederick Douglass,* 104; Foner, *Politics and Ideology,* 68.

Most commonly, abolitionists made individualist and liberal arguments that furthered the distance between organized labor and blacks. Believing that employers' economic interests would overcome racial prejudice, many abolitionists advised blacks to underbid white workers rather than attempt to join their unions.[41]

Though the Republican Party made more of an appeal to the working man than the abolitionists had and derived its principles from a wider range of sources, its members generally shared the self-ownership view of free labor. Most agreed with Massachusetts chief justice Lemuel Shaw's landmark 1842 opinion in *Commonwealth v. Hunt,* that workers had the right to organize and seek their goals collectively, and that unions should not be regarded per se as criminal conspiracies. Most Republicans supported the right to strike but believed that while workers should be free to quit their jobs, they could neither prevent their employers from continuing their businesses nor stop other workers from taking their places. Neither party should have the power to dictate terms to the other or to use force to compel obedience. Otherwise, unions would hold the same compulsory power that slaveholders held.[42]

Here again the crucial factor was coercion. Lincoln gave voice to these principles in March 1860, supporting the Lynn shoemakers strike. "I am glad to see that a system of labor prevails in New England under which laborers *can* strike when they want to, where they are not obliged to work under all circumstances, and are not tied down and obliged to labor whether you pay them or not! I *like* the system which lets a man quit when he wants to."[43] Lincoln was no liberal ideologue, but this statement expresses the fundamental liberal principle of voluntarism. Lincoln claimed not to know the details of the Lynn strike, and violent action by the strikers would have been an important factor in his judgment—but one that was not present in this case anyway.[44]

41. Litwack, *North of Slavery,* 172.

42. Earl Maltz, *Civil Rights, the Constitution, and Congress, 1863–69* (Lawrence, 1990), 4; Eric Foner, *Free Soil, Free Labor, Free Men: The Ideology of the Republican Party Before the Civil War* (New York, 1970), 26–27; David Montgomery, *Beyond Equality: Labor and the Radical Republicans, 1862–72* (Urbana, 1967), 31; Tomlins, *The State and the Unions,* 46. Herbert Hovenkamp, "Labor Conspiracies in American Law, 1880–1930," *Texas Law Review* 66 (1988), 944.

43. Roy P. Basler, ed., *Collected Works of Abraham Lincoln,* 9 vols. (New Brunswick, 1953–55), IV: 24.

44. Dulles, *Labor in America,* 90; James L. Hutson, "Facing an Angry Labor: The American Public Interprets the Shoemakers Strike of 1860," *Civil War History* 28 (1982), 197–212; Alan Dawley, *Class and Community: The Industrial Revolution in Lynn* (Cambridge, 1976), 82–88. G. S. Boritt, *Lincoln and the*

Liberals were accused of failing to see the invisible or impersonal coercion inherent in desperate men's labor contracts, but they could not countenance the more obvious violence of labor strikes, particularly the intimidation of or assault on workers who were willing to take jobs that strikers refused. Labor organizations, like all cartels, needed some kind of coercive power to enforce their demands, though violent strikes in the end usually hindered union efforts. To liberals, strike enforcement was the flip side of slavery, using coercion to prevent work, and often targeting blacks.[45]

The Republican Party's free labor philosophy became more focused once the Civil War began. Before the Emancipation Proclamation and the Thirteenth Amendment, the preference of northern white labor to avoid competition with slave labor in the West provided a powerful antislavery impetus, but the threat of having to compete with freedmen deterred support for emancipation.

During the war, the fear of an influx of emancipated black labor contributed to some of the worst racial unrest in American history. Most northern Republicans sought to dodge the black labor problem. General James Wadsworth, the Republican nominee for governor of New York in 1862, argued that emancipation would prompt northern free blacks to return to the South rather than cause emancipated slaves to come North. The *New York Times* agreed.[46] President Lincoln continued to endorse colonization along with emancipation, but he assured northerners that emancipation would not harm the interests of white workers. Lincoln explained the economics of the issue in as liberal terms as any. "Emancipation, even without deportation, would probably enhance the wages of white labor, and, very surely, would not reduce them," he told Congress in his December, 1862 annual message.

Economics of the American Dream (Memphis, 1978), 181–84, claims that Lincoln meant something more than the right to quit, but does not say that he favored coercive striking. Pp. 220–21 outline Lincoln's support of strikes during the Civil War. Herman Schluter, *Lincoln, Labor, and Slavery: A Chapter from the Social History of America* (New York, 1913), gives a Marxist analysis doubting Lincoln's sympathy toward the labor movement.

45. Dorfman, *Economic Mind*, II: 634, 967; Friedrich A. Hayek, *The Constitution of Liberty* (Chicago, 1960), 270; Morgan O. Reynolds, *Power and Privilege: Labor Unions in America* (New York, 1984), 12, 43, 48–50, 104; Arnold J. Thieblot Jr. and Thomas R. Haggard, *Union Violence: The Record and the Response by Courts, Legislatures, and the NLRB* (Philadelphia, 1983), 5–8; Philip Taft and Philip Ross, "American Labor Violence: Its Causes, Character, and Outcome," in Hugh Davis Graham and Ted Robert Gurr, eds., *The History of Violence in America* (New York, 1969), 281, 294, 381–83, 387. Hovenkamp, "Labor Conspiracies," 948.

46. "General Wadsworth's Acceptance," *New York Times*, 6 Oct. 1862, 4 [DH I: 311].

Thus, the customary amount of labor would still have to be performed; the freed people would surely not do more than their old proportion of it, and very probably, for a time, would do less, leaving an increased part to white laborers, bringing their labor into greater demand, and consequently, enhancing the wages of it. With deportation, even to a limited extent, enhanced wages to white labor is mathematically certain. Labor is like any other commodity in the market—increase the demand for it, and you increase the price of it. Reduce the supply of black labor, by colonizing the black laborer out of the country, and, by precisely so much, you increase the demand for, and wages of, white labor.[47]

Frederick Douglass echoed this analysis, dismissing the chimera of black labor competition during a wartime labor shortage when "no tolerably efficient white laborer" could fail to find remunerative work.[48] But slack from the 1857 panic, mechanization, and employment of women offset the expected war-induced labor shortage. However marginal black labor competition may have been, it could be fanned into calamitous proportions.[49]

In 1862 South Chicago butchers resolved to strike against any employer who hired black labor, and whites—predominantly Irish immigrants stirred up by Copperhead politicians—drove blacks out of Cincinnati waterfront work.[50] In New Orleans, quickly occupied by Union forces, German and Irish dockworkers tried to prevent blacks from breaking their monopoly on dock jobs. Legislative attempts to control black labor failed and, without violent strikes, blacks made significant inroads during the war.[51]

The bloodiest race riot in American history had its roots in fear of black labor competition in New York, a Democratic city already seething about war, emancipation, taxation, and conscription. Irish workers rioted against a tobacco manufacturer who employed blacks in 1862. The Longshoremen's United Benevolent So-

47. Basler, ed., *Collected Works of Abraham Lincoln*, V: 535.

48. *Douglass' Monthly*, Sep. 1862 [DH I: 279].

49. James M. McPherson, *Battle Cry of Freedom: The Civil War Era* (New York, 1988), 448–49; Williston H. Lofton, "Northern Labor and the Negro during the Civil War," *Journal of Negro History* 34 (1949), 252.

50. *Douglass' Monthly*, Nov. 1862; *Cincinnati Commercial*, 11 and 17 Jul. 1862 [DH I: 273–74, 277]; Lofton, "Northern Labor and the Negro," 260; Gerber, *Black Ohio and the Color Line*, 27.

51. Eric Arnesen, *Waterfront Workers of New Orleans: Race, Class, and Politics, 1863–1923* (Urbana, 1994), 6, 20.

ciety, formed in 1852 by Irish immigrants loyal to Tammany Hall, was able to force dockworkers to join their union and to get the shipping companies to pay higher wages. The union maintained an "all-white" (in fact all Irish) labor policy until the shipping companies decided to employ black workers in the spring of 1863 to break a strike. This strike was put down by federal troops, but the unionists used the July draft riots as a cover for a successful purge of black dockworkers. The most thorough history of the riot concludes that "In a sense, the racial violence of the draft riots was the quickening of an already accelerated tempo of intimidation and assault." [52]

Though the New York political establishment and some merchants sympathized with the white rioters, a group of businessmen associated with the Union League established a "Committee of Merchants for the Relief of Colored People, Suffering from the Late Riots." In addition to providing direct relief for the victims, the group resolved to defend the right of blacks to work and of merchants to hire them. They said, "The full and equal right of the colored man to work for whoever chooses to employ him, and the full and equal right of any citizen to employ whoever he will, is too manifest to need proof. Competition is indispensable to the successful management of commercial business; surely the energetic, enterprising merchants of this city will not allow any interference with their rights . . . The laws of the demand and supply of labor cannot be permanently changed by combinations or persecutions." [53] Given the wartime experience of black workers, it was little wonder that they often supported employers and were suspicious of organized labor. [54] The New York merchants combined their beliefs in competition and charity, and their principles of free labor would become the center of Republican policy once abolition was complete and colonization plans abandoned.

RECONSTRUCTION AND FREE LABOR

After the war, congressional policy and the behavior of the freedmen displayed the dominance of the antislavery, self-ownership definition of free labor. It was clear

52. Herman D. Bloch, "Labor and the Negro, 1866–1910," *Journal of Negro History* 50 (1965), 170. Albon P. Man Jr., "Labor Competition and the New York Draft Riots of 1863," *Journal of Negro History* 36 (1951), 375; Iver Bernstein, *The New York City Draft Riots: Their Significance for American Society and Politics in the Age of the Civil War* (New York, 1990), 117, 27.

53. Bernstein, *New York City Draft Riots*, 125; *Report of the Committee of Merchants for the Relief of Colored People, Suffering from the Late Riots in the City of New York* (New York, 1863), 12–13 [DH I: 291].

54. Lofton, "Northern Labor and the Negro," 272–73.

that the former rebel governments and most plantation owners meant to prevent genuine self-ownership. The civil and political status of the freedmen remained unclear at war's end, it being uncertain whether the Thirteenth Amendment did anything more than abolish the legal condition of chattel slavery.[55] Legislatures in the former Confederate states acted as if it had not when they enacted the "Black Codes" in 1865. "The Black Codes were the scaffolding for rebuilding agriculture on the pattern of the old regime: overseers, obtrusive discipline, gang labor, women and children in the labor force, and even a return to physical coercion," one historian notes.[56]

To a certain extent, however, even the Black Codes recognized free labor and property rights, and their coercive elements were often exaggerated.[57] Mississippi's 1865 Black Code permitted "freedmen, free Negroes, and mulattoes" to "sue and be sued, plead in all the courts of law and equity in this state, and acquire personal property . . . by descent or purchase, and . . . dispose of the same, in the same manner, and to the same extent that white persons may." But a series of restrictions limited black rights to own land, travel, and engage in certain occupations. Under Louisiana's Black Code, "Every negro is required to be in the regular service of some white person, or former owner, who shall be held responsible for the conduct of said negro," and blacks were required to have permits to travel and to obey a curfew. Florida's code provided that a person of color who refused or neglected to fulfill his terms of a labor contract "by willful disobedience of orders, wanton impudence, or disrespect to his employer," was to be treated as a vagrant, and made "enticement"—competition among planters that might bid up the wages of freedmen—a misdemeanor. Georgia's 1866 code prohibited enticing by higher wages but was not race-specific. Apprenticeship and vagrancy laws were particularly restrictive.[58] States also used licensing laws "to ease competition that white ar-

55. Michael W. Fitzgerald, *The Union League Movement in the Deep South: Politics and Agricultural Change during Reconstruction* (Baton Rouge, 1989), 232–35; Herman Belz, *A New Birth of Freedom: The Republican Party and Freedmen's Rights, 1861–66* (Westport, 1976), 119–27.

56. Fitzgerald, *Union League Movement*, 138; William Cohen, *At Freedom's Edge: Black Mobility and the Southern White Quest for Racial Control, 1861–1915* (Baton Rouge, 1991), 28; Ray Marshall, *Labor in the South* (Cambridge, 1967), 9.

57. Theodore B. Wilson, *The Black Codes of the South* (University, AL, 1965), 118.

58. Ibid.; Senate Executive Document 2, 39th Cong., 1st Sess., 93 [DH I: 338]; Acts and Resolutions of the General Assembly of Florida, 1865–66, in Walter L. Fleming, ed., *Documentary History of Reconstruction*, 2 vols. (Cleveland, 1906–07), I: 276.

tisans feared from blacks trained in mechanical crafts as slaves," an indication that the freedmen did not leave slavery with "nothing but freedom."[59]

The Union Army and Freedmen's Bureau also treated the newly emancipated blacks as less than completely free. In response to the devastation and disorder of the war, they continued to keep free blacks under a benevolent guardianship that did not give southern planters the control they desired but that appeared too restrictive and feudal to many abolitionists and radical Republicans.[60] Senator Thomas A. Hendricks, an Indiana Democrat who opposed the bureau, pointed out that it imposed the compulsion of specific performance in labor contracts, which had been done away with for white workers.[61] Republicans in Congress developed a policy of wage labor that went beyond the apprenticeship envisioned in the early Freedmen's Bureau policy and the Black Codes, but not as far as the land redistribution sought by some of the Radicals. The Freedmen's Bureau—itself a temporary agency—moved beyond its early transitional phase toward promoting a bona fide free labor system.[62]

Here, too, the basic principle of voluntarism provided the standard. Officers were not to impose compulsory labor except as punishment for crime, the assistant commissioners were told. "Suffering may result to some extent, but suffering is preferred to slavery, and is to some degree the necessary consequence of events. In all actions the officer should never forget that no substitute for slavery, like apprenticeship without proper consent or peonage . . . will be tolerated."[63] More regimented labor systems were "regarded as a make-shift, which it was hoped would disappear as confidence should grow out of experience on both sides, and leave to

59. Charles L. Flynn Jr., *White Land, Black Labor: Caste and Class in Late-Nineteenth-Century Georgia* (Baton Rouge, 1983), 85; Michael Les Benedict, *The Fruits of Victory: Alternatives to Restoring the Union, 1865–77*, rev. ed. (Lanham, MD, 1986), 91; Wesley, *Negro Labor in the United States*, 65.

60. Belz, *New Birth of Freedom*, 73–74; George R. Bentley, *A History of the Freedmen's Bureau* (Philadelphia, 1955), 140; Donald G. Nieman, *To Set the Law in Motion: The Freedmen's Bureau and the Legal Rights of Blacks, 1865–68* (Millwood, 1979), 53, 91, 110, 136. Wilson, *Black Codes of the South*, notes that the Freedmen's Bureau policies set an example that the Black Codes followed (58–59, 83, 142–46); Cohen, *At Freedom's Edge*, 9–11.

61. *Congressional Globe*, 39th Cong., 1st Sess. (15 Jul. 1864), 2972; Steinfeld, *Invention of Free Labor*, 147.

62. Belz, *New Birth of Freedom*, 41–47; Foner, *Politics and Ideology*, 101–2.

63. Instructions to Assistant Commissioners, 12 Jul. 1865, in Fleming, *Documentary History of Reconstruction*, I: 331.

each the benefit of an appeal at any time to competition," an Alabama Bureau official noted.[64] But even the early policies of the Freedmen's Bureau, which have been described as a "compulsory free labor system," outraged the former slave-holders. While the planters thought that force would be a necessary and permanent part of managing free blacks, the bureau saw it as a temporary expedient that would form no part of the final system of a free market in labor.[65]

President Andrew Johnson believed that the Black Codes provided enough protection for the freedmen. When he vetoed a bill to extend the Freedmen's Bureau in February 1866, he argued that military government in the former Confederacy must end. The freedmen's "condition is not so exposed as may at first be imagined," Johnson opined. The demand for labor in the South would "enable him to command almost his own terms. He also possesses a perfect right to change his place of abode" and was free to seek and find better working conditions. "The laws that regulate supply and demand will maintain their force," Johnson continued, "and the wages of the laborer will be regulated thereby." The president trusted that southern whites would not attempt to keep the freedmen in semi-bondage and judged that the freedmen must shift for themselves as best they could.[66]

Johnson's inattention to the Black Codes struck many in Congress as extraordinarily obtuse. Some southern conservatives, as well as Republicans, doubted that the Black Codes were compatible with market freedom.[67] Congressional Republicans recoiled, aghast at this sign of the president's resistance to their Reconstruction policy. Lyman Trumbull, principal author of the vetoed bill, concluded that testimony from the South showed that the freedmen were not "protected by the courts and by the civil authorities." "Is there not necessity for some supervising care of these people?" he asked. "Are they to be coldly told that they have a perfect right to change their place of abode, when if they are caught in a strange neighborhood without a pass they are liable to be whipped; when combinations exist against them that they shall not be permitted to hire unless to their former mas-

---

64. *Reports of Freedmen's Bureau Assistant Commissioners and Laws in Relation to the Freedmen,* Senate Exec. Doc. 6 (Washington, 1866), 6.

65. Cohen, *At Freedom's Edge,* 13.

66. *Senate Journal,* 39th Cong., 1st Sess. (19 Feb. 1866), 171.

67. Thomas Wagstaff, "Call Your Old Master—'Master': Southern Political Leaders and Negro Labor during Presidential Reconstruction," in Milton Cantor, ed., *Black Labor in America* (Westport, 1969), 3, 15.

ter?"[68] The Black Codes clearly compromised the fundamental element of consent in free labor. "The nation cannot thus lightly put aside its obligations to a defenseless race called to its aid in its day of peril," said Maine Republican senator Lot Morrill. "We all know that the freedman has no protection." Morrill replied that Johnson's statement that the freedmen could be left to the law of supply and demand without civil protection was "a sentiment . . . which shocks me, and which I fear will shock the sensibilities of mankind."[69]

Congress passed a revised Freedmen's Bureau Act over another Johnson veto in July and, more important, passed the Civil Rights Act of 1866 in March. The act emphasized the right to labor freely and to be secure in the protection of the fruits of one's labor as fundamental civil rights.[70] After taking the monumental step of defining all the freedmen as American citizens, it declared that they "shall have the same right in every State and Territory in the United States to make and enforce contracts, to sue, be parties, and give evidence, to inherit, purchase, lease, sell, hold, and convey real and personal property, and to full and equal benefit of all laws and proceedings for the security of person and property, as is enjoyed by white citizens, and shall be subject to like punishment, pains, and penalties, and to none other."[71] The Civil Rights Act did not strike at private discrimination but did aim to prevent force and fraud by giving blacks power to enforce private, voluntary contracts. The Reconstruction statutes and amendments articulated basic antislavery legal and constitutional principles of the freedom to dispose of one's labor. The Republican Reconstruction program meant to secure a range of limited but absolute equality of rights, the substance of which principally concerned free labor and property rights.[72] Congress wrote the Fourteenth Amendment, the outstanding expression of Reconstruction policy, to make permanent the terms of the Civil Rights Act.

The freedmen themselves defined free labor primarily in terms of self-

68. *Congressional Globe*, 39th Cong., 1st Sess. (20 Feb. 1866), 941; Gerald D. Jaynes, *Branches without Roots: Genesis of the Black Working Class in the American South, 1862–82* (New York, 1986), 18.

69. *Congressional Globe*, 39th Cong., 1st Sess. (8 Mar. 1866), A156.

70. Bernard H. Siegan, *Economic Liberties and the Constitution* (Chicago, 1980), 50; Alfred Avins, "The Right to Work and the Fourteenth Amendment: The Original Understanding," *Labor Law Journal* 18 (1967), 15–28.

71. 14 Stat. L. 27 (1866).

72. Belz, *New Birth of Freedom*, 168; Forbath, "Ambiguities of Free Labor," 786; Earl Maltz, "Reconstruction without Revolution: Republican Civil Rights Theory in the Era of the Fourteenth Amendment," *Houston Law Review* 24 (1987), 224–35.

ownership. Most blacks did not lament the putative paternalism of the slave system, and eagerly embraced the individual rights of the free market system.[73] The transformation of the South into a free labor economy was perhaps the most successful element of the Republican Reconstruction program. "At least in the legal sense, the Negro was transformed from a slave into a 'free' economic agent," one historian concludes. "If that freedom was sometimes limited—as it obviously was—the Negro had the same alternatives possessed by his northern white contemporary; he could submit, starve, or move. Even among Negroes themselves, few would have asked for more."[74]

Even before Congress installed Republican governments in the South, freedmen benefited from the evolution of slave labor into free labor. The new labor system provided many blacks with the fundamental freedoms to bargain with and choose among employers, and to move in search of better terms of work.[75] Planters almost always failed in their efforts to control the wages of freedmen and to reestablish the antebellum gang labor system, and blacks did exercise their freedom of mobility within the South—perhaps 10 percent of South Carolina freedmen left the state during Reconstruction; over 8 percent of the black population of Tennessee, Alabama, and Virginia moved out in the 1870s.[76]

Reconstruction governments repealed the Black Codes and defeated a number of devices by which the planters sought to control the black work force, from "anti-enticement" laws that prevented employers from bidding for labor to "sunset laws" that prohibited the sale of agricultural produce at night. Republican legislatures also enacted laws to benefit the poor and laboring classes. Homestead laws and taxation policies effected some redistribution of land; bankruptcy acts, stay laws, and lien laws attempted to give an advantage to debtors and employees. Perhaps most important of all was the administration of the law by Republican and black officials.[77] Some who believed that the political action of Reconstruction was

73. Eric Foner, *Reconstruction: America's Unfinished Revolution* (New York, 1988), 106.

74. Joel Williamson, *After Slavery: The Negro in South Carolina during Reconstruction, 1861–77* (Chapel Hill, 1965), 121.

75. Cohen, *At Freedom's Edge,* 22; Flynn, *White Land, Black Labor,* 59, 65, 68.

76. Foner, *Reconstruction,* 138; Robert Higgs, *Competition and Coercion: Blacks in the American Economy, 1865–1914* (Cambridge, 1977), 47; Williamson, *After Slavery,* 108; Cohen, *At Freedom's Edge,* Table 14; Benedict, *The Fruits of Victory,* 46.

77. Foner, *Reconstruction,* 372; Jay R. Mandle, *Not Slave, Not Free: The African-American Economic Experience Since the Civil War* (Durham, 1992), 10; Williamson, *After Slavery,* 113; Jaynes, *Branches without Roots,* 146, 296.

inadequate looked to labor organizations; others who believed that it had gone too far embraced Liberal Republicanism.

THE NATIONAL LABOR UNIONS

The Civil War sparked a revival of the labor movement which continued until the depression of 1873. Nationalization of the economy and wartime strains on labor—particularly the inflationary decline of real wages—fostered national labor organization. Abolition brought up the question of the place of black workers in the heretofore almost entirely white labor movement. In response to a mixed and often hostile reaction from white organizations, black workers wrestled with the question of labor organization.

A group of union delegates meeting in Baltimore in 1866 formed the germ of the National Labor Union (NLU). Open to all laborers—agricultural and industrial, skilled and unskilled—it was broadly political in orientation and utopian, tending to reject wage labor per se. Blacks hoped that this national organization would take up the issue of the near-total exclusion of black workers from white labor unions.[78]

Several voices in the NLU urged inclusion of blacks. Chief among them was William H. Sylvis. Born in 1828 near Pittsburgh, Sylvis was the son of an unsuccessful wagon-maker, grew up in the home of a Whig state legislator, and educated himself. He became a skilled iron molder, was active in the Methodist church and temperance movement, and joined the new Journeymen Stove and Hollow-Ware Moulders' Union in 1857. A Douglas Democrat, he pressed for compromise in the secession winter but then served in the Union Army. He helped to establish the International Moulders Union in 1863. Though Sylvis believed that trade unions and strikes were only temporary expedients on the way to the abolition of wage labor, he saw that blacks must be included in the movement.[79] He denounced Reconstruction and the Freedmen's Bureau, "a stupendous fraud upon the labor of the nation," and shared the racial views of most of the labor leaders of the day. Sylvis argued that emancipation had simply added 4 million chattel slaves to the millions of white wage slaves in the nation. "We are now all one fam-

---

78. Dulles, *Labor in America*, 95–100; Foner, *Organized Labor and the Black Worker*, 17–29.

79. James C. Sylvis, ed., *The Life, Speeches, Labors, and Essays of William H. Sylvis* (Philadelphia, 1968 [1872]), 45; Charlotte Todes, *William H. Sylvis and the National Labor Union* (New York, 1942), 73–79; "William H. Sylvis," ANB.

ily of slaves together, and the labor reform movement is a second emancipation proclamation."[80]

Andrew Carr Cameron was the other principal advocate of an interracial labor movement. Son of a Scots printer born in England in 1836, Cameron edited the *Workingman's Advocate,* which became the organ of the National Labor Union. As chairman of the NLU's committee on trade unions and strikes, Cameron prepared an address for the 1867 convention. It called for the eight-hour day and advised that strikes should be used only as a last resort. "The systematic organization and consolidation of labor must henceforth become the watchword of the true reformer," it asserted, and "to accomplish this the cooperation of the African race in America must be secured." If not, the African would become a strikebreaker. Every union should "inculcate the great, ennobling idea that the interests of labor are one; that there should be no distinction of race or nationality; no classification of Jew or Gentile, Christian or Infidel; that there is but one dividing line—that which separates mankind into two great classes, the class that labors and the class that lives by others' labors."[81]

The convention faced the race issue reluctantly. It referred the question to a Committee on Colored Labor, chaired by A. W. Phelps of the Carpenters and Joiners Union of New Haven, an organization whose constitution excluded Negroes.[82] He reported that his committee found the issue "involved in so much mystery, and upon it so wide diversity of opinion amongst our members," that it should be deferred for another year. Sylvis objected, arguing that "the time will come when the negro will take possession of the shops if we have not taken possession of the negro," but the members resolved that "the constitution already adopted prevents the necessity of reporting on the subject of negro labor" because it did not mention race at all.[83] The *Boston Daily Evening Voice* agreed. The question of Negro labor should not have come up at all, it argued, "any more than the question of red-headed labor, or blue-eyed labor."[84] Sylvis became the president of the NLU in

80. Sylvis, *Life, Speeches, Labors,* 232, 343; Jonathan P. Grossman, *William Sylvis, Pioneer of American Labor: A Study in the Labor Movement during the Era of the Civil War* (New York, 1945), 229–32.

81. DHIS IX: 158–59.

82. Foner, *Black Workers and Organized Labor,* 20.

83. DHIS IX: 185–88; *Workingman's Advocate,* 24 and 31 Aug. 1867 [DH I: 407].

84. *Boston Daily Evening Voice,* 27 Aug. 1867 [DH I: 408].

1868 and invited black delegates to the 1869 convention. At the same time, black leaders began planning a separate convention of black labor unions.

Because the vast majority of blacks worked the soil of the former Confederacy, the reorganization of southern agriculture was their primary concern, closely linked to the political questions of Reconstruction. Congress established free labor under the Civil Rights Act and Fourteenth Amendment to enable blacks to take advantage of market power and shape an independent and decentralized farming system. In addition to individual bargaining, the freedmen also adopted collective and direct action methods in dealing with the new economy.[85] "Your late owners are forming labor associations for the purpose of fixing and maintaining, without the least reference to your wishes or wants, the price to be paid for your labor," a committee of Norfolk blacks warned their fellows, "and we say to you, 'Go and do likewise,'" calling for black counter-organization.[86]

Collective labor action was often carried out under the auspices of the Union League. Freedmen boycotted offensive planters, seized crops when defrauded by them, and squatted on land after contracts expired.[87] Whites complained that a convention of South Carolina blacks "proposes to change the Union League into Labor Unions, and put into force upon the plantations and in every household, all the iron-handed despotism of the white labor unions, which in point of fact destroys *bargain* in the employment of labor, and makes the employer the victim of compulsion."[88] Freedmen showed a remarkable ability to organize and at times to enforce collective labor policies.[89]

Agrarian activism in the Reconstruction South displayed some resemblance to labor union tactics, but it usually observed the limits of the free labor philosophy. The Union League and Republican Party discouraged violent "wildcat strike" activity, and the freedmen usually did not engage in violence, which southern whites readily interpreted as "insurrection." Collective action was usually a response to planter violations of self-ownership, and even then it often invited reprisals—such as the Ku Klux Klan took up after 1868. Blacks could see the danger of organized coercion in white farm workers' efforts to push them out of the labor mar-

---

85. Williamson, *After Slavery*, 103.

86. "Address by a Committee of Norfolk Blacks," 26 Jun. 1865, in C. Peter Ripley, ed., *The Black Abolitionist Papers*, 5 vols. (Chapel Hill, 1985–92), IV: 342.

87. Fitzgerald, *Union League Movement*, 6, 104, 151–74.

88. *Macon Telegraph*, 22 Oct. 1869 [DH II: 8].

89. Jaynes, *Branches without Roots*, 117–18.

ket in order to raise their own wages. The white campaign for residential and oc-cupational segregation succeeded mainly in the upcountry.[90]

The Reconstruction agricultural settlement, with decentralized black farms under sharecropping or rental tenure, reflected concessions by both planters and freedmen within a free market. "Thus, by mutual consent occurred the marriage between the labor of the Negro and the capital of the white; a union of convenience certainly and possibly one of necessity, but no less a marriage for all that," a histo-rian notes.[91] Despite frequent complaints about "land monopoly," a significant re-ordering of the southern agricultural system occurred, and blacks made real eco-nomic progress. Land ownership was not the freedmen's central goal that many historians have depicted, and black farmers were able to improve their living stan-dards without it. Land ownership surely would have enhanced black economic progress, but it was not the panacea that is often counterfactually prescribed.[92]

Urban blacks faced perhaps greater challenges than the rural labor force. Free-born blacks in Richmond had to abide by early Black Codes meant to control those recently emancipated. Cities like Vicksburg and Mobile followed the example of antebellum New York and imposed high license fees on draymen to keep blacks out of that occupation. Immigrants in many border state and northern cities be-gan to edge blacks out of many of their traditional trades.[93] In Baltimore, whites completed their effort to exclude black shipyard workers in 1865. This provoked the organization of an independent black shipyard under the leadership of Isaac Myers, the most important black labor organizer of the era.

Myers was born of free black parents in Baltimore in 1835. Privately educated, he became an apprentice caulker at sixteen and was soon supervising large proj-ects. After some years in the wholesale grocery business, Myers returned to orga-nize a black shipyard. He raised ten thousand dollars in five-dollar shares—mostly in the Baltimore black community—and borrowed another thirty thousand to lease a shipyard and establish the Chesapeake Marine Railway and Dry Dock Com-

90. Flynn, *White Land, Black Labor,* 105; Jaynes, *Branches without Roots,* 255.

91. Williamson, *After Slavery,* 125.

92. *Proceedings of the Colored National Labor Convention* (Washington, 1870), 30; Higgs, *Competi-tion and Coercion,* 23, 42–52, 80; Fitzgerald, *Union League Movement,* 230; Williamson, *After Slavery,* 121–25; Greene and Woodson, *Negro Wage-Earner,* 27; Scott P. Marler, "Fables of the Reconstruction: Reconstruction of the Fables," *Journal of the Historical Society* 4 (2004), 122–28.

93. Peter Rachleff, *Black Labor in Richmond, 1865–90* (Urbana, 1984), 35; Fitzgerald, *Union League Movement,* 30; Greene and Woodson, *Negro Wage Earner,* 23.

pany. Several hundred black caulkers and carpenters were at work and were soon joined by whites, some of whom had lately tried to drive their new co-workers out of the trade.[94]

Myers's thinking, like Frederick Douglass's, displayed a combination of entrepreneurship and labor organization, of integration and racial self-help, and of liberal self-ownership and labor collectivist ideas of "free labor." Myers did not accept the supply-and-demand theory of labor value. A worker's wage, he said, should be based on what it costs him to afford a home, to educate his children, and to set aside money for old age, "not what a man or a combination of men would choose to pay you."[95] But he did argue that the state could not legislate wages, and he served as a delegate to a labor convention that accepted the proposition that "the price of labor, like that of any other commodity, is regulated by the law of supply and demand."[96] He emphasized the natural harmony of capital and labor, "founded on the soundest principles of political economy" and a "Divine economy ruling the world's affairs."[97] He explained the gap between labor and capital in personal, moral terms. "Capital is covetous, labor is prodigal. Capital seeks to gather in and increase its store, while labor squanders its surplus to gratify superficial tastes," he said. As a result, "millions of laborers are the absolute slaves of capital, receiving but a pittance of the wealth their labor produces."[98] But Myers's "wage slavery" language alternated with self-ownership, right-to-work terms. "American citizenship with the black man is a complete failure," he told the National Labor Union in 1869, "if he is proscribed from the workshops of the country—if any man cannot employ him who chooses, and if he cannot work for any man whom he will."[99] Organization held out the key to labor's success, but the means and methods of organization remained cautious and voluntary.

94. "Isaac Myers," ANB; "A Biographical Sketch of Isaac Myers," *The Freeman* (Indianapolis), 12 Oct. 1889 [DH I: 416]; Thomas, "A Nineteenth-Century Black Operated Shipyard"; August Meier and Elliott Rudwick, "Attitudes of Negro Leaders toward the American Labor Movement from the Civil War to World War One," in Julius Jacobson, ed., *The Negro and the American Labor Movement* (Garden City, 1968), 28.

95. Myers address to Virginia state convention, *New National Era*, 28 Apr. 1870 [DH II: 113].

96. Colored National Labor Union Annual Address, *New National Era*, 19 Jan. 1871 [DH II: 95]; *Proceedings of the Colored National Labor Convention*, 30.

97. "Address of the Colored Delegates," *New York Times*, 19 Aug. 1869, 1 [DH I: 413]; Colored National Labor Union Annual Address.

98. Colored National Labor Union Annual Address.

99. "Address of the Colored Delegates."

The admission of black delegates to the 1869 NLU convention was the first time that American labor reformers advocated and recognized the organization of black workers.[100] But the National Labor Union's acceptance of the delegates did not allay black suspicions of the white labor movement. White unionists congratulated themselves that "the barriers of class and caste have broken down," and NLU editors assured blacks that the admission of their delegates "must convince the most skeptical that we are sincere in our declarations."[101] Elizabeth Cady Stanton scolded blacks, saying that if they did not succeed in forming labor unions, it was their own fault.[102] But the NLU did nothing beyond admitting delegates from black unions. Most significantly, it remained silent about discrimination and exclusion in white unions. Even if national unions advocated a nondiscrimination policy, they left admission policies in the hands of discriminatory locals—like the Maryland bricklayers local that imposed fifty-dollar fines on members who worked with blacks.[103]

It was in this context that Myers in 1868 set out to establish the Colored National Labor Union (CNLU). Its goals went beyond economic organization, pushing for the ratification of the Fifteenth Amendment, public education, and loyalty to the Republican Party. But, Myers said, "The bestowing of the franchise upon the colored men would benefit them but little if they did not organize and protect themselves and their families" in trade unions.[104] Black workers from every state were encouraged to send delegates to a December convention in Washington, to combat the "organized and unjust effort" by white unionists "to prevent men of African descent from obtaining a living at any one of the trades."[105] The CNLU was needed, Myers explained, because "I find the white mechanics of the North and South organized for the extermination of colored labor and because I do not find the colored men organized for their protection."[106]

Job competition continued to be the chief source of hostility between white and black workers. Both the NLU and the CNLU disparaged strikes. "Unfortu-

100. Foner, *Organized Labor and the Black Worker,* 26.

101. "Labor," *New York Times,* 22 Aug. 1869, p. 1. *The American Workman* (Boston), 28 Aug. 1869 [DH I: 415]; *Workingman's Advocate,* 30 Apr. 1870 [DH II: 275].

102. *The American Workman* (Boston), 30 Apr. 1871 [DH II: 275]; Sumner E. Matison, "Labor Movement and the Negro during Reconstruction," *Journal of Negro History* 33 (1948), 436–37.

103. *Workingman's Advocate,* 28 Jan. 1871 [DH II: 277].

104. *Baltimore Sun,* 20 Jul. 1869 [DH I: 422].

105. *Christian Recorder,* 14 Aug. 1869 [DH I: 424].

106. Myers address to Virginia state convention.

nately," Myers observed, "by the unwise counsel of brainless leaders, *strikes* are the first means resorted to as a remedy."[107] Frequently, strikes begun by one race were broken by workers of the other race. "Capital knows no difference between white and black laborers; and labor cannot make any without undermining its own platform," warned the *Boston Daily Evening Voice*.[108] "Capital is no respecter of persons," the NLU organ noted, "and it is in the very nature of things a sheer impossibility to degrade one class of laborers without degrading all."[109] But blacks from Portsmouth broke a Boston caulker's eight-hour strike, and white workers broke a black strike in Portland, Maine. In Charleston, black and white painters had formed separate unions and struck together in 1869. Lower-paid black painters wanted higher wages; higher-paid whites wanted a larger share of the work that went to blacks. The strike was settled by giving the whites still higher wages, making the painting trade even more stratified.[110]

Skilled, white New Orleans dockworkers, pledged to an all-white union since 1850, struck at the end of 1865. Local authorities believed that the free labor principle supported the right of black non-unionists to take their jobs. The black work force was so numerous that the white workers had to appeal to, as well as to coerce, them. Eventually white and black unionists agreed to divide the work according to a half-and-half quota system. This level of interracial labor action was driven by the need to "control the labor supply" rather than by a commitment to racial equality.[111]

The *New Orleans Daily Tribune,* the nation's first black daily newspaper, gave voice to views similar to Douglass's and Myers's. It supported the eight-hour day in hopes that "The white laborer and the black laborer, whose interests are one and the same, will thus be brought together, and the prejudices of caste will eventually die away."[112] Expressing the individualism and liberalism that characterized the black elite, it denounced coercion and interference with freedom of contract and

107. *Proceedings of the Colored National Labor Convention,* 10; Colored National Labor Union Annual Address.

108. 16 Jan. 1866, quoted in Matison, "Labor Movement and the Negro during Reconstruction," 432.

109. *Workingman's Advocate,* 2 Jan. 1869 [DH I: 374].

110. Matison, "Labor Movement and the Negro during Reconstruction," 428–33; Montgomery, *Beyond Equality,* 243; William C. Hine, "Black Organized Labor in Reconstruction Charleston," *Labor History* 25 (1984), 510.

111. Arnesen, *Waterfront Workers of New Orleans,* 20–24.

112. *New Orleans Daily Tribune,* 7 Dec. 1865 [DH I: 330].

did not believe that illegitimate union power was justified, even if it promoted racial cooperation.[113]

A successful strike among black lumberjacks in western Florida involved the intimidation of French-speaking migrant workers from Canada. Local authorities did nothing to protect the Acadians, and the U.S. Navy came to their rescue after the British consulate alerted the government. There were more than enough workers, black and white, to replace the strikers, and the strike effort failed, but the political influence of blacks remained an important advantage. After the strike the Florida legislature required workers to meet a six-month residency requirement before being able to work on the docks, effectively excluding foreign migrant workers, and black strikers tried for assault were acquitted by predominantly black juries.[114]

The majority of these race-based job actions failed because the unionists could not "control the labor supply." Blacks saw that attempts to control the labor supply often meant controlling and excluding workers of another race. The actions of these strikebreakers represented what Myers called the right of any man to employ whomever he chose and of any man to work for whomever he chose.

One of the most high-profile clashes between white and black unionists involved Frederick Douglass's son, Lewis, secretary of the CNLU. Trained as a printer, Lewis Douglass could not win admission to the International Typographical Union in the District of Columbia. The typographers accused him of having worked as a "rat" (non-union member) in Denver, and a minority of the local was able to prevent his election, a super-majority of members being required for approval. The national union came to the defense of the minority, censuring the Government Printing Office for employing a "rat."[115] Though the Columbia Ty-

---

113. Arnesen, *Waterfront Workers of New Orleans,* 24, 51.

114. Jerrell H. Shofner, "Militant Negro Laborers in Reconstruction Florida," *Journal of Southern History* 39 (1973), 397–408; Shofner, "Negro Laborers and the Forest Industries in Reconstruction Florida," *Journal of Forest History* 19 (1975), 189; Shofner, "The Labor League of Jacksonville: A Negro Union and White Strikebreakers," *Florida Historical Quarterly* 50 (1972), 278–82; W. K. Hyer to J. J. Midland, 8 Jan. 1873, Notes from British Legation, Department of State, RG 59, NA [DH II: 141].

115. Douglass, "We Are Not Yet Quite Free," 232–33; Matison, "Labor Movement and the Negro during Reconstruction," 449–50; *National Anti-Slavery Standard,* 3 and 17 Jul. 1869 [DH I: 374–79]; Factor, *Black Response to America,* 40. All of the black delegates to the 1869 NLU convention supported the typographers' move to eject Susan B. Anthony for having worked as a "rat"; Montgomery, *Beyond Equality,* 398.

pographical Union eventually admitted blacks into the union, many black work-ers continued to suffer this peculiar circular affront: Their continued exclusion from unions ensued from their acceptance of non-union jobs due to their exclu-sion from those same unions.[116]

Other issues divided the National and Colored National Labor Unions. The NLU moved toward the formation of a third political party while the CNLU re-mained steadfastly Republican, and its loyalty became firmer when Frederick Douglass was elected CNLU president in 1871.[117] "Never before in the history of the country have the working people received so large a remuneration for their labor, and been so prosperous and happy, for which we are especially indebted to the Re-publican Congress" and the tariff, Douglass wrote in his newspaper, the CLNU or-gan.[118] Ohio lawyer and activist John M. Langston accused some white delegates to the 1869 CLNU convention of trying to detach blacks from the Republican Party, and Langston himself and other "politician delegates" were ousted from the 1870 NLU convention.[119] The next year the NLU warned, "Ultimately the colored race, like every other, must stand on their own merits; that if they shall prove themselves capable of competing with white labor, no legislation can keep them down; while on the other hand, if they are tried and found wanting, no class legislation can maintain them in a false position." Castigating blacks as strikebreakers and Re-publicans, the NLU accused black workers of allying themselves with the enemies of labor. It said that it refused to grant "special privileges" to blacks and did not "propose to allow one of its members to become the pillars of oppression, the stool pigeons of the very powers whose aggressions it was organized to resist." Black workers "must learn to respect the rights of others first."[120] The 1870 NLU con-vention was the last one that blacks attended. The CNLU held its last meeting in 1871, and the NLU disintegrated shortly after the failure of its Labor Reform Party in the 1872 election.

116. Spero and Harris, *The Black Worker*, 20. Bloch, "Labor and the Negro," 180.

117. *New National Era*, 15 Sep. 1870 [DH II: 170].

118. *New National Era*, 11 Apr. 1872 [DH II: 287].

119. *Proceedings of the Colored National Labor Convention*, 5; *American Workman* (Boston), 25 Dec. 1869 [DH II: 76]; Foner, *Organized Labor and the Black Worker*, 37; Commons et al., *History of Labor in the United States*, II: 145; William and Aimee Lee Cheek, "John Mercer Langston: Principle and Poli-tics," in Leon Litwack and August Meier, eds., *Black Leaders of the Nineteenth Century* (Urbana, 1988), 103–26.

120. *Workingman's Advocate*, 11 Nov. 1871 [DH II: 106].

THE LIBERAL REPUBLICAN REVOLT

Black workers resisted the pull of the collectivist "labor" movement and remained faithful to the Republican Party. They also faced the concurrent departure of liberal Republicans who feared that the party had become too close to groups that would use government power to stifle individual competition.

Though most abolitionist and antislavery Republicans remained loyal to President Ulysses S. Grant, a significant number of them, including Lyman Trumbull and Charles Sumner, rejected the party in 1872. Many antebellum liberals had always been uncomfortable with the statist aspects of the Republican Party—the protective tariff, subsidies for internal improvements, and wartime policies like fiat currency. The corruption of the Grant administration and the Republican governments in the southern states aggravated this sentiment. Impatience and disillusionment with the freedmen accounted for some of their discomfort, and the Liberal revolt of 1872 is usually depicted as the "abandonment" of the freedmen.[121] But there was merit in the liberals' concern that blacks "were learning their first lessons in civics from the worst of teachers."[122]

Though a generation of revisionist historians has discredited the legend of "Black Reconstruction," it remains true that southern Reconstruction governments displayed many of the worst traits of Gilded Age politics. That they were not unique, or that northern or white Redeemer regimes were equally corrupt and incompetent, did not alter the problem. To the extent that the Reconstruction governments exhibited "proletarian rule," they engaged in redistributive policies that most Americans would not accept until the New Deal.[123] Northern sympathy for white southerners manifested more than just renascent racism, for northerners committed to liberal principles were understandably alarmed when white south-

---

121. Hans L. Trefouse, *The Radical Republicans: Lincoln's Vanguard for Racial Justice* (Baton Rouge, 1968), 457; John G. Sproat, *"The Best Men": Liberal Reformers in the Gilded Age* (Chicago, 1968), 11–44; Patrick W. Riddleberger, "The Radicals' Abandonment of the Negro during Reconstruction," *Journal of Negro History* 45 (1960), 88–102.

122. Sproat, *"The Best Men,"* 39.

123. Foner, *Reconstruction,* 379–92; Jaynes, *Branches without Roots,* 287; Michael Les Benedict, "The Problem of Constitutionalism and Constitutional Liberty in the Reconstruction South," in Kermit Hall and James W. Ely Jr., eds., *An Uncertain Tradition: Constitutionalism and the History of the South* (Athens, GA, 1989), 237; Benedict, "Laissez-Faire and Liberty: A Re-Evaluation of the Meaning and Origins of Laissez-Faire Constitutionalism," *Law and History Review* 3 (1985), 293–331.

erners complained of the "class legislation" enacted by Reconstruction governments.[124] The Liberal revolt represented less of an abandonment of the freedmen
than a commitment to the principle of liberty, and suspicion of power and coercion, that promoted the antislavery effort in the first place.

Many liberals denied that bolting the Republican Party was tantamount to
abandoning the cause of the Negro. Blacks above all would benefit from sectional
reconciliation and the restoration of normal civil government in the South.[125]
Though they would regret the capture of the party by other interests, Liberals tried
to depict their effort as the extension of the Republican Party's founding principles.[126] There was some support for the Liberal ticket at the April 1872 Colored
National Convention in New Orleans, but Frederick Douglass kept most of them
loyal to the regular Republicans.[127] "The Republican party is the deck; all else is the
sea," he told the delegates.[128]

The Liberals' opposition to government interference with market forces led
them to condemn most labor organizations. The NLU convention, the liberal *Journal of Social Science* noted, "exhibited an ignorance of the very first principles of
social economy, coupled with an opinionated spirit, a defiance of common sense,

124. Benedict, "Problem of Constitutionalism," 240. This is a modified expression of the older
progressive view that their concern for "liberty" amounted to a bartering away of freedmen's rights to
prevent the disruption of class relations found in William B. Hesseltine, "Economic Factors in the
Abandonment of Reconstruction," *Mississippi Valley Historical Review* 22 (1935), 191–210; Montgomery,
Beyond Equality, 385; Richard F. Bensel, *Yankee Leviathan: The Origins of Central State Authority in
America, 1859–77* (Cambridge, 1990), 303, 350, 379.

125. James M. McPherson, "Grant or Greeley? The Abolitionist Dilemma in the Election of 1872,"
American Historical Review 71 (1965), 52; Wilbert H. Ahern, "Laissez-Faire Versus Equal Rights: Liberal
Republicans and the Negro, 1861–77" (Ph.D. diss., Northwestern University, 1968), 323; David Gerber,
"Peter H. Clark: The Dialogue of Hope and Despair," in Litwack and Meier, *Black Leaders of the Nine-
teenth Century*, 185.

126. David M. Tucker, *Mugwumps: Public Moralists of the Gilded Age* (Columbia, MO, 1998), 48,
113; Ahern, "Laissez-Faire Versus Equal Rights," 22; George Selden Henry Jr., "Radical Republican Policy toward the Negro during Reconstruction, 1862–72" (Ph.D. diss., Yale University, 1963), 331; Richard
Allan Gerber, "The Liberal Republicans of 1872 in Historiographical Perspective," *Journal of American
History* 62 (1975), 73.

127. Earle Dudley Ross, *The Liberal Republican Movement* (New York, 1971 [1919]), 78; Factor, *Black
Response to America*, 50.

128. "The Colored Citizens," *Harper's Weekly*, 11 May 1872, p. 363; "A Word with Some Republicans," ibid., 25 May 1872, p. 403.

a readiness to accept and advocate the wildest theories of European socialistic schools" and "confirmed the truth demonstrated in former years, that our working classes are not a whit more advanced than those of the Old World." It applauded the inclusion of black delegates and noted that the proceedings of the CNLU were "far more sensible" It commended the CNLU's lack of "empty discussion" and its appreciation that "it will be better for the freedmen in the end to depend in the future for their material improvement on their own efforts rather than on the assistance of the Government, and that public opinion inclines strongly to this view." [129]

In addition, the Reconstruction governments, based as they were on white disfranchisement and Union Army occupation, faced a fundamental problem of legitimacy. The reestablishment of white-Democratic governments was only a matter of time. Four of the eleven Confederate states had been "redeemed" by 1872, and sectional reconciliation was nearly complete. "No administration could have prolonged the process for more than a few years," one historian notes. [130]

Liberal principles did not prevail in 1872, but they remained a powerful force throughout the nineteenth century, particularly in constitutional law. Historians often depict an inherent conflict between economic and racial liberalism in the late nineteenth century and claim that the Fourteenth Amendment ended up protecting big business rather than the freedmen. [131] The often misunderstood relationship between economic and racial liberalism is manifest in the first interpretation of the Fourteenth Amendment by the Supreme Court, the year after the Liberal revolt.

In the *Slaughterhouse Cases,* a group of butchers challenged the monopoly that the state of Louisiana granted to the Crescent City Live-Stock Landing and Slaughtering Company. [132] Ostensibly enacted as an ordinary regulation to protect public health, the act was typical of the kind of special-interest legislation that liberals excoriated, by a notoriously corrupt Reconstruction regime. The butchers claimed that the Fourteenth Amendment's provision that "no state shall make or enforce any law which shall abridge the privileges or immunities of citizens of the United

---

129. "General Intelligence," *Journal of Social Science* 2 (1869–70), 206–14.

130. Sproat, *"The Best Men,"* 86; Benedict, *The Fruits of Victory,* 47.

131. David E. Bernstein, *Only One Place of Redress: African Americans, Labor Regulations, and the Courts from Reconstruction to the New Deal* (Durham, 2001), 54.

132. 83 U.S. 36 (1873).

States," protected every man's right to pursue a lawful trade. A narrow Court majority rejected this interpretation, saying that the "privileges and immunities" protected by the amendment were few and that Congress intended it to protect the freedmen almost exclusively. The dissenters accepted the butchers' argument that the amendment should prevent a state from depriving them of their right to pursue a legal trade. This broad-based defense of economic freedom, consonant with the free labor substance of the Civil Rights Act and Fourteenth Amendment, could have had great potential to protect black economic progress against discriminatory state interference. But it would prevail only after racial theory grabbed hold of social and political thought.[133]

The convection of liberal and labor ideas continued to stir the mind of Frederick Douglass. He remained loyal to Grant in 1872 but shared many liberal impulses. While a Garrisonian abolitionist he recognized the links between abolition and economic freedom. The world was becoming smaller via nineteenth-century technology, he said. "A change has now come over the affairs of mankind. Walled cities and empires have become unfashionable. The arm of commerce has borne away the gates of the strong city. Intelligence is penetrating the darkest corners of the globe. It makes its pathway over and under the sea, as well as on earth. Wind, steam, and lightning are its chartered agents."[134] Douglass also made occasional references to class conflict, arguing that leaving the freedmen to the control of their former masters was akin to "placing . . . the laborer in the power of the capitalist."[135] Though he remained confident that individual exertions, if protected by civil rights laws and the suffrage, would lead to success, he sometimes worried about the growth of a permanent, degraded American working class. "The government, in giving the negro his freedom, has given him the freedom to starve, and in giving him the ballot-box, has given him a coffin."[136] "It is a long step from slavery to the wage system . . . But it is also a long way from the wage system to the complete emancipation of working people. The relation of laborer to employer is servitude for a consideration—a modified slavery entered voluntarily by the laborer himself, and terminable at his pleasure." He also claimed that many labor re-

133. Bernstein, *Only One Place of Redress.*

134. "What to the Slave Is the Fourth of July?" *American Heritage: A Reader,* 2d ed. (Acton, MA, 2000), 297.

135. Factor, *Black Response to America,* 29, 36, 43.

136. *New National Era,* 19 Jan. 1871 [DH II: 99].

formers "are more or less adherents of communism" and "have no higher motive than that of obtaining a 'new deal' for themselves and theirs." He singled out Wendell Phillips, whom he said believed "that as soon as a man ceases to work for day wages and begins to hire other men, he is no longer entitled to the fruits of his enterprise, for the profit he makes on the labor of others, and hardly to the protection of the laws."[137]

Douglass seemed to understand that union exclusion was more the result of unsound economic thinking than of racism. "I cannot think so meanly of my fellow-citizens as to suppose that their opposition proceeds altogether from villainy," he said of union discrimination in 1869. "It is due in part to honest stupidity, and to that narrow notion of political economy which supposes every piece of bread that goes into the mouth of one man, is so much bread taken out of the mouth of another." This struck at the essential union idea that there was a surplus of labor and a scarcity of employment. Too many labor reformers overlooked the greed and selfishness of workers and their unions.[138] In arguing against the Labor Reform Party in 1870, Douglass said that no such party was needed so long as individual rights and legal equality were secured. "Any party which seeks or pretends to do more or less for the workingman is an injury both to him and to the country."[139]

His experience with the white labor movement was surely the source of much of Douglass's ambivalence about political economy and labor relations in general. His view of the role of labor unions could not be clearer. In 1874 he wrote an essay on "The Folly, Tyranny, and Wickedness of Labor Unions." "On more than one occasion we have attempted to convince the workingmen of the absolute injury to their interests of the labor unions of the country, and also their oppressions and tyrannical course toward fellow workmen, as well as to their employers," Douglass wrote. "The history of these organizations—generally managed, not by industrious workmen themselves, but by unprincipled demagogues who control them for their own benefit—furnishes abundant proof almost every day of their mischie-

137. *New National Era*, 20 Apr. 1871, 12 Oct. 1871, 14 Dec. 1871 [DH II: 171–76].

138. Douglass, "We Are Not Yet Quite Free," 3 Aug. 1869, in John W. Blassingame et al., eds., *The Frederick Douglass Papers*, 5 vols. to date (New Haven, 1979–), IV: 231; Clarence B. Carson, "The Impact of Unionism," in Hans F. Sennholz, ed., *American Unionism: Fallacies and Follies* (Irvington, NY, 1994), 129–42.

139. *New National Era*, 15 Sep. 1870 [DH II: 170].

vous influence upon every industrial interest in the country."[140] Though he conceded that not all unions were bad, the experience of the first labor organizations strengthened the libertarian side of Douglass, the one that answered the question, "What Should Be Done with Emancipated Slaves" in 1862: "Do nothing with them; mind your business, and let them mind theirs. Your *doing* with them is their greatest misfortune. They have been undone by your doings, and all they now ask, and really have need of at your hands, is just to let them alone. They suffer by every interference, and succeed best by being left alone. The great majority of human duties are of this negative character."[141] On the whole, Douglass carried the liberalism of the abolitionist movement through to the close of the century.

Coincident with the withdrawal of federal troops from the South was their use in the first nationwide labor clash, the great railroad strike of 1877. Historians have depicted this sequence as indicative of the advent of a national policy that would leave blacks at the mercy of southern whites and labor at the mercy of capital, as white supremacists of the South allied themselves with plutocrats of the North.[142] Such an interpretation is oversimplified, however. Reconstruction can be said to have "ended" in 1868 while its effects continued into the 1890s. The great strike was also complex in economic and racial terms.

Laissez-faire liberals recognized that railroads were no ordinary industry. They had been built through government subsidies that fed a corrupt system that led many liberals to leave the Republican Party in 1872.[143] Workers in this industry could claim that they demanded what the owners had gotten—privileged relief from market competition. As the U.S. Strike Commission noted after the 1894 Pullman strike, "Railroads have not the inherent rights of employers engaged in private business; they are creatures of the state, whose rights are conferred upon them for public purposes." That they sought such privileges through violence rather than bribery, however, turned public opinion against them. "The right to

140. *New National Era*, 7 May 1874 [DH II: 178].

141. *Douglass' Monthly*, Jan. 1862, in Michael Meyer, ed., *Frederick Douglass: The Narrative and Selected Writings* (New York, 1984), 374.

142. Foner, *Reconstruction*, 585; W. R. Brock, *An American Crisis: Congress and Reconstruction, 1865–67* (New York, 1963), 300–01.

143. Sidney Fine, *Laissez-Faire and the General Welfare State: A Study in Conflict in American Thought, 1865–1901* (Ann Arbor, 1956), 65–71; Charles Francis Adams, "The Prevention of Railroad Strikes," *The Nation* 636 (6 Sep. 1877), 99; Alan Jones, "Thomas M. Cooley and 'Laissez-Faire Constitutionalism': A Reconsideration," *Journal of American History* 53 (1967), 756.

strike is conceded by everybody," *The Nation* commented. "The right to seize other people's property and to prevent them from selling their labor on terms satisfactory to themselves is denied by the law of every civilized country."[144] Though liberals might regard the grievances of workers against railroads, corruption, and tariffs as legitimate, the labor movement proposed not to curb monopoly abuses but to create new monopolies to counteract them.[145] The great strike was a harbinger of the future, for though the strike was broken, the railroad workers would be among the first to organize successfully, under the aegis of federal government power.

Blacks worked as strikebreakers on the Union Pacific Railroad in 1877, but the great strike also displayed an unusual, if small and temporary, solidarity between white and black workers.[146] Though initially unconcerned about the black proletariat, St. Louis socialists united with black workers and controlled the city for a week in a brief interracial commune.[147] But Mississippi congressman John R. Lynch noted that "few" blacks took part in the great strikes and "were hunted down, arrested, tried, punished in the courts and kept out of employment by the same white working men who inaugurated the strikes."[148] On the other hand, the California labor movement turned the 1877 strike into an anti-Chinese campaign. "Anti-coolie" organizations had been formed before the Civil War, and the cigarmakers union began the "union label" campaign against Chinese-made cigars: "The cigars herein contained are made by WHITE MEN," the label testified. Organized into the Workingmen's Party under the slogan "The Chinese Must Go," California labor leaders pushed for an end to Chinese immigration and employment. California's 1879 constitution prohibited the state or corporations from employing Chinese; other states similarly prohibited the employment of immigrants in public works.[149] Agitation, often violent, against Asian immigrant labor became a

---

144. *Report on the Chicago Strike of June–July 1894*, Sen. Exec. Doc. 7 (Washington, 1895), 11; *The Nation* 632 (9 Aug. 1877), 85.

145. Montgomery, *Beyond Equality*, 337.

146. Quintard Taylor, *In Search of the Racial Frontier: African Americans in the American West, 1528–1990* (New York, 1998), 205.

147. Philip S. Foner, *The Great Labor Uprising of 1877* (New York, 1977), 181–208; David Roediger, *The Wages of Whiteness: Race and the Making of the American Working Class* (New York, 1991), 168.

148. *AME Church Review* 3 (Oct. 1886), 165–67 [DH III: 40].

149. Commons et al., *History of Labor in the United States*, II: 262; John Higham, *Strangers in the Land: Patterns of American Nativism, 1860–1925* (Westport, 1981 [1955]), 46.

mainstay of the California labor movement for the next several decades.[150] While the movement had little appeal beyond the Pacific Coast, the anti-Chinese campaign reveals the fundamental economic fact that the labor movement had to control the supply of labor in order to raise wages.[151] As labor editor Andrew Cameron explained it, "We desire protection against foreign pauper labor imported against our interests, to reduce the price of labor."[152]

The few voices opposed to Chinese exclusion were old abolitionists and liberals, along with business interests who employed the Chinese. Manufacturers who faced competition from Chinese entrepreneurs also favored exclusion. Though some Liberal Republicans joined the anti-Chinese movement in California, William Lloyd Garrison defended Calvin Sampson, a Massachusetts shoemaker who employed Chinese workers to replace his striking workers, and Julia Ward Howe and Lydia Maria Child attributed anti-coolie agitation to "labor monopolists."[153] Despite its generally negative depiction of the Chinese, the black press similarly denounced union agitation against them.[154] But, as in their failure to control the Republican party or to launch a liberal Republican party, the liberals, like the socialists, remained on the margins of the discussion of labor and race relations in the late nineteenth century. They would continue to have influence, particularly in the courts, but liberalism would gradually lose ground to varieties of statism. The liberalism of the antislavery period would come to a crisis point by the end of the century.

---

150. Alexander Saxton, *The Indispensable Enemy: Labor and the Anti-Chinese Movement in California* (Berkeley, 1971), 69–128; David Montgomery, *The Fall of the House of Labor: The Workplace, the State, and American Labor Activism, 1865–1925* (Cambridge, 1987), 85.

151. Saxton, *Indispensable Enemy*, 259; Higham, *Strangers in the Land*, 45, 70. Andrew Gyory, *Closing the Gate: Race, Politics, and the Chinese Exclusion Act* (Chapel Hill, 1998), and Robert Weir, "Blind in One Eye Only: Western and Eastern Knights of Labor View the Chinese Question," *Labor History* 41 (2000), 421–36, discount the appeal of anti-Chinese movement east of the Mississippi before 1882.

152. *Workingman's Advocate*, 1 Sep. 1866.

153. Martin Brown and Peter Philips, "Competition, Racism, and Hiring Practices among California Manufacturers, 1860–82," *Industrial and Labor Relations Review* 40 (1986), 61–74; Ross, *Liberal Republican Movement*, 171; Gyory, *Closing the Gate*, 55–58; Saxton, *Indispensable Enemy*, 133–35.

154. Arnold Shankman, *Ambivalent Friends: Afro-Americans View the Immigrant* (Westport, 1982), 19–22; David J. Hellwig, "Black Reactions to Chinese Immigration and the Anti-Chinese Movement: 1850–1910," *Amerasia* 6 (1979), 25–44.

2 / From Reconstruction to Jim Crow, 1877–1895

The black American population remained concentrated in the South in the last quarter of the nineteenth century, a fluid, dynamic, and experimental period in race relations. Taking advantage of market opportunities where they were not prevented by coercion, blacks accumulated land and saw a general rise in living standards. Fundamental indicators like mortality and fertility rates showed that blacks were making economic progress faster than whites, albeit when measured from the low starting point of slavery. With all its limitations, a substantial black business class also emerged in southern cities.[1]

By the 1890s, black economic success prompted a white reaction, most clearly seen in formal segregation.[2] "Beginning from the depths," one historian observes, "southern Negroes had risen markedly in literacy and property holding after the war, facts sometimes evident to the poorer whites and always easy to exaggerate. And as it happened, Negroes enjoyed rapid advance during the 1880s."[3] The triumph of trade unionism in the American Federation of Labor augmented this reaction, as competition gave way to coercion and the progressive search for order limited opportunity for blacks. Southern unions wavered in this period as to whether they should exclude black competitors or bring them into their membership. If southern whites adjusted their class differences at the expense of the Negro, white capital's agreement to white labor's demand for racial exclusion or segregation was no small part of the compromise.[4]

1. C. Vann Woodward, *Origins of the New South* (Baton Rouge, 1951); Woodward, *The Strange Career of Jim Crow*, 3d ed. (New York, 1974), 33–44; Edward L. Ayers, *The Promise of the New South: Life after Reconstruction* (New York, 1992), 70, 208; Robert Higgs, *Competition and Coercion: Blacks in the American Economy, 1865–1914* (Cambridge, 1977), 23, 90, 97–102, 123; Howard Rabinowitz, *Race Relations in the Urban South, 1865–90* (New York, 1978), 78–95.

2. Ayers, *Promise of the New South*, 140; Stephan and Abigail Thernstrom, *America in Black and White: One Nation, Indivisible* (New York, 1997), 32. For a similar development in South Africa, see W. H. Hutt, *The Economics of the Colour Bar: A Study of the Economic Origins and Consequences of Racial Segregation in South Africa* (London, 1964), 29.

3. Robert Wiebe, *The Search for Order, 1877–1920* (New York, 1967), 59; W. E. B. Du Bois, "The Passing of Jim Crow," *Independent*, 14 Jul. 1917 [DuBP LXXXI: 1648].

4. Woodward, *Origins of the New South*, 229; Woodward, *Strange Career of Jim Crow*, 6; Ayers, *Promise of the New South*, 431.

BLACK PHYSICAL AND SOCIAL MOBILITY

Physical mobility was the most important benefit of emancipation, enabling blacks to gain higher wages either by moving or threatening to move. Conspiracies among planters to keep wages low always failed, as landowners competed with one another for workers. While the resort to outright violence was not uncommon, planters also did all that they could within the law to inhibit black labor mobility. The Black Codes had been the clearest expression of this goal to limit black opportunity, but Republican Reconstruction governments repealed or prevented the enforcement of most of them. As Democrats regained power, they did not reenact the codes all at once, but did so gradually, so that most were again in force by the turn of the century. As with disfranchisement and segregation laws, they became more common and more stringent in the 1890s.[5]

Most blacks migrated westward, from one part of the South to another. Virginia, North Carolina, Kentucky, and Tennessee lost black population in every decade after 1870, while Mississippi gained black residents in the 1870s, as did Louisiana and Arkansas in the 1880s. Texas gained blacks during every decade before World War II, except for the 1900s. The Mississippi Delta especially attracted blacks; labor was so scarce there that they were able to get jobs in new industries that were reserved for whites in the older regions of the South. Blacks could also purchase land, and sometimes did so in greater proportions than the white population did.[6] Near the end of the century the *New Orleans Picayune* noted that Italian immigrants were supplanting blacks in the sugar fields. "The movement is the result of economic laws that have been silently but most potentially at work, and they will never cease to operate until they shall establish equilibrium."[7] Nevertheless, black migration remained regional. Overall, 90 percent of the black population remained in the South until World War I. Southern blacks still found themselves isolated and unaware of the opportunities that existed in the North, and such opportunities remained limited. Southern whites also prevented them from taking advantage of them.[8]

---

5. William Cohen, *At Freedom's Edge: Black Mobility and the Southern White Quest for Racial Control, 1861–1915* (Baton Rouge, 1991), xiv.

6. Ibid., table 13; Ayers, *Promise of the New South*, 195.

7. *New Orleans Picayune*, 10 Nov. 1898 [HNCF 264].

8. Higgs, *Competition and Coercion*, 28–30.

One of the devices that kept black labor in place was the convict-lease system. Though the effort to use vagrancy laws to turn the freedmen into a bound labor force failed during Reconstruction, the states often leased out to private employers prisoners convicted of ordinary crimes. Reconstruction Republicans devised the system to save the state the cost of imprisonment and to generate revenue, and the Redeemers continued it. It usually fell most heavily on blacks—89 percent of 734 convicts leased by Alabama in 1880 were black. The system provided one of the most persistent grievances of organized labor—Virginia's purchase of convict-made barrels provoked and sustained an interracial cooper union strike in Richmond in the 1870s.[9] While the use of the criminal justice system to coerce black labor dated from Reconstruction, debt-peonage laws—involuntary servitude as the means of debt repayment—did not emerge until the early twentieth century.

Redeemer governments attempted to revive laws that punished "enticement"— the offering of higher wages to workers under contract to another planter. But these laws affected employers rather than workers directly. Louisiana enacted a law that criminalized the breach of a labor contract in 1871, and in 1885 Alabama enacted a "false pretenses" act, punishing those who made labor contracts and received advances for work with the intent to leave before the end of the season. Three other states enacted false-pretenses acts before 1891, but since they required proof of intent to defraud, they were of little value before 1903, when Georgia declared that the making of the contract was presumptive of intent to defraud.[10]

States also attempted to use license requirements and heavy taxes to stop "emigrant agents" who worked for labor-hungry employers and informed workers of better opportunities—a risky business even in states that did not try to inhibit the practice legally. Virginia enacted the first emigrant-agent law in 1870. Georgia enacted one in 1876 and Alabama in 1877, the latter limited to Black Belt counties. In 1882 the Alabama Supreme Court held the act unconstitutional, and North Carolina's 1891 law was overturned in 1893. The status of emigrant-agent laws remained uncertain until 1900, when the U.S. Supreme Court upheld them. Several states responded to union attempts at job control by trying to prevent the "importation" of workers, federal courts struck such acts down. The panoply of labor-control de-

9. Cohen, *At Freedom's Edge*, 228; Daniel Letwin, *The Challenge of Interracial Unionism: Alabama Coal Miners, 1878–1921* (Chapel Hill, 1998), 29; Peter Rachleff, *Black Labor in Richmond, 1865–90* (Urbana, 1984), 82.

10. Cohen, *At Freedom's Edge*, 229–31.

vices—convict leasing and debt peonage, enticement and emigrant-agent laws— had been growing in fits and starts since Reconstruction but did not come together into a coherent and effective system until the 1890s, and especially after 1900.[11]

Behind these legal devices lurked such illegal means of controlling black competition as lynching and "whitecapping"—terror to prevent black ownership or rental of land or the destruction of black businesses. Historians remain divided over the impact of these laws and practices on black economic prospects. Some discount the impact of anti-enticement and debt peonage laws while others conclude that they had a "severely effective" deterrent effect and argue that "No government which allows its laboring population to mortgage its labor by enforcing debt peonage can claim to have free labor."[12]

Legal and illegal impediments notwithstanding, blacks made sustained economic progress between the end of Reconstruction and the establishment of formal segregation. Blacks had accumulated 586,000 acres of land, assessed at $1.5 million, by 1880. They saw their per capita incomes rise at 2–2.7 percent annually from the end of the Civil War to the end of the century. Their incomes grew faster than those of whites, so that black per capita income increased from 24 percent of the white average to 35 percent. This showed itself in higher standards of living in diet, housing, and education. Black entrepreneurs continued to prosper after the end of Reconstruction and beyond the 1890s. While chroniclers often exaggerate the extent of black migration to the frontier, particularly the Kansas "Exodus" of 1879, blacks did exploit opportunities in the West. They encountered no significant discrimination in the western cattle industry, and blacks found more opportunities for genuine freedom there than almost anywhere else.[13] "Writers who have por-

11. Ayers, *Promise of the New South,* 120, 150; Cohen, *At Freedom's Edge,* 232–38, 246, 275; David Bernstein, "The Law and Economics of Post–Civil War Restrictions on Interstate Migration by African-Americans," *Texas Law Review* 76 (1998), 791–801; "Record of Political Events," *Political Science Quarterly* 14 (1899), 373; *The Nation* 69 (1899), 198; "The Negroes Withdrawn," *Detroit Free Press,* 27 Jul. 1901 [HNCF 264].

12. Higgs, *Competition and Coercion,* 76; Gerald D. Jaynes, *Branches without Roots: Genesis of the Black Working Class in the American South, 1862–82* (New York, 1986), 308; Scott P. Marler, "Fables of the Reconstruction: Reconstruction of the Fables," *Journal of the Historical Society* 4 (2004), 122–28.

13. James P. Smith, "Race and Human Capital," *American Economic Review* 74 (1984), 688; Robert C. Kenzer, *Enterprising Southerners: Black Economic Success in North Carolina, 1865–1915* (Charlottesville, 1997); Kenzer, "The Black Businessman in the Postwar South: North Carolina, 1865–80," *Business History Review* 63 (1989), 61–87; Cohen, *At Freedom's Edge,* 196, 255; Bradley J. Birzer, "Ex-

trayed the economic condition of blacks in the late 19th century or early 20th century as having improved only slightly are surely mistaken," an economic historian concludes.[14]

Though they remained overwhelmingly agrarian, blacks had begun making inroads into the urban industrial work force in the years after Reconstruction. They took advantage of market opportunities in both the agricultural and the industrial labor markets but probably faced more discrimination in the latter. Exclusion of blacks from tobacco and textile industries contributed to the economic decline of urban black workers in the late nineteenth century.[15] These years also saw a burst of labor union activity that held out the possibility that unions might present a help rather than an obstacle to black economic progress.

THE KNIGHTS OF LABOR

Historians have depicted the principal labor federation of the late nineteenth century, the Knights of Labor, as the most racially egalitarian labor organization prior to the CIO. Where the National Labor Union had run from the issue and hidden behind its constitution's silence, the Knights of Labor faced it, however tentatively. But more important than its ambivalence about race was its amorphous nature as an organization and its position on strikes.

Like the NLU, the Knights established a "reform" federation. Backward-looking, it rejected the wage system and hoped to restore the imagined independence and harmony of pre-industrial society through a campaign of education and class conciliation. Its reaction to the industrial revolution was emotional rather than rational, resulting in many contradictory and confused positions.[16]

---

panding Creative Destruction: Entrepreneurship in the American Wests," *Western Historical Quarterly* 30 (1999), 59; Kenneth W. Porter, "Negro Labor in the Western Cattle Industry, 1866–1900," in Milton Cantor, ed., *Black Labor in America* (Westport, 1969), 41, 51.

14. Higgs, *Competition and Coercion,* 52, 97–116, 123; Higgs, "Black Progress and the Persistence of Racial Economic Inequalities, 1865–1940," in Steven Shulman and William Darity Jr., eds., *The Question of Discrimination: Racial Inequality in the U.S. Labor Market* (Middletown, CT, 1989), 12.

15. Higgs, *Competition and Coercion,* 60, 65, 89; Rayford Logan, *The Negro in American Life and Thought: The Nadir, 1877–1901* (New York, 1954), 152; Michelle Brattain, *The Politics of Whiteness: Race, Workers, and Culture in the Modern South* (Princeton, 2001), 19.

16. Gerald N. Grob, *Workers and Utopia: A Study of Ideological Conflict in the American Labor Movement, 1865–1900* (Evanston, IL, 1961).

Philadelphia tailor Uriah Stephens founded the Knights of Labor. An anti-slavery Republican, Stephens left the party when he concluded that "monopolists" dominated it. Stephens had established a Garment Cutters' Association in 1862 and attributed its failure to lack of secrecy. In 1869 he followed it with the "Noble and Holy Order of the Knights of Labor," whose members were bound to secrecy by oath. Stephens led the mostly Pennsylvanian organization until Terence V. Powderly succeeded him in 1879. Powderly was a railroad machinist and politician, elected mayor of Scranton in 1878 under the Greenback-Labor Party banner. He shared the reform unionism of Stephens and the Knights but, though he had been blacklisted for his organizing activities, ended the secrecy oath in 1882 to make the order more appealing to Catholics.[17]

The Knights of Labor comprised a variety of workingmen and associations. Trade unions composed some of the order's local assemblies, but more often these were "mixed" groupings that could include anyone except lawyers, stockbrokers, liquor dealers, gamblers, or bankers. Local assemblies sent delegates to district and state assemblies, which in turn sent delegates to a general assembly. The executive board of the general assembly was quite powerful on paper (one historian notes that its concentration of power "would have greatly endangered democratic institutions"), but in fact the Knights of Labor allowed the extensive local autonomy that has been typical of American labor organizations.[18]

The signals the locals got from Knights of Labor leaders regarding race were basically inclusive, but mixed. Powderly himself had egalitarian instincts that he attributed to his abolitionist mother, and he believed that the labor movement was the natural extension of the antislavery movement. But the Knights zealously supported the anti-Chinese movement, refusing to admit Chinese workers, recommending boycotts against Chinese goods and labor, and lobbying Congress for exclusion. Knights led the 1885 Spring Rock, Wyoming, riot that killed 28 Chinese railroad workers, and this caused Powderly to suspect that the organization's

17. Sidney H. Kessler, "The Negro in the Knights of Labor" (M.A. Thesis, Columbia University, 1950), 8; Leon Fink, *Workingmen's Democracy: The Knights of Labor and American Politics* (Urbana, 1983); Foster Rhea Dulles, *Labor in America: A History*, 3d ed. (New York, 1966), ch. 8; Jason Kaufman, "The Rise and Fall of a Nation of Joiners: The Knights of Labor Revisited," *Journal of Interdisciplinary History* 31 (2001), 6.

18. Dulles, *Labor in America*, 127–131; Robert E. Weir, *Beyond Labor's Veil: The Culture of the Knights of Labor* (University Park, PA, 1996), xvii; Melton A. McLaurin, *The Knights of Labor in the South* (Westport, 1978), 42.

anti-Chinese campaign had gone too far.[19] The Knights also favored immigration restriction.

Powderly showed more concern for the inclusion of blacks in the movement, but he maintained that industrial "wage slavery" was worse than antebellum chattel slavery, a common argument among anti-abolition Jacksonian labor leaders.[20] He displayed more egalitarian racial views than did most whites of the day.[21] "Since Powderly was uncompromising in demanding that white Knights realize their obligations to accept the Negro as an equal, he personally must have believed in Negro equality," one study concludes.[22] But he shared the white unionist view that most blacks served as a reservoir of "cheap labor." "The man who goes South with no capital and no trade can make but little headway," he wrote in 1885. "It makes no difference how much northern energy or push he brings with him, he will find that as a laborer he soon sinks to the level of the low white trash and the lazy, shiftless blacks who infest the cities and towns. I do not charge that all the colored men are lazy and shiftless or that some of those who are lazy will not work at times, but they are unsteady and will rather sit in the sun than work at any time, and no matter how ambitious a laboring man may be he soon finds that this element is the club which beats back every effort to improve his condition."[23] The need to include blacks stemmed from both egalitarian principle and the practical need to control their competition.[24]

The Knights recommended black-white labor unity but consistently advocated separate local organizations. Powderly concluded, "The color line cannot be rubbed out, nor can prejudice against the colored man be overcome in a day."[25] His speaking tour of the South in 1884 impressed many black leaders. Black locals, having formed first in Iowa in 1881, spread until the Knights were able to claim "hundreds" of colored locals by 1885. That year the general assembly resolved to

19. Terence Powderly, *Thirty Years of Labor, 1859–89* (New York, 1967 [1890]), 32, 168; Grob, *Workers and Utopia,* 57; Sidney Kessler, "The Organization of Negroes in the Knights of Labor," *Journal of Negro History* 37 (1952), 249.

20. Powderly, *Thirty Years of Labor,* 168.

21. McLaurin, *Knights of Labor in the South,* 133.

22. Sr. William Marie Turnbach, "The Attitudes of Terence V. Powderly toward Minority Groups, 1879–93" (M.A. Thesis, Catholic University of America, 1956), 56.

23. "The South of Today," *Scranton Truth,* 17 Mar. 1885 [DH III: 249].

24. Kessler, "Organization of Negroes in the Knights of Labor," 250; Kessler, "The Negro in the Knights of Labor," 8.

25. Turnbach, "Attitudes of Terence V. Powderly," 54–55; DH III: 246–60.

appoint Negro organizers in each southern state, though they never carried out this resolution.[26]

Blacks initially met the growing labor organization's overtures skeptically. A Detroit black newspaper complained that the Knights had not made strenuous efforts to organize blacks, and T. Thomas Fortune's *New York Freeman* took a gloomy view of labor union progress. Tyranny rather than justice seemed to be the normal condition of mankind, Fortune noted, though tyranny of labor might prove preferable to the current tyranny of capital. The *New York Age* recommended that, while remaining cautious, blacks be receptive to white appeals.[27]

Some black voices favored remaining outside of the organized labor movement and seizing the job opportunities created by white strikers.[28] The *Washington Bee* complained that black hodcarriers, satisfied with their wages, had been forced to strike on behalf of white construction workers who were making unreasonable demands. "Would it not be wiser to stand aloof and attract attention and sympathy by filling up the breaks which these strikes occasion, rather than manifest undue sympathy for a movement which in practice operates against the interests of colored labor?"[29] Fortune called this strategy "pernicious," and denied that blacks would suffer additional unemployment if employers were forced to pay them the same wages as white workers.[30]

At about the same time that the Knights began to reach out to blacks, the order began to expand dramatically. Blacks responded to the Noble and Holy Order in part because of its secret, fraternal, and even quasi-religious nature but, like most workers, looked to it primarily for economic benefits. The order began to display the power to confer such benefits in the early 1880s, but it did so by winning a series of strikes. The leaders of the order consistently condemned the strike as a tool of the labor movement and, while never forbidding its use, spoke out against it. Powderly adamantly believed that strikes at best won only short-term benefits that perpetuated the wage system that he ultimately hoped to abolish. At their

26. Kessler, "Organization of Negroes in the Knights of Labor," 255, 257; McLaurin, *The Knights of Labor in the South,* 45; Sterling Spero and Abram Harris, *The Black Worker: The Negro and the Labor Movement* (New York, 1931), 41.

27. *New York Freeman,* 20 Mar. 1886 [DH III: 38]; *New York Age,* 10 Apr. 1886 [DH III: 39].

28. Philip S. Foner, *Organized Labor and the Black Worker, 1619–1981* (New York, 1982), 51.

29. *Washington Bee,* 8 May 1886 [DH III: 43].

30. *New York Freeman,* 22 May and 2 Oct. 1886 [DH III: 44–45]; Emma Lou Thornbrough, *T. Thomas Fortune: Militant Journalist* (Chicago, 1972), 81.

worst they turned public opinion against labor unions, as the great strikes of the 1870s had.[31]

The Knights had engaged in several successful railroad strikes, culminating in the 1885 campaign against Jay Gould's Southwestern railroad system. The strikers resorted to sabotage and violence, preventing Gould from enlisting strikebreakers (black or white), and finally forced him to recognize the Knights' union.[32] Workers quickly joined the organization, and the order's rolls swelled from 100,000 to 700,000 in 1886. Estimates of black membership range to perhaps a hundred thousand, but may have been about half as many as that. But in 1886 the order's secretary reported, "The colored people of the South are flocking to us."[33]

New Orleans, an unusually open and integrated city with a sympathetic city government that kept police at bay, saw significant interracial labor solidarity in the 1880s, though the unionists were organized apart from the Knights of Labor. In 1880 dockworkers formed a Cotton Men's Council that included black and white unions. The most highly skilled and highly paid workers, the "screwmen," who packed cotton as tightly as possible into ships' holds, had limited blacks to 100 jobs in the 1870s, but they now forced shippers to equalize black and white wage rates and refused their offer of a racial job monopoly. In a pattern that became typical of waterfront labor, the unions divided the available work according to a racial quota, and whites and blacks shared union offices—whites serving as presidents and blacks as vice-presidents. New Orleans maintained a powerful labor movement until the 1890s. In Galveston, a general strike engineered by the Knights in 1885 failed when blacks acted as strikebreakers and shippers refused to accept a racial quota work-sharing formula.[34]

The Knights successfully organized black workers in Richmond, Virginia. Blacks organized in sufficient numbers to control an all-black district assembly alongside the all-white one, but their separation and political divisions had im-

31. McLaurin, *Knights of Labor in the South*, 52, 139.

32. Kenneth Kann, "The Knights of Labor and the Southern Black Worker," *Labor History* 18 (1977), 56; Dulles, *Labor in America*, 140.

33. *Record of Proceedings of the General Assembly of the Knights of Labor of America* (Minneapolis, 1886), 44; Weir, *Beyond Labor's Veil*, 8; Kessler, "The Negro in the Knights of Labor," 41.

34. Eric Arnesen, *Waterfront Workers of New Orleans: Race, Class, and Politics, 1863–1923* (Urbana, 1994), 74–118; Kann, "Knights of Labor and the Southern Black Worker," 57; "Knights of Labor on Strike," *New York Times*, 4 Nov. 1885, p. 1 [DH III: 77]; "The Mallory Boycotted Again," *New York Times*, 29 Jan. 1886, p. 1 [DH III: 84]; *Galveston Daily News*, 4 Nov. 1886 [DH III: 80]; Ernest Obadele-Starks, *Black Unionism in the Industrial South* (College Station, TX, 2000), 12, 38–47.

portant economic consequences. The white Knights organized a Workingmen's Reform Party and won municipal elections in 1886. Blacks remained loyal to the Republican Party, and the city council voted to exclude blacks from public works employment. In Jacksonville, Florida, a newly elected labor reform government shared patronage with blacks, but, after a calamitous yellow fever epidemic, the state legislature provided for a governor-appointed city council, disfranchising city voters.[35]

Richmond also hosted the October 1886 Knights of Labor general assembly, where the race issue manifested itself most disturbingly. After long battling them, Powderly by 1886 had allied himself with New York's district assembly 49, described by one historian as "a motley assortment of anarchists, Lasallean socialists, and old-line fundamentalists opposed to changes made in the Knights of Labor ritual since 1881."[36] French-born anarchist Victor Drury led this group, known as the "Home Club." They sought to protect local control of the order against centralization, favored secrecy, opposed trade unionism, and sympathized with the Haymarket bombers. The Home Club tried to organize Chinese workers in New York despite the almost universal animus against them, and it sent a black delegate, Frank Ferrell, to the 1886 Richmond convention where he mounted a challenge to the city's customary segregation. When Murphy's Hotel refused to accommodate Ferrell, the entire delegation left it for black-owned Harris Hall. Ferrell also defied racial custom by sitting in the orchestra section at the Academy of Music's performance of *Hamlet*. The Home Club suggested that Ferrell introduce Governor Fitzhugh Lee at the opening of the convention, but Powderly vetoed this affront to southern racial custom. Instead, after Governor Lee welcomed the 650 Knights to the city, Ferrell introduced Powderly and declared that the order sought the "abolition of distinctions maintained by creed and color."[37]

35. Rachleff, *Black Labor in Richmond*, 150–60; McLaurin, *Knights of Labor in the South*, 91, 96.

36. Robert Weir, "Powderly and the Home Club: The Knights of Labor Joust among Themselves," *Labor History* 34 (1993), 84. Cf. Craig Phelan, "The Warp of Fancy: The Knights of Labor and the Home Club Takeover Myth," *Labor History* 40 (1999), 283–99.

37. Robert E. Weir, *Knights Unhorsed: Internal Conflict in a Gilded Age Social Movement* (Detroit, 2000); *Record of Proceedings of the General Assembly of the Knights of Labor of America* (Minneapolis, 1886), 1–8; Kessler, "The Negro in the Knights of Labor"; "The Home Club's Victory," *New York Times*, 5 Oct. 1886, p. 1; Claudia Miner, "The 1886 Convention of the Knights of Labor," *Phylon* 44 (1983), 151; Rachleff, *Black Labor in Richmond*, 171; Fink, *Workingmen's Democracy*, 162–68; Foner, *Organized Labor and the Black Worker*, 53–57.

Powderly initially supported the challenge to southern racial mores, but he retreated when local opinion became outraged at the specter of "social equality" and local vigilantes threatened violence. He tried to explain the order's racial policy in economic terms. "Cheap southern labor is more of a menace to the American toiler than the Chinese," he wrote in a letter to the *Richmond Dispatch*. "There need be no further cause for alarm. The colored representatives of this Convention will not intrude where they are not wanted, and the time-honored laws of social equality will be allowed to slumber undisturbed . . . In the field of labor and American citizenship we recognize no line of race, creed, politics, or color."[38] He intended no "violation of the rules of social equality," he later explained. "My only wish was to do something to encourage the black workmen, and cause him to feel that, as a factor in the field of production, he stood the equal of all other men." Powderly made it clear that the Knights of Labor were concerned with the industrial question, not the race question.[39]

Most blacks who had embraced the Knights of Labor by 1886 were satisfied with Powderly's compromise. The *Pittsburgh Dispatch* accepted that "the acts and utterances of the leading Knights show plainly that the whole organized moral force of the Order is to be used in breaking down the social barriers that have heretofore existed between the races in the southern states." The real challenge would be to convince the white workers of the benefit of interracial organization.[40] T. Thomas Fortune criticized Powderly's retreat from his initial courageous stand but remained more concerned about the rank and file than about the leadership of the Noble and Holy Order.[41]

Contemporaries did not regard segregation per se as important an issue as it subsequently appeared. Many blacks themselves favored segregated local assemblies because these gave them the power to send black delegates to district, state, and general assemblies. Black Knights most often complained that their minority in the district assemblies, which were integrated, prevented them from electing delegates to the state and general assemblies. Even at the apex of interracial cooperation, white Knights did not often fight against black exclusion from skilled labor or oppose wage discrimination, adding to a mistrust that made blacks seek a

---

38. *Record of Proceedings*, 7–8; *Richmond Dispatch*, 12 Oct. 1886 [DH III: 106]; Powderly, *Thirty Years of Labor*, 350.

39. Powderly, *Thirty Years of Labor*, 352.

40. Kessler, "The Negro in the Knights of Labor," 80; *Pittsburgh Dispatch*, 21 Oct. 1886 [DH III: 131].

41. *New York Freeman*, 16, 23, and 30 Oct. 1886 [DH III: 130, 133].

racially identifiable cadre in the Order. Blacks continued to complain about discriminatory treatment from unions that did admit them and would continue to call for leadership or black power within labor organizations as a solution. Black workers sought mainly the economic benefits of the Order, rather than its social or political activity, showing the persistent bifurcation of elite and mass concerns among black Americans.[42]

The Knights rapidly collapsed in the year after the Richmond convention, but it would be a vast distortion to claim that it failed due to its lack of commitment to racial equality. Indeed, the issue may not have been all that significant even to the Home Club, whose chief aim was to "rule or ruin" the Knights of Labor and whose introduction of the racial issue may have been a tactical maneuver to derange the convention. Religious divisions presented more severe problems than racial ones within the order, and economic factors outweighed ethnocultural ones. If the 1885 Gould strike had provided a burst of enthusiasm, the failure of an 1886 strike against Gould deflated zeal. The chairman of the executive board of the district assembly had to be forced at gunpoint to order the strike, and the executive board of the general assembly opposed it once it was underway. Blacks took jobs as mechanics and helped break the strike. The Noble and Holy Order's leaders also did not support other high-profile strikes, such as the Chicago meatpackers'.[43]

The chasm between the Knights' leaders and its rank and file on the strike issue fed the conflict between the reformers and the trade unionists. The telegraphers union had withdrawn in 1883 when the order did not support its strike against Western Union. Though the reformers claimed to be at "war" with the industrial system, they refused to organize their forces along trade union lines or to use the weapon of the strike. They preferred to organize in mixed local assemblies,

42. McLaurin, *Knights of Labor in the South,* 134–35; Kann, "Knights of Labor and the Southern Black Worker," 57–59; August Meier, *Negro Thought in America* (Ann Arbor, 1963), 10–12.

43. William H. Harris, *The Harder We Run: Black Workers since the Civil War* (New York, 1982), 27; Miner, "The 1886 Convention of the Knights of Labor," 156; Weir, "Powderly and the Home Club," 110; Kaufman, "Rise and Fall of a Nation of Joiners," 6; David Montgomery, *Beyond Equality: Labor and the Radical Republicans, 1862–72* (Urbana, 1967), 31; Ruth A. Allen, *The Great Southwest Strike* (Austin, TX, 1942), 76; Grob, *Workers and Utopia,* 65–71; Kessler, "Organization of Negroes in the Knights of Labor," 253. For a recent explanation of the Knights' failure, see Kaufman, "Rise and Fall of a Nation of Joiners"; Kim Voss, "Disposition Is Not Action: The Rise and Demise of the Knights of Labor," *Studies in American Political Development* 6 (1992), 272–321; Howell John Harris, "Exceptionally Knights," *Reviews in American History* 23 (1995), 658–62.

which tended to produce feckless oratory and relied on conciliation, education, and cooperative ventures. These compromises clashed with the desire of most members for immediate benefits in wages, hours, and working conditions.[44] The few cooperative ventures that got off the ground showed the problem: When workers became owners, "the desire for profits often became so overwhelming that many cooperatives were transformed into joint stock companies," a historian observes. "Stockholders then became intent on paying low wages in the hope of securing higher profits. Dissension within labor's ranks was also responsible for the failure of many undertakings."[45] The trade unionists within the Knights of Labor formed the Federation of Trades and Labor Unions in 1881 and tried to remain part of the order. But in 1886 the same New York Lassalleans who led the assault on segregation forced the issue by demanding that members of the Cigar Makers International Union choose between their own union and the rival Progressive Cigar Makers Union. The leaders of the cigarmakers, Adolph Strasser and Samuel Gompers, convened a meeting in December that created the American Federation of Labor.[46]

Powderly and the leaders of the Knights refused to embrace the trade unionists' tactics of coercion. At the same time, trade unionists would find the use of coercion to be one of their chief problems. The reaction to the anarchist Haymarket bombing in 1886 showed part of the problem, but greater still was the routine violence of non-anarchist strikes.[47] Most Americans would accept the peaceful organizational methods of the Knights but balked at the threats and violence that often accompanied strikes, and which were usually directed at other, strikebreaking, workers. Black Americans were especially alert to the dangers of the extralegal use of force. Socialists and anarchists found few adherents among either black or white Americans. Ohio Republican George Washington Williams defended orthodox economics and warned blacks against socialist despotism associated with the 1877 strikes. *Cleveland Gazette* editor Harry Smith, less economically dogmatic, nevertheless feared that radicalism would undermine the rule of law and unleash racial violence. After the Haymarket executions he wrote, "It is time to put down the foot

44. Grob, *Workers and Utopia,* 100.

45. Ibid., 47.

46. Ibid., 102–12.

47. Ibid., 72, 137; Henry David, *The History of the Haymarket Affair: A Study in the American Social-Revolutionary and Labor Movements,* 2d ed. (New York, 1958), 535–37.

of American law, promptly and fearlessly, upon every effort, no matter how small, to rouse the people to revolution against it." The violence of the Knights' strikes eroded black support for the Noble and Holy Order.[48]

Labor violence erupted in the Louisiana sugar fields in 1887. Initially an area of high-wage agricultural labor, the Louisiana sugar country faced greater competition from foreign producers and the increasing concentration of the sugar refining industry by the 1880s, at the same time that new technology became available to the planters. However much they may have sought control over their labor force, the planters had never been able to establish it. By 1887 rising costs, falling prices, and poor crops depressed the industry. No longer able to command the relatively high wages to which they had been accustomed, black workers organized by the Knights of Labor struck for a wage increase (another strike denounced by Powderly) and used violence to force other workers to quit and to prevent the use of replacement workers, including the murder of white replacements. Planters prevailed upon the governor to send in the militia, and at least thirty, and perhaps sixty, strikers were killed.[49]

The Knights of Labor had its greatest success with blacks among farm workers, and the order grew in the rural South while it collapsed elsewhere in the country. But blacks soon joined the general exodus from the order, and by 1894 its frustrated national leaders devised a plan, said to enjoy overwhelming membership support, to petition Congress to subsidize a voluntary deportation of black Americans to Africa.[50] Expressing a confidence in black workers' ability to compete with whites, the *Christian Recorder* replied, "Because he may speedily open his eyes and elbow some less energetic competitor out of his way may account for the desire on

48. Meier, *Negro Thought in America,* 46–48; Robert L. Factor, *The Black Response to America: Men, Ideals, and Organization from Frederick Douglass to the NAACP* (Reading, MA, 1970), 53–55; David Gerber, *Black Ohio and the Color Line, 1860–1915* (Urbana, 1976), 175–76.

49. Louis Ferleger, "The Problem of 'Labor' in the Post-Reconstruction Sugar Industry," *Agricultural History* 72 (1998), 140–58; John C. Rodrigue, "'The Great Law of Demand and Supply': The Contest over Wages in Louisiana's Sugar Region, 1870–80," ibid., 159–82; Joseph P. Reidy, "Mules and Machines and Men: Field Labor on Louisiana Sugar Plantations, 1887–1915," ibid., 183–96; Jeffrey Gould, "Sugar War," *Southern Exposure* 12 (1984), 45–55; McLaurin, *Knights of Labor in the South,* 74, 141; Foner, *Organized Labor and the Black Worker,* 60; Kessler, "The Negro in the Knights of Labor," 98; DH III: 143–239.

50. "Wish to Be Rid of the Negroes," *New York Times,* 26 Feb. 1894, p. 10; Foner, *Organized Labor and the Black Worker,* 62; Kessler, "The Negro in the Knights of Labor," 81.

the part of the Knights of Labor to have him out of the country. If so, it were to be hoped that their most painful fears may be realized." [51]

CONFIDENCE AND CRISIS

A mixture of boldness and fear, of optimism and desperation, marked black opinion in these years—a mixture seen sometimes in the same mind—and influenced views on economic and labor relations. Journalist T. Thomas Fortune published *Black and White: Land, Labor, and Politics in the South,* in 1884. Fortune had been born in Florida in 1856, the son of a delegate to the state's Reconstruction constitutional convention and a member of its House of Representatives. The Ku Klux Klan expelled his father from the state in 1869. Fortune eventually completed some courses at Howard and Harvard Universities, returned to Florida, and settled in New York City. A radical before the 1890s, he began editing the *New York Globe,* which became the *New York Freeman* and then the *New York Age,* one of the most influential of black newspapers. [52] By 1884 Fortune had adopted the economic views of Henry George, and attributed the problems of the South to "land monopoly." The solution lay in the emancipation of the poor of both races. "The future conflict in that section will not be racial or political in character, but between capital on the one hand and labor on the other," he wrote. [53]

Fortune denounced the hypocrisy of the American founders for their treatment of Africans and Indians, the fruit of "the spirit of injustice, inborn in the Caucasian nature." The Civil War and emancipation, he insisted, actually left blacks worse off, under "industrial slavery; a slavery more excruciating in its exactions, more irresponsible in its machinations than that other slavery, which I once endured." [54] Quoting Henry George, Fortune explained, "We have not really abolished slavery; we have retained it in its most insidious and widespread form—in a form which applies to whites as well as to blacks." He denounced Republicans as well as Democrats, and held no romantic sentiments about Reconstruction. The South had been bankrupted, he wrote, "by the Carpet-Bag harpies, aided and abetted by the ignorant negroes whom our government had not given time to shake

51. *Christian Recorder,* 15 Mar. 1894 [DH III: 282].

52. Thornbrough, *T. Thomas Fortune;* "T. Thomas Fortune," ANB; Meier, *Negro Thought in America,* 31.

53. T. Thomas Fortune, *Black and White: Land, Labor, and Politics in the South* (New York, 1968 [1884]), iv.

54. Ibid., 28, 235; *New York Freeman,* 23 Nov. 1886 [DH III: 137].

the dust of the cornfield from their feet before it invited them to seats" in the legislature. He warned, "The American Negro is no better and no worse than the Haytian revolutionists . . . I do not indulge the luxury of prophecy when I declare that the American people are fostering in their bosoms a spirit of rebellion which will yet shake the pillars of popular government as they have never before been shaken, unless a wiser policy is inaugurated and honestly enforced." [55]

Fortune seemed to admire the modernizing North. While the South was concentrating on agriculture, politics, and hatred, the rest of the country was engaged in new economic pursuits, making them thrifty, wealthy, and content. But the industrial revolution would bring only ruin to workers. "Competition, it is declared, is the life of trade; if this be true, it is truer that it is the death of labor, of the poorer classes." He believed that blacks should "cultivate more cordial relations with the white men of the South" and that eventually the most talented among blacks, already making substantial economic progress, would rise to the top of southern society. Then they would "turn the tables upon the unscrupulous harpies who have robbed him for more than 200 years; and from having been the slave of these men, he, in turn, will enslave them . . . I strongly incline to the belief that the black men of the South will eventually become the large land-holding class, and, therefore, the future tyrants in that section." [56]

Fortune saw the labor troubles of the 1880s as the unfolding result of the tyranny of capital that he described in *Black and White*. He hoped that the Knights of Labor would effect the interracial labor organization that some of its leaders envisioned, and he remained a sympathetic critic as the Order struggled with the race problem. He went so far as to say that "The labor organizations of the country have shown a most magnanimous and fraternal disposition to put colored men on equal footing with white members, and to stand by them in all their efforts to better the common lot of the laborer." This most hopeful proponent of interracial unionism advised blacks to "make common cause with the white laborer. They cannot pursue any other course without mutual loss and permanent disadvantage." [57] But soon the scales fell from his eyes; he abandoned his radicalism and became an ally of Booker T. Washington. Though he never dropped his hostility to

55. Fortune, *Black and White*, 34, 39, 106.
56. Ibid., 115, 128, 166, 193–94, 205.
57. *New York Freeman*, 17 Jul. and 25 Dec. 1886 [DH IV: 43, 202].

the idea that blacks ought to compete with white workers as strikebreakers, he did denounce the discriminatory practices of white labor unions.[58]

From the other direction came William H. Councill, a staunch defender of laissez-faire. Born in 1848 and escaping from slavery in 1863, Councill settled in Alabama, became a prominent Republican during Reconstruction, and organized local branches of the National Labor Union. He left the Republican Party in 1874, and the Redeemer Democrats made him the principal of the State Normal and Industrial School in Huntsville. Contemporaries and most historians criticized Councill for his "accommodation" to white supremacy, yet in 1887 he filed a suit with the Interstate Commerce Commission (ICC), complaining that the Atlantic Railroad Company had refused to seat him in the first-class section for which he had purchased a ticket. (He won his case, but the ICC held that separate accommodations were acceptable if substantially equal.) Angry whites forced him out of his principalship, but he returned after a year.[59]

Councill published a pamphlet, "The Negro Laborer: A Word to Him," in 1887.[60] Far from Fortune's class consciousness, Councill told blacks that capital was simply accumulated labor to which all were equally entitled. "The little girl who peddles laces, or newspapers, or pins around the street, is as much a capitalist to the extent of her investment as Mr. Vanderbilt or Mr. Gould. Mr. Gould and Mr. Vanderbilt have simply by the exercise of more economy, sagacity, and energy

---

58. Meier, *Negro Thought in America*, 47; Thornbrough, *T. Thomas Fortune*, 158–62; August Meier and Elliott Rudwick, "Attitudes of Negro Leaders toward the American Labor Movement from the Civil War to World War One," in Julius Jacobson, ed., *The Negro and the American Labor Movement* (Garden City, 1968), 37; T. Thomas Fortune, "Loss of Gainful Occupations," Report to the Fifth Annual Convention of the National Negro Business League (1904) [NNBL I: 400].

59. "William H. Councill," ANB; Meier, *Negro Thought in America*, 209–10. Ironically, Councill's replacement as principal was Peter H. Clark, a free-born Cincinnatian who traversed an even more erratic political odyssey than Fortune or Councill. An antebellum Republican, Clark joined the Liberal Republicans in 1872, returned to the party to support Hayes in 1876, became a socialist at the time of the 1877 railroad strike, rejoined the Republicans, and became a Democrat in 1882. David Gerber, "Peter Humphries Clark: The Dialogue of Hope and Despair," in Leon Litwack and August Meier, eds., *Black Leaders of the Nineteenth Century* (Urbana, 1988), 173–90; Herbert G. Gutman, "Peter H. Clark: Pioneer Negro Socialist, 1877," *Journal of Negro Education* 34 (1965), 413–18; Philip S. Foner, *The Workingmen's Party of the United States: A History of the First Marxist Party in the Americas* (Minneapolis, 1984), 50.

60. *The Negro Laborer: A Word to Him* (Huntsville, AL, 1887) [DH III: 47].

accumulated more wealth than she." He denounced all forms of collectivism, including "Henry Georgism."

Admitting that laboring men had legitimate grievances, Councill denounced strikes, calling them "an appeal from reason to error, from justice to injustice, from order to disorder, from law to riot." He reminded black workers that they had frequently seen strikes used to push them out of jobs. Emphasizing the common element of compulsion in strikes, he warned, "If it is right [to strike] against the employer for higher wages, it is right [to strike] against a fellow workman on account of race or color. But it is not right at all."

Councill did not regard labor organizations as illegitimate. He argued that the right to organize them had long been secure in America, and that the laboring men in America were in fact the rulers of the country. "However, they are threatened with great danger growing out of the slavery entailed by labor organizations." Yet the one labor leader whom Councill quoted at length for his views against strikes and alcohol, P. M. Arthur of the Brotherhood of Locomotive Engineers, headed the most racially exclusive union in the country.

Historians often lament the failure of the Knights of Labor, depicted as the most racially enlightened labor organization before the 1930s. "On the whole it can be said that the Knights loomed in the mid-1880s as a beacon of racial enlightenment in a dark era," says one student of the Order. "In no other contemporary organization, it appears, was there such a quickening dynamic toward, rather than away from, race equality."[61] "The decline and disappearance of the Knights of Labor was a tragedy for all American workers, but especially for the black workers," says another. "The Knights contributed immensely toward a brief era of good feeling between black and white workingmen, even in the South."[62] It is hard, however, to credit the Knights of Labor with anything because of its uncertain identity. It flowered overnight almost despite its leaders, and the variety of agendas among its constituent elements, including race, caused its overnight collapse. It is true that its leaders faced the race issue more squarely than the National Labor Union had or the American Federation of Labor would, but its answers remained equivocal. Much of its racial liberalism was expressed before southern racial attitudes hardened into legalized segregation. These movements were developing simultane-

61. Fink, *Workingmen's Democracy,* 169.

62. Foner, *Organized Labor and the Black Worker,* 63. Cf. Herman D. Bloch, "Labor and the Negro, 1866-1910," *Journal of Negro History* 50 (1965), 175.

ously; there is no evidence that the success of the Knights or other reform organizations would have prevented the development of segregation, let alone that segregation was erected as a response to the threat of interracial populism.[63] Blacks would probably have suffered from a national labor movement that grew in tandem with disfranchisement and racial segregation, insofar as segregation served as "one big union" for southern whites.

COAL AND IRON

Particular local and national unions, rather than gestures and pronouncements of the Knights of Labor, demonstrate the racial policies of the labor movement in the Gilded Age. In the late-nineteenth-century South, whites sought to segregate and subordinate black workers in agriculture and industry. White farmers were more successful at doing this in upcountry areas with small black populations than they were in the Black Belt. So, too, white industrial workers excluded blacks when possible but were compelled to accommodate black workers where they were already established.[64]

The cotton textile industry, the symbol of "New South" modernization, provides an unusual example of nearly complete exclusion of black labor. This industry was distinct in that it was built largely by southern, rather than northern, capital. The cotton mill promoters represented a new generation of southern entrepreneurs who often did not come from the antebellum slaveholding class. They devised a strategy to win state support by depicting the industry as a philanthropic venture that would provide jobs for poor Confederate Army veterans, or to their widows and orphans. Besides his belief in the inherent inferiority of most blacks, one prominent mill owner said, "Another reason why I do not think the Negro should be put in the mills is that this industry furnishes almost the only refuge for the laboring white people of the South from the strong competition of cheap Negro labor."[65] Mill owners who tried to introduce black workers often met sponta-

---

63. Spero and Harris, *The Black Worker*, 45; McLaurin, *Knights of Labor in the South*, 148; C. Vann Woodward, *The Strange Career of Jim Crow*, 3d. ed. (New York, 1974), 80; Alex Lichtenstein, "Racial Conflict and Racial Solidarity in the Alabama Coal Strike of 1894: New Evidence for the Hill-Gutman Debate," *Labor History* 36 (1995), 75.

64. Jaynes, *Branches without Roots*, 255–257; Gerber, *Black Ohio and the Color Line*, 63.

65. Jaynes, *Branches without Roots*, 274–76; Ray Marshall, *Labor in the South* (Cambridge, 1967), 13; James L. Orr, "The Negro in the Mills," *The Independent* 53 (1901), 845–46; U.S. Industrial Commission, *Reports*, 19 vols. (Washington, 1900–02), VII: 63, XIV: lii; Brattain, *The Politics of Whiteness*, 35.

neous strikes by their white workers. A northern-owned firm provoked a strike when it tried to bring in a black machine tender in 1896 and subsequently hired a southern manager who better understood the region's customs. When the Fulton Bag and Cotton Mill hired twenty black spinners the following year, 1,400 white workers walked out until the managers dismissed or segregated them. Collective action among textile workers often aimed at keeping blacks out of the mills. Blacks fell from 20 percent to 3 percent of the cotton mill work force in the 1890s.[66]

Southern coal mining also showed the limits of interracial unionism. Blacks composed part of the industry from its earliest days, taking advantage of the great demand for miners. Simple market forces rather than managerial "divide and rule" tactics brought blacks into the mines. Black and white miners organized in local assemblies of the Knights of Labor and, while never striking against one another, sometimes did join in strikes against other groups. Black and white miners fought against the introduction of Italian contract labor in 1884 and 1885. The Italians were run out of town at first, then jailed for carrying concealed weapons, and finally segregated into one mine entrance. Zinc miners in the Knights of Labor also tried to get the Noble and Holy Order to stop the importation of Welsh miners from New York in 1889, but these southern miners, like the national Knights leadership, disclaimed any desire for social equality between black and white natives and tried to avoid the issue altogether. The Knights of Labor mining unions were not successful, and members formed the Alabama Federation of Miners in 1888, before the establishment of the United Mine Workers (UMW) in 1890.[67]

In other places, blacks gained their first entry into the industry as strikebreakers. Coal operators overcame local resistance to the introduction of blacks in the Hocking Valley of Ohio in 1873–74, and the Illinois militia protected blacks who had broken a strike by miners in Braidwood in 1877, an action witnessed by future United Mine Workers president John Mitchell. Blacks also helped to break strikes in Pennsylvania and Ohio in the early 1880s.[68]

66. Brattain, *The Politics of Whiteness*, 37; Clifford M. Kuhn, *Contesting the New South Order: The 1914–15 Strike at Atlanta's Fulton Mills* (Chapel Hill, 2001), 28; Dittmer, *Black Georgia in the Progressive Era*, 32–33; "Negro and White Labor," *The Outlook* 56 (1897), 980; "Strike against Negro Labor," *New York Times*, 7 Aug. 1897, p. 3; "Race Strike in Alabama," *New York Times*, 7 Oct. 1898, p. 3.

67. Ayers, *Promise of the New South*, 121; Letwin, *The Challenge of Interracial Unionism*, 54. Cf. U.S. Immigration Commission, *Reports*, 42 vols. (Washington, 1911), VI: 331, 424, 656, VII: 15, 21, 147, 221; Letwin, *Challenge of Interracial Unionism*, 73, 82; McLaurin, *Knights of Labor in the South*, 55–59.

68. Herbert Gutman, "Reconstruction in Ohio: Negroes in the Hocking Valley Coal Mines in 1873 and 1874," *Labor History* 3 (1962), 243–64; Gutman, "The Negro and the United Mine Workers of

The bloodiest and most prominent racial clashes came in the Illinois coalfields in 1898. When some mine owners refused to abide by an agreement between the UMW and other operators, white miners went on strike in the spring. After threatening to bring in Chinese replacements, the owners began to recruit southern black workers. The strikers' first effort to repel them was to ask the governor, Republican John R. Tanner, to investigate the alleged inefficiency of the black miners as a threat to public safety. Tanner agreed, and took the side of the strikers throughout the conflict. The UMW claimed that the operators were deceiving the black miners whom they recruited in the South to break the strike and that the owners chose criminals and hoped to provoke a violent clash.[69] Some of the recruits were unaware that a strike was in progress, and the union men were able to persuade some of them to join the UMW or return home, but the operators found more than enough willing replacements.

The strikers prevented the use of black replacements at Virden until October 12, when a bloody riot followed the attempt of migrant blacks to disembark from a train. The governor used the state militia to prevent the importation of any more black workers. A week later he said in a speech, "I reiterate that I will not tolerate this wholesale importation of foreigners into Illinois, and if I hear that a mob is to be brought into this state, such as was taken into Virden, I do not care on what railroad it comes or for whom, I will meet it at the state line and shoot it to pieces with Gatling Guns."[70] The militia captain at Pana swore to obey Tanner's orders. "If any Negroes are brought into Pana while I am in charge, and they refuse to retreat when ordered to do so, I will order my men to fire," he said. "If I lose every man under my command no Negroes shall land in Pana." The governor "admitted that he had no warrant of law for his action, but asserted that he was protecting the interests of the people of the state and enforcing their will."[71] More riots

America: The Career and Letters of Richard L. Davis and Something of Their Meaning, 1890–1900," in Jacobson, *The Negro and the American Labor Movement,* 50; Gerber, *Black Ohio and the Color Line,* 63; Cohen, *At Freedom's Edge,* 97–101; Spero and Harris, *The Black Worker,* 210.

69. *The American,* 27 Aug. 1898 [DH IV: 207]; John H. Keiser, "Black Strikebreakers and Racism in Illinois, 1865–1900," *Journal of the Illinois State Historical Society* 65 (1972), 320; *UMW Journal,* 22 Sep. 1898; *Birmingham Labor Advocate,* 1 Oct. 1898 [DH IV: 210, 215].

70. *Richmond Planet,* 5 Nov. 1898 [DH IV: 235]; Warren C. Whatley, "African-American Strikebreaking from the Civil War to the New Deal," *Social Science History* 17 (1993), 525–58.

71. "Aiding the Virden Miners," *New York Times,* 15 Oct. 1898, p. 12; "Record of Political Events," *Political Science Quarterly* 13 (1898), 760.

erupted at Pana in the spring of 1899, and five black miners who left the city were murdered when they sought work in Carterville.[72]

The liberal Republican and black press condemned the strikers and Governor Tanner in particular. "There is too much fear of these tyrannical labor trusts on the part of public officials," the *Colored American* complained. "The people's welfare is bartered away year after year to satisfy the ever-increasing demands of these selfish cormorants. They bar the Negro from the benefits that unions are designed to confer, and then proceed to terrify capitalists and politicians into connivance with their indefensible schemes."[73] Though the strikers may have had legitimate grievances, they had no right to prevent others from taking the places they refused.[74] "White miners of that region have combined and sworn that a black man shall not exist if they have anything to do with it," said the *Washington Bee*. The UMW was "no more than an abominable 'trust' so far as it relates to the still poorer blacks."[75] The *American* condemned Tanner as "a pusillanimous, villainous imbecile with a severe case of Negrophobia of the Ben Tillman type," and *The Nation* described him as "a demagogue who has no respect for justice or law."[76] "Tannerism" became a synonym for collusion between white politicians and unions against blacks and reinforced black animus against organized labor.[77]

A few years later, when a race riot broke out at Springfield, W. M. Hershaw, the co-editor of W. E. B. Du Bois's magazine, *The Horizon,* noted, "Illinois has contributed more than its share to the reputation of the United States for lawlessness and mob rule. In the Alton riots and the murder of Lovejoy she only did what she has repeated at Pana."[78] The United Mine Workers got an Arkansas court to enjoin the "importation" of "armed men of the low and lawless type of humanity," but a federal court overturned the order. The federal judge had earlier punished strikers for violating a court order and attacking black workers, "ostensibly because said employees were Negroes, but really because the company was operating its mines without the aid of the strikers." *The Nation* applauded the ruling, noting that "the fourteenth amendment guarantees equal protection to all, and he holds that un-

72. "Another Fatal Pana Riot," *New York Times,* 11 Apr. 1899, p. 3.

73. *Colored American,* 8 Oct. 1898 [DH IV: 230].

74. *Christian Recorder,* 20 Oct. 1898 [DH IV: 231].

75. *Washington Bee,* 7 Oct. 1899 [DH IV: 247].

76. *The American,* 15 Oct. 1898 [DH IV: 230]; *The Nation* 69 (1899), 216.

77. Foner, *Organized Labor and the Black Worker,* 78.

78. L. M. Hershaw, "Springfield," *The Horizon* 4 (Aug. 1908), 10.

der that amendment persons have a perfect right to go from one State into another in the pursuit of employment."[79] A grand jury indicted Tanner for his dereliction of duty in the riots, but an AFL resolution applauded his action at its 1898 convention. The United Mine Workers' membership certificate intoned, "Remember Virden, Pana, Latamar, and District 21."[80] Mary Harris ("Mother") Jones, the heroine of the mine workers, asked to be buried in Virden, among the miners who "are responsible for Illinois being the best organized labor state in America."[81] Their victory also helped to prevent the entry of black miners above the Ohio River.[82]

New Orleans dockworkers, whose organization preceded the Knights of Labor, stood out as the outstanding example of biracial organization, but relations between white and black workers remained uneasy throughout the Gilded Age. Like railroad and other transportation workers, dockworkers derived their power from their strategic position in the ports. Shippers were vulnerable to even short work stoppages, unable to pile up inventory to outlast a strike. The New Orleans unions also had the support of the cotton screwmen, who possessed valuable skills and used their power to support their fellow workers. The political support of the municipal "ring" also made New Orleans unions strong. Shippers and strikebreakers did not get the kind of protection that they did in most other cities.[83]

Black and white workers' mutual suspicions had defeated an 1873 dock strike. After that failure, the screwmen assisted blacks to organize their own union in exchange for their agreement to accept a 100-man limit. Other work was divided on a half-and-half racial basis. Black officers served on citywide trade councils, though whites always held the presidency. By 1887 black Republican politician J. Madison Vance could tell black workers, "white labor is no longer necessarily your foe, and the color line is no longer a dead line between the races."[84] But black resentment over the division of work (they constituted well above 50 percent of the

79. *Arkansas v. Kansas & Texas Coal Co.*, 96 F. 353 (1899); *U.S. v. Sweeney*, 95 F. 434 (1899), 446; *The Nation* 69 (1899), 198; "Record of Political Events," *Political Science Quarterly* 14 (1899), 373; Abram L. Harris, "The Negro in the Coal Mining Industry," *Opportunity* 4 (1926), 45.

80. "Governor Tanner Indicted," *New York Times*, 2 Dec. 1898, p. 2; AFL *Proceedings* (1898), 73, 130; Roger Butterfield, *The American Past* (New York, 1947), 321.

81. Rosemary Feurer, ed., *Remember Virden, 1898* (Chicago, n.d. [c. 1998]), 1.

82. Ronald L. Lewis, *Black Coal Miners in America: Race, Class, and Community Conflict, 1780–1980* (Lexington, KY, 1987), 100.

83. Arnesen, *Waterfront Workers of New Orleans;* Herbert Northrup, "The New Orleans Longshoremen," *Political Science Quarterly* 57 (1947), 526–44.

84. Arnesen, *Waterfront Workers of New Orleans*, 91.

work force) and jurisdictional disputes continued. Black organizations' sympathy with employers also raised white workers' suspicion. Black workers seeking allies against the rising tide of political and social discrimination believed they were more likely to find them among their employers than among their fellow workers.[85] By 1894 white screwmen moved to exclude blacks entirely, attacking black dockworkers with unprecedented fury, culminating in the March 1895 "Riverfront Massacre." By the end of the decade the former racial work-sharing arrangements had been restored and white and black unions maintained a tense coexistence.

Iron and steel workers displayed a more typical union racial policy. As in the cotton textile industry, New South promoters initially attempted to attract scarce skilled labor by promising to maintain an occupational hierarchy, with the best jobs reserved for whites. The southern iron and steel industry depended on lower labor costs to compete with northern producers. Its promoters claimed that, with blacks as a mudsill, Birmingham would avoid the class conflict that accompanied English industrialization. But white craftsmen surmised that the economic interests of their employers would override their racial loyalties, and they organized themselves to maintain job control. Racial discrimination, they understood, served their economic interests rather than their employers'. Thus the Amalgamated Association of Iron and Steel Workers (AAISW), formed in 1876, determined to prevent what had already happened in the coal industry.[86]

Economic distress in the early 1880s led to the first labor-management clashes in Birmingham and marked the introduction of black workers into skilled jobs. The AAISW did not formally bar black membership but allowed locals to do so. The skilled white workers usually dominated the Knights of Labor's mixed local assemblies, and blacks organized separate ones. When black ironworkers struck for higher wages in 1887, skilled whites refused to support them, and the effort, along with the Knights of Labor, collapsed. Over the next few years the labor market improved for both white and black workers, and black workers continued to move to Birmingham. Despite planter and Klan attempts to keep them on the farm, fifty thousand blacks moved to the city in the 1880s–90s.[87]

85. Ibid., 112.

86. Henry M. McKiven Jr., *Iron and Steel: Class, Race, and Community in Birmingham, Alabama, 1875–1920* (Chapel Hill, 1995), 4, 19, 28–29; W. David Lewis, *Sloss Furnaces and the Rise of the Birmingham District: An Industrial Epic* (Tuscaloosa, 1994), 91.

87. Frank T. Stockton, *The International Molders Union of North America* (Baltimore, 1921), 59; McKiven, *Iron and Steel*, 37, 44; McLaurin, *Knights of Labor in the South*, 146; Jaynes, *Branches without Roots*, 267.

Skilled white ironworkers remained convinced that exclusive unionism was in their interest. At the same time, black workers "exploited white class divisions to secure jobs traditionally closed to them," one historian observes. "Whites' commitment to a racial division of work allowed blacks such complete domination of certain jobs that they gained a degree of leverage in some sectors of the labor market. Black workers could and did exploit this monopoly, especially during boom times, to secure better wages and to define for themselves the terms of their employment." The traditional hostility between organized white workers and blacks in some cases worsened in the period of the Knights of Labor.[88]

Some black workers broke into steel employment in the North as strikebreakers, just as they had done in the coal industry. When labor was plentiful, owners were willing to acquiesce to white workers' preference for all-white shops. Some, like Asa Bushnell in Ohio or the Black Diamond Steel Company in Pittsburgh, extended job opportunities to blacks in the teeth of white union opposition, culminating in a 1906 race riot in Springfield, Ohio. More blacks won jobs breaking an 1886 Knights of Labor strike. An antiunion craftsman, Jack Whitehead, made a career of using forty skilled black ironworkers (called "the forty thieves" by defeated union men) to break strikes throughout the country in the 1890s. Black strikebreakers met a bloody reception in the 1892 Homestead strike, being among those assaulted and dynamited by AAISW members and their sympathizers. But total employment rose for the blacks and immigrants whom the union had excluded.[89] Blacks since emancipation had encountered "the opposition, not of capital, not of the men and syndicates who employ labor, and diffuse the benefits of invested wealth amongst the ranks of the 'toiling masses,'" a black newspaper commented, "but by labor, organized systematized labor itself . . . with organized opposition and a virulence of hate and hostility, that is a blistering reproach to American institutions."[90]

Another great railroad strike in the midst of another great depression showed

88. McKiven, *Iron and Steel*, 5, 41, 50. Cf. Paul Worthman, "Black Workers and Labor Unions in Birmingham, Alabama, 1897–1904," in Cantor, *Black Labor in America*, 54, 84.

89. F. B. McQuiston, "The Strike Breakers," *The Independent* 17 (1901), 2456–58; Robert D. Parmet, *Labor and Immigration in Industrial America* (Boston, 1981), 62; Gerber, *Black Ohio and the Color Line*, 63–65; "Springfield," *The Moon Illustrated Weekly*, 17 Mar. 1906, pp. 3–5; Greene and Woodson, *The Negro Wage-Earner*, 141–42; David Montgomery, *The Fall of the House of Labor: The Workplace, the State, and American Labor Activism, 1865–1925* (Cambridge, 1987), 40–42; Paul Krause, *The Battle for Homestead, 1880–92: Politics, Culture, and Steel* (Pittsburgh, 1992), 247, 346.

90. *Indianapolis Freeman*, 30 Jul. 1892 [DH IV: 278].

that little had been accomplished to ameliorate the relations of black and white workers. While the nearly defunct Knights of Labor was recommending colonization to solve the race problem, socialist Eugene V. Debs attempted to form an industrial union of all the nation's railroad workers. With 150,000 members by 1894, the American Railway Union (ARU) was among the largest ever formed. Though Debs urged the ARU to drop its exclusion of blacks, he did not oppose the white-only policies of the railroad unions such as his own Brotherhood of Locomotive Firemen. Debs edited the *Brotherhood of Locomotive Firemen Magazine* in the 1880s when the union pursued the elimination of black firemen in the South. In 1891 he warned against cheap immigrant labor, saying "The Dago works for small pay and lives far more like a savage or wild beast, than the Chinese." Decades later Debs attributed the defeat of the Pullman strike to the ARU's exclusion of blacks, but this came after a long gestation of his thought on American race relations.[91]

Not surprisingly, black workers did not support the Pullman strike. Blacks in Chicago formed an "Anti-Strikers Railroad Union" to fight the ARU. Many black leaders expressed the general American revulsion at labor violence, as the Pullman strike, like the 1877 rail strike, degenerated into violence and vandalism.[92] According to free labor principles, the unionists had no right to do more than quit and let others take their jobs. "Because of what I may deem sufficient reason to myself, I shall determine my labor is worth more than it is bringing in market," asked the *Indianapolis Freeman,* and "am I to be permitted to dictate to my brother, when and how he shall dispose of his toil, and how much he shall receive for it?"[93] The *Richmond Planet* likewise blamed immigrants and their foreign ideologies for the unrest and saw the strike as an opportunity to display the value of Negro labor. It denounced "anarchistic" Illinois governor Peter Altgeld for objecting to President Cleveland's intervention with federal troops, seeing it as the resurrection of the

91. Dulles, *Labor in America,* 173; Nick Salvatore, *Eugene V. Debs: Citizen and Socialist* (Urbana, 1982), 104–105, 227; J. Robert Constantine, ed., *Letters of Eugene V. Debs,* 3 vols. (Urbana, 1990), I: lvi; Gwendolyn Mink, *Old Labor and New Immigrants in American Political Development: Union, Party, and State, 1875–1920* (Ithaca, NY, 1986), 229. Some of Debs's detractors were slow to forget his former race-consciousness—Amanda Cheney to W. E. B. Du Bois, 5 Jan. 1921 [DuBP X: 701].

92. Susan E. Hirsch, "The Search for Unity among Railroad Workers: The Pullman Strike in Perspective," in Richard Schneirov, Shelton Stromquist, and Nick Salvatore, eds., *The Pullman Strike and the Crisis of the 1890s: Essays on Labor and Politics* (Urbana, 1999), 50. Herbert Hovenkamp, "Labor Conspiracies in American Law, 1880-1930," *Texas Law Review* 66 (1988), 952.

93. *Indianapolis Freeman,* 7 and 14 Jul. 1894 [DH IV: 78, 80].

Confederate doctrine of states' rights.[94] Though the black press could appeal to American nativism against immigrant labor competition, some black leaders welcomed such competition as a spur to elevate black Americans.[95] The competition should be a free one, they maintained. Thus the *Christian Recorder* lamented that the right to work was not adequately protected: "The man who wishes to earn his living by the sweat of his brow must fight his way as best he can. Let some poor fellow attempt to work in a place left vacant by a striker, and commonly he does so at the risk of his own life. . . . As in most great strikes the practical result of this upheaval is to give a chance to men who had no chance or small chance before, and the power of the Government can be in no better business than opening a path to work for men to whom it was before closed."[96] The strike showed "the folly and danger of cooperation with labor malcontents in their fight against capital."[97]

The crisis of the 1890s was the last one in which classical liberal principles, including the "free labor" idea, prevailed. Black American leaders adhered to them more closely than ever; perhaps as fervently as any group in the country. Frederick Douglass stood out in reiterating his concern for political and social equality, but he did not rethink his fundamental economic liberalism. T. Thomas Fortune had abandoned his Henry George socialism by the 1890s and come under the tutelage of the rising race leader, Booker T. Washington. The future leader of twentieth-century black collectivism, young W. E. B. Du Bois, was as liberal as the others of his day. He described himself as a free-trade, civil-service-reforming liberal in these years—a black Mugwump—who was horrified at the violence of the strikes of the 1880s and approved of the Haymarket hangings. A story he sketched while a graduate student in Germany at about the time of the Pullman strike concerned the destruction of a black entrepreneur's hopes by his white workers.[98]

94. *Richmond Planet,* 14 Jul. 1894 [DH IV: 79].

95. Arnold Shankman, *Ambivalent Friends: Afro-Americans View the Immigrant* (Westport, 1982), 156–59.

96. *Christian Recorder,* 12 Jul. 1894 [DH IV: 82].

97. Ibid., 19 Jul. 1894 [DH IV: 204].

98. Robert Higgs, *Crisis and Leviathan: Critical Episodes in the Growth of American Government* (New York, 1987), 79; Meier, *Negro Thought in America,* 76–77; Factor, *Black Response to America,* 36, 51, 62, 92, 254–58, 303; Louis R. Harlan, *Booker T. Washington: The Making of a Black Leader, 1856–1901* (New York, 1972), 225; Harlan, "Booker T. Washington and the National Negro Business League," in William G. Shade and Roy C. Herrenkohl, eds., *Seven on Black: Reflections on the Negro Experience in America* (Philadelphia, 1969), 77; Leon F. Litwack, *Trouble in Mind: Black Southerners in the Age of Jim Crow* (New York, 1998), 148; W. E. B. Du Bois, "Comments on My Life," *Freedomways* 5 (1965), 105; "A

Despite the potential of the Knights of Labor, the period left blacks and the labor movement farther apart than ever, but most Americans took the 1890s as a crisis never to be repeated and began to temper liberalism with "progressive" reforms, including an expanded role for organized labor. Changes were afoot that would make it more difficult for blacks to advance either inside or outside the labor movement.

SEGREGATION

Segregation and disfranchisement, along with other more labor-specific limitations on black Americans, began to accelerate and cohere into a system in the 1890s. Clearly, they did not erupt in sudden response to the crises of the decade. The uproar over the behavior of the New York delegates at the 1886 Richmond Knights of Labor convention signaled that segregation had already become customary. Southern states began to make customary segregation legally enforceable in the 1880s, particularly toward the latter part of the decade. Every southern state had enacted laws to make voting more difficult between 1871 and 1889; poll taxes in Virginia and Georgia prevented significant numbers of whites as well as blacks from voting. Mississippi took further steps in formal, constitutional disfranchisement. Black loss of voting power would have economic effects. Per-pupil educational expenditures for blacks fell in absolute terms from 1890 to 1910 in Alabama, Florida, Louisiana, North Carolina, and Virginia; counties with a black majority spent seven to thirty times as much on white as on black students. The various labor control laws that southern states experimented with became more numerous and stringent in the 1890s and especially in the first decade of the new century. Lynchings also became more frequent and intense in the first half of the 1890s. Southern whites had used devices of racial control all along, but in the 1890s they became more bold and unapologetic about the maintenance of white supremacy.[99]

Novel Idea," 7 Dec. 1892, in Herbert Aptheker, ed., *Against Racism: Unpublished Essays, Papers, Addresses, 1887–1961* (Amherst, 1985), 25–26; David Levering Lewis, *W. E. B. Du Bois: Biography of a Race, 1868–1919* (New York, 1993), 109, 133.

99. Cohen, *At Freedom's Edge*, 206, 212, 246; J. Morgan Kousser, *The Shaping of Southern Politics: Suffrage Restriction and the Establishment of the One-Party South, 1880–1910* (New Haven, 1974), 71; Gavin Wright, *Old South, New South: Revolutions in the Southern Economy since the Civil War* (New York, 1986), 123; Frederick Douglass, "What the Black Man Wants," in Philip S. Foner, ed., *The Life and Writings of Frederick Douglass,* 4 vols. (New York, 1950–75), IV: 158; James P. Smith, "Race and Human Capital," *American Economic Review* 74 (1984), 688–90; Jaynes, *Branches without Roots,* 314.

Segregation rarely applied directly to employment. South Carolina's 1915 statute requiring segregation of workers in cotton textile mills appears to be the only instance of legislative segregation in business. Still, Alabama required separate bathrooms for employers of twenty-five or more, and North Carolina enforced a similar ordinance. In most cases, southern whites could not explicitly bar blacks from competing with whites for jobs, for "liberty of contract" was more clearly written in Reconstruction legislation and was more vigorously enforced by the courts than was social equality. But segregation in nonoccupational spheres effectively raised the cost of employing blacks and thus kept them out of jobs. The difficulties of finding restaurant or hotel accommodations would inhibit any kind of work that involved travel, especially for blacks and whites working together.[100] "One cannot read those laws and examine the conditions under which they became effective without realizing that one of their prime purposes was to differentiate the Negro labor product and make it more expensive than that of whites," an economist observed. "The basic economics of segregation were thus carefully designed to limit the ability of Negroes to compete with whites for jobs by making it more costly to employ Negroes and most expensive to employ them on an integrated basis."[101]

Segregation began to take root and extend to more areas of southern life, but it was not something that the New South business class promoted. Segregation was a reaction to the effects of market forces and industrialization on southern life. The industrialization of the "New South" could have undermined the region's racial hierarchy, but segregation forced business to conform to it. Businessmen resisted the higher costs that segregation and a limited labor supply produced. Railroad owners balked at enforcing racial segregation and fought the laws in court—joining Homer Plessy, for example, in challenging the requirement of separate accommo-

100. Richard A. Epstein, *Forbidden Grounds: The Case against Employment Discrimination Laws* (Cambridge, 1993), 246; Jack Greenberg, *Race Relations and American Law* (New York, 1959), 383; Langston T. Hawley, "Negro Employment in the Birmingham Metropolitan Area," National Planning Association, *Selected Studies of Negro Employment in the South* (Washington, 1955), 271; Steven M. Gelber, *Black Men and Businessmen: The Growing Awareness of a Social Responsibility* (Port Washington, NY, 1974), 63; Carl B. King and Howard W. Risher Jr., *The Negro in the Petroleum Industry* (Philadelphia, 1969), 26; Richard D. Leone, *The Negro in the Trucking Industry* (Philadelphia, 1970), 28–29.

101. Herbert R. Northrup, "Industry's Racial Employment Practices," in Arthur M. Ross and Herbert Hill, eds., *Employment, Race, and Poverty* (New York, 1967), 291; Northrup, *The Negro in the Rubber Tire Industry* (Philadelphia, 1969), 117; Herbert Hill, "Recent Effects of Racial Conflict on Southern Industrial Development," *Phylon* 20 (1959), 323.

dations in New Orleans streetcars in *Plessy v. Ferguson*. Segregation appealed most to politicians, who could indulge white voters' racial prejudices without having to pay for it, and to white workers who benefited from exclusion of black competition. Labor unions clearly facilitated exclusion, but formal organization was often not necessary for it. White workers were able to keep blacks out of the textile industry without formal organization. Professional baseball also drew the color line in these years.[102]

Baseball was still an unstable and competitive industry in the 1880–90s. Principally a northern game, it would not have attracted many black players in any case. In 1884, about four hundred players worked for thirty-four major league teams, including one in Richmond and nine in border state cities. Of these, only seven players had been born in former Confederate states. Indeed, nearly as many came from abroad (30) as hailed from border states (48).[103] The first players union, the National Association of Baseball Players, formally excluded blacks in 1867. Its successor, the National Association of Professional Baseball Players, formed in 1871 without a formal color bar, and blacks made their way into the game as more formal business organization and player-owner divisions took hold. Only two black men, Moses Fleetwood Walker and his brother Welday, played for a major league (American Association) team, the Toledo Blue Stockings, in 1884, but several dozen blacks played for minor league teams.

White players often vented their unhappiness at playing with blacks by insults and violence. Their resentment culminated in the refusal of the Chicago White Stockings, led by Cap Anson, to play an exhibition game with a minor league team that included Fleet Walker and George Stovey in 1887. The New York Giants were rumored to be considering hiring Stovey at the time. John Montgomery Ward was attempting to establish a players union and supported Stovey's aspirations, but many of his fellow players resisted and wanted to exclude black competition. At

102. Ayers, *Promise of the New South*, 140–45, 312; Gavin Wright, "Black and White Labor in the Old New South," in Fred Bateman, ed., *Business in the New South: A Historical Perspective* (Sewanee, TN, 1981), 46; James C. Cobb, *Industrialization and Southern Society, 1877–1984* (Lexington, KY, 1984), 1; Jennifer Roback, "The Political Economy of Segregation: The Case of Segregated Streetcars," *Journal of Economic History* 46 (December 1986), 893–917; Barbara Young Welke, *Recasting American Liberty: Gender, Race, Law, and the Railroad Revolution, 1865–1920* (New York, 2001), 274, 345.

103. Rick Wolff et al., eds., *The Baseball Encyclopedia*, 8th ed. (New York, 1990), 81–88. Robert F. Burk, *Never Just a Game: Players, Owners, and American Baseball to 1920* (Chapel Hill, 1994), 131, notes that only 3 out of 168 National League players in 1897 were from as far South as Virginia.

the players' behest, the six International League owners with no black players forced the four owners who did employ blacks to agree to sign no more. The outcry among the press led the league to permit a quota of one black per team, and blacks continued to play in the minors until 1899. After the National League established a relatively stable cartel, their players' demand for a whites-only field was not an issue of contention, as the owners avoided provoking white player unrest.[104] Yet when Anson, the star player (and frustrated part-owner) who had led the effort to establish a racial labor monopoly, retired in 1897, he complained, "Baseball as at present conducted is a gigantic monopoly intolerant of opposition and run on a grab-all-that-there-is-in-sight basis that is alienating its friends and disgusting the public."[105]

As segregation settled on the South, Booker T. Washington acquired the mantle of racial leadership. Like Frederick Douglass, Washington was born on the margins of slavery, of an unknown and probably white father, enslaved to a small farmer in the Virginia upcountry. Part of the generation emancipated at a young age, he escaped poverty and an abusive stepfather, learning bourgeois virtues in personal service to Viola Ruffner and then at General Samuel Chapman Armstrong's Hampton Institute, founded in 1868 to train teachers for the freedmen. He returned to West Virginia in 1874 to find the area in depression and coal miners on strike. He worked as a miner and later claimed to have been "a member, for a number of years, of the Knights of Labor." He concluded, however, that unions and strikes benefited only "professional labor agitators."[106] After returning to Hampton to educate Indian prisoners of war, Washington established an institute of his own at Tuskegee, Alabama. Supporters of black education won state funding for Tuskegee by swinging black votes to an influential Democratic state senator.

Washington believed that slavery had prepared blacks for economic success,

104. David W. Zang, *Fleet Walker's Divided Heart: The Life of Baseball's First Black Major Leaguer* (Lincoln, NE, 1995), 40–41, 54–56; Geoffrey C. Ward, *Baseball: An Illustrated History* (New York, 1994), 39–44; Jerry Malloy, ed., *Sol White's History of Colored Base Ball, with Other Documents on the Early Black Game, 1886–1936* (Lincoln, NE, 1995), xvi–xx; Robert Peterson, *Only the Ball Was White: A History of Legendary Black Players and All-Black Professional Teams before Black Men Played in the Major Leagues* (New York, 1984), 16–28; Mark Ribowsky, *A Complete History of the Negro Leagues* (New York, 1995), 13–32; Dick Clark and Larry Lester, eds., *The Negro Leagues Book* (Cleveland, 1994), 15; Burk, *Never Just a Game*, 76, 89–98.

105. David Okrent and Harris Lewine, eds., *The Ultimate Baseball Book* (Boston, 1979), 28.

106. Harlan, *Booker T. Washington*, 71; Washington to editor, *St. Louis Post Dispatch*, 18 Nov. 1910 [BTWP X: 475]; Factor, *Black Response to America*, 201.

rescuing them from an African situation where men knew neither labor nor progress, but that it also deranged their view of labor by associating it with compulsion. Thus, in the years after emancipation, blacks hoped to escape labor and imitate the leisure class of the antebellum southern whites. Impractical, liberal education contributed to this problem, so Washington advocated industrial education, which would provide blacks with skills to compete in a sophisticated industrial economy.

Washington concisely expressed his program in the famous Atlanta Exposition speech of 1895. His advice to blacks to "cast down your bucket where you are"—to start from the bottom, cultivate good relations with southern whites, cultivate opportunities rather than grievances, and leave political and social equality until a firm economic base had been established—is the better known part of the formula. He also called on southern whites to "Cast down your bucket among these people who have, without strikes and labor wars, tilled your fields, cleared your forests, builded your railroads and cities, and brought forth treasures from the bowels of the earth." He believed that southern whites had already shown more openness to blacks in the economic sphere where he advised blacks to concentrate their efforts. "Whatever other sins the South may be called to bear," he said, "when it comes to business, pure and simple, it is in the South that the Negro is given a man's chance in the commercial world." Associating immigrant labor with industrial conflict, Washington praised the Negro American as "the most patient, faithful, law-abiding, and unresentful people that the world has seen." Economic progress would pave the way for ultimate social and political equality, for "No race that has anything to contribute to the markets of the world is long in any degree ostracized." Segregation and disfranchisement would not prevent this economic progress, which needed only the barest minimum of public protection. "It is important and right that all privileges of the law be ours," he noted, "but it is vastly more important that we be prepared for the exercise of these privileges." [107] If whites would provide black vocational education and legal protection, blacks would abjure political and social aspirations and provide a reliable labor force. Segregation and disfranchisement would be acceptable if blacks were allowed to participate in the economic opportunities of the New South.[108]

107. "The Standard Printed Version of the Atlanta Exposition Address," 18 Sep. 1895 [BTWP III: 583–87].

108. Factor, *Black Response to America,* 162; John Sibley Butler, "Why Booker T. Washington Was Right: A Reconsideration of the Economics of Race," in Thomas D. Boston, ed., *A Different Vision: African-American Economic Thought,* 2 vols. (New York, 1997), I: 182.

More than Frederick Douglass or T. Thomas Fortune before him or W. E. B. Du Bois after him, Washington's theory of the primacy of economics in race relations was clear and coherent. Blacks would cultivate their own business class, an economic elite, whether they be captains of industry or petty entrepreneurs. Washington believed that the laws of trade would overcome men's racial prejudices and that blacks would gain political and social equality as they accumulated property. "The white man on whose house the mortgage rests will not try to prevent that negro from voting when he goes to the polls," he said. "Whether he will or not, a white man respects a negro who owns a two-story brick house."[109]

Washington outlined a pattern that has been seen all over the world, of excluded ethnic groups turning to small enterprise, serving as "middlemen minorities." "But Washington missed the fact that it is the success of business middlemen groups that creates hostility against them," a recent scholar observes. Lynching might, as Frederick Douglass and Washington both suggested, actually be a sign of black progress—triggering white hostility to black success—but that it went unpunished assured that it would hinder black progress. Washington depicted industrial education as more acceptable to southern whites than liberal education that might provoke social and political aspirations among blacks, but the economic competition that effective industrial education would provide would also provoke white reaction. Black entrepreneurship had emerged even in slavery, but it was usually followed by white interference. Moreover, segregation deprived black businesses of the larger, integrated market they needed to flourish. Above all, the white South did not provide basic civil rights protecting life and property—the right to make and enforce contracts or security against force and fraud. Washington ignored the limited but indispensable public protection that economic freedom needs. In turning away from utopia he sped past the minimal state and ultimately expected blacks to succeed in an environment of anarchy.[110]

Later interpreted as a generational blueprint for race relations, the "Atlanta

---

109. Harlan, "Booker T. Washington and the National Negro Business League," in Shade and Herrenkohl, *Seven on Black,* 84; Washington, "The Awakening of the Negro," *Atlantic Monthly* 78 (1896), 326, in Emma Lou Thornbrough, ed., *Booker T. Washington* (Englewood Cliffs, NJ, 1969), 44.

110. John Edward Bruce, "White Opposition to the Negro" (c. 1900) in Peter Gilbert, ed., *The Selected Writings of John Edward Bruce: Militant Black Journalist* (New York, 1971), 61–62; Leon F. Litwack, *Trouble in Mind: Black Southerners in the Age of Jim Crow* (New York, 1998), 151, 160, 320; Butler, "Why Booker T. Washington Was Right," 182–87; Elizabeth Wright, "Booker T. Washington," *The American Enterprise* 6 (1995), 57–59; Factor, *Black Response to America,* 143; Robert Nozick, *Anarchy, State, and Utopia* (New York, 1974).

Compromise" speech was not widely regarded as such at the time. Blacks had anticipated Washington's advice in the 1870–80s, and his speech was more of a recognition of conditions than a new departure—like the Compromise of 1877, the Atlanta Compromise is more of a useful chronological milestone than a real event. Despite the weak basis of his proposal—already apparent to some and to become more so over the next two decades—Washington's message had broad appeal to both black and white opinion.[111]

Despite his faith that the free market would recognize and reward merit, Washington was more of a rural, southern traditionalist than a laissez-faire liberal. He has been described as a "peasant conservative" who had "a deep suspicion of the marketplace and market forces as a tool for positively reconstructing black life."[112] His antiunion tone was usually less strident than that of many black editors, but he shared the suspicion of organized labor common among late-nineteenth-century black leaders. An 1893 Hampton alumni conference unanimously agreed that labor unions drew the color line. In 1897 Washington declared that trade unions were placing obstacles in the way of the material advancement of the Negro.[113] The next year he claimed, "There is almost no prejudice against the Negro in the South in matters of business, so far as the native whites are concerned, and here is the entering wedge for the solution of the race problem. Where the white mechanic or factory operative gets a hold, the trades union soon follows, and the Negro is crowded to the wall."[114] Washington advised against northern migration due to the hostility of labor unions there.[115] He told southern whites that it was only in the South, "by reason of the presence of the Negro, that capital is freed from tyranny and despotism that prevents you from employing whom you please and for that wage that is mutually agreeable and profitable. It is here that that form of slav-

111. Harlan, *Booker T. Washington*, 224–27; Thornbrough, *T. Thomas Fortune*, 162; Meier, *Negro Thought in America*, 99, 116–18; Gerber, *Black Ohio and the Color Line*, 173; Brian Kelly, *Race, Class, and Power in the Alabama Coalfields, 1908–21* (Urbana, 2001), 98.

112. Louis R. Harlan, *Booker T. Washington: The Wizard of Tuskegee, 1901–1915* (New York 1983), 437; Peter Eisenstadt, "Southern Black Conservatism, 1865–1945: An Introduction," in Eisenstadt, ed., *Black Conservatism: Essays in Intellectual and Political History* (New York, 1999), 72.

113. "Proceedings of the Triennial Reunion of the Hampton Alumni Association," 28 May 1893 [BTWP III: 337]; AFL *Proceedings* (1897), 82–83 [BTWP IV: 351].

114. "Industrial Training for the Negro," *Independent* (27 Jan. and 3 Feb. 1898) [BTWP IV: 366].

115. "The Case of the Negro," *Atlantic Monthly* 84 (Nov. 1899), 577, in Thornbrough, ed., *Booker T. Washington*, 44.

ery which prevents a man from selling his labor to whom he pleases on account of his color is almost unknown. We have had slavery, now dead, that forced an individual to labor without a salary, but none that compelled a man to remain in idleness while his family starved." [116] "The Negro is not given to strikes and lockouts," he wrote. "He believes in letting individuals to be free to work where and for whom he pleases." [117]

The American labor movement that took shape in the 1890s confirmed most of the suspicions that black Americans had developed in the preceding decades. Samuel Gompers, the president of the American Federation of Labor for all but one year from its creation in 1886 until his death in 1924, in many ways resembled his Tuskegeean antagonist. Both led what they believed to be the only possible labor and race movements in the 1890s. What they thought practical and prudent their detractors called opportunism and selling out. Washington's rejection of political and social agitation paralleled Gompers's rejection of Lassallean socialism, with its belief that workers' political power must precede the creation of strong trade unions. But both men were only superficially apolitical. Just as Washington acted secretly to challenge segregation and disfranchisement, the AFL used political action whenever it felt that it safely could. While Washington often spoke of accommodation to inequality while acting to challenge it, however, Gompers increasingly voiced racial inclusion while practicing exclusion. [118]

Gompers led the trade unionists as a group within the Knights of Labor in the 1880s, fearing that the Knights would be subverted by politicians as its predecessors had. The labor movement had to be kept separate from bourgeois subversion and would gain political influence as the result of the economic power of well-organized unions. These were basic Marxist principles that Gompers and his allies fashioned into their trade union socialism. Gompers believed that should trade unions follow the cartel model of business, to reduce competition and achieve stability and higher wages, they would eventually replace capitalists as the trustee of the national product. To the chagrin of the Knights of Labor leaders, the trade union socialists were willing to use, or threaten to use, force to achieve their goals. Although nonpartisan, the federation was not apolitical. It acted as a political lobby in the 1880s, fighting to end tenement, child, and convict labor, and sup-

116. Address before the Southern Industrial Convention, 12 Oct. 1899, in Ibid., 46.
117. "The Best Labor in the World," *Southern Farm States Magazine* (Jan. 1898) [BTWP IV: 374].
118. Wiebe, *Search for Order*, 125.

porting the eight-hour day and Chinese exclusion.[119] Gompers's break with the Knights of Labor came rapidly in 1886. Powderly's decision to support the Lassalleans and the New York "Home Club" added to deep personal animosity between the prim, abstemious, and aloof Knight and the garrulous, sometimes irascible, but always convivial trade unionist.

Analysts often attribute the AFL's inattention to black workers to the federation's lack of interest in the organization of unskilled labor. While it is certainly true that it was more difficult to organize the unskilled, the early AFL had no principled aversion to the effort.[120] Despite Adolph Strasser's oft-quoted claim that "we have no ultimate aims," Gompers often spoke of the "ultimate emancipation of the working class" and in 1887 wrote that trade unionists shared "certain ultimate ends, including the abolition of the wage system."[121] Since labor costs were the overwhelming majority of employer costs, to take them out of competition amounted to taking competition out of the economy. Political socialists remained a powerful influence in the AFL in the 1890s, nearly passing a ten-point political program in 1894 that included worker control of the means of production and successfully ousting Gompers from the federation presidency for a year.[122]

While open to socialism and broad organization, the leaders of the AFL were even more vexed by the racial problem than the Knights of Labor had been. The AFL admitted black delegates from the outset. Its predecessor organization, the Federation of Organized Trades and Labor Unions, was so named because a black delegate had pointed out that "it would be dangerous to skilled mechanics to exclude from this organization the common laborers who might, in an emergency, be employed in positions they could readily qualify themselves to fill."[123] White AFL members supported black strikers in the 1892 New Orleans general strike, a display of white sacrifice that Gompers would extol for decades. "Never in the his-

119. Stuart Kaufman, *Samuel Gompers and the Origins of the American Federation of Labor, 1848–96* (Westport, 1973), xiv, 33; William M. Dick, *Labor and Socialism in America: The Gompers Era* (Port Washington, 1972), 21; Kaufman, *Samuel Gompers,* 115, 124, 173, 185; Sidney Fine, *Laissez-Faire and the General Welfare State: A Study in Conflict in American Thought, 1865–1901* (Ann Arbor, 1956), 316–21.

120. Kaufman, *Samuel Gompers,* 170; Dick, *Labor and Socialism,* 18, 24.

121. Dick, *Labor and Socialism,* 31, 38.

122. Grob, *Workers and Utopia,* 171; Dick, *Labor and Socialism,* 42; Fine, *Laissez-Faire and the General Welfare State,* 321; Philip G. Wright, "The Contest between Organized Labor and Organized Business," *Quarterly Journal of Economics* 29 (1915), 238.

123. Report, *First Annual Session, Federation of Organized Trades and Labor Unions,* 15–18 Sep. 1881 (Cincinnati, 1882), 16–17 [DH IV: 3].

tory of the world was such an exhibition, where with all the prejudices existing against the black man, when the white wage-earners of New Orleans would sacrifice their means of livelihood to defend and protect their colored fellow workers," he boasted. "With one fell swoop the economic barrier of color was broken down."[124]

Though Gompers left the organization of southern workers mostly to whites, he did appoint two black organizers, George L. Norton and Joseph Amstead. He implored them to respect southern racial feelings, to organize separate locals, and to leave white workers alone if they objected to black leadership. "The race prejudice exists to such an extent that it seems that it were better under the circumstances to give the white men and the colored men the opportunity of organizing separate unions rather than to have them not organize at all," Gompers concluded. "It is only when men begin to organize that they also begin to realize that their interests are much more closely allied regardless of color, nationality, or prejudice."[125]

Even these modest efforts provoked opposition from those who believed that the organization of blacks would alienate white support for the AFL. Some argued that blacks would undermine white standards within unions as much as outside of them—their willingness to work harder would tempt employers to use all-black work forces.[126] So Gompers treaded lightly on the issue, usually sacrificing substantial equality while repeating verbal commitments to it. When the National Association of Machinists (NAM) applied for an AFL charter, Gompers urged them to drop their constitution's white-only limitation of membership. He and NAM president James O'Connell exhorted the machinists in terms of self-interest. "Employers care very little what nationality or color or previous conditions of life the wage-worker has been or is in so long as he will consent to work cheap," Gompers told the Grand Master Machinist.[127] "If we don't [organize black machinists] they bid against us, and competition in labor is the very thing that labor organizations

124. Foner, *Organized Labor and the Black Worker,* 65–67; Gompers to John M. Callaghan, 21 Nov. 1892 [DH IV: 23]; U.S. Industrial Commission, *Reports,* VII: 647.

125. Bernard Mandel, "Samuel Gompers and the Negro Workers, 1886–1914," *Journal of Negro History* 40 (1955), 43–44; Gompers to George L. Norton, 16 and 17 May 1892, Gompers Letterbooks, LC [DH IV: 41–42].

126. C. C. Taber to Gompers, 24 Apr. 1892, Gompers Letterbooks, LC [DH IV: 30]; *Machinists Journal,* Apr. 1895, p. 128 [DH IV: 53].

127. Gompers to Thomas Talbot, 15 Apr. 1890 [SGP II: 296]; Mark Perlman, *The Machinists: A New Study in American Trade Unionism* (Cambridge, MA, 1961), 16.

are agitating against," he told the 1893 machinists convention.[128] Gompers went so far as to charter a rival, the International Machinists Union (IMU), that did not have a color bar. The NAM renamed itself the International Association of Machinists and simply shifted the racial restriction from its constitution to its ritual of initiation, and the AFL accepted it. Gompers revoked the charter of the rival IMU, whose members were forced to seek admission to the IAM as individuals—its black members were rejected.[129]

Some unions were unwilling to make even the gesture that the machinists did. William S. Carter, Eugene Debs's successor as editor of the *Locomotive Firemen's Magazine,* told Gompers in 1896 that "our members will never consent to admitting the negro firemen of the South to membership in our organization, but I do believe that they will consent to eliminating the word 'white' from our Constitution, and depend upon each Lodge to regulate its own affairs as to who shall become members . . . I believe that if we would remove the word 'white' from our Constitution, the American Federation of Labor would accept our application, and not compel us to admit negroes as members."[130] Carter reminded Gompers that "The southern negro occupies the same relative position to the Brotherhood of Locomotive Firemen as does the Chinaman to the Cigar Makers Union," and he confided that "if we did not decide to affiliate with the AFL, I believe it would be beneficial to place the word 'white' in our ritual instead of the Constitution, inasmuch as the Negroes could not say that we were fighting them."[131] Still the firemen resisted, saying that they did "not care to belong to an organization that is not honest enough to make public its qualifications of membership."[132]

The boilermakers union followed the machinists' gesture, but by the end of the century, the AFL no longer required even such constitutional stratagems. It ad-

---

128. *Indianapolis Freeman,* 27 May 1893 [DH IV: 52].

129. AFL, 1891 *Proceedings,* 12; Mandel, "Samuel Gompers and the Negro Workers," 34–37; Spero and Harris, *The Black Worker,* 89; Perlman, *The Machinists,* 17; Logan, *The Negro in American Life and Thought,* 148. The IAM was admitted during the one year that Gompers was not president of the AFL, but the move was entirely consistent with his policy.

130. Carter to Gompers, 19 Feb. 1896 [SGP IV: 125–26].

131. Carter to Gompers, 3 and 26 Oct. 1896 [DH IV: 86–87]. The cigarmakers union had led the anti-Chinese movement in California, and expressly excluded blacks in its 1865 constitution, but by 1879 forbade antiblack discrimination. F. E. Wolfe, *Admission to American Trade Unions* (Baltimore, 1912), 18.

132. Foner, *Organized Labor and the Black Worker,* 69; U.S. Industrial Commission, *Reports,* XVII: 36.

mitted unions with constitutional color bars and permitted affiliated unions to add color bars to their constitutions. Gompers's only concrete action was to forbid AFL members to refuse to work alongside nonunion black workers. In 1900 the AFL amended its constitution to permit separate black locals to affiliate directly with the AFL as "federal" labor unions.[133] These federal labor unions were at the mercy of the national unions that dominated the AFL and had no representation within them. Black carpenters in a federal labor union, for example, would only be able to press as far as the national carpenters union, which excluded them, would allow, and while the national union would send a large number of delegates to annual AFL conventions, the federal union would send but one.

Originally conceived as temporary organizations, to exist until a large enough number of workers were able to form a national union, the federal unions became the predominant and permanent Jim Crow organization in the AFL.[134] Gompers later explained that he had tried to keep out unions that maintained color bars, "but this course did not result in the representation of colored men in the central bodies; it simply acted in disrupting the organizations. Experience has demonstrated that such a course neither accorded rights to the colored men but destroyed the interests of the white men." Segregation, then, was preferable to complete exclusion. The federal policy "has been fraught with success; not all the advancement and success for which we hope, but yet considerably more than was achieved by the former policy."[135] In separate-but-equal phrasing similar to Washington's Atlanta Compromise address, Gompers said in 1892, "We want to make the trade union movement under the AFL as distinct as the billows, yet one as the sea."[136]

Despite the obvious subterfuge of the machinists episode, Gompers continued to boast that it was proof of the racial egalitarianism of the AFL.[137] "I am sure that anyone who charges organized labor as being antagonistic to the colored race must be entirely ignorant of the history of our organization, or willfully and maliciously misrepresents it," he told the secretary of the Tobacco Workers Union in 1896.[138]

---

133. Spero and Harris, *The Black Worker*, 89; AFL, 1900 *Proceedings*, 12–13; Wolfe, *Admission to American Trade Unions*, 118.

134. Spero and Harris, *The Black Worker*, 99; Foner, *Organized Labor and the Black Worker*, 72.

135. Gompers to Frank Duffy, 2 Mar. 1906 [SGP VII: 533].

136. 1892 *Proceedings*, 16, in Grob, *Workers and Utopia*, 151.

137. Some historians continue to try to regard it as such. David Montgomery, "The Pullman Boycott and the Making of Modern America," in Schneirov et al., *The Pullman Strike*, 236; cf. Ibid., 242.

138. Gompers to J. F. Brown, 2 Mar. 1896 [SGP IV: 130]; Gompers to R. T. Cole, 28 Apr. 1891, Gompers Letterbooks, LC [DH IV: 29].

At the 1897 AFL convention, Henry Lloyd of the carpenters union took exception to Booker T. Washington's claim that labor unions posed obstacles to black economic progress. He and Gompers, over the objections of some southern delegates, reaffirmed that no AFL affiliate could discriminate on the basis of race.[139] Within weeks of admitting the Order of Railway Telegraphers, which barred blacks, Gompers told a congressional committee that the AFL "consistently and persistently insisted that organizations which become affiliated with the AFL must of necessity eliminate the color clause from any constitution or laws which the organization may have."[140]

Gompers increasingly blamed black workers themselves for their depressed economic condition. "There are few instances I know of where the colored workers are discriminated against by reason of their color," he wrote in 1896.[141] "The real difficulty in the matter is that the colored workers have allowed themselves to be used with too frequent telling effect by their employers as to injure the cause and interests of themselves as well as of the white workers," he concluded. Following Booker T. Washington's advice, blacks had made themselves "cheap men" and sold themselves to white employers. Black workers were treated fairly by organized labor, he claimed, and the complaints of black leaders were in fact demands for "special privileges."[142]

Yet Gompers continued to claim that "If we fail to organize the colored wage-earners, we cannot blame them very well if they accept our challenge of enmity and do all they can to frustrate our purposes. If we fail to make friends of them, the employing class won't be so shortsighted and play them against us. Thus if common humanity will not prompt us to have their cooperation, then enlightened self-interest should."[143] One black newspaper commented that interracial unity as matter of self-preservation did not provide a secure basis for cooperation. Gompers's argument was "good as far as it goes. But being not unmindful of past expe-

139. 1897 *Proceedings,* 82–83 [SGP IV: 406]; Mandel, "Samuel Gompers and the Negro Workers," 45.

140. Gompers testimony, 18 Apr. 1900, U.S. Industrial Commission, *Reports,* VII: 162–790 [DH IV: 326]; Mandel, "Samuel Gompers and the Black Workers," 51.

141. Gompers to William Stokes, 27 Aug. 1896 [SGP IV: 220].

142. "Trade Union Attitude toward Colored Workers," *American Federationist* 8 (1901), 116–18 [DH IV: 10].

143. Gompers to James H. White, 14 Sep. 1899, Incoming Correspondence, AFL Archives, LC [DH IV: 25].

riences in the labor world when the interests of the Negro have been at stake, we can hardly help feeling that the proposed course is dictated 'as a matter of self-protection' rather than the natural and spontaneous triumph of fundamental principle." Black enrollment in union ranks might do more harm than good, and blacks ought not to allow themselves to be taken for granted as they were in the Republican Party.[144]

The abandonment of racial inclusiveness took place long before Gompers and the AFL began to tone down socialism and adopt an apparently conservative "business unionism." There was probably little that Gompers could have done to make the AFL more racially inclusive. He was not zealously egalitarian, and the federation was the creature of the discriminatory member unions. While Gompers often made his egalitarian appeals in economic terms, the economic interests of labor union members worked against racial inclusion. The economic basis for the intense hostility labor unionists felt toward Chinese immigrants, and their wariness about unlimited European immigration, applied to blacks as well. Organized labor became more hostile to black competition at the same time that it embraced more restrictive immigration laws.[145] "Economic motive, always hostile to any increase in the number of workers and possible decrease in wages, has probably been the strongest single factor in the exclusion of Negroes from trade organizations," a 1912 study of union admission practices concluded. "The desire to maintain wages, rather than race prejudice, in the last analysis controls the acts and policies of unions."[146] A later study commented, "While race prejudice is a very fundamental fact in the exclusion of the Negro, the desire to restrict competition so as to safeguard job monopoly and to control wages is inextricably interwoven with it."[147] The early years of the new century would show that racial exclusion was not inimical to the success of the new labor movement.

144. "Color Line in Labor Unions," *Baltimore American,* 7 Dec. 1900; "Colored Men and Labor Unions," *Afro-American Ledger,* 15 Dec. 1900 [HNCF 264].

145. Parmet, *Labor and Immigration,* 145.

146. Wolfe, *Admission to American Trade Unions,* 133.

147. Spero and Harris, *The Black Worker,* 55–56; Marshall, *Organized Labor and the Negro,* 19.

3 / Blacks and Labor in the Progressive Era, 1900–1920

The "progressive" era marked the nadir of American race relations. It was also a period of great flux in the economic position of black Americans and their relations to the labor movement. The effects of disfranchisement, segregation, and discrimination in the labor market began to retard black economic progress in these years. Some black leaders began to develop "progressive" departures from the anti-union mindset that prevailed in the 1890s, most evident in the steps toward socialism by W. E. B. Du Bois and A. Philip Randolph. The most significant change of these years was the Great Migration from southern farms to northern cities, fueled by the choking off of immigration and labor demand during World War I. The war years saw a vast but temporary government fillip to organized labor, some of the worst race riots in American history between white and black workers, and the first steps toward a reconsideration of the AFL's racial policies.

BLACK ECONOMIC PROGRESS 1900–1914

Although discriminatory state policy began to affect black economic progress in the first decades of the new century, the impact was gradual. Black land and capital accumulation continued after the 1890s despite disfranchisement, segregation, and lynching, though the gains would certainly have been greater without them. Blacks had acquired 15 million acres of land by 1910; the value of their real property increased by 90 percent in the first decade of the century. Most black businessmen failed, "But such was also the fate of most white businessmen," a historian observes. "What is remarkable is the degree to which a significant segment of the black business community, through a combination of personal character and an ability to adjust to market forces, survived and in many cases thrived." [1] "The reality of the black historical experience between 1865 and 1915 seemed to lend support to [Booker T. Washington's] Jeffersonian vision of a future society of prosperous small black farmers," one historian notes. "Washington was not alone in such a perspective." [2] But black land ownership fell by one-third between 1910 and

1. Robert C. Kenzer, *Enterprising Southerners: Black Economic Success in North Carolina, 1865–1915* (Charlottesville, 1997), 6, 106, 128.
2. Robert Higgs, "Black Progress and the Persistence of Racial Economic Inequalities, 1865–1940," in Steven Shulman and William Darity Jr., eds, *The Question of Discrimination: Racial Inequality in the U.S. Labor Market* (Middletown, CT, 1989), 11–14.

1930. Black income growth is estimated to have slowed down to a rate equal to white income growth, where it had exceeded the white rate before 1900. The real wages of American workers continued to increase between 1900 and World War I, with the American economy growing at least as rapidly as it had since the Civil War. However, as unionization took hold among skilled workers, inequality among American workers increased. The earnings gap between skilled and unskilled workers was greater in America than anywhere else in the world. Wealth being a "lagging indicator" of economic health, an older generation of black workers continued to acquire property while the younger generation began to suffer the effects of discrimination.[3]

Blacks in the South lived in an economic system that included both competition and coercion, and the coercive elements reached their peak in the early twentieth century. Harsh conditions affected all farmers in the region and were aggravated by laws that made it a crime to "entice" labor away from planters, imposed onerous licensing fees on labor agents, punished vagrancy severely, and provided for the leasing of state prisoners. All of these were designed to limit competition for black labor and to ensure a cheap labor supply for planters. Economists and historians have disputed the effectiveness of these laws, and the safest conclusion seems to be that the level of exploitation and control was real but limited.[4]

Laws designed to keep black hands on the farm clashed with the southern industrialists' need for labor. The convict-lease system, the most exploitative of these devices, provided labor to some industries. Free labor organizations and businesses that could not obtain convict labor opposed the system, and it was abolished in most southern states by 1890. Convict labor continued in the Alabama coal industry until 1928, effectively lowering the wages of free workers. The system

3. W. E. B. Du Bois, *The Negro American Artisan* (Atlanta, 1912), 142; Kevern Verney, *The Art of the Possible: Booker T. Washington and Black Leadership in the United States, 1881–1925* (London, 2001), 70; W. D. Walker, *Critical Reflections on Black History* (Westport, 2002), 43–68; Robert C. Allen, "Real Incomes in the English-Speaking World, 1879–1913," in George Grantham and Mary MacKinnon, eds., *Labour Market Evolution: The Economic History of Market Integration, Wage Flexibility, and the Employment Relation* (New York, 1994), 123; Robert Higgs, *The Transformation of the American Economy, 1865–1914: An Essay in Interpretation* (New York, 1971), 22; Robert Higgs, *Crisis and Leviathan: Critical Episodes in the Growth of American Government* (New York, 1987), 80, 107; Edward L. Ayers, *The Promise of the New South: Life after Reconstruction* (New York, 1992), 429–30.

4. Jennifer Roback, "Southern Labor in the Jim Crow Era: Exploitative or Competitive?" *University of Chicago Law Review* 51 (1984), 1161–92; Charles L. Flynn Jr., *White Land, Black Labor: Caste and Class in Late-Nineteenth-Century Georgia* (Baton Rouge, 1983), 68, 110.

represented a compromise between Black Belt planters and New South industrial-ists—the planters had to avoid appearing to promote industrial development but needed to give something to the new interests. The system did have some value for black workers, providing them with a sort of vocational education. Convicts received clothing and cash at the end of their term, and a significant proportion of them kept their jobs in the mines. It was essentially the sort of apprenticeship system that the Reconstruction Black Codes had envisioned. Unfree labor meant that, to some extent, states like Alabama, if not the entire South, followed a statist, almost Prussian, model of economic development rather than the free-market, antebellum, northern one.[5]

The federal government appeared to have abandoned the Negro to the control of southern whites by 1900, but it did impose some limits on state control of black labor. The Supreme Court sustained federal prosecutions against the enforcement of state debt-peonage laws, primarily in a series of Alabama cases adjudicated by district court judge Thomas Jones, who had broken the 1894 Alabama coal strike and had been appointed to the federal bench at Booker T. Washington's behest. More important, though, the federal government failed to secure the rights of black workers, not against state laws, but against private lawlessness.

At the same time that the Supreme Court struck down state peonage laws, it also held that the federal government did not have the power to protect black workers whom white workers had driven out of an Arkansas lumber mill. Justice John Marshall Harlan, the lone dissenter in the *Plessy* case, argued that the Thirteenth Amendment abolished slavery and all its "badges and incidents," one of which was the inability to make and enforce contracts. "If . . . a person is prevented, because of his race, from living and working where and for whom he will, or from earning his livelihood by any lawful calling that he may elect to pursue, then he is hindered in the exercise of rights and privileges secured to freemen by the Constitution of the United States." The Court had denied to black Americans "the right to appeal for national protection against lawless combinations of individuals who seek, by force, and solely because of the race of such laborers, to de-

5. Ronald Lewis, *Black Coal Miners in America: Race, Class, and Community in Conflict, 1780–1980* (Lexington, 1987), 13, 32; Brian Kelly, *Race, Class, and Power in the Alabama Coalfields, 1908–21* (Urbana, 2001), 30–43; U.S. Immigration Commission, *Reports*, 42 vols. (Washington, 1911), VII: 218; Gavin Wright, "The Strange Career of the New Southern Economic History," *Reviews in American History* 10 (1982), 172; Judith Stein, "'Of Mr. Booker T. Washington and Others': The Political Economy of Racism in the United States," *Science and Society* 38 (1974–75), 428.

prive them of the freedom . . . to earn a living in all lawful ways, and to dispose of their labor by contract." Harlan noted that the Court had thrown up protections to businesses against state infringements of the "liberty of contract," and believed that this protection should be extended to all individuals.[6]

Black employment in skilled trades also had risen in the last decades of the nineteenth century but began to fall after AFL organization accelerated. This was especially true in the building trades, where blacks had made important gains after emancipation but fell behind as new technologies altered the nature of the work.[7] "Wherever trade unions flourished, black men lived in fear of exclusion from opportunities for employment," a historian notes.[8]

Booker T. Washington's National Negro Business League (NNBL), established in 1900, attempted to promote black capitalism. The league's appeal to racial solidarity rather than to market standards appeared to conflict with Washington's frequent appeals to the color-blind dollar, and this was perhaps one among the Compromiser's many compromises. Like most Americans, blacks in the late nineteenth century were economic individualists at the same time that they supported a number of mutual-aid voluntary associations.[9] There was certainly an aspect of wishful thinking in the league's boosterism, as Washington publicly denied the economic discrimination he knew existed in the South. "Black Americans were all too obviously denied equal opportunities in their civil, political, and social life in the South. This left economic advancement as the only means of racial uplift for Washington to encourage," one historian observes. "If, even in this area, opportunity was severely limited, there was no alternative agenda for Washington to pursue other

6. *Hodges v. U.S.*, 203 U.S. 1 (1906); William Cohen, *At Freedom's Edge: Black Mobility and the Southern White Quest for Racial Control, 1861–1915* (Baton Rouge, 1991), 275–90; Robert Higgs, *Competition and Coercion: Blacks in the American Economy, 1865–1914* (Cambridge, 1977), 74–76; Flynn, *White Land, Black Labor*, 110. The first peonage case was *Clyatt v. U.S.*, 197 U.S. 207 (1905). *Bailey v. Alabama*, 219 U.S. 219 (1911) and *U.S. v. Reynolds*, 235 U.S. 133 (1914) were the Alabama cases.

7. Claudia D. Goldin, *Urban Slavery in the American South, 1820–60: A Quantitative History* (Chicago, 1976), 129–31; Herbert Northrup, *Organized Labor and the Negro* (New York, 1944), 20–23; John Dittmer, *Black Georgia in the Progressive Era, 1900–20* (Urbana, 1977), 29–30; Neil R. McMillen, *Dark Journey: Black Mississippians in the Age of Jim Crow* (Urbana, 1990), 164.

8. Higgs, *Competition and Coercion*, 81–85.

9. Verney, *The Art of the Possible*, 61; Sterling D. Spero and Abram L. Harris, *The Black Worker: The Negro and the Labor Movement* (New York, 1968 [1931]), 51; August Meier, *Negro Thought in America, 1880–1915: Racial Ideologies in the Age of Booker T. Washington* (Ann Arbor, 1963), 124–27, 140; David A. Gerber, *Black Ohio and the Color Line, 1860–1915* (Urbana, 1976), 178, 379.

than to give up altogether in despair." [10] Washington's critics and later historians and economists have denigrated black capitalism as pure illusion and have obscured real accomplishments in the early twentieth century. The 1910 census showed that there was a roughly equal "entrepreneurship rate" (defined as employers and those "working on their own account") between whites (29 percent) and blacks (26 percent). While black enterprises were dwarfed by the giant white businesses, they were quite healthy when compared to recent immigrant groups. In addition to the NNBL, the Masons and other voluntary associations promoted black economic success, particularly among smaller businessmen. After 1900, though, black businesses suffered from the effects of social segregation and disfranchisement, as well as the concentration of blacks in the agricultural sector of the economy. The spirit of entrepreneurship, strongest among the first generation of freedmen and immigrants, also tended to fade over time. The Great Migration may also have undermined southern black economic success by disrupting business networks and drawing off the more energetic and ambitious of the southern black population.[11]

W. E. B. DU BOIS

Washington launched the National Negro Business League at the height of his popularity and power. His prestige began to erode during the first decade of the new century, however. Though Washington acted as an informal adviser to President Theodore Roosevelt on black affairs, Roosevelt and his successors began to curtail black patronage positions in the South and to court the "lily white" elements in the region. Washington's 1901 luncheon with the president raised a chorus of protest among white supremacists that led Roosevelt never to repeat it and to scale back his association with black interests. Bloody race riots in Atlanta demoralized those who hoped that the white South would respect the terms of the 1895 "Compro-

10. Verney, *The Art of the Possible*, 62; John H. Burrows, *The Necessity of Myth: A History of the National Negro Business League, 1900–45* (Auburn, AL, 1988), 72, 174; Louis R. Harlan, "Booker T. Washington and the National Negro Business League," in William G. Shade and Roy C. Herrenkohl, eds., *Seven on Black: Reflections on the Negro Experience in America* (Philadelphia, 1969), 73–91.

11. Juliet E. K. Walker, *The History of Black Business in America: Capitalism, Race, Entrepreneurship* (New York, 1998), xviii–xxv; Burrows, *The Necessity of Myth*; Abram L. Harris, *The Negro as Capitalist* (Philadelphia, 1936); E. Franklin Frazier, *Black Bourgeoisie: The Rise of a New Middle Class in the United States* (Glencoe, IL, 1957); Margaret Levenstein, "African American Entrepreneurship: The View from the 1910 Census," *Business and Economic History* 24 (1995), 106–22; Kenzer, *Enterprising Southerners*, 4, 85; John Sibley Butler, *Entrepreneurship and Self-Help among Black Americans: A Reconsideration of Race and Economics* (Albany, 1991), 229, 292; Donald Dewey, "Negro Employment in Southern Industry," *Journal of Political Economy* 60 (1952), 288.

mise" articulated in that city, and in 1908 riots spread to Abraham Lincoln's own Springfield, Illinois. Roosevelt's summary dishonorable discharge of three companies of black soldiers for their alleged role in a Brownsville, Texas, shooting incident in 1906 further undermined Washington's role as racial intermediary. Black political influence in the nation's capital would dwindle under William H. Taft and virtually disappear under Woodrow Wilson.[12]

Black leaders in the early years of the new century began to move away from the views of Booker T. Washington and of classical liberalism. The last serious attempt to revive classical liberalism after the crisis of the 1890s involved two future leaders of the civil rights movement, Oswald Garrison Villard and Moorfield Storey. Villard was the grandson of the abolitionist William Lloyd Garrison and publisher of the *Nation* and *New York Evening-Post.* Storey had been the personal secretary of Senator Charles Sumner. They joined the National Democratic (or "Gold Democrat") party in 1900, which embraced a "conservative libertarianism" that sought to restore the liberal principles of the Republican Party. These future founders of the National Association for the Advancement of Colored People (NAACP) were among the many party members who joined racial egalitarianism with free-market economic principles, but their cause was the last gasp of nineteenth-century liberalism.[13]

Black thinkers dissatisfied with the program of Booker T. Washington came together in the American Negro Academy in 1897. Alexander Crummell led the movement to form a black professional society, to offset the opportunism of black politicians and the excessive emphasis on industrial education that they associated with Tuskegee. Crummell feared the effects of anarchy in the labor movement and tried to convince his audience that blacks were naturally conservative and more reliable than foreign workers.[14] "I am forced to say that I do not sympathize with the

12. David W. Southern, *The Malignant Heritage: Yankee Progressives and the Negro Question, 1901–14* (Chicago, 1968), 68–72; Louis R. Harlan, *Booker T. Washington: The Wizard of Tuskegee, 1901–15* (New York, 1983), 295.

13. David T. and Linda R. Beito, "Gold Democrats and the Decline of Classical Liberalism, 1896–1900," *Independent Review* 4 (2000), 555–75. Villard was removed as an NAACP vice-president in 1946 for his antiunion views. Kenneth Robert Janken, *White: The Biography of Walter White, Mr. NAACP* (New York, 2003), 302.

14. Alfred A. Moss Jr., *The American Negro Academy: Voice of the Talented Tenth* (Baton Rouge, 1981); Wilson J. Moses, *Alexander Crummell: A Study of Civilization and Discontent* (New York, 1988), 230–31; Gregory U. Rigsby, *Alexander Crummell: Pioneer in Nineteenth-Century Pan-African Thought* (New York, 1987), 166–67.

attitude of labor in its conflict with capital, and I feel desirous that the black race should keep clear of it," Crummell wrote. He discounted the claims of white workers that they were oppressed. "Abuses of capital there are: and they must be corrected; but the white laborer in this land is *not* a wage slave. He is the freest, best paid, most highly endowed politically than any other laborer in the world." Crummell denounced the "savagery and fanaticism of blatant American democracy" and believed that blacks would be an effective force to counter it.[15] Most members of the academy assumed the classical liberal model of free and lawful individual competition.[16]

William Edward Burghardt Du Bois was the most important figure associated with the American Negro Academy. Born in Great Barrington, Massachusetts, in 1868, Du Bois graduated from an integrated high school in 1884 and wrote for the *Springfield Republican* and T. Thomas Fortune's *New York Globe*. An academic prodigy, he graduated from Fisk University and taught in the Tennessee backcountry before enrolling at Harvard. He earned another bachelor's degree and, after study at the University of Berlin, earned a Ph.D. in history from Harvard in 1895.

Du Bois found himself in the middle of the *Methodenstreit* raging in the Berlin department of political economy between the classicists like Carl Menger and the historicists like Werner Sombart and Max Weber.[17] His writings displayed a mixture of orthodox liberalism and Crummell-style conservatism. In his 1897 American Negro Academy paper, "The Conservation of Races," he outlined a communal, race-based view of black progress that clashed with the liberal tradition of those "reared and trained under the individualistic philosophy of the Declaration of Independence and the laisser-faire philosophy of Adam Smith," philosophies "of which the Negro people are especially fond." Du Bois emphasized the "spiritual, psychical" gifts of the black race, ones that would "soften the whiteness of the Teutonic today. We are that people whose subtle sense of sound has given America its only American music, its only American fairy tales, its only touch of pathos and humor amid its mad money-getting plutocracy."[18]

15. Alexander Crummell, "The Negro as a Source of Conservative Power," in Wilson J. Moses, ed., *Destiny and Race: Selected Writings, 1840–98* (Amherst, 1992), 236.

16. Robert L. Factor, *The Black Response to America: Men, Ideals, and Organization from Frederick Douglass to the NAACP* (Reading, MA, 1970), 254.

17. Thomas D. Boston, "W. E. B. Du Bois and the Historical School of Economics," *American Economic Review* 81 (1991), 303; Raymond Wolters, *Du Bois and His Rivals* (Columbia, MO, 2002), 21.

18. "The Conservation of Races," in Nathan Huggins, ed., *Du Bois: Writings* (New York, 1986), 815–26; Leon F. Litwack, *Trouble in Mind: Black Southerners in the Age of Jim Crow* (New York, 1998), 148.

Though this sounded like a radical challenge to Washington's gospel of black economic achievement, Du Bois was on good terms with Washington in these years. He praised the Atlanta Compromise speech, telling him that it was "a word fitly spoken" and wrote in the *New York Age* that "Here might be the basis of a real settlement between whites and blacks in the South," if the South opened to the Negroes the doors of economic opportunity and the Negroes cooperated with the white South in political sympathy.[19] But Du Bois was also exposed to and admired Prussian state socialism while a graduate student in Germany—he had delivered a paean to Bismarck as his Fisk commencement address and sported the Kaiser's moustache and goatee for the rest of his life. He had sketched a novel whose protagonist became a Socialist, much as Du Bois would, and his dissertation on the suppression of the African slave trade had traces of Marxian analysis.[20]

Du Bois's first sociological studies displayed a liberal cast of mind. *The Philadelphia Negro* called attention to the discrimination blacks suffered but also to their own cultural deficiencies, and it exhorted Americans to be faithful to liberal principles. "Industrial freedom of opportunity has by long experience proven to be generally best for all," he wrote. "This does not contemplate the wholesale replacing of white workmen for Negroes out of sympathy or philanthropy; it does mean that talent should be rewarded, and aptness used in commerce and industry whether its owner be black or white; that the same incentive to good, honest, effective work be placed before a black office boy as before the white one."[21] An early Atlanta University study, *The Negro in Business*, recommended, "Negroes ought to enter into business life in increasing numbers. The present disproportion in the distribution of Negroes in the various occupations is unfortunate. It gives the race a one-sided development, unnecessarily increases competition in certain lines of industry, and puts the mass of the Negro people out of sympathy and thought with the industrial and mercantile spirit of the age."[22] Its call for "Negro Businessmen's Leagues" was the germ of Washington's National Negro Business League. Du Bois's economic thought at this point was no more radical than Washington's and "indistinguishable from the conventional American laissez-faire orthodoxy of per-

19. Du Bois to Washington, 24 Sep. 1895 [BTWP IV: 26].

20. David Levering Lewis, *W. E. B. Du Bois: Biography of a Race, 1868–1919* (New York, 1993), 77, 142, 154, 159.

21. Julius Lester, ed., *The Seventh Son: The Thought and Writings of W. E. B. Du Bois*, 2 vols. (New York, 1971), I: 226.

22. W. E. B. Du Bois, ed., *The Negro in Business* (Atlanta, 1899), 50.

sonal and collective bootstrap improvement," a biographer observes.[23] Decades later Du Bois noted that he had a conventionally liberal outlook in the late nineteenth century.[24]

Du Bois's later radicalism often obscures his early "conservatism."[25] His commitment to socialism was never complete or consistent, but he did begin to take steps along this road after his break with Booker T. Washington. Their conflict had more to do with Washington's use of power and patronage, and the stifling effect of the "Tuskegee Machine," than it did with any particular issues, economic ones least of all. There was little indication of a novel economic agenda in *The Souls of Black Folk*—its Carlylean disdain for the production of wealth and its critique of materialism, dialectical or other, were poor starting points toward Marxism. A correspondent's suggestion that Du Bois look at the race problem in class terms seems to have nudged him in this direction.[26]

As Du Bois came into contact with white socialists in the Niagara movement, especially William English Walling, his views began to shift. The movement's 1909 "Declaration of Principles" blamed employers and unions equally for discrimination against blacks. "We hold up for public execration the conduct of two opposite classes of men: The practice among employers of importing ignorant Negro-American laborers in emergencies, and then affording them neither protection nor permanent employment; and the practice of labor unions in proscribing and boycotting and oppressing thousands of their fellow-toilers, simply because they are black. These methods have accentuated and will accentuate the war of labor and capital, and they are disgraceful to both sides."[27] But Du Bois's most sustained analysis of the labor problem before the Great War, *The Negro American Artisan*, laid nearly all the blame on labor unions. A detailed survey of American unions found that about half of them excluded blacks explicitly, while most of the remainder kept them out unofficially. "In only a few unions, mostly unskilled, is the

23. Lewis, *W. E. B. Du Bois: Biography of a Race*, 221.

24. Du Bois, "Comments on My Life," *Freedomways* 5 (1965), 105.

25. Verney, *The Art of the Possible*, 86; Wolters, *Du Bois and His Rivals*. Lewis notes that Du Bois edited Crummell out of his autobiography's index after he became a Marxist: *W. E. B. Du Bois: Biography of a Race*, 168.

26. Verney, *The Art of the Possible*, 89; Factor, *Black Response to America*, 217; Wolters, *Du Bois and His Rivals*, 54; Lewis, *W. E. B. Du Bois: Biography of a Race*, 295.

27. Niagara Movement, "Declaration of Principles," *The Horizon* (Dec. 1909), in Lester, *The Seventh Son*, I: 430.

Negro welcomed, as in the case of the miners. In a few others the economic foothold of the Negro has been good enough to prevent his expulsion, as in some of the building trades." Even when brought into white unions, black workers often suffered discrimination. As strikebreakers, blacks were forced to gain entry into industrial jobs "only by degrading labor conditions." This situation would continue until the next economic depression, when "the present wave of extraordinary prosperity and exploitation passes and the ordinary everyday level of economic struggle begins. If the Negro can hold his own until then his development is certain." [28]

Du Bois saw labor unions as part of the general frustration of economic opportunity for black workers. He focused on the governmental obstacles to blacks in a 1909 address to the National Negro Committee (soon to become the NAACP). The principal source of black powerlessness was disfranchisement, he explained. "One thing that is impossible and proven so again and again is to train two sets of workers side by side in economic competition and make one set voters and deprive the other of all participation in government." Southern states had repeatedly attempted "to keep down economic competition between the races by confining the Negroes by law and custom to certain vocations." Armed with the ballot, "the white workingman can enforce his feeling of prejudice and repulsion. Other things being equal, the employer is forced to discharge the black man and hire the white man—public opinion demands it, the administrators of government, including police, magistrates, etc., render it easier, since by preferring the white, many intricate questions of social contact are avoided and political influence is vastly increased."

When blacks attempted to underbid white workers, "the next step is to enforce by law and administration that which they cannot gain by competition." Alabama's law making breach of an employment contract a criminal offense was limited to farm laborers, since most of them were black. Other oppressive labor laws applied only to counties that voted for their enforcement. "Counties with white workmen vote it down. Counties with disfranchised black workmen vote it in." Blacks were excluded from public employment, and government contractors bowed to public

---

28. Du Bois, *The Negro American Artisan,* 129–39. Ten years earlier Du Bois had concluded that "Opposition on the part of southern white workmen, and the eagerness of union organizers to replace Negro by white laborers explains the difficulty of extending the union movement and the justifiably suspicious attitude of Negroes toward it," but gave a more favorable view of the attitude of labor leaders than he did in 1912—*The Negro Artisan* (Atlanta, 1902), 157, 162.

pressure to exclude or segregate and subordinate black workers. The legal system failed to protect black life and property; "so much that it is a widespread custom among Negroes of property never to take a civil suit to court but to let the white complainant settle it." The efforts of black entrepreneurs to establish a separate economy were impeded by public license and tax laws. "This is not always done, but it is done just as soon as any white man or group of white men begin to feel the competition." White unions were among these groups. Du Bois feared that the process was still growing. "The fear of Negro competition in all lines is increasing in the South. The demand of tomorrow is going to be increasingly not to protect white people from ignorance and degradation but from knowledge and efficiency—that is, to so arrange the matter by law and custom as to make it possible for the inefficient and lazy white workman to be able to crush and keep down his black competitor at all hazards." [29]

Du Bois edited *The Crisis,* the organ of the NAACP, and employed union men, despite the fact that the printers union excluded blacks. Repeating the findings of *The Negro American Artisan,* Du Bois wrote, "Whatever the tactics, the result is the same for the mass of white workingmen in America: beat or starve the Negro out of his job if you can by keeping him out of the union; or if you must admit him, do the same thing inside union lines." He hoped that organized labor would someday live up to its professed ideals. "So long as union labor fights for humanity, its mission is divine; but when it fights for a clique of Americans, Irish or German monopolists who have cornered or are trying to corner the market in a certain type of service, and are seeking to sell that service at a premium, while other competent workmen starve, they deserve themselves the starvation which they plan for their darker and poorer fellows." [30]

On the eve of World War I, Du Bois's commitment to organized labor was based on little more than faith that white unionists would see the light and give up their racial privileges. While he was preparing *The Negro American Artisan,* he asked AFL president Samuel Gompers to review its findings. The labor chieftain called it "neither fair nor accurate. After careful perusal of the summing up of the attitude of the AFL toward the colored worker, I should say that you are inclined, not only to be pessimistic on the subject, but you are even unwilling to give credit

---

29. "Politics and Industry," *Proceedings of the National Negro Conference* (New York, 1909), 79–86.

30. "Organized Labor," *Crisis* 4 (Jul. 1912), 131, in Lester, *The Seventh Son,* II: 301; Wolters, *Du Bois and His Rivals,* 213.

where credit is due. Let me say further," he concluded peevishly, "that I have more important work to attend to than correct 'copy' for your paper."[31] Almost nothing in the next decade would improve this relationship, and the changes wrought by the Great War would exacerbate black-union tension but also open possibilities for cooperation.

THE GROWTH OF UNION POWER AND BLACK WORKERS

The AFL consolidated its position as the principal labor organization in the United States as the new century dawned. After the turmoil of the 1890s, many large "progressive" employers reached out to the AFL in an attempt to stabilize industrial relations. The first years of the century became known as the "honeymoon of capital and labor," as groups like the National Civic Federation tried to promote management cooperation with labor organizations. The federal government also began to alter its position regarding labor. In the late nineteenth century the federal government usually intervened in labor disputes to protect property and strikebreakers when state and local authorities could or would not. In 1898 Congress passed the Erdman Act to facilitate negotiation of disputes in the railroad system. The act recognized railroad workers' right to organize by outlawing the "yellow dog" contract, in which employees promised not to join a union as a condition of employment. The act also provided for voluntary mediation to avert strikes. President Theodore Roosevelt's promotion of a settlement in the 1902 anthracite coal strike showed that the federal government could go beyond enforcement of property rights and toward conciliation of labor grievances.

Through its own stronger organization and a new "Square Deal" attitude of some employers and state officials, the AFL grew in numbers and power, representing 2 million workers by 1904. Though it reiterated its "voluntarist" and apolitical principles, the federation slowly increased its use of state power. Mine workers president John Mitchell said in 1903, "The trade union movement in this country can make progress only by identifying itself with the state." Though the federation itself remained nonpartisan, many state federations and local unions aligned themselves with the Democrats from 1896 onward.[32] Alliances between local and

31. Gompers to Du Bois, 5 Jan. 1903 [SGP VI: 90; DuBP I: 67]; W. E. B. Du Bois, ed., *The Negro Artisan* (Atlanta, 1902), 157.

32. Gwendolyn Mink, *Old Labor and New Immigrants in American Political Development: Union, Party, and State, 1875–1920* (Ithaca, NY, 1986), 117, 144–46; Robert Wiebe, *Search for Order, 1877–1920* (New York, 1967), 204.

state federations and city and state governments grew, and labor organizations often used state police power to enact legislation favorable to their members. Among the chief goals of the AFL was the elimination of the injunction during strikes. Courts issued injunctions in cases where the law did not provide an adequate remedy—in strikes, where irreparable damage might be done to a business. Unions execrated injunctions because they could be issued with only the employer's testimony, without defendant answer or jury trial, and violations of injunctions incurred criminal penalties. Courts also issued injunctions to prevent union organizers from appealing to workers to breach "yellow-dog contracts." Organized labor regarded the judiciary as biased against unions and the injunction as a tool of class oppression. Gompers claimed that the AFL sought no special privileges from the state, only freedom from laws that added to employer power. Others regarded the power to strike—usually involving intimidation or violence—as a grant of sovereign power to ostensibly private organizations, in line with the syndicalist tendencies of the AFL. By 1906 the AFL was promoting pro-union congressional candidates, and the Democratic Party adopted an anti-injunction plank in its 1908 platform. The alliance of the AFL and the Democrats grew close and peaked during the Wilson administration.[33]

The AFL adopted a policy of "voluntarism" because the American regime was a voluntarist one, its economy based on the principle of liberty of contract. Tactics moving from contract to coercion would be illegal. The federation did try to change the law to outlaw certain kinds of contracts (women and child labor, Asian exclusion) and to exempt labor organizations from laws that prohibited coercion (its campaign against labor injunctions). The federation used political action prudently, when unions could gain without too much risk. Coercion would also be used prudently—only strikes that had a good chance of success would be ap-

33. William M. Dick, *Labor and Socialism in America: The Gompers Era* (Port Washington, NY, 1972), 116, 124; Philip Taft, *Organized Labor in American History* (New York, 1964), 232–39; Dewey Grantham, *Southern Progressivism: The Reconciliation of Progress and Tradition* (Knoxville, 1983), 295; Howard Dickman, *Industrial Democracy in America: Ideological Origins of National Labor Relations Policy* (La Salle, IL, 1987), 18; Armand J. Thieblot Jr., and Thomas R. Haggard, *Union Violence: The Record and the Response by Courts, Legislatures, and the NLRB* (Philadelphia, 1983); Foster Rhea Dulles, *Labor in America: A History*, 3d ed. (New York, 1966), 201–3; Mink, *Old Labor and New Immigrants*, 204; Philip G. Wright, "The Contest Between Organized Labor and Organized Business," *Quarterly Journal of Economics* 29 (1915), 244; Morgan O. Reynolds, "An Economic Analysis of the Norris-LaGuardia Act, the Wagner Act, and the Labor Representation Industry," *Journal of Libertarian Studies* 6 (1982), 253.

proved. In fact, AFL "voluntarism" was the antithesis of the laissez-faire idea of "voluntarism." The federation sought to exercise sovereign power or exemption from general law, a kind of private law (*privilege*) closest to anarcho-syndicalism.[34]

Interest groups have always used local "police power" regulations to promote their own economic advantage. As part of the anti-Chinese campaign in California, a San Francisco ordinance required that all laundries be operated in brick buildings, as a precaution against fires. The city council could grant exceptions for laundries to be operated in wooden dwellings—exemptions that were always granted to whites and denied to Chinese. This act was so transparently discriminatory that the Supreme Court struck it down in 1886—one of the few occasions in which the Court explicitly protected minority rights in the course of its protection of property rights. Organized labor began to lobby for restrictions on the employment of aliens in public employment after the ban on contract labor failed to stem the influx of immigrants.[35] Unionists were behind another regulation that was struck down by the "laissez-faire Court": the limitation on the number of hours worked by bakers in *Lochner v. New York* was aimed at new immigrant bakers who worked longer hours and undersold the established, German bakers. Recent immigrants with little capital would be the ones driven out of business.[36] Justice Rufus Peckham, one of the most laissez-faire justices on the late-nineteenth-century

34. Dickman, *Industrial Democracy*, 253.

35. David E. Bernstein, *Only One Place of Redress: African Americans, Labor Regulations, and the Courts from Reconstruction to the New Deal* (Durham, 2001), 29; *Yick Wo v. Hopkins*, 118 U.S. 356 (1886); Mink, *Old Labor and New Immigrants*, 123; Robert D. Parmet, *Labor and Immigration in Industrial America* (Boston, 1981), 148. In 1915 the Supreme Court struck down an Arizona statute requiring employers to maintain an 80 percent citizen work force—*Truax v. Raich*, 239 U.S. 33 (1915).

36. Bernard H. Siegan, *Economic Liberties and the Constitution* (Chicago, 1980), 116–18; Paul Kens, *Judicial Power and Reform Politics: The Anatomy of* Lochner v. New York (Lawrence, KS, 1990); Sidney G. Tarrow, "Lochner Versus New York: A Political Analysis," *Labor History* 5 (1964), 280–81; Susan Olzak, "Labor Unrest, Immigration, and Ethnic Conflict in Urban America, 1880–1914," *American Journal of Sociology* 94 (1989), 1303–33. The leader of the movement for the maximum hours law, Henry Weismann—though he switched sides before the case was finally decided—had been an anti-Chinese agitator in California. In his attack on the Court's decision, Gompers asked, apparently unaware of the *Yick Wo* decision, "Pray when did the court heretofore assume to declare unconstitutional a law enacted by a sovereign state because it suspected the motive of the legislature enacting the law to be other than that for which it declared?" Gompers, "Bakers Lose at Law but Win in Fact," *American Federationist* 12 (1905), 363; Alfred H. Kelly, Winfred A. Harbison, and Herman Belz, *The American Constitution: Its Origins and Development*, 7th ed., 2 vols. (New York, 1991), II: 405.

Court, had dissented in a New York case that upheld plumbing regulations used against immigrant Russian Jews and noted that "interference with the ordinary trades and occupations seems to be on the increase." But, as in the *Plessy* case, the Court usually allowed such progressive socioeconomic regulation.[37]

The building trades were among the strongest of AFL unions. Many of them—plumbers, electricians, sheet metal workers, ironworkers—used local ordinances controlling licensing and apprenticeship to keep blacks out of their trades. A Virginia act made plumbers union members part of the board of examiners to license the trade, and a Norfolk plumber recommended that his national union support the law as a device to disqualify black plumbers. Twenty-four states enacted similar laws.[38] Virginia barbers sought to require haircutters to graduate from barber school, while no such school in the state admitted blacks. This plan was defeated, but every state except Virginia and New York had local barber regulations by 1941.[39] Control of public employment also reserved employment for whites. Richmond prohibited the employment of blacks on public works in 1902, and a Richmond contractor was threatened with the loss of his job because he employed blacks.[40] The electricians union forced blacks into segregated auxiliary unions. Labor lobbyists usually justified these restrictions on the basis of black incompetence; electrician union leader J. P. Noonan was among the few to call attention to the inconsistency in denigrating Negro inferiority while fearing Negro competition.[41]

37. Bernstein, *Only One Place of Redress,* 33; *Lochner v. NY,* 198 U.S. 45 (1905), 63.

38. Taft, *Organized Labor in American History,* 203; Ray Marshall, *Labor in the South* (Cambridge, 1967), 48; Gerber, *Black Ohio and the Color Line,* 303; Clyde W. Summers, "Admission Policies of Labor Unions," *Quarterly Journal of Economics* 61 (1946), 83; Marshall, *The Negro Worker,* 76; Spero and Harris, *The Black Worker,* 59, 477–81.

39. Ira De A. Reid, *Negro Membership in American Labor* Unions (New York, 1969 [1930]), 155; Bernstein, *Only One Place of Redress,* 38; W. Scott Hall, *The Journeymen Barbers' International Union* (Baltimore, 1936), 44; Doug Bristol, "The Victory of Black Barbers over Reform in Ohio, 1902–13," *Essays in Economic and Business History* 16 (1998), 251–60.

40. Lorenzo Greene and Carter G. Woodson, *The Negro Wage Earner* (New York, 1970 [1930]), 184; W. P. Burrell, "Report of the Committee on Business and Labor Conditions in Richmond, VA," *Proceedings of the Hampton Negro Conference* (Hampton, VA, 1904), 42; "Don't Want Negroes Used as Linemen," *Richmond Times,* 7 Nov. 1902 [HNCF 264]; Bernard E. Anderson, *The Negro in the Public Utilities Industry* (Philadelphia, 1970), 38.

41. Marshall, *The Negro Worker,* 74; Herman D. Bloch, "Labor and the Negro, 1866–1910," *Journal of Negro History* 50 (1965), 181; Barbara J. Fields, "Ideology and Race in American History," in J. Morgan Kousser and James M. McPherson, eds., *Region, Race, and Reconstruction: Essays in Honor of C. Vann Woodward* (New York, 1982), 156.

These efforts made many blacks believe that unions had driven them from skilled employment and that, even where unions did not exclude blacks, their ultimate goal was to limit or ultimately drive them out.[42] A.M.E. bishop Alexander Walters warned of "a determined effort on the part of the white labor unions of the country to exclude the Negro from the industrial avenues in which he can make an honest living," though some New York unionists disputed the contention.[43] "This is the age of combination, both of capital and of labor," Howard University mathematician and sociologist Kelly Miller wrote in 1903. "What the trusts are to capital, trades unions are to labor . . . Combination among whites always proves inimical to the interests of the Negro. The black workman is accorded a fair chance only in those localities where labor unions do not dominate."[44] The *Colored American* denounced "labor barons" as "autocratic and overbearing . . . narrow, dictatorial and full of prejudice. By their dicta no Negro, however well qualified, can be either as a motorman or conductor on the street railways systems of the great cities . . . The trade and labor unions are the greatest enemies of the Negro in America and are doing more to foster and encourage race hatred and the caste spirit than any other agency we know of."[45]

Many black workers practiced their trades where unions did not control the labor supply, and unions were quite weak throughout the South. They worked in the segregated market that white competitors did not deign to serve—the construction of black houses or the cutting of black hair remained open to them.[46] Some of the Tuskegeeans warned blacks not to exaggerate union discrimination and use it as an excuse for failure. An engineering instructor at Tuskegee noted, "There are numerous localities, both North and South, where the union movement has never existed, and yet we find the same scarcity of colored mechanics that we find in the union cities."[47] Kelly Miller denied that "shiftlessness and inefficiency" accounted

42. Greene and Woodson, *The Negro Wage Earner,* 186, 191, 319, 346.

43. "The Race Problem Again," *New York Times,* 14 Mar. 1898, p. 7; "Negroes and Trades Unions," *New York Times,* 20 Nov. 1898, p. 11.

44. Kelly Miller, "The City Negro: Industrial Status," *Southern Workman* 30 (1903), 340–45 [DH V: 11].

45. *Colored American,* 25 May 1901 [DH V: 94].

46. W. E. B. Du Bois, "The Economic Future of the Negro," *Publications of the American Economic Association* 7 (1906), 222; Marshall, *Labor in the South,* 49; Gavin Wright, *Old South, New South: Revolutions in the Southern Economy since the Civil War* (New York, 1986), 178; Higgs, "Black Progress," 10, 23.

47. Harry E. Thomas, "Handicaps of Negro Mechanics," *Southern Workman* 31 (1902), 614–16 [DH V: 40].

for black occupational decline in the North. "The smallness of his numbers is the negro's industrial weakness in the North," he noted. Growing numbers of black workers and a firm stand by employers would facilitate their advancement.[48]

The Negro's "industrial advancement is now checked by the interference of the labor organizations. In the labor movement, the old guild idea of exclusiveness is yet opposed to the more recent idea of inclusiveness; and the negro's fate is involved in this struggle," wrote the lawyer and diplomat James S. Durham. But he detected an "uncertainty of the labor unions' attitude" in which "the colored man finds whatever hope he may for the future."[49] The *Nation* agreed. Reviewing the generally gloomy account in Du Bois's *Negro Artisan,* it concluded, "The employers have no objection to him as a worker, but rather welcome him. Therefore, his competition will be a progressive factor in the industrial world, and the question is, whether his competition shall be controlled as far as possible under union rules, or whether it shall come in conflict with unionism and takes sides with the employer. When this issue becomes a serious one, it is hardly doubtful that race prejudice will yield to pecuniary interest."[50] Mary White Ovington, a settlement house activist, defended northern unionists, saying that organized labor "has found caste feeling and has at times been unable to overcome it, but it has not created it. If it had, we should have seen the Negro strongest in those pursuits which were unorganized; yet many occupations are closed to him because of the prejudice of white employees who have never formed a union."[51] Richard R. Wright Jr., a Philadelphia sociologist, businessman, editor, and African Methodist Episcopal priest (later bishop), believed that Chicago unionists had learned from a series of defeats and believed that "Today, as never before, unionism, which has often meant the crowding out of Negro laborers, is in an increasingly friendly attitude toward black men."[52]

The railroad brotherhoods, remaining outside the AFL, led the way in using political power to achieve their ends and showed how union power often harmed black interests. Railroad workers were particularly well situated to exercise collec-

48. Kelly Miller, "The Economic Handicap of the Negro in the North," *Annals of the American Academy of Political and Social Science* 27 (1906), 84; Mary White Ovington, "The Negro in the Trades Unions in New York," ibid., 91.

49. James Stephens Durham, "The Labor Unions and the Negro," *Atlantic Monthly* 81 (1898), 223, 230; U.S. Industrial Commission, *Reports,* 19 vols. (Washington, 1900–02), XVII: xxix.

50. "The Negro and the Trade Unions," *The Nation* 76 (1903), 186–87.

51. Ovington, "The Negro in the Trades Unions in New York," 92.

52. R. R. Wright Jr., "The Negro in Times of Industrial Unrest," *Charities* 15 (1905–06), 69–73.

tive power. They were skilled and occupied a strategic position in the economy. Strikes could cripple national commerce, and nineteenth-century railroad strikes were especially dramatic and traumatic. Thus Congress' first intervention in national economic regulation concerned the railroads in the Interstate Commerce Act of 1887, and its first foray into labor relations concerned them in the 1898 Erdman Act.[53]

The "Big Four" brotherhoods—engineers, conductors, firemen and enginemen, and trainmen—dominated the work force. Blacks were completely excluded from these unions and from their trades in the North, but in the South there were too many black firemen and trainmen for railroad operators willingly to dispense with them. These unions nevertheless pressed for exclusion rather than try to organize black workers. In 1898 the Grand Master of the Brotherhood of Locomotive Firemen declared that "the avenue to the locomotive should be open to whites alone."[54] Firemen and trainmen had agitated for black exclusion repeatedly but failed. The campaign reached its climax in the 1909 "race strike" against the Georgia Railroad.[55]

The firemen's position usually served as an apprenticeship for the engineer's job, but blacks were considered "unpromotable" and kept feeding the engine box. As a result, they accumulated seniority that enabled them to win preferable job assignments or "runs." The Georgia Railroad increased its employment of black firemen because they worked more cheaply than whites. When the Atlanta Terminal Company replaced ten white hostlers with blacks in May 1909, the Brotherhood of Locomotive Firemen and Enginemen used this as the occasion to strike against the Georgia Railroad. It demanded the replacement of all black firemen with whites. The railroad refused. The white firemen's demands, general manager Thomas K. Scott told the Interstate Commerce Commission, would eliminate "all rights of seniority in runs as firemen from the Negro firemen who have been in our service for years" and ultimately remove them from the service altogether.[56] The railroad

53. Marshall, *Labor in the South,* 52; Dean Dutcher, *The Negro in Modern Industrial Society: An Analysis of Changes in the Occupations of Negro Workers, 1910–20* (Lancaster, PA, 1930), 53.

54. "The Labor Factor in Race Troubles," *The Literary Digest* 17 (1898), 740; Greene and Woodson, *The Negro Wage Earner,* 104.

55. Eric Arnesen, *Brotherhoods of Color: Black Railroad Workers and the Struggle for Equality* (Cambridge, 2001), 30–34; Arnesen, "'Like Banquo's Ghost, It Will Not Down': The Race Question and the American Railroad Brotherhoods, 1880–1920," *American Historical Review* 99 (1994), 1601–33.

56. Thomas K. Scott to Martin Knapp, 22 May 1909, Records of the National Mediation Board, RG 13, NA [BWGM V: 1007]; "Driving the Negro," *Chattanooga News,* 20 May 1909 [HNCF 296].

hired black and white firemen replacements, and the engineers refused to strike with the firemen. The engineers preferred black firemen, it was said, because they were more servile and, unlike white firemen, would act as their personal valets. Being unpromotable, they also decreased the number of potential competitors as engineers.[57] The Brotherhood then embarked on an appeal to the public along the railway line, raising vigilante mobs to attack trains on which black firemen worked. The engineers finally refused to work without better protection, but Governor Hoke Smith, who had campaigned on a platform of white supremacy and black disfranchisement, refused to intervene. Smith feared that his rival, Tom Watson, would exploit any sympathy he showed toward blacks.[58]

The Taft administration stepped in to mediate under the terms of the Erdman Act, and the railroad and the union agreed to let three mediators settle the dispute. The union argued that the black firemen were incompetent, while the railroad insisted that it could not remain in business without the more efficient black labor. General Manager Scott warned that this action was the first step toward the complete exclusion of blacks from industrial work in the South. The mediators, by a two-to-one vote, took the side of the railroad on every point but required that it pay blacks and whites an equal wage. Some union men lobbied for a state act that would require educational tests for black railroad workers or prohibit their employment entirely.[59] Other Brotherhood members considered the decision a victory, assuming that the railroad would not employ blacks unless they worked more cheaply than whites. Thomas W. Hardwick, the dissenting mediator, agreed, saying that the equal-pay order, "by removing the principal incentive for their employment, will result in the speedy elimination of this cheaper labor, and a consequent improvement of the service."[60] But the railroad maintained its black work force at pre-strike levels.

Despite its defeat, the Brotherhood clung to its racially exclusive principles and maintained its white-only constitution until the 1960s. It would continue its campaign for an all-white firemen force, by legal and illegal means, for the next several

---

57. Joseph B. Cumming to *Augusta Chronicle,* 22 May 1909 [DH V: 200]; Greene and Woodson, *The Negro Wage-Earner,* 104.

58. John Michael Matthews, "The Georgia 'Race Strike' of 1909," *Journal of Southern History* 40 (1974), 613–30; Hugh B. Hammett, "Labor and Race: The Georgia Railroad Strike of 1909," *Labor History* 16 (1975), 470–84.

59. "Want No Negro Firemen," *New York Times,* 30 Jun. 1909, p. 12 [DH V: 221].

60. Settlement, Records of the National Mediation Board, RG 13, NA [BWGM V: 1032].

decades. The *Springfield Republican* denounced the hypocrisy of the railroad. "If the southern corporations seek to abolish the color line among their workmen, or to protect in their jobs those Negroes whom they already employ, it is manifest from all the other circumstances of the political, social, and industrial life of the South that they act from selfish motives. It is their antagonism to white trade unionism that governs their course rather than a desire to uplift the Negro."[61] But most blacks believed that such employer selfishness uplifted them incidentally and that white trade unionism was their mutual antagonist. Though one black newspaper warned that the railroad "can play off blacks against whites and whites against blacks and individual against individual, and have no effective opposition to its will," it was hard to believe that it was not the Brotherhood that was attempting to "divide and conquer" in Georgia.[62]

"It is a race issue pure and simple," said *The Nation.* "The Governor, like the labor unions, probably fails to see that, quite aside from the American tradition of fair play to every man who is doing an honest day's work, he is wrong from a strictly business point of view."[63] A Richmond paper commented, "The attack is not upon the lazy, loafing Negroes but upon the honest, industrious ones."[64] "The railroad has stood its ground to the end with admirable firmness," concluded the *Baltimore Afro-American.* "The railroad had absolute justice on its side, and fought tenaciously for employees of proved worth and long service, whose sole offense was the color of their skins."[65] The *New York Times* believed that the settlement vindicated Booker T. Washington's argument that business, rather than politics, would solve the race problem in America. "Business draws no color line," it wrote. "The commission awards an equal right to equal pay for equal work, and an equal right to work."[66] Washington himself wrote to one of the mediators, "The Negro people everywhere feel under the greatest obligation to you . . . I think that I can say that every one of them with whom I have talked feels that this decision

61. "Southern Trade Unionism and the Negro," *Springfield Republican,* 27 May 1909 [HNCF 296].

62. *New York Call,* 26 May 1909 [DH V: 206]. This conclusion has been reiterated by Matthews, "Georgia 'Race Strike,'" and Kelly, *Race, Class, and Power in the Alabama Coalfields,* 206.

63. *The Nation* 88 (1909), 523; "The Georgia Railroad Strike and Its Menaces," *Atlanta Independent,* 29 May 1909 [HNCF 296].

64. "Organized Labor and the Negro," *Richmond Planet,* 26 May 1909 [HNCF 296]; Du Bois, "Politics and Industry."

65. *Baltimore Afro-American,* 12 Jun. 1909 [DH V: 218].

66. "Georgia Firemen Satisfied," *New York Times,* 29 Jun. 1909, p. 2 [DH V: 220].

rendered by southern men will be as far-reaching in effect as any single thing in helping forward the progress of the Negro people."[67]

White railroad unionists continued to press for limitations on black employment, and employers became more accommodating to their demands. Mediators in the next decade limited black firemen to work in the South and placed quotas on the number of black firemen. White brakemen persuaded the Ohio legislature to enact a "full crew" law that enabled them to oust black "porter-brakemen"— blacks who were officially classified as porters but did brakemen's jobs. W. E. B. Du Bois commented that "the various 'full crew' laws were simply methods of driving out Negro competition." But blacks were able to maintain their numbers in railroading until World War I.[68]

If the building trades and railroad brotherhoods were the unions most hostile to blacks, the mine workers were among the most friendly. The largest industrial union in the craft-dominated AFL, the UMW included twenty thousand black members, or more than half of the AFL's entire black membership.[69] In the South the United Mine Workers faced the most serious racial problems and was usually defeated despite its strong interracial solidarity. Indeed, in Alabama the union's interracialism contributed to its defeat: where the union used antiblack sentiment in its battle with the Georgia Railway, Alabama coal operators used the specter of "social equality" to defeat the UMW. In the northern coal fields, whites were able to exclude blacks for the most part. In between, in West Virginia, blacks enjoyed greater economic equality and freedom than almost anywhere else in American industry.

The UMW benefited from the "honeymoon of capital and labor" after its defeats in the 1890s, as operators signed union contracts North and South. By 1902, one-half of all the miners in America were UMW members. By 1904 the *modus vivendi* broke down, and the cycle of strikes and violence returned to the Alabama

---

67. Washington to Hilary Abner Herbert, 12 Aug. 1909 [BTWP X: 155].

68. "Statement of the Firemen's Position in the Strike" (c. 1910), Settlement, 25 Mar. 1911, Records of the National Mediation Board, RG 13, NA [BWGM V: 1143, 1181]; Arnesen, *Brotherhoods of Color*, 37; David E. Bernstein, "Racism, Railroad Unions, and Labor Regulations," *Independent Review* 5 (2000), 237–47; W. E. B. Du Bois, "The Hosts of Black Labor," *The Nation* 116 (1923), 539–41 [DH VI: 3]; Roy Wilkins to Roy Ellis, 31 Mar. 1934 [NAACP 10, III: 237]; Spero and Harris, *The Black Worker*, 291.

69. Gerber, *Black Ohio and the Color Line*, 300–303; Philip S. Foner, *Organized Labor and the Black Worker, 1619–1981* (New York, 1982), 83.

pits. Blacks again composed a significant part of the replacement work force, but the strike did not provoke much racial disorder.[70] Blacks now comprised a majority of Alabama coal miners, so the UMW had little choice but to reach out to them. But the fundamental problem that the union faced—that there were more than enough replacements, black and white, willing to work at wages below those demanded by the union—doomed their every effort. Shooting the replacements and dynamiting mine equipment only worsened the strikers' position. When the miners continued a 1907 strike months after such action, the Birmingham press tried to stir up public opinion against the UMW by accusing it of advocating "social equality." White supremacists were particularly upset by the specter of black and white families living together in tent colonies set up after the miners had been evicted from company housing. Union leaders were "daily instilling into the minds of the blacks ideas of social equality," wrote Frank V. Evans of the *Birmingham Age-Herald,* "which if they do take root will result in a worse condition than now exists—of bloodshed and absolute annihilation."[71]

Because some of the companies had shown in the 1890s that they were willing to "play the race card" in their antiunion efforts, and because they paid $3,500 to two newspapers in this campaign, this was a clear case of a "divide and conquer" tactic on their part.[72] But the UMW attempted to draw a line between job equality and social equality and "paid rhetorical ransom to the claims of white supremacy," one historian notes. Indeed, the white miners blamed the operators for threatening white supremacy by having introduced blacks in the first place, using blacks as strikebreakers and forcing whites and blacks to work together. The UMW offered "to transport out of the state every Negro who was on strike and make it a white man's fight."[73] Still, "whatever local discrimination blacks encountered in their

70. Price Van Meter Fishback, *Soft Coal, Hard Choices: The Economic Welfare of Bituminous Coal Miners, 1890–1930* (New York, 1992), 23; Daniel Letwin, *The Challenge of Interracial Unionism: Alabama Coal Miners, 1878–1921* (Chapel Hill, 1998), 143.

71. Richard A. Straw, "The Collapse of Biracial Unionism: The Alabama Coal Strike of 1908," *Alabama Historical Quarterly* 37 (1975), 92–114; "Social Equality Talk Evil Feature of Strike," *Birmingham Age-Herald,* 22 Aug. 1908 [DH V: 185].

72. Letwin, *Challenge of Interracial Unionism,* 114, 145–51; Herbert Gutman, "The Negro and the United Mine Workers of America: The Career and Letters of Richard L. Davis and Something of Their Meaning, 1890–1900," in Julius Jacobson, ed., *The Negro and the American Labor Movement* (Garden City, NY, 1968), 52.

73. Kelly, *Race, Class, and Power in the Alabama Coalfields,* 24.

dealings with white miners," another historian concludes, "in the context of southern society the UMW was the most progressive force in their lives."[74] Alabama hosted some of the most bitter labor conflicts in American history, and these owners represented the most vociferous proponents of the open shop. The De-Bardeleben family especially opposed unionism, and would go to extraordinary and even absurd lengths to destroy it.[75] Nor were the operators united in their tactics. While DeBardeleben and Sloss took a bare-knuckles approach to labor relations, the Tennessee Coal, Iron, and Railroad Company, especially after U.S. Steel acquired it, adopted "welfare capitalist" methods. Withal, the UMW was devastated by the 1908 defeat and could count but twenty-eight members in Alabama by 1915.[76]

Though some blacks had broken into northern mines, whites were usually able to keep them out, as in Pana and Virden. White manipulation of apprenticeship rules had long kept black miners out of the Pennsylvania anthracite mines, the scene of the intense 1902 strike that President Roosevelt mediated.[77] "The crafty labor leaders and some of their followers, most of whom are of foreign birth, have gotten the idea into their heads that they have the undoubted right to dictate to these operators not only what they shall pay for their labor but who shall perform that labor," complained Bruce Grit (the pen-name of John Edward Bruce) in the *Colored American.* "If Negro miners were set to work in these coal fields tomorrow it is not unlikely that every labor organization in this country would go out on strike." Grit exhorted the operators, far from meeting their workers halfway, to vindicate the principle "that every man of whatever race he may be may have the unquestioned right to sell his labor wherever he can find a purchaser."[78] Although

74. Lewis, *Black Coal Miners,* 64.

75. "Between 1933 and 1935, for example, a so-called 'mystery man' appeared at the . . . mines. This character was draped in a black robe outlined with white markings resembling a skeleton, and wore white gloves to which were attached long claws. His hood was adorned with horns to which flashing electric lights were attached. Presumably the superstitious black miners were supposed to be frightened by this masquerade. The mystery man would sneak up behind them while they were working and listen to them talk." Lewis, *Black Coal Miners,* 73.

76. Letwin, *Challenge of Interracial Unionism,* 159; Kelly, *Race, Class, and Power in the Alabama Coalfields,* 31; Lewis, *Black Coal Miners,* 58; Marshall, *Labor in the South,* 74; Spero and Harris, *The Black Worker,* 247.

77. Lewis, *Black Coal Miners,* xii.

78. "Bruce Grit on the Strike Situation," *Colored American,* 18 Oct. 1902, p. 7.

the UMW constitution committed it to nondiscrimination, whites in control of local unions were able to exclude blacks from the work force entirely or to marginalize them within the union, denying them official positions. When black members demanded race-based representation in the body, whites replied that this would constitute "preferential treatment" in violation of the union's nondiscrimination policy. Local discrimination would lead the black miners to support John L. Lewis's effort to centralize control of the mine union between the world wars.[79]

West Virginia provides the best example of the benefits of a competitive labor market for black Americans. Organization conferred few benefits even when successful, but black workers more often used the strategy of "exit" to improve their situation. Taking advantage of the fundamental freedom of physical mobility, blacks moved from southern coal mines to the central Appalachian fields, just as they had moved from cotton fields to the southern mines. As early as the 1880s an adumbration of the later Great Migration was underway. Historians often neglect "exit" as an alternative to unionization, for it worked gradually and individually and did not produce dramatic and violent conflicts, but it was probably the most important factor in black economic progress. In addition, the *threat* of exit often gave workers more bargaining power.[80]

Black miners ventured into West Virginia in the decades before World War I, and the competitive labor market and company towns in the remote Appalachian countryside created a new social environment.[81] The mining life provided a transition from southern farm to northern urban industrial life for many blacks. They earned the same as whites—payment by the ton helped to eliminate racial bias. Black miners largely escaped white supervision during the workday, an independence greatly sought after. Most company towns provided blacks with housing of identical quality to that provided for whites, and it was usually not segregated. State law segregated local schools, but the black vote and company influence ensured that spending on black education was not slighted. Black teacher salaries were actually higher than whites' in West Virginia, and the state spent more per pupil on

79. Lewis, *Black Coal Miners,* 100; Lewis, "Job Control and Race Relations in the Coal Fields, 1870 – 1920," *Journal of Ethnic Studies* 12 (1985), 44.

80. Fishback, *Soft Coal, Hard Choices,* 4; Lewis, "From Peasant to Proletarian: The Migration of Southern Blacks to the Central Appalachian Coalfields," *Journal of Southern History* 55 (1989), 77–102; Kelly, *Race, Class, and Power in the Alabama Coalfields,* 96.

81. David Corbin, *Life, Work, and Rebellion in the Coal Fields: The Southern West Virginia Miners, 1880–1922* (Urbana, 1981), 61.

blacks than on whites, five times as much as most southern states. As one historian concludes, "In many ways West Virginia was a haven for black workers."[82]

The initial attractiveness of the West Virginia coal mines eventually diminished, and black workers joined whites of various ethnic backgrounds in the UMW. Growing public discrimination helped limit black progress—the state required written exams for mine foremen in 1910 and established management training at the white-only state university.[83] The operators had brought together a diverse set of workers—what has been called a "judicious mixture"—but this was not part of a "divide and conquer" strategy.[84] Employers responded to labor market availability and to the variety of work cultures that they believed the miners brought with them. "Blacks tended to work only long enough to fulfill their basic needs, about three days a week, and then they laid off to enjoy themselves," operators observed. "Foreigners, on the other hand, worked as long and as often as they could but insisted on celebrating numberless religious and national holidays by getting roaring drunk. Native white mountaineers, for their part, were unaccustomed to rigid work routines, and mine managers considered them lazy and shiftless." Stereotyping work habits of national groups, followed by recruitment through family and ethnic networks, was a way of reducing search costs.[85] The operators' racial egalitarianism facilitated the growth of interracial solidarity among the miners. On the eve of World War I, Appalachian labor relations had degenerated to those of the South, with bloody strikes at Paint Creek and Cabin Creek. Blacks zealously supported the UMW in West Virginia, where strikes were more often broken by poor whites.[86]

Southern iron- and steelworkers did not make the attempt that the UMW did

82. Corbin, *Life, Work, and Rebellion,* 64–74; Lewis, "From Peasant to Proletarian," 90–93; Fishback, *Soft Coal, Hard Choices,* 175–90.

83. Joe William Trotter Jr., *Coal, Class, and Color: Blacks in Southern West Virginia, 1915–32* (Urbana, 1990), 27.

84. Kenneth R. Bailey, "A Judicious Mixture: Negroes and Immigrants in the West Virginia Mines, 1880–1917," *West Virginia History* 34 (1973), 157.

85. Judith Stein, *Running Steel, Running America: Race, Economic Policy and the Decline of Liberalism* (Chapel Hill, 1998), 44; U.S. Immigration Commission, *Reports,* IX: 68; Hugh Davis Graham, *Collision Course: The Strange Convergence of Affirmative Action and Immigration Policy in America* (New York, 2002), 157.

86. Corbin, *Life, Work, and Rebellion in the Coal Fields,* 77; Lewis, *Black Coal Miners,* 121, 134–35; Lewis, "Job Control and Race Relations in the Coal Fields," 52.

to include blacks. Blacks clearly gained more from the "welfare capitalism" policies of the new, progressive steel operators when U.S. Steel moved into the South
in the early decades of the century. Blacks enjoyed more occupational mobility and
access to skilled jobs as employers redefined racial lines.[87] Employers complained
that the region's occupational caste system made southern steel less competitive.
Reformers complained that racial discrimination wasted black talent, gave white
workers unearned rewards, and inflated the prices of southern products. But employers did not go so far as to challenge segregation, and they continued to acquiesce to a racial division of labor while they eroded it. The AFL made some attempts
to form segregated black locals of iron and steel workers, but rank-and-file opposition to cooperation with blacks was more powerful than the federation's commitment to it. The Alabama molders union reaffirmed its white-only policy in
1902, and many unions withdrew from the Alabama Federation of Labor when it
voted to admit black delegates. An ironworkers local ended a strike in 1906 when
company officials agreed to its demand to "discharge all niggers."[88]

RIVALS ON THE LEFT

As the AFL became less attentive to the race issue in the twentieth century, it faced
a growing challenge from the left. Socialists advocated a fuller political program for
the labor movement, particularly in the establishment of a labor party. Syndicalists, by contrast, would push the economic direct action of the AFL to the goal of
destruction of the capitalist system. Though the syndicalist Industrial Workers of
the World (IWW, or "Wobblies") did articulate and sometimes act on racially egalitarian principles, neither the socialists nor the syndicalists made much of an impression on black Americans.[89]

In 1901 the Socialist Party recognized a special dimension to the racial problem
within capitalism. Capitalists sought to maintain the subordination of blacks "and
to foster and increase color prejudice and race hatred between the white worker
and the black, so as to make their social and economic interests appear to be sep-

87. Robert J. Norrell, "Caste in Steel: Jim Crow Careers in Birmingham, Alabama," *Journal of
American History* 73 (1986), 671–72.

88. McKiven, *Iron and Steel*, 114–25; Herbert R. Northrup, "The Negro and Unionism in the Birmingham, Alabama, Iron and Steel Industry," *Southern Economic Journal* 10 (1943), 32.

89. John R. Commons et al., *History of Labor in the United States*, 4 vols. (New York, 1966 [1918–
35]), III: 533.

arate and antagonistic, in order that the workers of both races may thereby be more easily and completely exploited."[90] But Socialist Party leaders spent the next two decades either ignoring or revising this position. Most often they declared that the race issue would disappear once the class issue was solved. Since racial prejudice was the result of capitalist manipulation, it would vanish along with capitalism. Leaders like Eugene V. Debs, while sympathetic to the problems of black labor, would not make any specific race-based appeals. Though he told a Harlem audience in 1923 that "One reason why I became a Socialist was because I was opposed to this cruel discrimination against human beings on account of the color of their skin," the problem of discrimination did not enter into his economic or political strategy. "The race question as we come to understand it resolves itself into a class question . . . The capitalist cares no more about the white worker than about the black worker. What he wants is labor power—cheap labor power; he does not care whether it is wrapped up in a white skin or a black skin. Has he one bit more consideration for the white slave than he has for the black slave?"[91] Such observations, echoing both Marxist and liberal principles, left the problem of racial bias untouched.

Debs and Socialist Party leader Morris Hillquit claimed that to call attention to the particular problems of black workers would only serve to divide the working class and declared, "We have nothing special to offer the Negro." Other Socialists, like Milwaukee's Victor Berger, linked the triumph of the working class to the triumph of the white race. "There can be no doubt that the Negroes and mulattoes constitute a lower race," he wrote in 1902. "The many cases of rape which occur whenever Negroes are settled in large numbers proves, moreover, that the free contact with the whites has led to the further degeneration of the Negroes." He asked "whether the United States and Canada are to remain a white country or become peopled by a yellowish black race with a white admixture," and in Congress warned against "modern white coolies . . . Slavians, Italians, Greeks, Russians and Armenians" who were taking jobs from "Americans, Germans, Englishmen and Irishmen." As Ernest Untermann, the aptly named party theoretician and Idaho gubernatorial candidate, put it, "the question as to what race shall dominate the globe must be met as surely as the question of what class shall own the world." "I

90. R. Laurence Moore, "Flawed Fraternity: American Socialist Response to the Negro, 1901–12," *The Historian* 32 (1969), 2.

91. Eugene V. Debs, *The Negro Workers* (New York, 1923), 6, 12.

am determined that my race shall not go the way of the Aztec and the Indian . . .
I am determined that my race shall be supreme in this country and the world."
Seattle socialist Herman Titus noted, "Racial incompatibility was a fact, and no
amount of Proletarian Solidarity or International Unity can ignore it. We must
face the facts."[92]

Other Socialists blamed capitalism for bringing white and black workers together, where socialism would allow them to follow their natural racial antipathy
and remain separate. Nearly all Socialists abjured any designs of "social equality,"
and few raised any significant protest against AFL racial policy. Many of the socialist unionists who remained in the AFL, like the Machinists, were among the
most discriminatory of its affiliates. Debs opposed party resolutions to restrict immigration or declare nonwhite inferiority but overlooked much of the racism of
the left. He claimed in 1903 that "the labor movement in general, in America,
stands unequivocally committed to receive and treat the Negro upon terms of absolute equality," and he praised the efforts of Georgia segregationist Tom Watson
on behalf of the "common people."[93]

The Industrial Workers of the World, a revolutionary syndicalist organization
devoted to the violent overthrow of capitalism, was formed in 1905, but it did not
undertake any serious labor organization until after 1910. It grew out of the Western Federation of Miners and made its greatest efforts in the industrial Northeast
and so had few black members. Its most successful efforts were among longshoremen and timber workers, where it fought conditions even more harsh than those
of the southern coal miners, and it openly challenged segregation. In the southern
lumber industry, the Brotherhood of Timber Workers formed the basis for IWW
organization. The lumber camps were racially mixed, and both blacks and whites
resisted and joined the BTW's organization efforts. Like the United Mine Workers,
the BTW carefully pointed out that its interracial union did not advocate "social
equality." One large operator feared that the BTW's interracial appeal would make
it more powerful but also suspected that the white members "have no concern
about our colored citizens except insofar as they can use the Negroes for their personal advantage . . . [I]f they succeed in establishing the organization and getting

92. Moore, "Flawed Fraternity," 3–77; Ira Kipnis, *The American Socialist Movement, 1897–1912*
(New York, 1952), 278; Seymour Martin Lipset and Gary Marks, *It Didn't Happen Here: Why Socialism
Failed in the United* States (New York, 2000), 155–56; Southern, *Malignant Heritage*, 72–73.

93. Moore, "Flawed Fraternity," 10–14; Kipnis, *The American Socialist Movement*, 278.

control of the mills they intend to drive every colored man off the job and supply his place with some inferior white fellow." When the BTW affiliated with the IWW and sought their guidance, the IWW made the principle of racial equality more explicit but also raised the fear of socialism and violence.[94]

Like the Socialists, the Wobblies also did not recognize the peculiar racial dimension of the southern labor system. "Despite its advanced position against race prejudice and segregation in the labor movement, the failure of the IWW to understand the special aspect of the Negro problem restricted its appeal to the black masses," one historian notes.[95] When the Wobblies did address the race question, the tone and language of its appeals could also inflame racial passions. "A grave situation is rapidly developing in the South which all Negroes who care for their race's advancement would do well to take note of and use all their power against," warned the timber workers newspaper in 1913, "and that is the using of the lowest type of their race, the Niggers, as scabs in every struggle of the workers to better their condition." The IWW had tried earnestly to bring blacks into their "one big union," it continued, "but, if the Negroes of the South lay down on the job and allow the Niggers to continue to disgrace their race, no earthly power can prevent a disaster to their people."[96] This was as alienating as anything that the AFL published.

The IWW did impress some civil rights activists. Mary White Ovington noted that its president, William ("Big Bill") Haywood, was the only delegate to express any concern about the race issue at the Socialist Party convention in 1912, and that the Wobblies and the NAACP were the only organizations that took clear stands against segregation.[97] Its most enthusiastic black advocate was A. Philip Randolph, who would rival W. E. B. Du Bois for longevity and mercurialism on the issue of blacks in the labor movement. A Socialist Party member who attempted to organize blacks in New York, Randolph in 1917 launched *The Messenger* with

94. James F. Fickle, "Race, Class, and the Wobblies in the Southern Lumber Industry, 1900–16," in Joseph R. Conlin, ed., *At the Point of Production: The Local History of the IWW* (Westport, 1981), 98, 101, 103.

95. Philip S. Foner, "The IWW and the Black Worker," *Journal of Negro History* 55 (1970), 49; Leland V. Bell, "Radicalism and Race: The IWW and the Black Worker," *Journal of Intergroup Relations* 19 (1971), 53–54.

96. "The Nigger Scab," *The Lumberjack* 10 (Jul. 1913) [DH V: 510].

97. Mary White Ovington, "The Status of the Negro in the United States," *New Review* 1 (1913), 747–49 [DH V: 510].

his law school friend Chandler Owen. It was bumptious, calling Robert Russa Moton (Washington's successor as president of the Tuskegee Institute), J. Emmett Scott (Washington's secretary), and George E. Haynes (National Urban League founder), "political fossils, mental manikins, intellectual Lilliputians," who had done nothing to gain recognition for blacks in the labor movement. He credited the IWW with forcing the AFL to appeal to blacks. As for the AFL, "The very thing which they are fighting is one of the chief factors in securing for Negroes their rights. That is Bolshevism." Randolph in 1919 denounced the AFL as "the most wicked machine for the propagation of race prejudices in the country."[98] Du Bois remained wary of the Wobblies' motives and methods. As he would later say about the Communists, "American Negroes do not propose to be the shock troops of the Communist Revolution, driven out in front to death, cruelty, and humiliation in order to win victories for white workers. They are picking no chestnuts from the fire, neither for capital nor white labor."[99] Blacks who did join or support the IWW usually did so for its practical, economic benefits. The Marine Transport Workers (MTW), for example, when it won control of dock work, behaved very much like any AFL local. In Philadelphia, a port controlled by the MTW for several years, the union focused on bread-and-butter issues and adopted the AFL waterfront formula of alternating the local chairmanship monthly between blacks and whites. The successor unions to the IWW had mixed records on racial issues. Black Americans shared the religious faith and bourgeois aspirations of their white fellows, so the appeals of atheist socialism fell on deaf ears.[100]

NORTHERN INDUSTRIES BEFORE THE WAR

Black workers' steady migration into northern industries continued before World War I. In the North blacks found a wider range of jobs open to them, but they still faced occupational discrimination. Most companies sought no unnecessary antag-

---

98. *The Messenger* 2 (Aug. 1919), 10–12 [DH V: 448]; *The Messenger* 2 (May–Jun. 1919), 7, in Spero and Harris, *The Black Worker,* 390.

99. "The Negro and Communism," *Crisis* 40 (Sep. 1931), 313, in Lester, *The Seventh Son,* II: 278; Lewis, *W. E. B. Du Bois,* 420.

100. Spero and Harris, *The Black Worker,* 396, 413; Bell, "Radicalism and Race," 51; Kelly Miller, *The Everlasting Stain* (Washington, 1924), 22; Paula Pfeffer, *A. Philip Randolph: Pioneer of the Civil Rights Movement* (Baton Rouge, 1990), 296; Michael Goldfield, "Race and the CIO: The Possibilities for Racial Egalitarianism during the 1930s and 1940s," *International Labor and Working Class History* 44 (1993), 13.

onism with their white workers, who wanted to keep the better jobs to themselves. Chicago attracted blacks as it did European immigrants. The meatpacking industry became the largest industrial employer of Chicago blacks. When the Knights of Labor butchers union went out on strike in sympathy with Debs's white-only American Railway Union in 1894, blacks made their first significant inroads into the packinghouses. Ten years later, when a reformed union of skilled butcher workers struck to establish a minimum wage for unskilled labor, to protect their own jobs, the unskilled—new immigrants and blacks—did not join them and took their jobs.[101] There was "very little system" in the recruitment of the strikebreakers, R. R. Wright reported.[102] Though strikebreakers were as often Italian or Greek as black, resentment focused on the blacks, and the press provided lurid reports of the new workers as a gang of depraved desperadoes.[103] Upton Sinclair broadcast the image in his best-selling socialist realist novel, *The Jungle*.

> Any night, in the big open space in front of Brown's, one might see brawny Negroes stripped to the waist and pounding each other for money, while a howling throng of three or four thousand surged about, men and women, young white girls from the country rubbing elbows with big buck Negroes with daggers in their boots, while rows of wooly heads peered down from every window in the surrounding factories. The ancestors of these black people had been savages in Africa; and since then they had been chattel slaves, or had been held down by a community ruled by the traditions of slavery. Now for the first time they were free—free to gratify every passion, free to wreck themselves . . . They lodged the men and women on the same floor; and with the night there began a saturnalia of debauchery—scenes such as never before had been witnessed in America. And as the women were the dregs from the brothels of Chicago, and the men were for the most

101. Paul Norgren et al., "Negro Labor and Its Problems" (unpublished ms. for the Carnegie-Myrdal Study, 1940), 339, 581–88; Alma Herbst, *The Negro in the Slaughtering and Meat-Packing Industry in Chicago* (New York, 1932), 18, 23; William M. Tuttle Jr., *Race Riot: Chicago in the Red Summer of 1919* (Urbana, 1996 [1970]), 114.

102. Wright, "The Negro in Times of Industrial Unrest," 70.

103. James R. Barrett, *Work and Community in the Jungle: Chicago's Packinghouse Workers, 1894–1922* (Urbana, 1987), 172; Herbst, *Negro in the Slaughtering and Meat-Packing Industry*, 26; Stephen H. Norwood, *Strikebreaking and Intimidation: Mercenaries and Masculinity in Twentieth-Century America* (Chapel Hill, 2002), 91–94.

part ignorant country Negroes, the nameless diseases of vice were soon rife; and this where food was being handled which was sent out to every corner of the civilized world.[104]

An effective propagandist, Sinclair knew that "No issue would arouse the public to urge the companies to bargain with the unions more effectively than that of young African-American men taking the factory jobs of whites, sleeping with white women, and learning the pleasures of debauchery."[105] Yet Sinclair tried to blame the packers for manipulating racial feelings, claiming that they brought in arch-segregationist Ben Tillman in the aftermath to confound the Socialists.[106]

AFL leader John J. Fitzpatrick telegrammed Booker T. Washington, asking him to come to Chicago and discourage blacks from breaking the strike. Washington claimed that his schedule did not permit it but wrote to President Roosevelt, "Of course I shall not go to Chicago for any such purpose and shall keep clear of the whole business." The National Negro Business League, meeting in New York during the strike, denounced the racial bias and violence of the strikers and praised the courage of the strikebreakers.[107] The *New York Age* commented, "There are those who think that Negroes should not allow themselves to be used to help corporations against striking employees, but we are not of the number, on the theory that a man has the right to quit work if he is dissatisfied and another man has the right to take the job if he wants the work and is satisfied with the conditions of employment. The theory that he may also prevent others from working is an absurdity which cannot be recognized or tolerated without destruction of personal liberty and of business enterprise." Labor union monopoly was as illegitimate as any trust.[108] Some complained that the packers continued to favor white immigrant labor to black, and blacks usually lost positions that they won during the strikes because the returning strikers outperformed them or forcibly ousted them. In any event, only six hundred remained by 1910. This remained a significant achieve-

---

104. Upton Sinclair, *The Jungle* (New York, 1990 [1905]), 270–71.

105. Emory Elliott, "Afterword," ibid., 348. This may have been a vestige of Sinclair's early hack writing that often targeted ethnic minorities and blacks—William A. Bloodworth, *Upton Sinclair* (Boston, 1977), 20.

106. Sinclair, *The Jungle*, 234; Stephen Kantrowitz, *Ben Tillman and the Reconstruction of White Supremacy* (Chapel Hill, 2000), 278.

107. Washington to Roosevelt, 27 Aug. 1904 [BTWP VIII: 58].

108. "Strikers and Strikebreakers," *New York Age*, 4 Aug. 1904 [NHCF 264].

ment, however. "Throughout this era when many industries remained closed to blacks because of employer or union hostility, the packers offered them relatively high wages and continued to employ them even during economic decline," one historian notes.[109]

As in the Alabama steel industry, black entry into the Chicago packinghouses illustrated how black workers could take advantage of competition among white workers and bargaining between employers and employees. This was the sort of economic competition that tended to erode racial discrimination, rather than a conscious effort by the packers to use race to "divide and conquer" their work force. Owners could be as prejudiced as, or even more prejudiced than, their workers, but there was a limit to how much they would be willing to pay for it. Packers appeared to benefit from racial animosity among their workers, but this is not to say that they were the cause of or encouraged it. Blacks were simply one of many new ethnic groups that made their way into the packinghouses—not always as strikebreakers, nor as the only group to break strikes when they did.[110]

Many claimed that black strikebreaking caused white workers' hostility to blacks; in fact, black strikebreaking was the result of decades of white union exclusion. The packinghouses would be among the most important employers of blacks, who moved up the occupational skill ladder and by the 1920s had earned a measure of equality with whites in the industry.[111] "Strikebreaking is wrong from the point of view of the union just as the strike is wrong from the point of view of the employer," Richard R. Wright observed. "But it is one of the few methods which Negroes have to force recognition from the unions, and has been possibly an economic necessity." It might be "the worst form of competition," he wrote, "Still, after all is said and done, it is probably true that the Negro has been the gainer."[112] A labor historian has recently observed that "black strikebreaking was

109. Walter A. Fogel, *The Negro in the Meat Industry* (Philadelphia, 1970), 23; U.S. Immigration Commission, *Reports,* XIII: 93; Barrett, *Work and Community in the Jungle,* 47.

110. John R. Commons, "Labor Conditions in Meat Packing and the Recent Strike," *Quarterly Journal of Economics* 19 (1904) [DH V: 103]. T. J. Woofter Jr., "The Negro and Industrial Peace," *The Survey* 45 (1920), 420–21, refers to white waiters who tricked blacks into striking with them and then made the discharge of blacks a condition of settling the strike, but dates this to 1912.

111. Paul Street, "The Logic and Limits of 'Plant Loyalty': Black Workers, White Labor, and Corporate Racial Paternalism in Chicago's Stockyards, 1916–40," *Journal of Social History* 29 (1996), 663.

112. Richard R. Wright Jr., "The Negro Skilled Mechanic in the North," *Southern Workman* 38 (1909), 155–68 [DH V: 46].

nothing less than a form of working-class activism designed to advance the interests of black workers and their families." It was "in many instances a collective
strategy as much as trade unionism," in which blacks appealed to the American
heritage of equal citizenship, liberty of contract, and open competition.[113] Another
historian notes that in addition to the economic gains, black strike breakers were
able to assert courage and manliness "in a period of steadily increasing subordination to whites." "For many whites it undermined the image of black male passiv-
ity and obsequiousness."[114] Harvard president Charles W. Eliot told a congrega-
tion of Boston unionists that strike breakers should be regarded as heroes.[115]

The stockyards strike was one of several racially divisive actions in Chicago in
the first decade of the century. The powerful building trades unions had excluded
blacks in order to limit competition, but they made overtures to them in an unsuccessful 1900 strike and began to adopt a more open policy afterward. By contrast, in a brutal teamsters strike in 1905, blacks were the target of both white
strikers and white strikebreakers, as well as the strike's public supporters. While a
Methodist minister accused the employers of using black drivers to "foment race
hatred," Ida B. Wells Barnett proposed a resolution for black leaders that praised
the strike breakers as "men who proved their value by risking their lives to obtain
work" and endorsed "the constitutional right of all men to earn a living and to protect themselves in the exercise of that right." Employers agreed to stop hiring
blacks as replacement drivers but refused to discharge ones already hired. White
strikers assaulted black Chicagoans indiscriminately, not distinguishing between
"scabs" and blacks in general. Black waiters felt that they had been betrayed by
white waiters after joining them in a 1903 strike.[116] Journalist Ray Stannard Baker

113. Eric Arnesen, "Specter of the Black Strikebreaker: Race, Employment, and Labor Activism in
the Industrial Era," *Labor History* 44 (2003), 322, 328–30.

114. Norwood, *Strikebreaking and Intimidation*, 77–79, 105.

115. Henry James, *Charles William Eliot: President of Harvard, 1869–1909*, 2 vols. (Boston, 1930), II:
155. Eliot distinguished between what were commonly called "scabs" and "finks," claiming that the former might be a "fair type of hero" while the latter was more likely "an humble sort of hero."

116. Tuttle, *Race Riot*, 119; John Cummings, "The Chicago Teamsters' Strike—A Study in Industrial Democracy," *Journal of Political Economy* 13 (1905), 536–73; Norwood, *Strikebreaking and Intimidation*, 103; William W. Tuttle Jr., "Labor Conflict and Racial Violence: The Black Worker in Chicago,
1894–1919," in Milton Cantor, ed., *Black Labor in America* (Westport, 1969), 88; Wright, "The Negro
Skilled Mechanic in the North"; Chicago Commission on Race Relations, *The Negro in Chicago: A Study
of Race Relations and a Race Riot* (Chicago, 1922), 426; Walter White, "Chicago and Its Eight Reasons,"
Crisis 16 (1919), 293; "Shall We Unionize?" *Chicago Defender*, 23 Aug. 1919 [HNCF 302].

explained, "Color prejudice is used like any other weapon for strengthening the monopoly of the labor union. I know several unions which are practically monopolistic corporations into which any outsider, white, yellow, or black, penetrates with the greatest difficulty . . . Of course these unions, like any other closely organized group of men, employ every weapon to further their cause. They use prejudice as a competitive fighting weapon, they seize upon the color of the Negro, or the pig-tail and curious habits of the Chinaman, or the low-living standard of the Hindu, to fight competition and protect them in their labor monopoly." [117]

Increasingly convinced that black hostility to unions rather than union hostility to blacks was the source of the problem, Gompers concluded, "I have stood as a champion of the colored man and have sacrificed self and much of the movement that the colored man should get a chance. But the Caucasians are not going to let their standard of living be destroyed by Negroes, Chinamen, Japs, or any other." With regard to Negro strikebreakers, Gompers said, "If the colored man continues to lend himself to the work of tearing down what the white man has built up, a race hatred worse than any ever known before will result. Caucasian civilization will serve notice that its uplifting process is not to be interfered with in any such way." [118]

Blacks continued to make inroads into the northern steel industry in the first decades of the twentieth century—indeed, these were the years of their greatest progress. Blacks helped break the 1901 steel strike, and the *Colored American* noted, "The corporation offers him bread. The labor unions turn him away with a stone . . . If the labor unions are so besotten that they cannot see their folly in ignoring the skilled Negro, they deserve the disaster that is rapidly overtaking them." [119] In the aftermath of the Pana and Virden coal conflict, Illinois enacted a law prohibiting the importation of armed workmen or anyone who agreed to work for stipulated wages, but this did not prevent an attempt to bring blacks to replace Chicago steel strikers in 1901. "Of course this . . . law is daily being violated, being passed for demagogical reasons without intention of enforcement," a Detroit newspaper observed. [120] But the Amalgamated Association of Iron, Steel, and Tin Workers con-

117. Ray Stannard Baker, *Following the Color Line: An Account of Negro Citizenship in the American Democracy* (Williamstown, MA, 1973 [1908]), 134.

118. Samuel Gompers, "Talks on Labor," *American Federationist* 12 (Sep. 1905), 636, 638 [DH V: 124].

119. *Colored American*, 31 Aug. 1901 [DH V: 96].

120. *Detroit Free Press*, 27 Jul. 1901 [HNCF 264].

tinued to oppose black membership, its 1902 annual convention resolved against inclusion of black workers, fearing that they might leave the South and compete with northern white ironmongers. In 1907 the association reversed itself and called for black organization "wherever possible." But black workers continued to be suspicious of the association's motives, believing that its ultimate goal was to eliminate black competition. This seemed confirmed when the puddlers left the association and revived the Sons of Vulcan. Most black entry into the Pennsylvania steel mills resulted not from strikebreaking or employer recruitment but from the continued migration of southern workers into northern cities. Employer receptivity varied: some wanted segregation; others, like the Black Diamond Company in Pittsburgh and Midvale Steel in Philadelphia were open; and others employed no blacks. They held a variety of jobs and sometimes gained skilled jobs as rapidly as whites.[121]

THE WILSON ADMINISTRATION

The advent of Woodrow Wilson's first administration in 1913 set off some of the most rapid and profound changes in the history of American labor and race relations. Though officially nonpartisan and making no endorsement in the 1912 election, the AFL clearly favored the Democrats, and Wilson responded with the creation of the Department of Labor and the appointment of William B. Wilson, a former United Mine Workers official, as its secretary. The U.S. Commission on Industrial Relations issued a report in 1915 that was so radically pro-union that a majority of its members, including John R. Commons, filed a dissenting report.[122] W. E. B. Du Bois and many of the new voices of the civil rights movement deserted the Republican Party and supported Wilson in 1912. Though he remained critical of organized labor, the Socialist Party, and the IWW, Du Bois was clearly leading the activists of the new NAACP toward an alliance with organized labor.

121. Dennis C. Dickerson, *Out of the Crucible: Black Steelworkers in Western Pennsylvania, 1875–1980* (Albany, NY, 1986), 14–26; Spero and Harris, *The Black Worker*, 250–58; Mansel G. Blackford, *A Portrait Cast in Steel: Buckeye International and Columbus, Ohio, 1881–1980* (Westport, 1982), 62; U.S. Industrial Commission, *Reports*, XIV: xcvii, 353; U.S. Immigration Commission, *Reports*, IX: 68.

122. Joseph A. McCartin, *Labor's Great War: The Struggle for Industrial Democracy and the Origins of Modern American Labor Relations, 1912–21* (Chapel Hill, 1997), 15. Nor did the report pay any attention to black labor. Julie Greene, "Negotiating the State: Frank Walsh and the Transformation of Labor's Political Culture in Progressive America," in Kevin Boyle, ed., *Organized Labor and American Politics, 1894–1994: The Labor-Liberal Alliance* (Albany, NY, 1998), 81; Edward T. Devine to W. E. B. Du Bois, 21 Feb. 1912 [DuBP IV: 351].

By 1913, Booker T. Washington also sounded more receptive than ever to the idea of a black alliance with organized labor. In an article for the *Atlantic Monthly* he explained that he believed the antagonism of blacks toward organized labor was rooted in their rural origins. "The average Negro laborer in the country districts has rarely had the experience of looking for work; work has always looked for him," he noted, and "he does not understand the necessity or advantage of a labor organization, which stands between him and his employer and aims apparently to make a monopoly of the opportunities for labor." Southern black Americans customarily regarded employment in personal terms, relying on the paternalism of white employers, and thus were suspicious of unions that appeared "to be founded on a sort of impersonal enmity to the man by whom he is employed." But he also attributed the antagonism to the racial discrimination that was prevalent among unionists. When blacks responded to this animus by acting as strikebreakers, white unionists became even more prejudiced. Reiterating his faith in free labor principles, Washington noted that blacks "are engaged in a struggle to maintain their right to labor as free men, which, with the right to own property, is, in my opinion, the most important privilege that was granted to black men as a result of the Civil War." [123]

Washington also praised the response to a survey that he conducted among labor unions, which showed "a sympathy and an understanding of the difficulties under which the Negro labors that I did not expect to find." He attributed union exclusion more to economic than to racial motives. "Labor unions are not primarily philanthropic organizations. They have been formed to meet conditions as they exist in a competitive system where, under ordinary circumstances, every individual and every class of individuals is seeking to improve its own condition at the expense, if necessary, of every other individual and class. It is natural enough, under such conditions, that union men should be disposed to take advantage of race prejudice to shut out others from the advantages which they enjoy." Where black workers were too numerous to exclude, as in the case of the mine workers, blacks were brought in to the organization. He also noted that employers used prejudice to defeat unions.[124] But Washington concluded that recent years had

123. "The Negro and the Labor Unions," *Atlantic Monthly* 111 (1913), 756–67 [BTWP XII: 206–23; DH V: 109].

124. The general secretary of the Journeymen Barbers Association told Washington that black barbershop owners had begun a rumor that the union was trying to displace black barbers, as a means to dissuade them from joining the union. In this case, however, the rumor was based on substantial evi-

shown that "the Negro, as a matter of fact, can and does compete with the white laborer, wherever he has the opportunity to do so" and that "on the whole, the effect of this competition is not to increase but to lessen racial prejudice." He was confident that, in time, unions would realize they had more to gain by including blacks, and "I am convinced that these organizations can and will become an important means of doing away with the prejudice that now exists in many parts of the country against the Negro laborer."

Washington had never been as critical of labor unions as many other early-twentieth-century black leaders had been. He helped promote the National Urban League, which retained many of his pro-business instincts but also reflected many of the attitudes of the rival NAACP, including ambivalence rather than outright hostility to unions. The Negro Press Association, for example, declared itself "against all forms of unionism and economic radicalism" in 1914.[125] Washington's relations with Gompers and the AFL were generally cool but polite. He also noted privately that the article "did not mean or intend . . . to indicate that I had sympathy with the labor unions. As a rule, they have treated my race unfairly."[126] But the article may have signaled that, in the last years of his life, Washington had begun to reconsider the alliances that he had made in the late nineteenth century. The deteriorating condition of American race relations in the Progressive era, as well as the acquittal of a white man who had assaulted him in 1911 and the efforts of his Huntington, Long Island, neighbors to convince him to sell his estate, had begun to alter his views. The success of his opponents in the NAACP, as well as the complete loss of his already dwindling patronage with the end of Republican control of the executive branch in 1913, may have set him to seek new allies.[127] In any

---

dence. Reid, *Negro Membership in American Labor Unions*, 155; Bernstein, *Only One Place of Redress*, 38; Hall, *The Journeymen Barbers' International Union*, 44; Bristol, "The Victory of Black Barbers over Reform in Ohio," 251–60.

125. BTWP XIII: xxi–xxii; *Baltimore Afro-American*, 14 Mar. 1914 [DH V: 118]. The *Afro-American* condemned this declaration and called for blacks to join the labor movement. Black newspaper owners had an obvious interest in maintaining the open shop in their own establishments but also faced the fact that the typographers union did not admit blacks. "Organized Labor," *Crisis* 4 (Jul. 1912), 131, in Lester, *The Seventh Son*, II: 301; Wolters, *Du Bois and His Rivals*, 213. The *Chicago Defender* faced the same situation when it became a union shop in 1921. Roi Ottley, *The Lonely Warrior: The Life and Times of Robert S. Abbott* (Chicago, 1955), 194.

126. Washington to William Robert Ware, 6 Jun. 1913 [BTWP XII: 196].

127. Factor, *Black Response to America*, 347–48; Harlan, *Booker T. Washington: The Wizard of Tuskegee, 1901–15* (New York, 1983) 295–309.

event, Washington's death two years later left unanswerable the question of his reorientation.

Du Bois and other black supporters of Woodrow Wilson soon smarted at the president's racial policies, but AFL leaders reaped considerable rewards for their backing. Even worse for black leaders, many of the Democrats' pro-union policies hobbled black workers. The AFL won the Clayton Antitrust Act's exemption of labor unions from prosecution and its limitation on federal courts' power to issue injunctions in labor disputes. Gompers hailed the act's declaration "that the labor of a human being is not a commodity or article of commerce" as "the industrial Magna Charta [*sic*] upon which the working people will rear their construction of industrial freedom." For those who regarded labor unions as cartels, the Act granted a special privilege; it implied that union labor was not a commodity but that nonunion labor would continue to be. Black workers had reason to fear unfettered union power to strike, for the chief object of strikes was to stop the operations of businesses, primarily by halting the use of replacement workers. Injunctions had helped blacks to break strikes by discriminatory unions, and would continue to do so through the 1920s. The act limited its protection to strikes that did not threaten "irreparable injury to property, or to a property right," and to those using "peaceful means" of persuasion. This sounded like nothing more than a restatement of rights already protected. Since almost every strike that had been curtailed by injunctions involved violence and intimidation, courts continued to issue injunctions. As one historian observes, "Never did a statute backfire so badly." [128]

The next piece of New Freedom labor legislation, Progressive senator Robert M. La Follette's Seamen's Act, derived largely from the inroads that nonwhite seamen had made in the merchant marine. Seamen union leader Andrew Furuseth's goal was to improve the conditions on ships so that white men would find the work appealing. "The focus of the La Follette bill, on safety at sea and seamen's

---

128. Dickman, *Industrial Democracy*, 204, 224; Edwin F. Witte, *The Government in Labor Disputes* (New York, 1932), 66–68, 266; Bernstein, *Only One Place of Redress*, 55; W. E. B. Du Bois, "Injunctions" (n.d.) [DuBP LXXXIII: 882]; Sylvester Petro, "Injunctions and Labor Disputes, 1880–1932," *Wake Forest Law Review* 14 (1978), 345, 437, 448, 462; Kelly, Harbison, and Belz, *The American Constitution*, II: 450; George I. Lovell, *Legislative Deferrals: Statutory Ambiguity, Judicial Power, and American Democracy* (Cambridge, 2002); Herbert Hovenkamp, "Labor Conspiracies in American Law, 1880–1930," *Texas Law Review* 66 (1988), 964; Wright, "Contest between Organized Labor and Organized Business," 244.

rights, obscured but did not blunt Furuseth's cardinal goal: to drive Asiatics from American vessels," a historian notes. The AFL championed the bill; Gompers told La Follette that current conditions were "driving not only the American but all white men from the sea." The race-based appeal was essential to the passage of the Act, particularly among the southern delegation.[129]

The railroad brotherhoods showed themselves to be the most racially exclusive, as well as the most powerful, unions in America. As the U.S. government began to prepare for war in 1916, the brotherhoods took the opportunity to press their demand for the eight-hour day, with extra pay for overtime. The railroads had already lost their power to set prices; they were now faced with the loss of their power to control their largest expense. Faced with a shutdown of the national economy, President Wilson intervened, personally addressing Congress with a request for a settlement, and the September 1916 Adamson Act gave the unions most of what they wanted. The Act was symbolic of the shift of unions to state power in the progressive era. "Union men had learned that railroads under archaic Progressive regulation were *losers,* and they were determined to move onto the winning side." The Adamson Act's unprecedented intervention of the federal government into the national economy showed the growing power of the Democrat-union alliance.[130]

GREAT MIGRATION AND WAR

The massive demographic shift known as the Great Migration profoundly altered the relations between black workers and the union movement, as southern blacks moved into northern cities during the World War I. Perhaps half a million blacks left the South between 1915 and 1920, and as many as 300,000 in the summers of 1916 and 1917 alone. There were considerable forces pushing blacks out of the South: the increasingly oppressive Jim Crow system along with the devastation of the cotton economy by the boll weevil and floods. More important, as in earlier migrations, was the pull from the North, especially the availability of jobs due to the cut off of European immigration and an industrial boom driven by the demands of the belligerent powers and U.S. war preparation. A half century of vir-

129. Jerold S. Auerbach, "Progressives at Sea: The La Follette Act of 1915," *Labor History* 2 (1961), 344–60; Dick, *Labor and Socialism,* 122.

130. Albro Martin, *Enterprise Denied: Origins of the Decline of American Railroads, 1897–1917* (New York, 1971), 128, 323; Higgs, *Crisis and Leviathan,* 116–21.

tually unprecedented immigration restriction had dramatic social and economic consequences.[131]

Southern planters became alarmed at the loss of their work force and redoubled their efforts to hinder the agents of northern companies who recruited blacks. Booker T. Washington and other southern black leaders had long doubted emigration's value as a solution to the race problem, and many southern black businessmen had an interest in keeping workers and customers in the South. Nevertheless, most southern black leaders supported the movement. Du Bois enthusiastically promoted it at *The Crisis,* and perhaps nobody did more than Robert S. Abbott, the pioneer of northern black journalism, in the *Chicago Defender.*[132]

As the election of 1916 and war approached, the alliance of the Wilson administration and the AFL intensified. Initially opposed to the war, Gompers came to support it and became one of Wilson's leading advisers. The federal government intervened dramatically in the national economy, taking over the railroads in 1917 and establishing the National War Labor Board to manage industrial labor relations. All government contracts included union standards, and labor representatives served on important government agencies, with Gompers himself on the Advisory Commission of the National Council of Defense. With the federal government's support, AFL membership soared to 5 million before the war ended. The AFL responded with an implicit no-strike pledge and support for maximum production.[133]

The administration made efforts to deal with the Great Migration and to mo-

131. U.S. Department of Labor, Division of Negro Economics, *Negro Migration in 1916–17* (New York, 1969 [1919]), 11; *The Negro at Work during the World War and during Reconstruction* (Washington, 1921), 10; R. R. Wright, "The Migration of Negroes to the North," *Annals of the American Academy of Political and Social Science* 27 (1906) [DH V: 229]; Chicago Commission on Race Relations, *The Negro in Chicago,* 80–92; William J. Collins, "When the Tide Turned: Immigration and the Delay of the Great Black Migration," *Journal of Economic History* 57 (1997), 607–32; John E. Bodnar, "The Impact of the 'New Immigration' on the Black Worker: Steelton, Pennsylvania, 1880–1920," *Labor History* 17 (1976), 214–29.

132. James R. Grossman, "Black Labor Is the Best Labor: Southern White Reactions to the Great Migration," in Alferdteen Harrison, ed., *Black Exodus: The Great Migration from the American South* (Jackson, MS, 1991), 51–71; Gunnar Myrdal, *An American Dilemma: The Negro Problem and Modern Democracy* (New York, 1944), 305; U.S. Department of Labor, *Negro Migration,* 31–32; Kelly, *Race, Class, and Power in the Alabama Coalfields,* 135–40; Lewis, *W. E. B. Du Bois: Biography of a Race,* 516; Ottley, *The Lonely Warrior.*

133. Dulles, *Labor in America,* 224–41; McCartin, *Labor's Great War,* 56–58.

bilize black Americans. Emmett J. Scott became a special adviser for black affairs to the Secretary of War, and the Labor Department established a Division of Negro Economics in 1918, which acted as an informal employment agency for blacks. It operated until 1920, the first federal agency dedicated to black welfare since Reconstruction. While southern planters and Gompers were disappointed that the division did not strive to keep blacks in the South, black militants believed that its head, social worker and National Urban League founder George E. Haynes, was too accommodating to white supremacy. W. E. B. Du Bois, however, welcomed the appointment. A local committee of the agency was able to negotiate an agreement with Pittsburgh-area steelmakers to retain one-third of the black workers that they employed at the peak of war production. Though some companies retained blacks only to thwart threats of unionization, Haynes believed the programs were beneficial. Organizations like the Urban League continued to acculturate black migrants to urban, industrial conditions.[134]

Some black leaders regarded the hostility of white unions as a reason for blacks to stay in the South. Northern labor agents and editors should honestly tell blacks that the North was no paradise, the *Pittsburgh Courier* warned. "Also, let them be informed that unions of the North will not take him into their organization. Let him know that labor unions of the North are opposed to their coming."[135] Blacks remained suspicious of white unionists' motives. Indeed, some white unions used their increased wartime power against black workers. Missouri lead miners exploited wartime patriotic passion to oust blacks and immigrants from their jobs.[136]

134. Jane Lang and Harry N. Scheiber, "The Wilson Administration and the Wartime Mobilization of Black Americans, 1917–18," *Labor History* 10 (1969), 436–40; U.S. Department of Labor, *Negro at Work during the World War,* 12; Henry P. Guzda, "Social Experiment of the Labor Department: The Division of Negro Economics," *The Public Historian* 4 (1982), 7–37; Guzda, "Labor Department's First Program to Assist Black Workers," *Monthly Labor Review* 105 (Jun. 1982), 39–43; James B. Stewart, "The Rise and Fall of Negro Economics: The Economic Thought of George Edmund Haynes," *American Economic Review* 81 (1991), 311–14; William Cohen, "The Great Migration as a Lever for Social Change," in Alferdteen Harrison, ed., *Black Exodus: The Great Migration from the American South* (Jackson, MS, 1991), 72–82; James R. Grossman, *Land of Hope: Chicago, Black Southerners, and the Great Migration* (Chicago, 1989), 202; Gerber, *Black Ohio and the Color Line,* 272–95; George E. Haynes to W. E. B. Du Bois, 31 May 1918 [DuBP VII: 469].

135. *Pittsburgh Courier,* quoted in *Norfolk Journal and Guide,* 24 Mar. 1917 [DH V: 254].

136. "White Women Object to Negro Co-Workers," *Kansas City Post,* 24 Mar. 1916; "Union Leaders Try to Capture Colored Competitors," *Philadelphia Tribune,* 30 Sep. 1916 [HNCF 264]; McCartin, *Labor's Great War,* 46.

White Chicago grain handlers seceded from an AFL local, formed their own union, and expelled blacks. An AFL organizer told the War Labor Board that such action was "treason . . . pro-German, and as such should be dealt with summarily."[137] White members of the socialist-leaning machinists union went on strike in June 1917 to force the removal of a black college student who took a summer job at a Schenectady General Electric plant. The company defused the situation by assuring the union that it did not intend to hire blacks as substitutes.[138] While government railroad administrators ordered equal pay and revised job classifications for black workers, they also abetted white unions' efforts to remove black employees altogether.[139] But the Division of Negro Economics concluded that "While there is an undeniable hostility to Negroes on the part of white workers, the objection is frequently exaggerated by prejudiced gang bosses." Despite occasional conflict, "When the extent of the movement of Negroes to the North is considered, the amount of race friction reported is remarkably small."[140] But problems of job competition combined with labor organization drives led to two of the worst race riots in American history.

The Great Migration into East St. Louis continued earlier patterns; the city's black population had tripled, from two to six thousand, in the first decade of the century. Labor leaders exaggerated the numbers of black migrants and accused employers of "importing" black labor into the city.[141] It was perfectly legal to transport workers in this way, but, like southern planters, the AFL attributed black migration to the blandishments of unscrupulous employers and their labor agents. As in West Virginia, the issue became a politically important one, with Democrats accusing Republicans of trying to pack black voters into Illinois to win the 1916 presidential election. "During the months after the election local labor leaders, who had supported Wilson, took a leaf from the Democratic party's campaign hand-

137. John Riley to W. Jett Lauck, 26 Aug. 1918, Records of the National War Labor Board, RG 2, NA [BWGM IV: 959].

138. Theodore V. Purcell and Daniel P. Mulvey, *The Negro in the Electrical Manufacturing Industry* (Philadelphia, 1971), 30; "Negro Wins in Big Strike," *New York World,* 27 Jun. 1917 [HNCF 299]; McCartin, *Labor's Great War,* 133.

139. Spero and Harris, *The Black Worker,* 300–305; McCartin, *Labor's Great War,* 116; Malcolm Ross, *All Manner of Men* (New York, 1948), 119.

140. U.S. Department of Labor, *Negro Migration,* 126–28.

141. Elliott Rudwick, *Race Riot at East St. Louis: July 2, 1917* (Carbondale, 1964), 160–70.

book, and anti-Negro propaganda emanated from the economic as well as the political front," the principal historian of the riot notes. "White labor leaders, like
politicians in the 1916 presidential election, were prepared to use racist propaganda
when, in their view, legitimate goals were jeopardized."[142] The Aluminum Ore
Company used black strikebreakers to defeat a unionization drive in May 1917. The
city's Central Trades and Labor Union issued a circular saying that black migrants
were being used "to the detriment of our white citizens by some of the capitalists
and a few real estate owners," and it called for "drastic action" to "retard this growing menace, and also devise a way to get rid of a certain portion of those who are
already here." While labor leaders pressed the mayor and city council to take action a few days later, the first riots broke out.[143] On July 2 the major riot began,
which resulted in at least nine white and thirty-nine black deaths.

While there was no evidence that labor leaders plotted to cause the riot, they
did arouse racial hostility in their campaign.[144] There was a long pattern of labor
mobilization accompanied by attacks on ethnic and racial minorities.[145] "The terrible July riots did not grow out of the May meeting," the Division of Negro Economics concluded, "but they probably developed out of the dispositions of jealousy and hatred revealed there."[146] President Wilson remained silent about the
matter. Former president Theodore Roosevelt, appearing with Gompers at a Carnegie Hall reception for the new Russian ambassador, said that the riots "had no
real provocation, and, whether there was provocation or not, waged with such ap-
palling brutality as to leave a stain on the name of America." Gompers took exception to this statement and blamed the riot on employers' "importation of cheap
labor." Roosevelt then "shook his fist in [Gompers's] face so closely that to people
in the auditorium it must have appeared that he was striking him." This spectacle
nearly caused another riot. Gompers alleged that Roosevelt was bitter that the AFL
did not endorse him or the Republican nominee in the last election, and the *New*

142. Ibid., 15–16.

143. Ibid., 19–23; Chicago Commission on Race Relations, *The Negro in Chicago*, 74–75.

144. Rudwick, *Race Riot at East St. Louis*, 142; Spero and Harris, *The Black Worker*, 112; Nancy J.
Weiss, *The National Urban League, 1910–40* (New York, 1974), 207.

145. Susan Olzak, "Labor Unrest, Immigration, and Ethnic Conflict in Urban America, 1880–
1914," *American Journal of Sociology* 94 (1989), 1303–33.

146. U.S. Department of Labor, *Negro Migration*, 129; Woofter, "The Negro and Industrial
Peace," 420.

York Times chided the ex-president for acting like a "spoiled child." But W. E. B. Du Bois thanked Roosevelt "from the bottom of my heart."[147]

The AFL's effort to pin the blame for the riot on the employers' use of blacks as a cheap labor source was generally unsuccessful. Most black commentators blamed organized labor.[148] "It was not labor masquerading under race prejudice, or even prejudice using the labor troubles as a pretence that caused the riots in East St. Louis," wrote *The Crisis*'s literary editor, "it was the absolute conviction on the part of labor leaders that no Negro has a right to any position or privilege which the white man wants."[149] A. Philip Randolph's *Messenger* tried to depict the riot as a capitalist plot, but Du Bois could not swallow this. "Socialist though he continued to proclaim himself, he must have hooted at *The Messenger* when Randolph and Owen wrote that it was the stifling of class solidarity by capital rather than the force of racism that was behind East St. Louis," a biographer observes.[150]

"Evidently, the leaders of the labor unions thought something must be done, some measure sufficiently drastic must be taken to drive these interlopers away and to restore to white Americans their privileges," Du Bois wrote. "By all accounts of eye-witnesses, both white and black, the East St. Louis outrage was deliberately planned and executed."[151] Du Bois called himself "one of the few colored men who have tried conscientiously to bring about understanding and cooperation between American Negroes and the labor unions." Organized labor offered an alternative to Washington and his philanthropist supporters' plan to solve the race problem by "playing off black workers against white," he argued. Now it was apparent "that it is the labor unions themselves that have given this movement its

---

147. "Roosevelt and Gompers Row at Russian Meeting," *New York Times,* 7 Jul. 1917, p. 1; "Roosevelt Piqued, Gompers Asserts," *New York Times,* 8 Jul. 1917, sec. I, p. 5; "The Spoiled Child," *New York Times,* 8 Jul. 1917, sec. II, p. 1; *Outlook* 116 (18 Jul. 1917), 435–36 [DH V: 307]; Rudwick, *Race Riot at East St. Louis,* 134; Du Bois to Roosevelt, 7 Jul. 1917 [DuBP V: 1119].

148. Rudwick, *Race Riot at East St. Louis,* 64; "The Negro and the Nation," *The Nation* 105 (1917), 86. Roosevelt was an honorary member of the Brotherhood of Locomotive Firemen and Enginemen, perhaps the most racially exclusive union in the country. "President Addresses Railroad Firemen," *New York Times,* 9 Sep. 1902, p. 2.

149. Jesse Fauset, *Survey* 38 (1917), 448 [DH V: 312].

150. Lewis, *W. E. B. Du Bois: Biography of a Race,* 540; Manning Marable, "A. Philip Randolph and the Foundations of Black American Socialism," *Radical America* 14 (1980), 13–14.

151. "The Massacre of East St. Louis," *Crisis* (Sep. 1917), in Lester, *The Seventh Son,* II: 80.

greatest impulse and that today, at last, in East St. Louis have brought the most un-willing of us to acknowledge that in the present union movement, as represented by the American Federation of Labor, there is absolutely no hope of justice for an American of Negro descent." [152]

Though President Wilson remained silent about the riot, a congressional com-mittee held hearings and issued a report that emphasized employer rather than union culpability. Dominated by Democrats and chaired by a Kentuckian, the committee attributed the hostility to "natural racial aversion," aggravated by the appallingly corrupt politics of the "plague spot" of East St. Louis. The committee accepted union claims about the numbers of black migrants and the charge that labor agents had "enticed them to abandon profitable employment in the South." Absentee corporations, "money grubbers . . . pitted white labor against black, drove organized labor from their plants, brought thousands of inefficient Negroes from the South, crowding the white men from their positions." The principal his-torian of the riot concluded that "Although the corporate managers were most heavily responsible for the social climate which culminated in the race riot, they were also most directly responsible for helping to create a public determination to avoid a repetition of the event," including the congressional investigation that cas-tigated them. [153]

As the war came to an end, organized labor lost the power that the federal gov-ernment had provided for its efforts. This withdrawal of state power was the es-sential reason for the great defeats and contraction that unions endured in the postwar years, but black American opposition was also a factor. The association between the Bolshevik revolution and left-wing elements in the American labor movement also turned state support into state suppression.

While businessmen complained that a socialist AFL had taken over the gov-ernment, left-wing labor leaders complained that Gompers had sold out to gov-ernment and big business, although Wilson's policies had helped many left-wing unions. [154] The IWW's opposition to the war ran it afoul of the Espionage Act, and

152. "The Black Man and the Unions," *Crisis* (Mar. 1918), in Huggins, *Du Bois: Writings*, 1173–75.

153. "Report of the Special Committee to Investigate the East St. Louis Riot," House Doc. 1231, 65th Cong., 2d Sess. (1918) [DH V: 285]; Rudwick, *Race Riot at East St. Louis*, 148, 170; U.S. Department of Labor, *Negro Migration*, 134.

154. McCartin, *Labor's Great War*, 81.

in September 1917 its leaders were arrested and it was effectively destroyed. Many syndicalists and socialists remained in the AFL, however; Chicago in particular saw efforts to expand and intensify labor organization efforts.

John Fitzpatrick, president of the Chicago Federation of Labor, and William Z. Foster, a Railway Carmen Union organizer, led the Chicago effort to organize industrial unions in the stockyards and steel mills. Radical syndicalists (Foster later became secretary of the Communist Party of the USA), Fitzpatrick and Foster were attempting to turn the AFL to socialism by "boring from within." They formed the Stockyards Labor Council (SLC) to unite all of the packinghouse workers. The most powerful workers belonged to the skilled Amalgamated Meat Cutters, which admitted blacks but had very few black members. Various other less skilled unions banned or segregated blacks, so the SLC and AFL established a special, federal local that blacks could join.[155]

The SLC pressed the federal government to nationalize the meatpacking industry as it had the railroads, but the administration opted to appoint a mediator, federal judge Samuel Alschuler, to settle labor-management grievances. In March 1918 the judge gave the workers the eight-hour day and significant wage increases, and this boosted the popularity of the SLC immensely. Yet the award increased racial hostility among white workers who believed that blacks won the benefits of the union-initiated award without paying their dues.[156] As the end of the war approached, the SLC began to press for a "100 percent union" agreement with the packers, and blacks were the chief impediment to their goal. By the summer of 1919, 90 percent of white workers, but only 25 percent of blacks, were members. The NAACP's Walter White observed that employers had eagerly sought black workers, "and there was little doubt that this was done in part so that Negro labor might be used as a club over the heads of the unions . . . On the other hand, the Negro workman is not at all sure as to the sincerity of the unions themselves."[157] *Chicago Defender* publisher Robert Abbott, still open to the idea of black unionization despite his experiences, countered that "Something must be done to re-

155. Rick Halpern, *Down on the Killing Floor: Black and White Workers in Chicago's Packinghouses, 1904–54* (Urbana, 1997), 51; Barrett, *Work and Community in the Jungle*, 194; Tuttle, *Race Riot*, 125.

156. Herbst, *Negro in the Slaughtering and Meat Packing Industry*, 38; Chicago Commission on Race Relations, *The Negro in Chicago*, 413.

157. White, "Chicago and Its Eight Reasons."

move from the mind of the white laboring man the notion that large employers of labor are using us as a big stick over their heads." [158] One historian concludes, "It is evident that black men and women had very real reasons for resisting unionization, if indeed they had the opportunity to join in the first place." The Chicago unions either barred blacks or admitted them grudgingly. "The exclusionist policies of southern unions had likewise alienated the black workers from the labor movement, and some of the migrants to Chicago during the war had traveled there to escape the job control exercised by the unions." [159]

Black leaders remained guarded about the organization drive. The National Urban League attempted to mediate between unions and black workers but generally sided with the employers who supported the league financially and for whom it acted as an employment agency. The *Chicago Defender* took a similar position, while the city's smaller black newspapers were split. The *Defender* ignored an interracial march planned for July 6, one that the police segregated at the suggestion, it seems, of black politicians and the packing companies. The SLC interpreted the packers' claim that they feared that a race riot would result from the interracial march as an attempt to frustrate their organizing drive. Though the march took place on separate sides of the street and organizers made warm appeals to black workers, the SLC continued to enjoy little success in getting blacks to join.[160]

Self-appointed "race man" Richard E. Parker took advantage of the antagonism of black workers and white unions and established his own American Unity Labor Union. As the Chicago Commission on Race Relations noted, "The rift between employers and labor unions has provided a field of exploitation for certain less responsible Negroes." [161] But one scholar notes, "Parker was a demagogue and he was doubtless on the payroll of employers, but he might also have been working in the race's interest, as he perceived it." [162] The fact was that Parker was able to

158. "Shall We Unionize?"

159. Tuttle, *Race Riot,* 142–46; Tuttle, "Labor Conflict and Racial Violence," 103–4; David Brody, *The Butcher Workmen: A Study of Unionization* (Cambridge, 1964), 85.

160. Tuttle, *Race Riot,* 148; Grossman, *Land of Hope,* 202, 209; Barrett, *Work and Community in the Jungle,* 206, 211; Arvarh E. Strickland, *History of the Chicago Urban League* (Urbana, 1966), 59.

161. Chicago Commission on Race Relations, *The Negro in Chicago,* 422; James R. Barrett, "Unity and Fragmentation: Class, Race, and Ethnicity on Chicago's South Side, 1900–20," *Journal of Social History* 18 (1984), 41, 47.

162. Tuttle, *Race Riot,* 153.

strike a responsive chord in the black community, whose experience led them to trust white unions less than white employers.[163] Black migrants felt that employers had given them their first opportunities, the Chicago Commission on Race Relations pointed out. "They have also been affected by experiences with labor unions which in the past have not been disposed to accept Negroes freely into membership with them. Although the interest of employers in securing Negroes has not always been merely the granting of an opportunity for work, where Negroes have entered as strikebreakers they have usually remained. This recent entrance into industry has made them, for the first time, a considerable factor, and they feel that the unions, recognizing their importance to the accomplishment of union aims, are making appeals to them for membership, not out of a spirit of brotherhood, but merely to advance their purposes." [164]

Divisions within the SLC between skilled and unskilled workers—themselves often related to ethnic differences—posed problems as serious as those between white and black workers. In May 1919 the Amalgamated Meat Cutters made an agreement with the packers to extend Alschuler's mediation agreement for a year, with its no-strike provision, and left the largely unskilled SLC unions to fend for themselves. This decision intensified the SLC's need to have a "100 percent union" front to present to the packers, and reinforced pressure on black workers to join or quit.[165]

The July race riot ended whatever chance there had been for a successful accommodation of black workers and the SLC. "Above all, it was conflict between the white rank and file and their black counterparts that retarded unionization," a historian notes. "Overriding everything else, though, was the fact that, for the most part, black men and women in the stockyards were nonunion; and because of it, hundreds of white workers walked out in late June, vowing that they would not return until nonunion blacks were either fired or forced to wear the union button as members." The hostility of the white workers ended whatever appeal the union might have had for blacks, but the SLC leaders tried to use the riot as an opportunity to complete their organizing campaign, arguing that the riot was based on labor rather than racial antagonism, which would be healed by a union shop. "Hav-

163. Barrett, *Work and Community in the Jungle*, 217.

164. Chicago Commission on Race Relations, *The Negro in Chicago*, 421.

165. Barrett, *Work and Community in the Jungle*, 223–25; Halpern, *Down on the Killing Floor*, 62–63.

ing failed to convert the Negroes to unionism, the council was now using the explosive situation to force organization on them."[166]

As in East St. Louis, contemporaries and historians dispute the connection between the packinghouse labor movement and the 1919 Chicago race riot. The riot was set off by the drowning of a black boy who had crossed over into the traditionally white section of a Lake Michigan beach, and most of the mayhem was attributed to gangs of Irish hoodlums. But job competition was certainly among the causes of the riot.[167] The Chicago Commission on Race Relations conducted an investigation after the riot, and it emphasized the generally amicable relations among workers in the city's workplaces and noted that little violence occurred near the packinghouses. "But this is a simple matter to explain," a later account concluded, "fearing bodily harm, black workers stayed home," and violence and one murder ensued when they returned to work.[168] Labor leaders blamed the packers' use of black strikebreakers as the cause of racial friction and, as in East St. Louis, accused them of "importing" black labor to prevent unionization. When Irish gangs in blackface set fire to the Lithuanian section of Packingtown and burned down fifty tenements, the labor press claimed that it was a packers' scheme to stir up racial hostility. The commission sought evidence for such action, but the AFL did not produce any. It concluded that both sides played upon prejudice in the conflict.[169] Undoubtedly the packers' effort to prevent unionization exacerbated racial hostility, but the relationship of cause and effect was not what the SLC claimed. "It is true the packers were endeavoring to influence public opinion, but their objective was rather to secure strike-breakers to meet specific need than to stimulate race antagonism," one account concluded.[170]

The ambivalent attitude of Chicago's black leaders in 1919 turned to clear hostility by 1921, when the packers issued a decisive blow to the SLC and the stockyards

---

166. Tuttle, *Race Riot*, 154; Brody, *The Butcher Workmen*, 87–88; Norgren et al., "Negro Labor and Its Problems," 689.

167. DH V: 284.

168. Tuttle, *Race Riot*, 109–12; cf. Barrett, *Work and Community in the Jungle*, 203.

169. Barrett, *Work and Community in the Jungle*, 223; Chicago Commission on Race Relations, *The Negro in Chicago*, 363–64, 647. For a recent analysis discerning packer manipulation of racial divisions, see Cliff Brown, "The Role of Employers in Split Labor Markets: An Event-Structure Analysis of Racial Conflict and AFL Organizing, 1917–19," *Social Forces* 79 (2000), 653–81.

170. Herbst, *Negro in Slaughtering and Meat Packing Industry*, 63; Barrett, *Work and Community in the Jungle*, 224.

returned to open-shop conditions. Labor leaders blamed blacks for their failure, with Foster concluding that blacks were "constitutionally opposed" to unions and Fitzpatrick lamenting that the packers had been able to exploit a succession of ethnic immigrants until they reached the most "hopeless, discouraged, lowest rung" with the southern black migrants.[171]

Steel unionists also sought to make their wartime gains permanent and enjoyed greater public support at the outset. The open-shop principle of employment at will was losing its appeal, especially when Americans sought order at the end of the war. The Soviet revolution, domestic bombings, and strikes undercut this support, especially in light of the radical background of the steel organizers. The steel organizers did less than the Stockyards Labor Council to reach out to blacks—not enough to overcome their memories of racial exclusion—and faced the same problem of divergent interests between skilled and unskilled workers. No blacks joined the strike, except for in Cleveland and Wheeling, and perhaps 30,000 blacks came into the mills as strikebreakers.[172]

Although they were not the only group to act as strikebreakers, blacks were again singled out as having been the cause of the defeat. Foster noted "The indifference, verging often on open hostility, with which Negroes generally regard organized labor's activities, manifested itself strongly in the steel campaign." Though some blacks joined the strikers, for the most part "they made a wretched showing ... Most of them seemed to take a keen delight in stealing the white men's jobs and crushing their strike." The steel magnates were turning blacks into "a race of strikebreakers," using them as the czars used the Cossacks, to keep other minorities under control. The situation threatened to turn labor disputes into race wars, which was exactly what the Negro "intellegencia" believed they were, but Foster

---

171. Grossman, *Land of Hope,* 226, 242.

172. David Brody, *Steelworkers in America: The Nonunion Era* (Cambridge, 1960), 243–49; Grossman, *Land of Hope,* 211; David Brody, *Labor in Crisis: The Steel Strike of 1919,* rev. ed. (Urbana, 1987), 162; James R. Barrett, *William Z. Foster and the Tragedy of American Radicalism* (Urbana, 1999), 96, 162; Cliff Brown and Terry Boswell, "Strikebreaking or Solidarity in the Great Steel Strike of 1919: A Split Labor Market, Game-Theoretic, and QCA Analysis," *American Journal of Sociology* 100 (1995), 1479–1519. The mayor of Cleveland prohibited strikebreakers from entering the city—Brody, *Steelworkers in America,* 249. Earlier in the year a New York newspaper reported that a Coatesville, Pennsylvania, steel company allowed workers to vote on the twelve-hour day and on whether to deport their Negro coworkers. "Deporting Negro Steel Laborers," *New York Post,* 1 Mar. 1919; "Protests Union Deportation," *New York Post,* 6 Mar. 1919 [HNCF 300].

was probably blaming blacks for his own failure. Doubts persisted for years among socialists about Foster's commitment to black organizing.[173] Another commentator pointed out that blacks would have rejected earnest union appeals had they been made, "for the experiences of the Negro seeking work in steel had forced him to believe that there was as much sacredness about the principles involved in his rights to earn a living as were involved in the principles for which white steel workers were striking."[174]

The effort to maintain wartime gains also failed in the South. Federal wartime labor policies had a mixed effect here, sometimes helping black workers, sometimes reinforcing the power of discriminatory unions. They posed enough of a threat to state power and segregation for southern congressmen to press for their speedy abolition.[175]

The United Mine Workers regained a strong position in the southern coalfields under the wartime tutelage of the U.S. Fuel Administration, created by the Lever Act of 1917. Even before this act, migration out of the South gave workers who remained more bargaining power with coal operators in the region. When the war ended, they returned to the open shop, aided again by the specter of "social equality" in the UMW, the nationwide apprehension about bolshevism, and, above all, the postwar labor surplus. The UMW went out on strike in 1919 despite an injunction won by Attorney General A. Mitchell Palmer, and by 1920 the strike was lost in the usual cycle of violence and sabotage. The houses of a dozen black strikebreakers were dynamited, and arson of equipment and railroad stock turned public opinion against the miners.[176] The union again disclaimed any advocacy of "social equality," attempting to drape its efforts in the wartime garment of patriotic "industrial democracy," but it was frustrated by both white supremacists, who

173. William Z. Foster, *The Great Steel Strike and Its Lessons* (New York, 1920), 202–11; Mark Solomon, *The Cry Was Unity: Communists and African Americans, 1917–36* (Jackson, MS, 1998), 45; Brown, "The Role of Employers in Split Labor Markets," 653–81, finds a "laissez-faire" approach by U.S. Steel in Gary, Indiana.

174. John T. Clark, "The Negro in Steel," *Opportunity* 2 (1924), 299.

175. Joseph A. McCartin, "Abortive Reconstruction: Federal War Labor Policies, Union Organization, and the Politics of Race, 1917–20," *Journal of Policy History* 9 (1997), 155–83.

176. McCartin, *Labor's Great War*, 123–27; Kelly, *Race, Class, and Power in the Alabama Coalfields*, 157, 178–85; Letwin, *Challenge of Interracial Unionism*, 159, 185; Hywell Davies, "On the Salient Facts Developed in the Alabama Coal Strike," c. 1921, Records of the Federal Mediation and Conciliation Service, RG 280, NA [BWGM I: 623]; Lewis, *Black Coal Miners in America*, 60.

turned wartime patriotism into xenophobia, and race-conscious leaders among the black middle class. One white union leader advised black strikers that if they had any black leaders who opposed the strike, "you should take them out and hang them by the neck."[177] Though cognizant of injustice perpetrated by the mine owners, P. Colfax Rameau, the president of the Southern Federation of Afro-American Industrial Brotherhood, denounced the "socialistic" UMW. He wrote to President Wilson that "we are sick and tired of this business of coercion and agitation and the inciting of some of our people to violence and even murder."[178]

While blacks increased from 72 to 77 percent of the work force in Alabama iron and steel mines and mills in the 1910s, Alabama's white workers were again slow to recognize the importance of black workers in their organizing efforts.[179] They did, however, move from a strategy of complete exclusion to one of segregation. The skilled white strikers encouraged unskilled blacks to join the International Union of Mine, Mill, and Smelter Workers. This provoked a hostile reaction from white supremacists and also aroused suspicion among black workers, who detected an effort to control them. Rameau told federal authorities that he feared the strike would "force white man's unionism on my people."[180] The National War Labor Board decided not to intervene, since black steel workers in Alabama "had learned that they stood to gain more by exploiting class divisions among whites than by uniting with them as separate and unequal allies," as one historian puts it. Here, too, blacks kept out of the great steel strike of 1919.[181]

Despite—or because of—their wartime clashes, many observers hoped that the postwar years would lead to greater amity between blacks and organized labor. The AFL leadership made several restatements of its nondiscrimination policy in its annual conventions during the war years, and members of its executive board met with representatives of black organizations.[182] The *New York Age* praised "the

177. Kelly, *Race, Class, and Power in the Alabama Coalfields,* 172–75.

178. P. Colfax Rameau to James J. Davis, 23 May 1921, Rameau to Woodrow Wilson, 26 Oct. 1920, Records of the Federal Mediation and Conciliation Service, RG 280, NA [BWGM I: 682, 549].

179. Northrup, "The Negro and Unionism," 28.

180. McCartin, "Abortive Reconstruction," 172.

181. McKiven, *Iron and Steel,* 125–27; Letwin, *Challenge of Interracial Unionism,* 182; McCartin, *Labor's Great War,* 161, 186; Spero and Harris, *The Black Worker,* 247, 258.

182. Foner, *Organized Labor and the Black Worker,* 140; "The Negro's Brighter Outlook," *The Nation* 105 (1917), 627.

progressive policy of Samuel Gompers" and noted that the likely continuation of immigration restriction would augment the power of black labor. "With equal opportunity and equal wages and membership in the Federation," editor Fred Moore said, "the colored man will not lend himself to strikebreaking." [183] An economist concluded that, as white unionists saw the growing power of black workers, "racial prejudice will yield more and more to the demands of their economic interests." [184] Shortly after the war another analyst argued, "While there have been in the past cases of discrimination against the Negro on account of his color, it would appear that at last organized labor deems the economic value of such workers so well established as to make it unwise as well as unjust to refuse them admission to unions." [185]

But the AFL remained largely unable to control the behavior of its national and local unions, and its leaders remained divided and unrepentant about the federation's racial policy. When the 1918 convention declared its intention to cooperate with black leaders in organizing blacks, it noted, "We wish it understood, however, that in doing so no fault is or can be found with the work done in the past." [186] Union leaders continued to assert that black leaders were in fact demanding preferential treatment. "In many instances the conduct of colored workmen, and those who have spoken for them, has not been in asking or demanding that equal rights be accorded to them as to white workmen, but somehow conveying the idea that they are to be petted or coddled and given special consideration and special privilege," Gompers told the AFL executive council in 1917. "Of course that can't be done." [187]

Black organizations were understandably cool toward the AFL's efforts. The federation's gesture "may mean a great deal; it may mean nothing," said the Urban League's Eugene Kinckle Jones. Despite audiences with Gompers and the executive

---

183. "The Negro Enters the Labor Union," *Literary Digest* 61 (28 Jun. 1919), 12; Fred R. Moore, "Letting Him into the Labor Union," *World Outlook* 5 (1919), 28; George E. Haynes, "The Negro Laborer and the Immigrant," *Survey* 46 (1921), 209–10.

184. William O. Weyforth, *The Organizability of Labor* (Baltimore, 1917), 170.

185. John L. Sewall, "The Industrial Revolution and the Negro," *Scribner's* 69 (1921), 339.

186. *Report of Proceedings of the 38th Annual Convention of the AFL* (Washington, 1918) [DH V: 420]; Abram L. Harris, "Negro Labor's Quarrel with White Workingmen," *Current History,* Sep. 1926, pp. 903–08 [SCCF 2713].

187. Ray Marshall, *The Negro Worker* (New York, 1967), 19.

board, Jones reported that "numerous instances have shown themselves of gross discrimination against Negro labor on the part of local labor unions."[188] A black newspaper observed, "This is a rather sudden change of heart on the part of the AFL to be taken at face value . . . [I]t would be well for us to stand aloof and put the AFL on probation."[189] It was more important to make the most of the economic opportunities opened by the war. "We have an opportunity to barter both with the capitalist on the one hand and with union labor on the other, an opportunity of which we must take advantage as it may never come again."[190] Much of the black press remained skeptical and continued to advise that blacks align themselves with employers rather than with unions. "Northern employers have learned his value during the experience of the past six years," Haynes wrote. "The labor shortage in many parts of the South following the Negro migration has led to the increase of wages to new levels, has opened the minds of employers to the possibilities of Negro development and is enlisting them in behalf of Negro education, justice in the courts and protection in the enjoyment of community opportunities."[191] The National Urban League also cooled its hopes for cooperation with organized labor after the Chicago riot.[192] "Since management is so pleased to have the Negro added to the labor supply it is almost always through the prejudice of unions, foremen, or groups of employees who have been with the company for a long time that Negroes are barred from positions," wrote another commentator. "Unions have shown more active prejudice to Negro labor than any other northern group."[193] "It was organized capital and not organized labor that gave to black labor the position it now occupies," concluded the *Richmond Planet*.[194] As the tide ebbed from the great flow of wartime progressivism, it appeared that little had changed in black-union relations.

188. Eugene Kinckle Jones to Archibald Grimke and others, 19 Nov. 1918 [NUL I: 1].

189. "Shall the Negro Unionize?" *Southwest Christian Advocate*, 4 Sep. 1919 [HNCF 300].

190. Eugene Kinckle Jones, "The Negro in Labor and Industry," address to 1919 NAACP conference [NAACP 1, VIII: 548].

191. Haynes, "The Negro Laborer and the Immigrant."

192. Grossman, *Land of Hope*, 239; Barrett, *Work and Community in the Jungle*, 211.

193. Woofter, "The Negro and Industrial Peace."

194. "The Negro Enters the Labor Union."

4 / From Progressivism to the New Deal, 1920–1935

The national reaction against wartime statism shaped the political economy of the 1920s, particularly in labor relations, but the decade saw no wholesale abandonment of progressive economic regulation, and many prewar innovations were preserved and extended in the return to "normalcy." The Republicans, still divided between conservative and progressive wings, never embraced the agenda of the extreme "open shop" advocates in their campaigns or policies. Herbert Hoover engineered national labor policy in the 1920s, serving as secretary of commerce and then as president. Hoover was a Bull Moose progressive who favored an active government role in promoting the harmony of capital and labor, seeking to avoid laissez-faire conflict but also preserving individualism and voluntarism. New Era Republicans sought to avoid what they called wasteful "cut-throat" competition among employers as well as among workers. They hoped to regulate rather than abolish trusts among both producers and labor. Indeed, they argued, if producers could stabilize production, prices, and profits, they would be able to afford better wages for their workers. By the 1920s, many economists and policymakers had come to advocate a "high-wage" program that would boost employee purchasing power and consumption. Large employers who supported the American Association for Labor Legislation, a successor to the National Civic Federation, were on the same page. This thinking was in line with many labor leaders of the day who regarded unions as workers' trusts, serving as countervailing forces to producer trusts. The budding progressive theory would come to flower and fruition in the New Deal.[1]

1. Robert H. Zieger, *Republicans and Labor, 1919–29* (Lexington, KY, 1969); Robert Higgs, *Crisis and Leviathan: Critical Episodes in the Growth of American Government* (New York, 1987), 150–58; Ellis Hawley, *The New Deal and the Problem of Monopoly: A Study in Economic Ambivalence* (Princeton, 1966), 1–11, 39; Ruth Ann O'Brien, *Workers' Paradox: The Republican Origins of New Deal Labor Policy, 1886–1935* (Chapel Hill, 1998), 66; Howard Dickman, *Industrial Democracy in America: Ideological Origins of National Labor Relations Policy* (La Salle, IL, 1987), 166; Christopher L. Tomlins, *The State and the Unions: Labor Relations, Law, and the Organized Labor Movement in America, 1880–1960* (Cambridge, MA, 1985), 90; Morgan O. Reynolds, "An Economic Analysis of the Norris–LaGuardia Act, the Wagner Act, and the Labor Representation Industry," *Journal of Libertarian Studies* 6 (1982), 256; Daniel Nelson, "The Other New Deal and Labor: The Regulatory State and the Unions, 1933–40," *Journal of Policy History* 13 (2001), 367–90; Gene Smiley, *Rethinking the Great Depression* (Chicago, 2002), 12, 60; George I. Lovell, *Legislative Deferrals: Statutory Ambiguity, Judicial Power, and American Democracy* (Cambridge, 2002).

The Supreme Court followed a similar line. Though it appeared to revive and defend many of the judicial devices that most frustrated organized labor—injunctions, yellow-dog contracts, antitrust prosecution, and liberty of contract—here too the government actually continued the progressive extension of state regulation of labor relations. William Howard Taft, appointed chief justice by President Harding in 1921, regarded the open shop movement as a dangerous overreaction to the wartime radicalism and militancy of organized labor, as did conservative justice George Sutherland. The national judiciary, like the political branches, reflected the fundamental ambivalence of the American people on the question of economic regulation.[2] It is remarkable how many of the assumptions of the labor movement had been adopted even by those regarded as its opponents. Even as Taft upheld an injunction against picketing in a 1921 case, he noted that labor unions had long been recognized as legitimate and useful organizations, "essential to give laborers opportunity to deal on equality with their employer." He described the strike as a "lawful instrument in a lawful economic struggle or competition between employer and employees as to the share or division between them of the joint product of labor and capital." Though suspicious of radicals in the labor movement, Taft noted that "the day of the industrial autocrats is passing and should pass." This opinion adumbrated the theory behind New Deal labor legislation.[3]

The wartime curtailment of immigration had helped to increase the power of American workers, and Republicans enacted restrictive legislation that the AFL had been seeking for forty years. Annual immigration frequently exceeded a million before the war, fell to a quarter of that during the war, and returned to over 800,000 by 1921. Republican leaders defied open shop partisans who regarded unrestricted immigration as a means to maintain labor supply and curtail union power. Republican Congresses passed restrictive immigration legislation in 1921 and 1924. "In effect, if not in intent," a historian concludes, "the party supported

2. Alfred H. Kelly, Winfred A. Harbison, and Herman Belz, *The American Constitution: Its Origins and Development*, 7th ed., 2 vols. (New York, 1991), II: 442–50; Zieger, *Republicans and Labor*, 75; Morton Keller, "The Pluralist State: American Economic Regulation in Comparative Perspective, 1900–30," in Thomas K. McCraw, ed., *Regulation in Perspective: Historical Essays* (Cambridge, 1981), 69.

3. *American Steel Foundries v. Tri-City Central Trades Council*, 257 U.S. 184 (1921), 209; *Adkins v. Children's Hospital*, 261 U.S. 525 (1923), 562; *In Re Phelan*, 62 F. 803 (1894), 817; Sylvester Petro, "Injunctions and Labor Disputes: 1880–1932," *Wake Forest Law Review* 14 (1978), 354–56, 410; Joseph A. McCartin, *Labor's Great War: The Struggle for Industrial Democracy and the Origins of Modern American Labor Relations, 1912–21* (Chapel Hill, 1997), 186.

labor's position, opposing the demands of business, and, in the view of many businessmen, hindering the Open Shop movement."[4]

The organized core of railroad workers tried to use federal government power to impose collective bargaining on the entire industry. The AFL and railroad brotherhoods wanted permanent government ownership of the railroads, a proposal embodied in the "Plumb Plan" after the war. Though Congress rejected this plan and returned the roads to private ownership in the 1920 Transportation Act, the carriers were subject to so much government regulation that they had been nationalized in all but name. As part of the new system, Congress created a Railroad Labor Board to mediate labor disputes in the industry. The board was to promote the progressive view of "responsible unionism," to facilitate collective bargaining while continuing to protect the rights of workers to bargain individually. The board alienated both the unions and the owners and could not prevent the great shopmen's strike of 1922, the first nationwide rail strike since 1894.[5] In 1926 the Republicans enacted the Railway Labor Act, replacing the discredited Railroad Labor Board with a more powerful U.S. Mediation Board, which had the power to conclude legally enforceable agreements between unions and carriers. The government now compelled the railroads to bargain with recognized unions. Persistently extending the power unions had won in the Adamson Act of 1916, railroad labor law in the 1920s served as a model for the New Deal.[6]

Overall, the power of organized labor declined in the 1920s, with AFL membership falling from its wartime peak of 5 million to 3.5 million by 1923. Private employers made vigorous efforts to manage their personnel without independent labor unions. "Industrial relations" or "welfare capitalism" became the manager's version of the "industrial democracy" sought by wartime labor activists. This project of "scientific management," which included antiunion aspects known as the "open-shop drive" or "American Plan," intended to provide a stable, efficient, and contented work force. Personnel policy became more rational, elaborately structured training and promotion systems evolved, and employers relied more on in-

4. Zieger, *Republicans and Labor,* 75–80; William J. Collins, "When the Tide Turned: Immigration and the Delay of the Great Black Migration," *Journal of Economic History* 57 (1997), 607–32; John Higham, *Strangers in the Land: Patterns of American Nativism, 1860–1925* (Westport, 1981 [1955]), 70.

5. Higgs, *Crisis and Leviathan,* 153; Reynolds, "An Economic Analysis," 230; O'Brien, *Workers' Paradox,* 9, 72–119.

6. David Bernstein, "Racism, Railroad Unions, and Labor Regulations," *Independent Review* 5 (2000), 242; Dickman, *Industrial Democracy,* 243–47; O'Brien, *Workers' Paradox,* 17.

centives than threats. An important part of this system was the "employee representation plan" or company union.[7]

The political economy of the "New Era" affected blacks in conflicting ways. Curtailing immigration, for example, probably helped to preserve wartime gains that black workers had made. W. E. B. Du Bois criticized black leaders who favored immigration restriction for the benefits it would bestow on black workers. Employee representation plans could be more inclusive than the unions they substituted for—the Swift and Armour plans had clear statements of nondiscrimination. There appears to have been very little or no gain in black occupational status and relative income in the decade.[8] But the 1920s were not good years to break into industrial employment. Employer policies promoted higher wages for more skilled and efficient workers, but companies reduced total employment. As commerce secretary and then as president, Hoover encouraged these high-wage policies, and AFL president William Green applauded him for it.[9] As sociologist Charles S. Johnson noted, "A paradox is observed at this point in the two observable phenomena which can be measured: high wages appear along with increasing unemployment, and this is a manifest contradiction of the law of supply and demand."[10] Unemployment remained a considerable problem throughout the decade.[11] Employers who adopted new, scientific personnel policies were less apt to experiment

7. Lizabeth Cohen, *Making a New Deal: Industrial Workers in Chicago, 1919–39* (New York, 1990), 161; McCartin, *Labor's Great War,* 202–18; Dickman, *Industrial Democracy,* 217; Thomas N. Maloney, "Personnel Policy and Racial Inequality in the Pre–World War II North," *Journal of Interdisciplinary History* 30 (1999), 235–58.

8. Herman Feldman, *Racial Factors in American Industry* (New York, 1931), 18, 249; George E. Haynes, "The Negro Laborer and the Immigrant," *The Survey* 46 (1921), 209–10; David Levering Lewis, *W. E. B. Du Bois: The Fight for Equality and the American Century, 1919–63* (New York, 2000), 90; Horace R. Catyon and George S. Mitchell, *Black Workers and the New Unions* (Chapel Hill, 1939), 62–63, 110; McCartin, *Labor's Great War,* 218; Harold D. Gould to Frances Perkins, 23 Jun. 1934 [NUL IV: 2]; Robert Higgs, "Black Progress and the Persistence of Racial Economic Inequalities, 1865–1940," in Steven Shulman and William Darity Jr., eds., *The Question of Discrimination: Racial Inequality in the U.S. Labor Market* (Middletown, CT, 1989), 13.

9. Morgan O. Reynolds, *Making America Poorer: The Cost of Labor Law* (Washington, 1987), 90–91.

10. Charles S. Johnson, "Present Trends in the Employment of Negro Labor," *Opportunity* 7 (1929), 146–48 [DH VI: 63].

11. Gavin Wright, *Old South, New South: Revolutions in the Southern Economy since the Civil War* (New York, 1986), 206; Cohen, *Making a New Deal,* 161–84. Cohen notes that manufacturing unemployment was higher, 1923–27, than in any other nondepression half-decade.

with new sources of labor such as blacks.[12] Machines and skilled white workers were more likely than black workers to replace the immigrant newcomer.

The weakened condition of organized labor and its continued inattention to the problem of racial discrimination left most black leaders and workers at least as hostile to unionization as they had been before the war. The AFL continued to ignore black pleas for inclusion in the labor movement. At its 1920 convention, the delegates refused to support a resolution that the federation "use every means in its power to have the words 'only white' members stricken out of the constitution of the Brotherhood of Railway Carmen," instead voting to "request" that the carmen do so. Even this proposal had to overcome the objections of southerners and the committee on organization. Nor would the federation grant an international charter to the black Railway Coach Cleaners, whom the Carmen excluded, claiming that the AFL "does not organize workers of any trade or calling along racial lines."[13] Not surprisingly, blacks took the jobs of whites during the 1922 shopmen's strike, in the face of union violence that produced 1,500 cases of attempted murder and dozens of cases of kidnappings, dynamitings, and other vandalism.[14] The Labor Department noted that "avenues for employment in the transportation industry are rapidly being opened to the colored worker and . . . his future in this phase of employment has a particularly bright aspect." The industrial secretary of the Urban League, William L. Evans, noted that blacks would continue to act as strikebreakers until white unions realized that their own success depended on including blacks.[15]

Gompers's death in 1924 raised hopes that a new AFL president might be more receptive to black concerns. His successor, William Green, had been a member of the United Mine Workers, reputed to be the least discriminatory of AFL-affiliated

12. Maloney, "Personnel Policy and Racial Inequality," 243.

13. Philip Taft, *Organized Labor in American History* (New York, 1964), 672–73; *Report of Proceedings of the 40th Annual Convention of the AFL* (Washington, 1920) [DH VI: 351]; *Birmingham Reporter*, 19 Jun. 1920 [DH VI: 313].

14. Colin J. Davis, *Power at Odds: The 1922 National Railroad Shopmen's Strike* (Urbana, 1997), 29; Reynolds, "An Economic Analysis," 237. George Schuyler describes his brief foray into this strike in *Black and Conservative* (New Rochelle, NY, 1966), 127.

15. Ira De A. Reid, *Negro Membership in American Labor Unions* (New York, 1969 [1930]), 166; William L. Evans, "The Negro in Chicago Industries," *Opportunity* 1 (1923), 15–16 [DH VI: 20]; Arvarh E. Strickland, *History of the Chicago Urban League* (Urbana, 1966), 73; "Employment of Negroes on Railroads," *Monthly Labor Review* 19 (1924), 1105.

unions. Green did attempt to let black workers know that they were welcome in the ranks of organized labor, but he continued to deny that discrimination was a problem in the AFL and blamed blacks for their problems with unions. His presidency largely maintained the policies adopted or tolerated by Gompers.[16] In an open letter to the AFL in 1924, the NAACP observed that despite AFL resolutions, most blacks remained outside of the unions because "white union labor does not want black labor, and, secondly, black labor has ceased to beg admittance to union ranks because of its increasing value and efficiency outside of the unions." Since immigration had dwindled, the black worker was gaining "tremendous advantage ... He broke the great steel strike. He will soon be in a position to break any strike when he can gain economic advantage for himself." The whole working class was weakened as a result. The letter called for the NAACP, AFL, and the railroad brotherhoods to launch an interracial labor conference that would investigate and end discrimination in labor. The appeal met no reply.[17]

The difficulty of forming a black-labor alliance baffled many observers on the left. "The Negro may be continually admonished of being exploited by white capitalists," the progressive black economist Abram Harris wrote in 1925, "but experience and tradition, perhaps, lead him to wonder if working for a white employer at a wage slightly below that paid his white competitor is as great a handicap as ostracism or double-dealing by the union. His calculations are usually in favor of the employer."[18]

Blacks were caught in the midst of both racial and economic conflict, explained the more conservative Howard University sociologist and dean Kelly Miller. "Logic aligns him with labor, but good sense arrays him on the side of capital. The race issue frustrates all the conclusions of logic." Whatever common interests white and black workers might share, "the issue between the white and colored workman is sharper than that between capital and labor." Miller saw employer discrimination as a function of their workers' prejudices. "If the capitalist shows race prejudice in his operations, it is merely the reflected attitude of the white workman ... In all the

16. Craig Phelan, *William Green: Biography of a Labor Leader* (Albany, NY, 1989), 153; Philip S. Foner, *Organized Labor and the Black Worker* (New York, 1982), 170; William Green, "Our Negro Worker," *Messenger* 7 (1925), 332 [DH VI: 340].

17. "Are Negroes 'Workers'?" *The Nation* 119 (1924), 89; *Monthly Labor Review* 19 (1924), 678.

18. Abram L. Harris, "A White and Black World in American Labor and Politics," *Social Forces* 4 (1925), 380.

leading lines of industry the white workmen organize and either shut out the Negro or shunt him aside in separate lines with a lower level of dignity and compensation." When unions did include blacks, it was because employers forced them to do so. "The capitalist stands for an open shop which gives to every man the unhindered right to work according to his ability and skill. In this proposition the capitalist and the Negro are as one." White workers were responsible for black disfranchisement and lynching, while the employing class provided some security against such lawlessness. "But the laborers outnumber the capitalists more than ten to one, and under spur of the democratic ideal must in the long run gain the essential ends for which they strive." To the prospect of being on the losing side of this battle, Miller could only conclude, "Sufficient unto today is the industrial wisdom thereof. The Negro would rather risk the ills he has than fly to those he knows not of." [19]

T. Arnold Hill, director of the Urban League's Department of Industrial Relations, echoed this conclusion. "When capital uses its power in [the black worker's] favor, as it does in all issues when it cares to do so, it will be time for him to decide to oppose organized labor," he wrote, "or when labor removes barriers that rob him of positions, he will decide in their favor. Until then he will go his way resolved to let coming events decide his course of action." [20]

BLACK NATIONALISM AND THE LEFT

Miller's emphasis on race consciousness was reflected in the most visible manifestation of black organization in the postwar years, Marcus Garvey's Universal Negro Improvement and Conservation Association and African Communities League, usually called the Universal Negro Improvement Association (UNIA). The UNIA expressed the growing assertiveness of the "New Negro," particularly those who had migrated North and served in World War I. Garvey assembled the first great mass movement among American blacks and challenged the established civil rights organizations. Born in Jamaica in 1887, Garvey emigrated to Harlem in 1916. He was profoundly influenced by Booker T. Washington's doctrine of racial self-

---

19. Kelly Miller, *The Everlasting Stain* (Washington, 1924), 279–89; Miller, "The Negro as a Workingman," *American Mercury* 6 (1925), 310–13. For a contemporary critique, see "Labor and Race Relations," *Opportunity* 4 (1926), 4.

20. T. Arnold Hill, "The Dilemma of Negro Workers," *Opportunity* 4 (1926), 39.

help and the anticolonialism of Duse Mohammed Ali of Egypt, and he devised a program of self-segregation among American blacks and a movement for them to return to and redeem Africa.[21]

Garvey worked as a printer in Jamaica and, as a foreman, joined and became a leader of a 1907 printers strike in Kingston. The strike failed, and he was black-listed; the experience permanently soured his view of labor organizations. While he could be critical of unrestrained capitalism, he most often advocated free-market economics for contemporary black progress and warned against labor unions. He regarded capitalism as a stage in human progress, and launched a number of business ventures himself, but believed that ultimately Leninism would dominate the world.[22]

He admired the influence that Gompers and the AFL had attained during the war, and he urged blacks to follow their example and organize. But he saw white labor unions as enemies to blacks. "If I must advise the Negro workingman and laborer, I should warn him against the present brand of Communism or Workers' Partizanship [sic] as taught in America, and to be careful of the traps and pitfalls of white trade unionism, in affiliation with the American Federation of White workers or laborers." He advised black workers to underbid white workers, who would only take blacks into their unions in order ultimately to eliminate their competition. "If the Negro takes my advice he will organize by himself and always keep his scale of wage a little lower than the whites until he is able to become, through proper leadership, his own employer; by so doing he will keep the good will of the white employer and live a little longer under the present scheme of things." Communists, he said, would take over "not only as communists but as whitemen" and would exterminate blacks. Garvey went so far as to condemn the NAACP as hypocrites and lauded the Ku Klux Klan for providing a spur to black self-help. "Between the Ku Klux Klan and the Morefield [sic] Storey National Association for the Advancement of 'Colored' People group, give me the Klan for

---

21. "Marcus Garvey," ANB.

22. Edmund David Cronon, *Black Moses: The Story of Marcus Garvey and the Universal Negro Improvement Association* (Madison, 1955), 12; Tony Martin, *Race First: The Ideological and Organizational Struggles of Marcus Garvey and the Universal Negro Improvement Association* (Westport, 1976), 53–55, 248; Clarence E. Walker, *Deromanticizing Black History: Critical Essays and Reappraisals* (Knoxville, 1991), 52; Marcus Garvey, "Capitalism and the State," Amy Jacques-Garvey, ed., *Philosophy and Opinions of Marcus Garvey*, 2 vols. (New York, 1968–69 [1923–35]), I: 72.

their honesty of purpose towards the Negro. They are better friends of my race, for telling us what they are, and what they mean, thereby giving us a chance to stir for ourselves, than all of the hypocrites put together with their false gods and religions, notwithstanding." [23]

Garvey's defense of the Klan, disdain for light-skinned black leaders, and fraudulent business practices ruined his movement and earned him the enmity of nearly every black leader. (T. Thomas Fortune, a broken man at the end of a long career, was among the few journalists to adhere to him.) He was tried for mail fraud in 1922, began a prison sentence in 1925, and was finally deported in 1927. Yet he continued to operate the UNIA from his Atlanta prison cell, and his supporters played rough with his opponents. Union leader A. Philip Randolph received a severed hand in the mail as a warning to stop opposing Garvey, and a former UNIA officer was assassinated by Garveyites.[24] W. E. B. Du Bois was a particularly bitter foe of Garvey. "In his righteous determination to destroy Garvey as a leader, Du Bois seems never to have honestly considered the possibility that personal loathing of Garvey prevented him from taking even the most minimal steps toward finding an accommodation," a Du Bois biographer writes, though Du Bois would later come to embrace many of the main points of Washington's and Garvey's strategies.[25]

Independent black unions were a device that could combine black nationalism and labor unionism, adapting the Booker T. Washington strategy to labor organization.[26] The National Brotherhood Workers formed one such organization. Frustrated by the AFL's indifference to their concerns, black unionists sought to put together an organization equivalent to the United Hebrew Trades. The AFL had initially resisted the organization of the needle trades in New York City, and cen-

23. *Negro World*, 1 Feb. 1919 [UNIA I: 353]; Cronon, *Black Moses,* 195–96; "The Negro, Communism, Trade Unionism and His (?) Friend: 'Beware of Greeks Bearing Gifts,' " (c. 1925) [UNIA VI: 214].

24. FBI File on A. Philip Randolph (microfilm, Wilmington, DE, 1990); Kenneth O'Reilly and David Gallen, eds., *Black Americans: The FBI Files* (New York, 1994), 309; Kevern Verney, *The Art of the Possible: Booker T. Washington and Black Leadership in the United States, 1881–1925* (London, 2001), 119; Paula Pfeffer, *A. Philip Randolph, Pioneer of the Civil Rights Movement* (Baton Rouge, 1990), 13–16; Wolters, *Du Bois and His Rivals,* 161.

25. Lewis, *W. E. B. Du Bois: The Fight for Equality,* 61, 148–52; Manning Marable, "A. Philip Randolph and the Foundations of Black American Socialism," *Radical America* 14 (1980), 14–15.

26. Ernest Obadele-Starks, *Black Unionism in the Industrial South* (College Station, TX, 2000), 27–28; Dean Dutcher, *The Negro and Modern Industrial Society: An Analysis of Changes in the Occupations of Negro Workers, 1910–20* (Lancaster, PA, 1930), 116.

sured the United Hebrew Trades for "associating along race lines," but by 1912 the federation began to cooperate with them.[27] Some hoped that the AFL might end its neglect of black workers if they followed a similar route. "I fail to see how the black man can get justice so long denied to him" in the AFL, one wrote in 1919, arguing that the Brotherhood had forced the AFL to make the rhetorical concessions that it did during the war.[28] A. Philip Randolph and Chandler Owen flirted with the organization before its demise in 1921, with their magazine, *The Messenger,* serving as the Brotherhood's official organ. But after a falling out with the Brotherhood and Owen's departure for Chicago, Randolph accepted the invitation to lead what would become the most successful black union, the Brotherhood of Sleeping Car Porters. Having denounced the AFL as "the most wicked machine for the propagation of race prejudice in the country" in 1919, Randolph spent the 1920s trying to win affiliation for the porters in the AFL.[29]

Though the porters complained of long hours and low pay, many blacks looked on the job as a desirable one, the only kind of work available to many college-educated Negroes. Many felt gratitude toward the Pullman Company in particular for allowing them this job monopoly, and they often opposed unions. Pullman's company union also presented a powerful rival to Randolph's efforts. Established in 1920 and given a wage increase in 1924, it had effectively defused a postwar organization effort among the porters. The drive to organize the porters divided the black community, with the NAACP in support but many black newspapers, most notably the *Chicago Defender,* opposed. By means not altogether clear, Randolph was able to force publisher Robert S. Abbott to reverse the paper's position and, by November 1927, in "the unprecedented spectacle of a newspaper denouncing itself in terms approaching libel," the influential *Defender* joined the union's crusade.[30]

27. Gwendolyn Mink, *Old Labor and New Immigrants in American Political Development: Union, Party, and State, 1875–1920* (Ithaca, NY, 1986), 201–2; A. Philip Randolph, "The Trade Union Movement and the Negro," *Journal of Negro Education* 5 (1936), 56.

28. Sterling D. Spero and Abram L. Harris, *The Black Worker: The Negro and the Labor Movement* (New York, 1931), 117–19; Walter Green to editor, *Negro World,* 19 Jul. 1919 [UNIA I: 467].

29. Harris, *Keeping the Faith,* 34; Spero and Harris, *The Black Worker,* 390–94.

30. William H. Harris, *Keeping the Faith: A. Philip Randolph, Milton P. Webster, and the Brotherhood of Sleeping Car Porters, 1925–37* (Urbana, 1977), 15, 41–47, 129–38; Eric Arneson, *Brotherhoods of Color: Black Railroad Workers and the Struggle for Equality* (Cambridge, 2001), 86–94; Roi Ottley, *The Lonely Warrior: The Life and Times of Robert S. Abbott* (Chicago, 1955), 261. Randolph believed that Pullman was no longer bribing Abbott; others surmise that the porters themselves threatened to stop de-

Randolph was so eager to keep the support of the AFL and the railroad brotherhoods that he refrained from bringing the porters' complaints to the Railroad Labor Board because the brotherhoods wanted to abolish it. Other black railroad unionists warned Randolph that the pending legislation, the Railway Labor Act, would only help the stronger white unions and would enable them more effectively to exclude black workers.[31] When its replacement, the U.S. Mediation Board, refused to consider the porters' appeal, and the Pullman Company refused to submit to arbitration, Randolph threatened a strike in the hopes that it would so impair interstate commerce that the president would use his power under the Railway Labor Act to impose arbitration. At the eleventh hour, on the advice of AFL president William Green, Randolph called off the strike. Communists attacked Randolph for having sold out to the AFL, and membership in the demoralized union plummeted. The Hotel and Restaurant Employees union, which claimed jurisdiction over the porters, refused to allow the AFL to grant the porters a national charter, and in 1929 Randolph accepted nine federal charters instead. Randolph and Webster were satisfied that keeping the union intact and getting a foot in the door to the AFL was worth the sacrifice. Green hoped that he had gained a goodwill ambassador to the black community. When he welcomed the New York local into the AFL, Randolph hailed Green as "the second Abraham Lincoln, come to relieve industrial bondage."[32] Randolph would spend the rest of his long life exhorting blacks to see their interests as aligned with those of white unionists, but his philosophy had limited appeal on account of its atheistic premises and its dissonance with the experience of many black workers.[33]

Randolph had become much less radical since the war as he warmed up to the AFL. He attacked the communists as bitterly as he had the AFL, or even the Pullman Company. "Negro communists are a menace," he wrote in the *Messenger*. "They are either lunatics or *agents provocateurs,* stool pigeons of the U.S. Depart-

---

livering the *Defender* to southern towns. For reasons equally unclear, the *Pittsburgh Courier,* an influential weekly rival to the *Defender,* shifted from support to opposition to the union.

31. Harris, *Keeping the Faith,* 58, 96; "Protest against the Adoption of the Howell-Barkley Bill," 7 Apr. 1924 [NAACP 10, IV: 88].

32. Harris, *Keeping the Faith,* 153–60; Spero and Harris, *The Black Worker,* 449–55; Foner, *Organized Labor and the Black Worker,* 177–87; Pfeffer, *A. Philip Randolph,* 26–30; Milton Webster to Morris Moore, 11 Jun. 1928, BSCP Papers, Chicago Historical Society [DH VI: 286]; Schuyler, *Black and Conservative,* 137.

33. Pfeffer, *A. Philip Randolph,* 296.

ment of Justice. . . . [T]heir statements have revealed that they are ultimately de-
void of any respect for fact, truth, or honesty."[34] The communists vacillated
throughout the decade, first supporting the "internationalist" position linking
black oppression in America with global imperialism. Eventually they returned to
the socialist argument of Eugene Debs, that the race problem would resolve itself
when the class question was settled, and then shifted toward an endorsement of a
separate black nation in America.

The Soviets were in the midst of the power struggle that brought Josef Stalin,
erstwhile commissar for nationalities, to the state's fore. American communists
awkwardly hung on sudden and unacknowledged ideological jerks.[35] Whereas the
Comintern had previously blamed black strikebreaking on AFL exclusion, it now
said that black workers had to earn their way to equality within the working class,
and the party handed over the "Negro Question" to James Allen, who embraced
the "Black Belt" idea of an independent state for black Americans in the deep
South. Despite the objections of most black American communists, this "self-
determination," or separatist, position remained the Communist Party position
into the 1950s. Stalin and the Politburo delayed implementing the policy until they
could find a black American to embrace it, which they did with Harry Haywood.[36]

The American Communist Party (called the Workers Party until 1929) created

34. Harris, *Keeping the Faith*, 32; Marable, "A. Philip Randolph and the Foundations of Black
American Socialism," 16–18; Harris, "A White and Black World in American Labor and Politics," 380;
"Investigation of Communist Propaganda," Hearings before a Special Committee to Investigate Communist Activities in the U.S.," House of Representatives, 71st Cong., 2d Sess. (1930), I: 242–51 [DH VI:
474]; *Messenger* 5 (1923), 784 [DH VI: 387]; "The American Negro Labor Congress," *Messenger* 7 (1925),
304–5 [DH VI: 437]; Abram L. Harris, "Negro Labor's Quarrel with White Workingmen," *Current History*, Sep. 1926, pp. 903–8 [SCCF 2713]; Paula F. Pfeffer, "The Evolution of A. Philip Randolph and Bayard Rustin from Radicalism to Conservatism," in Peter Eisenstadt, ed., *Black Conservatism: Essays in
Intellectual and Political History* (New York, 1999), 201.

35. Keith P. Griffler, *What Price Alliance? Black Radicals Confront White Labor, 1918–38* (New York,
1995), 12, 64; John W. Van Zanten, "Communist Theory and the American Negro Question," *Review of
Politics* 29 (1967), 435–56; Theodore Draper, *American Communism and Soviet Russia: The Formative
Period* (New York, 1960), 322–31; Wilson Record, *The Negro and the Communist Party* (Chapel Hill,
1951), 15–23.

36. Griffler, *What Price Alliance?* 77–84; Harvey Klehr and William Thompson, "Self-Determination in the Black Belt: Origins of a Communist Policy," *Labor History* 30 (1989), 354–66; Draper, *American Communism and Soviet Russia*, 343–55; James R. Barrett, *William Z. Foster and the Tragedy of
American Radicalism* (Urbana, 1999), 243.

the American Negro Labor Congress in 1925, designing it to bring blacks into communist unions. From 1928 to 1935 the party adopted an "ultra left" line, rejecting cooperation with other left-wing parties, which were denounced as "social fascist" organizations.[37] The party adopted the "Black Belt" plan and shifted from "boring from within" to establishing separate communist unions but implemented neither principle consistently.[38] The National Urban League observed that the Congress did little actual organizing; the AFL and Randolph dismissed it as a mask for Soviet efforts to take over foreign labor movements, one that would "simply pit the American Negro in an organization under foreign control against the American Negro in a labor movement under American control."[39] Shifting Comintern policy made it difficult for black communists to attract followers, and it sometimes endangered their lives. Lovett Fort-Whiteman, a leading black American communist, was imprisoned for "anti-Soviet activity" and killed near Kolyma, the notorious Siberian gold mine, in 1939.[40]

BLACK POLITICAL ACTION

Black leaders also turned to political activity to frustrate the potentially discriminatory aims of labor organizations or to wrest concessions from them. In the 1920s, the AFL continued its campaign against yellow-dog contracts and labor injunctions. (The devices were tied together, as courts often issued injunctions to prohibit organizers from trying to get workers to breach yellow-dog contracts.) The federal government had prohibited yellow-dog contracts in railroad employment under the Erdman Act of 1898, but the Supreme Court overturned the provision

---

37. Earl Browder, Speech at 13th Plenum of the Executive Committee of the Communist International, Jan. 1934, in Robert V. Daniels, ed., *A Documentary History of Communism,* 2 vols. (New York, 1960), II: 108–10. The ANLC was funded by the Soviets: Secretariat of the ECCI to the CEC of the Workers Party of America, 3 Feb. 1925, in Harvey Klehr, John Earl Haynes, and Kyrill M. Anderson, eds., *The Soviet World of American Communism* (New Haven, 1998), 125.

38. Foner, *Organized Labor and the Black Worker,* 193; Cayton and Mitchell, *Black Workers and the New Unions,* 111; "Communists Boring into Negro Labor," *New York Times,* 17 Jan. 1926, sec. II, p. 1; "Report on 17 Apr. 1937 Politburo Meeting, Central Committee, CPUSA, Cleveland," John Frey Papers, Box 5, LC.

39. Reid, *Negro Membership in American Labor Unions,* 127; "The American Negro Labor Congress," *Messenger* 7 (1925), 304–95 [DH VI: 437]; Schuyler, *Black and Conservative,* 145.

40. Jeff Woods, *Black Struggle, Red Scare: Segregation and Anticommunism in the South, 1948–68* (Baton Rouge, 2004), 22; Record, *The Negro and the Communist Party,* 25; Klehr, Haynes, and Anderson, *The Soviet World of American Communism,* 220.

ten years later. Organized labor and progressives denounced the decision, but it hindered the railroad unions' campaign to establish racial job monopolies. The Supreme Court again upheld judicial power to issue injunctions to honor yellow-dog contracts against the UMW in 1917. Here the miners themselves wanted the protection of yellow-dog contracts against union incursion. Unorganized West Virginia miners earned more than those in the UMW's organized fields, and workers wanted protection from union-induced violence and disorder.[41]

In Illinois in 1925, black legislators voted against a state anti-injunction bill because its building trade union sponsors discriminated against black workers. The president of the Illinois Federation of Labor warned the lathers union that it must change its racial policy or the federation would be unable to accomplish anything in the legislature. The black legislators dropped their opposition when AFL leaders promised to ease entry into the electricians union.[42]

Prominent Ohio novelist, attorney, and NAACP activist Charles W. Chesnutt testified against the Shipstead anti-injunction bill in 1928, along with state legislator Harry E. Davis. Andrew Furuseth, the AFL legislative director responsible for the La Follette Seamen Act, had drafted Shipstead's bill. Chesnutt admitted that unions had improved the lot of working men, but "so far they have been used very slightly for the benefit of Negro labor and very often exercised against its interests . . . I make the charge baldly that the labor unions of the United States, broadly speaking, are unfriendly to colored labor, and I challenge them to prove the contrary." Chesnutt described the ways that Cleveland trade unionists had prevented black electricians from working, a scenario similar to that among Illinois electricians. Court injunctions provided one of the few protections that black workers had against the power of discriminatory unions. He warned the committee that black voting strength was growing, and that blacks "do not desire to see what little protection they have or may have through the courts against union discrimination

41. David Bernstein, *Only One Place of Redress: African Americans, Labor Regulations, and the Courts from Reconstruction to the New Deal* (Durham, NC, 2001), 55; Price Van Meter Fishback, *Soft Coal, Hard Choices: The Economic Welfare of Bituminous Coal Miners, 1890–1930* (New York, 1992), 91; Reynolds, *Power and Privilege,* 98–100; Petro, "Injunctions and Labor Disputes," 394, 426; Reynolds, "An Economic Analysis," 232–33.

42. John H. Walker to Ben F. Ferris, 1 Apr. 1925, Victor A. Olander Papers, Chicago Historical Society [DH VI: 517]; T. Arnold Hill, "The Negro in Industry, 1926," *Opportunity* 5 (1927), 51; Spero and Harris, *The Black Worker,* 138–39.

and tyranny taken away from them by this bill." Though he denounced the bill as "class legislation pure and simple," he did suggest that "it would be only human nature, if colored working men . . . benefit[ed] equally by whatever union labor might achieve in the way of power or influence or reward, that they might not oppose" it. Davis said that the bill would endanger blacks' right to make a living, and "it seems to me absolutely unjust for Congress to even think of passing a law which would deny [blacks] their only appeal, an appeal to the courts for their redress."[43] Davis's argument impressed Senator George Norris, who admitted that the legislation might burden black workers.[44]

The national office of the NAACP did not have enough time to join the Ohioans. Special legal assistant William T. Andrews studied the bill for Secretary James Weldon Johnson. New York socialist and labor lawyer Morris Hillquit told Andrews that the bill would neither curb injunctions nor harm unorganized workers. Civil rights lawyer Louis Marshall, in contrast, concluded that "There is no doubt that unorganized labor would suffer seriously from such legislation, and especially that of Negroes . . . If they were left to the tender mercies of unions which regard them as unfit for membership, and the courts would have their hands tied by an act of Congress inspired by the unions, they would be placed in a most unfortunate position." Andrews told Johnson that "its effect upon the rights of Negro employees who happen not to be members of the union will be immense" and recommended that the association not support it.[45] W. E. B. Du Bois shared these sentiments but saw the whole issue as a "dilemma which repeatedly faces the NAACP. This association has always been an organization of liberals and even of radicals on many matters of social advance." While they supported unionization, they had to be concerned about the potential abuse of union power. Injunctions might be unjust, "But this power of injunction has been used, not simply to protect capitalists and employers, it has been used to protect minority groups of

43. Lovell, *Legislative Deferrals,* 169; Bernstein, *Only One Place of Redress,* 56–57; Spero and Harris, *The Black Worker,* 139.

44. "Limiting Scope of Injunctions in Labor Disputes," Part 4: Hearings before the U.S. Senate Committee on the Judiciary, 70th Cong., 1st Sess. (15 Mar. 1928), 603–14; Davis statement on S. 1482 and clippings from *Cleveland Press* and *Cleveland News,* 16 Mar. 1928 [NAACP 10, IV: 366].

45. James Weldon Johnson to Clark L. Mock, 16 Mar. 1928 [NAACP 10, IV: 343]; Morris Hillquit to William T. Andrews, 1 May 1928 [NAACP 10, IV: 356]; Louis Marshall to Johnson, 10 May 1928 [NAACP 10, IV: 361]; Andrews to Johnson, 4 Jan. 1929 [NAACP 10, IV: 375].

employees against whom union labor discriminates. This is true especially of Ne-groes." Whatever position the association took on the injunction issue, the prob-lem of nearly universal racial discrimination in unions would have to be faced.[46]

Not all union leaders opposed labor injunctions as adamantly as did the AFL leaders. Many large employers repudiated yellow-dog contracts during the 1920s in favor of more conciliatory employee-representation plans. Though unions were usually the aggressors, and thus unable to press equity claims, almost one in eight injunctions between 1880 and 1932 was sought by a union. Progressive unionists like Sidney Hillman believed that judicial power might be turned to unions' ad-vantage and wanted to preserve the injunction power. New York judge Robert Wagner also saw the benefits of pro-union injunctions.[47]

MIGRATION

The wartime Great Migration remained strong in the 1920s, and black workers continued to make their way into the open shops of the North. The black urban population outside of the South rose by 70 percent in the 1920s. Chicago's black population doubled, to some 300,000, and they elected the first black congressman from the North.[48] Some breakthroughs occurred via strikebreaking, in the railroad shops and coal mines early in the decade, but for the most part black workers held on to jobs or pushed ahead in industries previously open to them. In steel, owners retained many of the black workers who broke the 1919 strike and brought them into the widening system of welfare capitalism.[49] Though the numbers of black

46. "Injunctions" (n.d.) [DuBP LXXXIII: 882].

47. Daniel Ernst, "The Yellow-Dog Contract and Liberal Reform, 1917–32," *Labor History* 30 (1989), 261; Petro, "Injunctions and Labor Disputes," 383–89; Edwin E. Witte, *The Government in La-bor Disputes* (New York, 1932), 231–34; *The Nation* 69 (14 Sep. 1899), 198; Bonnett, *History of Employers' Associations*, 435; William C. Liller to Hugh L. Kerwin, 6 May 1920, Records of the Federal Mediation and Conciliation Service, RG 280, NA [BWGM I: 273]; William E. Forbath, *Law and the Shaping of the American Labor Movement* (Cambridge, 1991), 119–24; Lovell, *Legislative Deferrals*, 177.

48. Sanford M. Jacoby, *Employing Bureaucracy: Managers, Unions, and the Transformation of Work in American Industry, 1900–45* (New York, 1985), 170; T. Arnold Hill, "The Present Status of Negro La-bor," *Opportunity* 7 (1929), 143–45 [DH VI: 60].

49. Dennis C. Dickerson, *Out of the Crucible: Black Steelworkers in Western Pennsylvania, 1875–1980* (Albany, NY, 1986), 93–117; U.S. Department of Labor, "Industrial Employment of the Negro in Pennsylvania," *Monthly Labor Review* 22 (1926), 48–51 [DH VI: 36]; John T. Clark, "Negro in Steel," *Op-portunity* 4 (1926), 87; Jacoby, *Employing Bureaucracy*, 194. These revise the view of Spero and Harris,

steelworkers declined in Alabama in the 1920s, they remained about the same in the United States at large. While whites maintained their hold on skilled labor in the southern steel industry, blacks also advanced into skilled positions.[50] Blacks became a more important part of the meatpacking work force in the 1920s and made greater gains here than in steel. In the country, total male employment in the industry fell by one-fifth, and black male employment by one-third, but blacks increased their share of employment in the major packing centers and gained considerable integration into skilled jobs. Weekly wages of black males in the industry were over 90 percent of those of whites, a significantly higher ratio than in any other industry. Black workers participated actively in the company unions, where they found less discrimination than in the independent unions. Large employers carefully prevented racial hostility among the new groups of workers they had brought into their plants. Blacks played an important role in the "Americanization" of the industrial work force in the 1920s, as ethnic identification diminished.[51]

Black coal miners increased their presence in the industry in the 1920s. The nonunion fields of Appalachia continued to gain market share at the expense of the UMW stronghold in the bituminous "Central Competitive Field" north of the Ohio River from Illinois to western Pennsylvania and in the eastern Pennsylvania anthracite region. Blacks had long been excluded from the North, but the nonunion Appalachian area exceeded the North in coal production by the end of the decade. Black employment rose by 5 percent while total employment fell 14 percent. Unionized operators were able to stay in business due to high demand for coal and cheaper transportation, but these advantages ran out in the 1920s. By 1927,

---

The Black Worker, 262, and Norgren et al., "Negro Labor and Its Problems," 460, who suggest that the black strikebreakers were dismissed in order to minimize racial friction.

50. Herbert R. Northrup, "The Negro and Unionism in the Birmingham, Alabama, Iron and Steel Industry," Southern Economic Journal 10 (1943), 28; Robert J. Norrell, "Caste in Steel: Jim Crow Careers in Birmingham, Alabama," Journal of American History 73 (1986), 671–72.

51. Thomas N. Maloney, "Degrees of Inequality: The Advance of Black Male Workers in the Northern Meat Packing and Steel Industries before World War II," Social Science History 19 (1995), 31–62; Robert A. Fogel, The Negro in the Meat Industry (Philadelphia, 1970), 46; Rick Halpern, Down on the Killing Floor: Black and White Workers in Chicago's Packinghouses, 1904–54 (Urbana, 1997), 77–95; Cohen, Making a New Deal, 204–05; Spero and Harris, The Black Worker, 267; Feldman, Racial Factors in American Industry, 272; American Management Association, The Negro in Industry (New York, 1923), 21, 24; Steven Fraser, Labor Will Rule: Sidney Hillman and the Rise of American Labor (Ithaca, NY, 1991), 228.

the northern operators broke their collective agreement with the UMW, and the union's strength collapsed. In 1922, union miners dug 70 percent of the nation's soft coal; ten years later the proportion had fallen to 20 percent. Yet, while the UMW went to pieces, its president, John L. Lewis, consolidated his own power in the organization and turned it into one of the most centralized unions in the country. Lewis had tried to work with Commerce Secretary Hoover to stabilize the industry, and though he believed that Hoover had not done enough to protect the union, he maintained his belief that government should do more to manage labor relations in the industry.[52]

Blacks also entered the automobile manufacturing industry, which enjoyed a reputation for harmonious labor relations. The demographic and labor market changes of the war and the 1920s brought blacks into the industry. They were usually restricted to unskilled, hot, heavy, unpleasant jobs, though these paid better than plant averages, and blacks seem to have been paid equally for equal work. Managers commonly explained this job segregation as helping to prevent racial tension in the plant.[53] Ford stood out, employing the greatest number of blacks and placing them at all skill levels, without incident.[54] In 1921, Ford adopted a racial quota system for black workers following an appeal from Detroit ministers; according to Ford's quotas, blacks would compose the same proportion of the factory work force that they did in Detroit and would be included in every department. By the mid-1920s, Ford employed ten thousand blacks in his Dearborn River Rouge plant, over half of all black autoworkers in the country. Ford was able to take advantage of this pool of workers virtually alone and chose the best workers in the black community, thus benefiting from the discrimination of his competitors. It is possible that Ford was able to get his black employees to work harder or more efficiently than white workers at the same wage, which amounted to a kind

52. Norgren et al., "Negro Labor and Its Problems," 413; Herbert R. Northrup, *Organized Labor and the Negro* (New York, 1944), 158–64; Ray Marshall, *Labor in the South* (Cambridge, MA, 1967), 78; Robert H. Zieger, *John L. Lewis: Labor Leader* (Boston, 1988), 32–47; Zieger, *Republicans and Labor,* 228–56.

53. Joyce Shaw Peterson, "Black Automobile Workers in Detroit, 1910–30," *Journal of Negro History* 64 (1979), 181, 188; Lloyd Bailer, "The Negro Automobile Worker," *Journal of Political Economy* 51 (1943), 419–20; Feldman, *Racial Factors in American Industry,* 271; Norgren et al., "Negro Labor and Its Problems," 581–88.

54. Bailer, "The Negro Automobile Worker," 422; Herbert R. Northrup, *The Negro in the Automobile Industry* (Philadelphia, 1968), 65.

of wage discrimination. Still, the city's black population widely hailed the automakers, and Ford in particular.[55]

Ford's example demonstrates an interesting example of the neoclassical "economics of discrimination" theory on the erosion of racial discrimination in labor markets—Ford profited by the discrimination that other automakers paid for. It also points out the limitations of this process—Ford's competitors seem not to have lost much by gratifying their taste for discrimination. Nobody has provided a clear explanation for Henry Ford's openness to blacks. His detractors claimed that he sought blacks because they were less susceptible to radicalism and unionism. Ford used his black workers as "strike insurance," a typical employer device to "divide and conquer" his employees. There is no evidence, however, that these were his motives, and it is more likely that his unorthodox stance derived from a combination of economics and philanthropy.[56]

On the eve of the Great Depression, very little suggested that the traditional animosity between blacks and organized labor was about to change. A bitter exchange between NAACP executive secretary Walter White and John P. Frey, the head of the AFL's metal trades department, early in 1929 revealed how deeply the wounds ran. Frey tried to explain the federation's position on the organization of blacks to the December 1928 National Interracial Conference. He denied that organized labor had played any role in establishing prejudice against blacks or foreigners, explaining that union exclusion was not racial or social but economic. Unions acted in simple self-preservation, to prevent an excess supply of labor.

55. Gunnar Myrdal, *An American Dilemma: The Negro Problem and Modern Democracy* (New York, 1962 [1944]), 1121; Thomas N. Maloney and Warren C. Whatley, "Making the Effort: The Contours of Racial Discrimination in Detroit's Labor Markets, 1920–40," *Journal of Economic History* 55 (1995), 478, 489–490; Warren Whatley and Gavin Wright, "Getting Started in the Auto Industry: Black Workers at the Ford Motor Company, 1918–47," *Cliometrics Society Newsletter* 5 (1990), 10–16; Christopher L. Foote, Warren C. Whatley, and Gavin Wright, "Arbitraging a Discriminatory Labor Market: Black Workers at the Ford Motor Company, 1918–47," *Journal of Labor Economics* 21 (2003), 493–532; August Meier and Elliott M. Rudwick, *Black Detroit and the Rise of the UAW* (New York, 1979), 5; Northrup, *Organized Labor and the Negro,* 189.

56. Maloney and Whatley, "Making the Effort," 469–70; Art Preis, *Labor's Giant Step: Twenty Years of the CIO* (New York, 1964), 107; John Brueggemann, "The Power and Collapse of Paternalism: The Ford Motor Company and Black Workers, 1937–41," *Social Problems* 47 (2000), 220–40. Christopher C. Alston, *Henry Ford and the Negro People* (Washington, 1941), a Communist and National Negro Congress member, emphasized Ford's anti-Semitism and the harshness of his industrial relations system. Meier and Rudwick, *Black Detroit and the Rise of the UAW,* 11–14.

"The American workman has to protect himself, and at times has been compelled to restrict members of his own group, and I think that in doing so very often he has been ethically sound." The chief source of problems in black-union relations lay in race leaders like Booker T. Washington and the black press, who allied themselves with employers. Frey accepted their antagonism as justifiable but insisted that blacks could not simultaneously adopt strikebreaking as their strategy and say that union hostility was unwarranted.[57]

Reviewing the conference, Walter White summed up Frey's presentation in *The Nation*. "'Unskilled labor must become skilled before it can gain rights,' he declared; union labor keeps the Negro out of the skilled trades—and the spokesman of the AFL calmly faces an intelligent audience and coolly justifies to his own satisfaction such a course."[58] Frey told William English Walling, a socialist activist and founder of the NAACP, that White's account misrepresented his speech and "is similar to other articles relative to the Negro and our trade union movement which *The Nation* has published in the past," complaining that W. E. B. Du Bois had also made defamatory statements about the AFL.[59] White, unmoved by Frey's complaint, told Walling, "I am inclined to believe that I was very gentle with him."[60] White may have distorted some of Frey's language, but he grasped the upshot of his message. Frey had simply looked at the economics of unionism, explaining that it benefited its members by job control and that nonmembers paid for it. It was cold comfort for blacks to understand that they were not the only outsiders who suffered.[61]

The National Urban League issued a study in 1930 noting that the AFL passed resolutions and "vacuous decrees" on equality, and that it used some black organizers but segregated black members in federal unions and allowed discriminatory national unions to run amok. "It has attempted to live up to its philosophy of liberalism without performing the mechanics necessary to make that liberalism a reality." The AFL, it concluded, had less appeal to blacks now "than at any other time

57. John P. Frey, "Attempts to Organize Negro Workers," *American Federationist* 36 (1929), 296–305 [DH VI: 325].

58. Walter White, "Solving America's Race Problem," *The Nation* 128 (1929), 42–43 [DH VI: 323].

59. Frey to William English Walling, 10 Jan. 1929, Walling Papers, Wisconsin Historical Society [DH VI: 324].

60. White to Walling, 18 Jan. 1929 [NAACP 10, IX: 110].

61. Mary Van Vleck to John Frey, 15 Jan. 1929; Mary White Ovington to Walling, 27 Apr. 1929, John Frey Papers, Box 12, LC; American Management Association, *The Negro in Industry*, 17.

in its history."[62] T. Arnold Hill, the most pro-union official at the league, saw "no real advance in the attitude of organized labor toward colored workers. I can discover no change in practice during the past fifteen years, save the partial victory of the Brotherhood of Sleeping Car Porters."[63]

Black workers had made the best bargain they could in the open-shop part of the economy that recognized them. "Realizing that bemoaning his fate is of little avail, the Negro worker has employed strategies"—individual bargaining, strike-breaking, separate unionism, the use of political influence, and "passing" for white—"that have accelerated his purpose, and in so doing has left open for debate many of the most widely accepted theories of racial inferiority and employment."[64] Like Booker T. Washington, the league believed that blacks could compete economically and that successful competition reduced prejudice. Strike-breaking secured both economic and social benefits. Once the market had brought them into industry, they were in a stronger position to bargain with unions. Thus blacks would receive overtures from white unionists with caution because black workers, feeling their increased power, would suspect that they were ruses.[65] Harvard Law School student and future Communist leader John P. Davis wrote in 1929 that

> Capital has never presented as sinister and malevolent a front to the Negro laborer as have the white labor unions . . . Our liberal white "friends" urge us to wait until they can persuade the white unions to see the light. But who can wait when winter has come and there is no coal, no food? . . . In the face of these facts can you give me any good reason for being a Socialist or joining with the "organized forces of labor to overthrow a despotic capitalistic regime"? Why shouldn't Negro labor organize to defeat every attempt of

62. Reid, *Negro Membership in American Labor Unions*, 32; Charles S. Johnson, "Negro Workers and the Unions," *Survey*, 15 Apr. 1928, pp. 113–15 [SCCF 2719].

63. Hill, "The Present Status of Negro Labor"; Karl F. Phillips to T. Arnold Hill, 15 Jan. 1930 [NUL IV: 1].

64. Reid, *Negro Membership in American Labor Unions*, 23; Scott A. Greer, *Last Man In: Racial Access to Union Power* (Glencoe, 1959), 39.

65. Warren C. Whatley, "African-American Strikebreaking from the Civil War to the New Deal," *Social Science History* 17 (1993), 539, 546; Ira De A. Reid, "The Decline of the Negro Strikebreaker," *New Leader* 21 (1928), 21 [DH VI: 526]. Whatley points out that, while the number of times in which blacks broke strikes in the 1920s may have declined, the percentage of them increased, as there were fewer strikes overall.

white labor to bargain collectively with capital? Why shouldn't we join in this cutthroat game and help capital throttle white labor? This it seems to me is the only way to make white labor see the light. And so I urge all Negro laborers to adopt as their motto: "Hurrah for the Scab and the Open Shop and to Hell with the Unions." [66]

But significant pro-union sentiment had taken root among young black intellectuals. While Davis wrote, Abram Harris was in the middle of his doctoral dissertation at Columbia that soon became a landmark book, *The Black Worker: The Negro and the Labor Movement,* co-authored with Sterling Spero. Harris was born into the Richmond, Virginia, black bourgeoisie in 1899, in the third free generation in his family. He earned a master's degree at the University of Pittsburgh and taught economics at West Virginia Collegiate Institute and then, after a period as head of the Minneapolis Urban League, at Howard University until after World War II. He was one of the leading voices among black Americans for the socialist elements in the "mixed economy" that the New Deal would bring.[67]

Though it catalogued the many attempts by white unions to exclude blacks from jobs, and the black response to them, *The Black Worker* concluded that blacks were no longer an "industrial reserve" but "a regular element in the labor force of nearly every basic industry." He was now "face to face with the problem of working conditions which, though they may contain special elements, are essentially the same as the problems of other workers. They are consequently problems with which the Negro cannot cope successfully without the cooperation of his fellow white workers." The chief obstacles were the craft-consciousness of white unions and the race-consciousness of the black bourgeoisie. Technology might erode the former; the latter might give way to a more sophisticated political consciousness that recognized that "industrial stablilization" was the best hope for the race. Rejecting the competitive strategy of the Urban League, Harris argued that federal control of the economy would "eliminate those competitive elements in industry

---

66. John P. Davis, "The Black Man's Burden," The *Nation* 128 (1929), 44.

67. "Abram Harris," ANB; William Darity Jr., *Race, Radicalism, and Reform: Selected Papers, Abram L. Harris* (New Brunswick, 1989); William Darity Jr. and Julian Ellison, "Abram Harris Jr.: The Economics of Race and Social Reform," *History of Political Economy* 22 (1990), 611–27; Griffler, *What Price Alliance?* 127–28. After moving to the University of Chicago in 1946, Harris turned toward neo-classical economics, though not perhaps as fully as some have claimed. He may also have helped to break a strike by white brickmakers who refused to work with blacks—William M. Ashby to Eugene K. Jones, 23 Sep. 1940 [NUL I: 1].

that redound to the disadvantage of the employees generally and minorities in particular." As much as the white majority, the black minority had to change its habits if the solution of interracial socialism were to be realized. Harris was one of the most important of a group of young black intellectuals who tried to get black organizations like the NAACP to recognize this and to act accordingly.[68]

THE DEPRESSION

The Great Depression of 1929 set in motion seismic economic and political changes, fundamentally altering the labor movement, the black community, and the relationship between the two. Most important, the depression destroyed most of the ambivalence that Americans had maintained since the 1890s about the government's role in the economy. An unprecedentedly activist state would provide opportunities and challenges for radicals and conservatives in both the labor movement and the black world. By the end of the 1930s, the revolutionary National Labor Relations Act (NLRA) had made possible industrial unionism that would organize one-third of American workers. Black Americans were included in these new unions and went from being ardent opponents of organized labor to some of its most fervent allies. Loyal Republicans since emancipation, blacks composed the most committed group in the New Deal Democratic coalition.

Yet many of the first steps toward the New Deal, through the NLRA itself, suggested that the new era might drive blacks and organized labor even farther apart. By 1930, President Hoover had lost control of Congress, as progressive Republicans began to join Democrats, who took control of the House of Representatives in 1931. Hoover ended up presiding over the early stages of what Franklin D. Roosevelt would call the New Deal. His appointment of John J. Parker, a federal appeals court justice from North Carolina, to the Supreme Court provided a rare opportunity for cooperation between black organizations and labor leaders. The AFL mobilized against Parker because he had upheld injunctions and yellow-dog contracts in a 1921 United Mine Workers strike in West Virginia. The NAACP charged that Parker was a racist because he had declared in a 1920 gubernatorial campaign that blacks ought to remain disfranchised.[69]

Parker did get some support from the black community, but the Negro press

---

68. "Abram Harris," ANB; Spero and Harris, *The Black Worker*, 461–49; Lewis, *W. E. B. Du Bois: The Fight for Equality*, 320.

69. O'Brien, *Workers' Paradox*, 160–62; Richard L. Watson Jr., "The Defeat of Judge Parker: A Study in Pressure Groups and Politics," *Mississippi Valley Historical Review* 50 (1963), 213–34.

was solidly behind the NAACP and believed that the AFL would have failed with-out black support.[70] But black opponents did not make any objections to Parker's labor decisions, and the AFL showed no concern for his civil rights record. As Wal-ter White recalled, "The AFL was exceedingly anxious to prevent identification of its opposition to Parker with that of Negroes. Throughout the fight, the AFL state-ments abstemiously refrained from mentioning Parker's anti-Negro stand. Wil-liam Green, president of the AFL, and I entered the hearings room at the same time. Although I had met with him on several occasions before that day, he ap-peared conspicuously to avoid speaking lest senators on the committee, news-papermen, or spectators believe that we were fighting as allies in a common battle."[71] Only Senator Robert F. Wagner of New York attempted to link Parker's opinions on unions and blacks as part of a pattern of indifference to the rights of the vulnerable, a point impressed upon him by A. Philip Randolph.

I see a deep and fundamental consistency between Judge Parker's views of labor relations and his reported attitude toward the colored people of the United States. They both spring from a single trait of character. Judged by the available record, he is obviously incapable of viewing with sympathy the aspirations of those who are aiming for a higher and better place in the world. His sympathies naturally flow out to those who are already on top, and he has used the authority of his office and the influence of his opinion to keep them on top and to restrain the strivings of the others, whether they be an exploited economic group or a minority racial group. Otherwise, would it not be strange that the man whose *Red Jacket* opinion is defended as resulting from the constraint of a Supreme Court precedent should feel so lightly the restraints of the Constitution itself in his expressed views of the colored people?[72]

Most other opponents believed that calling attention to the issue of black vot-ing might turn southern Democratic senators to favor the judge.[73] Some black lib-

---

70. *Congressional Record,* 71st Cong., 2d Sess. (1930), 7811–14; Watson, "The Defeat of Judge Par-ker," 220; Kenneth W. Goings, *The NAACP Comes of Age: The Defeat of Judge John J. Parker* (Blooming-ton, IN, 1990), 29.

71. Walter White, *A Man Called White: The Autobiography of Walter White* (New York, 1948), 106.

72. *Congressional Record,* 71st Cong., 2d Sess. (1930), 8037; Harris, *Keeping the Faith,* 167; Beth Tompkins Bates, *Pullman Porters and the Rise of Protest Politics in Black America, 1925–45* (Chapel Hill, 2001), 109.

73. Goings, *The NAACP Comes of Age,* 31.

erals like Du Bois wishfully saw blacks and the AFL in a joint effort; "The real significance of the vote is the degree to which it foreshadows a union of forces between the liberals and the labor unions, on the one side, and the Negroes, on the other," the editor asserted. But he had to admit that the result showed more coincidence than cooperation. "There was no union of effort as far as the Parker vote was concerned. The AFL in its rejoicing over the result, did not mention the Negro side, and few Negroes said anything about the labor unions."[74] Despite energetic efforts by Hoover and Parker to win confirmation, the Senate rejected the nomination by a vote of 47–49. While there is no telling how Parker might have evolved had he been elevated, the man who won his seat, Owen J. Roberts, ended up providing the crucial fifth vote to uphold New Deal legislation in 1937.[75]

Labor union advocates secured a national "prevailing wage" law to protect white construction workers in the North from competition from black migrants. The New York building trades had persuaded the state legislature to require that building contractors pay the "prevailing," or union, wage on state-funded projects, in order to remove the incentive for contractors to hire nonunion labor. A court had struck down such an act in 1901, but the New York State Court of Appeals sustained the new legislation in 1927. The act did not cover federal construction projects, and Long Island representative Robert Bacon introduced a bill to do so in 1928 after an Alabama contractor used black workers to build a veteran's hospital in his district. A Georgia congressman teased Bacon at his "reaction to that real problem you are confronted with in any community with a superabundance or large aggregation of Negro labor," but Bacon denied that he was motivated by any racial animus. Supporters complained about "imported," "cheap," and "bootleg" labor and saw the act as an extension of the principles of Chinese exclusion and immigration restriction acts. Union witnesses for the bill testified more explicitly. AFL president Green noted that "colored labor is being brought in to demoralize wage rates" in federal projects. Bacon's bill was sponsored in the Senate by James J. Davis, a former iron puddler who had served as Secretary of Labor since 1921 and was elected senator from Pennsylvania in 1930. Davis had been a leading advocate of immigration restriction in the Republican Party. Congress passed and President Hoover signed the Davis-Bacon Act in March 1931. With private construction wiped out by the depression, and the federal government about

74. W. E. B. Du Bois, "The Defeat of Judge Parker," *Crisis* 37 (1930), 248; Lewis, *W. E. B. Du Bois: The Fight for Equality*, 252.

75. Barry Cushman, *Rethinking the New Deal Court: The Structure of a Constitutional Revolution* (New York, 1998), 225.

to become the most important builder in the next decade, the act was a tremendous boost to the power of the AFL building trades.[76]

The AFL also won the enactment of a new federal anti-injunction act. Opponents believed that injunctions were necessary to protect the rights of employers and nonunion workers against the lawless violence and destruction of property that accompanied strikes. The Supreme Court had struck down state anti-injunction acts because they deprived employers of protection of life and property and had also overturned or strictly interpreted federal acts that limited the courts' power to issue injunctions. by 1930, the progressive argument that injunctions had been used unfairly by the courts to cripple labor unions prevailed. Felix Frankfurter's monograph, *The Labor Injunction,* encapsulated law professors' emerging hostility to the labor injunction, and large, progressive industrialists had come around. both political parties called for injunction reform in their 1928 platforms. President Hoover initially tried to derail the bill but in the end signed it and attempted to take credit for its enactment.[77]

Most notably, the Norris–La Guardia Act's statement of national policy expressed the labor movement's premises of industrial conflict. Government had helped corporations attain power, but now "the individual unorganized worker is commonly helpless to exercise actual liberty of contract and to protect his freedom of labor, and thereby to obtain acceptable terms and conditions of employment." Norris–La Guardia recognized the right of an individual worker to stay out of labor organizations, but it was aimed principally at promoting collective bargaining. It outlawed yellow-dog contracts and exempted unions from antitrust prosecution. It widened the definition of "labor disputes" beyond those of employer and employee. Unless actual fraud or violence were involved, federal courts were prohibited from issuing injunctions in labor disputes, and the procedures by which they could do so in cases of fraud and violence were narrowed.[78]

---

76. Bernstein, *Only One Place of Redress,* 71–79; Bernstein, "The Davis-Bacon Act: Vestige of Jim Crow," *National Black Law Journal* 13 (1994), 276–97; Armand Thieblot Jr., *The Davis-Bacon Act* (Philadelphia, 1975), 6–10.

77. *Truax v. Corrigan,* 257 U.S. 312 (1921); *Adair v. U.S.,* 208 U.S. 161 (1908); *Hitchman Coal and Coke Co. v. Mitchell,* 245 U.S. 229 (1917); Felix Frankfurter and Nathan Greene, *The Labor Injunction* (New York, 1930); Dickman, *Industrial Democracy,* 233–41; Lovell, *Legislative Deferrals,* 208; Ernst, "The Yellow-Dog Contract and Liberal Reform, 1917–32," 251–75; Petro, "Injunctions and Labor Disputes"; O'Brien, *Workers' Paradox,* 170.

78. 47 Stat. L. 70 (1932); Reynolds, "An Economic Analysis," 231.

The Norris–La Guardia Act seemed to exemplify AFL "voluntarism," reflecting its argument that unions wanted no special favors from the government—indeed, were suspicious of state grants of privilege that might turn into restrictions—and merely sought to be free from governmental restraint. But by 1932, in the depths of the depression, the AFL had moved beyond any semblance of voluntarism to embrace vigorous state support for unions.[79] The uses to which unions and others would put the act, and the judicial reception and interpretation of it, remained to be seen. These labor acts were part of a general acceleration of a turn away from competition and encouragement of cartels that marked the progressive era. The cutoff of immigration and a higher-than-ever tariff in 1930 were other important pieces.

EARLY NEW DEAL LEGISLATION

The new Roosevelt administration faced many crises in 1933. Black workers had felt the effects of the depression earlier than most Americans, enduring significant unemployment as early as 1927. Black workers tended to be concentrated in "sick industries" like coal, or those affected first in the downturn, like the building trades. As the most recent entrants into many factories, they were the first ones to be laid off, according to both the rule of seniority and the application of discriminatory standards. As the depression worsened, undesirable jobs traditionally held by blacks became attractive to whites, and displacement became a serious problem. Several southern cities enacted ordinances prohibiting black labor from engaging in certain occupations, and vigilante groups like the Atlanta "Black Shirts" attempted to force employers to discharge blacks.[80] Though nobody knew what Roosevelt's promise of a "New Deal" meant for anyone, blacks had good reason to

---

79. Dickman, *Industrial Democracy*, 17; Forbath, *Law and the Shaping of the American Labor Movement*, 165; Lovell, *Legislative Deferrals*, 210.

80. Charles S. Johnson, "Incidence upon the Negroes," *American Journal of Sociology* 40 (1935), 737–45; "Present Trends in Negro Labor"; "Negroes Out of Work," *The Nation* 132 (1931), 441; U.S. Department of Labor, *Monthly Labor Review* 32 (1931), 1326 [DH VI: 76]; T. Arnold Hill, "The Plight of the Negro Industrial Worker," *Journal of Negro Education* 5 (1936), 43; William A. Sundstrom, "Last Hired, First Fired? Unemployment and Urban Black Workers during the Great Depression," *Journal of Economic History* 52 (1992), 415–29; "Instances of Displacement of Negroes with Whites" (1933) [NAACP 10, XI: 942]; Raymond Wolters, *Negroes and the Great Depression: The Problem of Economic Recovery* (Westport, 1970), 114–15; Helen G. Norton, "Whites Force Negroes Out of Jobs in South," Federated Press, 11 May 1929 [SCCF 2708].

be apprehensive about the priorities of a Democratic administration, solidly supported by the AFL and southern whites, for whom very few blacks had voted.

The New Dealers' initial response to the depression was to try to limit competition and production, and to raise prices. Government would encourage and lend force to industrial coordination and cooperation. This was largely an extension of the associationalist policies of the Hoover administration, but Roosevelt added an emphasis on consumer "underconsumption." It would make an effort to redistribute income so that workers would be able to purchase more of the goods that they produced. These elements came together in the bold experiment of the National Industrial Recovery Act (NIRA) of 1933.

The NIRA authorized trade associations and the president to devise "codes of fair competition" for American industries, and it allowed the president to impose a code if industries could not agree on one. Though its language attempted to prohibit "monopoly" and to protect small business, the act was a scheme of government-enforced cartelization. Based on a congressional declaration of "national emergency," it was a tremendous expansion of the associationalist efforts of the Hoover administration, delegating tremendous power to private interests. The act gave trade associations power to enforce virtually whatever standards they wanted.[81] The act also provided two pieces for labor interests: minimum wages in the codes of fair competition, and protection for collective bargaining.

Black organizations soon saw that the wage provisions in the codes of fair competition could be manipulated to harm black workers. Southern manufacturers pressed the National Recovery Administration (NRA, the agency that administered the NIRA) for a racial wage differential, claiming that high industrial wages would lure blacks away from agricultural labor and that black workers were less efficient and could live on lower incomes than whites. Some black leaders recognized that since blacks were concentrated in less efficient, "sweatshop" industries that could stay in business only by their lower labor costs, they were likely to become unemployed if such businesses went bankrupt. It was also likely that white workers would be given jobs that blacks held if the wages for those jobs were increased, aggravating the problem of racial displacement.[82] One of the architects of

81. 48 Stat. 194 (1933); Hawley, *The New Deal and the Problem of Monopoly*, 25; Kelly, Harbison, and Belz, *The American Constitution*, II: 471–74.

82. Wolters, *Negroes and the Great Depression*, 98–135; Donna Cooper Hamilton, "The NAACP and New Deal Reform Legislation: A Dual Agenda," *Social Service Review* 68 (1994), 488–502.

the NRA estimated that its minimum wage provisions cost half a million black Americans their jobs.[83]

Black spokesmen were divided over the issue, but most rejected the idea of a racial wage differential.[84] Robert Russa Moton, Booker T. Washington's successor as president of the Tuskegee Institute, recognized the dilemma, on occasion favoring a differential and on others concluding that "it was preferable that the Negro should be placed on an equal pay basis even if it resulted in hardships caused by their discharge to make way for unemployed whites."[85] The Urban League's T. Arnold Hill called the proposal "economically unsound and morally unjust."[86] Walter White of the NAACP was chagrined that Hill would even discuss the issue. Economist Robert C. Weaver said that it would undermine the progress that Negroes had made proving their efficiency in the last decade and would undermine working-class solidarity. George E. Haynes and John P. Davis formed the Joint Committee on National Recovery, a coalition of twenty-two organizations seeking "the integration of Negroes into the federal recovery program," to lobby for equal treatment in NRA codes. Senator Robert Wagner proposed an amendment to the NIRA to prohibit discrimination, but Congress ignored it. The NRA ultimately did not approve of any explicit racial wage differentials, but black organizations still believed that the act was harming black workers. Clark Foreman, the Interior Department's adviser on Negro affairs, and Gustav Peck, the head of the NRA Labor Advisory Board, argued that black workers had probably benefited more than others from the codes, but their message met a hostile reception. The NRA did nothing for the agricultural and domestic sectors, where most blacks were concentrated.[87]

83. Bernstein, *Only One Place of Redress,* 89.

84. William Pickens, "NRA—Negro Removal Act?" *The World Tomorrow,* 28 Sep. 1933, pp. 539–40 [SCCF 2708]; A. Howard Myers, "The Negro Worker under NRA," *Journal of Negro Education* 5 (1936), 50.

85. Hamilton, "The NAACP and New Deal Reform Legislation," 491; Wolters, *Negroes and the Great Depression,* 104; Julian Harris, "Whites Oust Negro under NRA in South," *New York Times,* 27 Aug. 1933, p. E6 [DH VI: 534].

86. T. Arnold Hill, "An Emergency Is On!" *Opportunity* 11 (1933), 280–81 [DH VI: 85].

87. Walter White to Rose M. Coe, 9 Dec. 1933 [NAACP 10, IX: 441]; Robert C. Weaver, "A Wage Differential Based on Race," *Crisis* 41 (1934), 236 [DH VI: 97]; Walter White to Robert F. Wagner, 29 May 1933 [NAACP 10, IV: 915]; Myers, "The Negro Worker under the NRA"; Gustav Peck, "The Negro Worker and the NRA," *Crisis* 41 (1934), 263 [DH VI: 107]; John P. Davis, "NRA Codifies Wage Slavery," *Crisis* 41 (1934), 298 [DH VI: 110]; Suzanne La Follette, "A Message to Uncle Tom," *The Nation* 139

While it did not approve racial wage differentials, the act did permit regional wage differentials for the South, which often acted as proxies for racial differentials. Blacks were also frequently placed in lower-paid job categories while doing the same work as whites in higher-paid classifications. Yet such loopholes probably preserved black employment. Like most workers and consumers, blacks suffered because the NIRA likely retarded recovery, and raised prices that consumers had to pay. Thus the NRA acquired the sobriquets "Negro Removal Act" and "Negro Run-Around."[88]

The NIRA also tried to raise wages by encouraging collective bargaining. Section 7(a) of the act stated:

> Every code of fair competition, agreement, and license approved, prescribed, or issued under this title shall contain the following conditions: (1) That employees shall have the right to organize and bargain collectively through representatives of their own choosing, and shall be free from the interference, restraint, or coercion of employers of labor, or their agents, in the designation of such representatives or in self-organization or in other concerted activities for the purpose of collective bargaining or other mutual aid or protection (2) that no employee and no one seeking employment shall be required as a condition of employment to join any company union or to refrain from joining, organizing, or assisting a labor organization of his own choosing.

The administration supported this section to win the AFL away from Alabama senator Hugo Black's bill to limit the work week to thirty hours. But it contained no means of enforcement, even after the president established a National Labor Board to mediate disputes under it. Since it did not specify what kinds of representation were acceptable, most employers continued to use "company unions." Though the AFL added some 2 million new members, including new organizations in the

---

(1934), 265; The Agricultural Adjustment Act, which raised farm prices by lowering production, drove thousands if not hundreds of thousands of black tenants and sharecroppers off the land. It is widely regarded as the New Deal policy that was most inimical to blacks. Paul Moreno, "An Ambivalent Legacy: Black Americans and the New Deal Political Economy," *Independent Review* 6 (2002), 513–39.

88. Jim F. Couch and William F. Shugart, *The Political Economy of the New Deal* (Cheltenham, UK, 1998), xiv, 77; Harvard Sitkoff, *A New Deal for Blacks: The Emergence of Civil Rights as a National Issue* (New York, 1978), 54.

mass-production industries, these gains were uncertain, and there were more strikes in 1933 than in any year since 1921.[89]

Black leaders feared that AFL unions would use section 7(a) to monopolize jobs for white craftsmen, and several examples of their doing so confirmed those concerns. Roy Wilkins, NAACP secretary, wrote in 1934, "While the AFL was seizing upon section 7(a) to carry out the most stupendous drive for membership in its history, it was doing little or nothing to include Negroes in the organizing. As a matter of fact, we strongly suspect, although we cannot prove, that AFL unions have attempted to use section 7(a) to drive Negroes out of certain occupations." The Urban League charged that a steel workers' strike in Milwaukee was aimed at the discharge of black workers. In Kansas City, the Urban League feared that politically influential AFL building trades would use city ordinances to prevent black janitors from "chiseling" on plumbing jobs.[90] Du Bois wrote in *The Crisis* that "the most sinister power that the NRA has reinforced is the American Federation of Labor." "Seeking to avail itself of the powers granted under section 7(a) of the NRA, union labor strategy seems to be to form a union in a given plant, strike to obtain the right to bargain with the employer as the sole representative of labor, and then to close the union to black workers, effectively cutting them off from employment." These officials hoped that the AFL would soften its position and continued to support the organization of black workers under section 7(a), but their local affiliates sometimes actively undermined the unionization effort. Black community leaders often depended on the philanthropy of industrialists and had experienced the discriminatory treatment of white unionists. Some recognized the opportunities to blacks of a free labor market. "If the Negro exercises his position as a minority group and plays the management against the remaining workers, he will get more thereby," wrote a Chicago Urban League member in 1934. "I would go further and even suggest that Negroes go in as strikebreakers, provided they were retained when the strike was over."[91]

The separate field of railroad labor legislation showed more clearly the effect of discriminatory union power. Railroad employment fell from 1.6 million to less

89. James A. Gross, *The Making of the National Labor Relations Board: A Study in Economics, Politics, and the Law* (Albany, NY, 1974), 11–23; Zieger, *John L. Lewis*, 67–75.

90. Thomas A. Webster to T. Arnold Hill, 2 Aug. 1933 [NUL IV: 1].

91. Wolters, *Negroes and the Great Depression*, 169–78, 182; Catyon and Mitchell, *Black Workers and the New Unions*, 413, 407; *Crisis* 40 (1933), 292 [DH VI: 338]; "Union Labor Again," *Crisis* 41 (1934), 300.

than 1 million during the depression, and black jobs as firemen and trainmen became increasingly coveted. In the Deep South, assaults and assassinations, widely believed to be orchestrated by the Brotherhood of Locomotive Firemen, removed ten blacks from the roads.[92] The railroad unions acquired more power by amendments to the Railway Labor Act in 1934, which provided for exclusive, majority-rule unionism. The 1926 act required operators to bargain with worker organizations, but there might be several unions in each craft—separate black organizations among them. The new act also abolished company unions. The white railroad unions used this power to intensify their campaign to eliminate black railroad workers.

T. Arnold Hill warned, "During recent years considerable new federal legislation has been enacted to improve the railroads and promote the welfare of employees working on them. Concurrently with this legislation, the condition of Negroes engaged in train and yard service has grown steadily worse." The National Mediation Board (NMB) and National Railroad Adjustment Board recognized only white unions and aided their efforts to displace black workers—indeed, they seemed to try to accelerate the campaign. "One cannot avoid receiving the impression that the Board regards collective bargaining in the train and engine services as strictly a white man's affair," economist Herbert Northrup concluded in 1944. "In no other industry has collective bargaining had such disastrous results for Negroes." Though the act would help A. Philip Randolph's Brotherhood of Sleeping Car Porters gain recognition from the Pullman Company and get an international charter from the AFL, it deprived most other black railroad workers of bargaining rights and jobs. Black railroad employment was halved in the 1930s, from 143,000 to 75,000. Congress ignored black appeals to amend the Railway Labor Act. In 1943, black station porters ("red caps") were able to overturn a NMB ruling, convincing a federal court that the white freight handlers union could not fairly represent blacks when it barred them from membership, but the Supreme Court overturned the decision, ruling that NMB orders were entitled to overwhelming judicial deference.[93]

In 1936 Congress extended the Railway Labor Act to air transportation, ensur-

---

92. *Pittsburgh Courier,* 4 Feb. 1933; Hilton Butler, "Murder for the Job," *The Nation* 137 (1933), 44; Ira De A. Reid to *The Nation* 137 (1933), 273 [DH VI: 306–8].

93. Bernstein, *Only One Place of Redress,* 59–62; Northrup, *Organized Labor and the Negro,* 52–100; Arnesen, *Brotherhoods of Color,* 86, 116–38; T. Arnold Hill, "Railway Employees Rally to Save Their Jobs," *Opportunity* 12 (1934), 346 [DH VI: 309].

ing that blacks would not be able to enter this growing field even as they were being eliminated from the railroads. The machinists, airline clerks, and pilot unions all barred blacks from membership. "In retrospect," two economists wrote, "it is likely that few public policy decisions pertaining to industrial relations have been more unfortunate. This is so for industrial relations in general; it is even more the case insofar as Negro air transport employment is concerned."[94]

Neither the NRA codes nor section 7(a) was vigorously enforced, which probably prevented them from inflicting too much harm on black workers. "Colored workers were fortunate that section 7(a) did not adequately safeguard labor's right to organize independent unions," one historian has concluded.[95] But Roosevelt and the New Deal continued to gain black support, particularly due to relief payments, and black organizations hoped that labor legislation could be improved.

RACE-SPECIFIC NEW DEAL POLICIES

Some New Dealers did make special efforts to take black concerns into consideration. Harold Ickes, the Secretary of the Interior who oversaw $3 billion in Public Works Administration spending under the NRA, tried to ensure that blacks received a fair share of federal largesse. Ickes had been the president of the Chicago NAACP in the 1920s and established an "Interdepartmental Group Concerned with the Special Problems of the Negro Population" in the Interior Department, led by Clark Foreman, a southern white liberal, and Robert C. Weaver. Ickes issued a nondiscrimination order in September 1933, and the Interdepartmental Group devised a definition of discrimination to help enforce it. Contractors were required to employ, at a minimum, the same percentage of Negroes in various skilled trades in a city as was found in each of these trades in the 1930 census. Forty years later, Weaver called this "the first affirmative action program in the federal government." Contractors usually met their quotas, though they were of doubtful legality, and the government did not go beyond this effort to preserve the 1930 status quo. Several other New Deal agencies applied similar quota systems, particularly the U.S. Housing Administration, when Weaver moved there in 1937.[96] "It might

94. Herbert R. Northrup and Armand J. Thieblot Jr., *The Negro in the Air Transport Industry* (Philadelphia, 1971), 62.

95. Wolters, *Negroes and the Great Depression*, 147, 182.

96. Paul Moreno, "Racial Proportionalism and the Origins of Employment Discrimination Policy, 1933–50," *Journal of Policy History* 8 (Fall 1996), 426–28; Sigmund Shipp, "Building Bricks without Straw: Robert C. Weaver and Negro Industrial Employment, 1934–44," in Henry Louis Taylor Jr., and

be rationally argued that Negroes should receive their pro-rata share of unskilled, skilled, and even professional positions according to their population proportion," Charles S. Johnson mused in 1932, "But there is no dictator to enforce such specious evenhandedness."[97]

Some black activists tried to turn the growing power of labor organization to their own ends in the "Don't Buy Where You Can't Work" campaigns that erupted in nearly every large city in the 1930s. Black organizations, usually of middle-class and often of nationalist or Garveyite orientation, boycotted and picketed businesses that did not employ blacks in black neighborhoods. This was the sort of petit bourgeois self-help strategy that Booker T. Washington had recommended, but it used the tactics of labor unions. Many states had followed Congress and enacted "little Norris–La Guardia acts" that prohibited courts from issuing injunctions in "labor disputes." Though several state courts and the District of Columbia courts refused to extend the definition of "labor dispute" to these kinds of actions, by 1938 the U.S. Supreme Court approved of picketing to protest job discrimination. In New York, the protesters formed a permanent black AFL—the Afro-American Federation of Labor, later the Harlem Labor Union.[98]

Black leaders were divided over the direct action campaigns. The young, class-conscious group led by Abram Harris was trying to bring blacks into an alliance with the labor movement and saw the boycott campaign as a divisive distraction. Blacks might gain a handful of jobs in their neighborhoods, but they would make no inroads into the mass-production industries at the center of the economy. They invited white retaliation and further isolated blacks from cooperation with white labor. William Hastie, by contrast, lent his support to the campaign, arguing that

---

Walter Hill, eds., *Historical Roots of the Urban Crisis: African Americans in the Industrial City, 1900–50* (New York, 2000), 233; Robert C. Weaver, "An Experiment in Negro Labor," *Opportunity* 14 (1936), 295–98; Northrup, *Organized Labor and the Negro*, 33, 37, 44; Mark W. Kruman, "Quotas for Blacks: The PWA and the Black Construction Worker," *Labor History* 16 (1975), 37–49; Wolters, *Negroes and the Great Depression*, 196–209.

97. Charles S. Johnson, "The New Frontier of Negro Labor," *Opportunity* 10 (1932), 168–73 [DH VI: 79].

98. Moreno, "Racial Proportionalism," 410–26; August Meier and Elliott Rudwick, "The Origins of Nonviolent Direct Action," in Meier and Rudwick, eds., *Along the Color Line* (Urbana, 1976), 313–88; *New Negro Alliance v. Sanitary Grocery Co.*, 303 U.S. 552 (1938); Charles Lionel Franklin, *The Negro Labor Unionist of New York* (New York, 1936), 137; Claude McKay, "Labor Steps Out in Harlem," *The Nation* 145 (1937), 399.

"intelligently controlled racialism" could help bring about the end of discrimination. W. E. B. Du Bois had also embraced the idea of "segregation without discrimination" in 1934, a bold and controversial ideological statement that ended his formal association with the integrationist NAACP. Twenty-five years after helping to found the association in opposition to Washington's leadership, Du Bois had embraced some of his ideas, and he now accused his critics in the NAACP of not being black or race-conscious enough, as he had been accused by Garvey a decade before. The NAACP and the Urban League gave tepid support to the boycott strategy, which never developed into a sustained, large-scale movement.[99]

<h2 style="text-align:center">THE NATIONAL LABOR RELATIONS ACT</h2>

The weakness of section 7(a) led Senator Wagner to prepare a stronger measure to promote organized labor. Wagner's bill—the Trade Disputes Act of 1934, revised into the National Labor Relations Act of 1935—put into statutory form the protections for unions that the NRA labor boards had tried to develop. The act embraced the principles of compulsory and majority unionism, which would compel employers to bargain exclusively with the organization chosen by a majority of their employees. It would prohibit a number of "unfair practices," outlawing company unions and any employer interference with the right of workers to form independent unions. In particular, employers could not discriminate against workers on the basis of union activity. Employers would also be obliged to bargain with these organizations. In addition to the right to strike and picket that the Norris–La Guardia Act protected, the act explicitly allowed strikes and implied that striking workers would be given preference over replacements after a strike was settled. The act established a new, independent, "quasi-judicial" National Labor Relations Board empowered to issue enforceable orders, no longer attempting to bring management and unions together to mediate disputes.[100]

The Wagner Act provided no protection for black workers against discrimination by these more powerful unions. This raised the larger problem of "minority rights" in a system of majority unionism. Employers complained that workers who did not want to join independent unions would be forced into them; union advo-

---

99. "To Boycott or Not to Boycott," *Crisis* 41 (1934), 258; Lewis, *W. E. B. Du Bois: The Struggle for Equality*, 331–42.

100. 49 Stat. L. 449 (1935); Irving Bernstein, *The New Deal Collective Bargaining Policy* (Berkeley, 1950), 18, 129; Gross, *The Making of the National Labor Relations Board*, 52, 88.

cates saw this concern for minority rights as a pretext for preserving the open shop. Nor did the bill define any union activity as an "unfair labor practice" or impose any obligations on labor organizations. An early draft of Wagner's bill contained a nondiscrimination clause, but the AFL insisted that it be dropped.[101]

The NAACP believed that the majority-rule provision was "fraught with grave danger to Negro labor. This is an act which rigidly enforces and legalizes the closed shop . . . [T]he act plainly empowers organized labor to exclude from employment in any industry all workers who do not belong to a union. It is needless to point out the fact that thousands of Negro workers are barred from membership in American labor unions and, therefore, that if the closed shop is legalized by this act Negro workers will be absolutely shut out of employment." The association recommended an amendment that would ensure that closed shops be "valid only when it can be shown by such labor organization that it imposes no inequitable restrictions on its membership, such as limiting it because of race, creed, or color." William Green, president of the AFL, refused to support any such amendment.[102] At its annual convention in June, the NAACP resolved, "We welcome the growth of labor consciousness but we again warn the leadership of organized white labor, especially the AFL and railroad brotherhoods, they can never attain freedom for their groups by climbing on the backs of black labor. We urge all workers, white and black, to speed industrial as against craft unionism."[103]

While the NAACP held back and hoped to win a floor amendment, the National Urban League testified against the bill in Senate hearings. T. Arnold Hill noted that the league approved of "any measure that seeks to equalize the bargaining power of employers and employees, and encourage the amicable settlement of disputes . . . But, inequalities of bargaining power handicapping more than 5,000,000 Negro workers compel us to register this definite protest against the adoption of the Wagner bill in its present form." The bill would continue to allow unions to bar blacks from membership and would provide no protection for blacks who were admitted to white unions but discriminated against within them.

101. Gross, *Making of the National Labor Relations Board,* 97; Bernstein, *New Deal Collective Bargaining Policy,* 98–105; Dulles, *Labor in America,* 275; Walter White to Harry E. Davis, 23 Mar. 1934 [NAACP 10, IV: 976]; Wolters, *Negroes and the Great Depression,* 185 .

102. "Suggested amendment to Wagner bill," 23 Mar. 1934 [NAACP 10, IV: 975]; Walter White to William Green, 17 Apr. 1934; Green to White, 2 May 1934 [NAACP 10, IV: 1011, 1023].

103. *Crisis* 42 (1935), 250; Walter White to Matthew Dunn, 7 Jun. 1940 [NAACP 13-B, XXIII: 793].

Nor did the bill provide any protection for black strikebreakers. "While we deplore the necessity for strikebreaking, we hold that it is the one weapon left to the Negro worker whereby he may break the stranglehold that certain organized labor groups have utilized in preventing his complete absorption into the American labor market." Blacks would remain in segregated unions, which would weaken the bargaining power of all workers.[104] An attorney noted, "One does not have to be a pessimist to see danger to the Negro worker in the program that organized labor is seeking." The *Indianapolis Recorder* called the bill "nothing but a contraption of the labor unions intended to legalize what is now a fixed determination on the part of those organizations to deny the Negro of his right to earn a living."[105]

Wagner did not have President Roosevelt's support for his bill until after the Supreme Court struck down the NIRA late in May 1935, and FDR was unwilling to antagonize the AFL. When the president threw his weight behind the bill it passed quickly, without any substantial amendment. Thirty-five years later, Lester Granger of the Urban League called the Wagner Act "the worst piece of legislation ever passed by the Congress." While black organizations feared its effect, many believed along with many of the act's framers and supporters that it would be overturned by the Court as unconstitutional.[106]

Events at the annual AFL convention later that year reinforced the fear that organized labor did not take black interests seriously but offered hope that new forces in the federation might provide an egalitarian alternative. In 1934 the AFL had resolved to appoint a committee to study the problem of discrimination and recommend remedies. President William Green appointed a committee of five, which held a set of hearings in Washington in July 1935. Though all white, none of the committee members represented a constitutionally exclusive union and one, John Brophy of the mine workers, had a reputation for concern for black interests. Though civil rights groups were preparing for further hearings, Green told the

104. Brief of T. Arnold Hill, *Legislative History of the National Labor Relations Act, 1935* (Washington, 1985), 1058–60; Eugene Kinckle Jones to Walter White, 10 May 1940 [NAACP 13-B, XXIII: 733]; T. Arnold Hill, "Labor Marches On," *Opportunity* 12 (1934), 121.

105. Leon P. Miller, "The Negro and the 'Closed Shop,'" *Opportunity* 13 (1935), 168; Emma Lou Thornbrough, *Indiana Blacks in the Twentieth Century* (Bloomington, 2000), 109.

106. Gross, *Making of the National Labor Relations Board*, 140–49; O'Brien, *Workers' Paradox*, 198; Nancy J. Weiss, *The National Urban League, 1910–40* (New York, 1974), 275; Hamilton, "The NAACP and New Deal Reform Legislation," 493; Marian C. McKenna, *Franklin Roosevelt and the Great Constitutional War: The Court-Packing Crisis of 1937* (New York, 2002), 327.

committee to prepare a report after its initial one. The committee recommended that all discriminatory unions revise their constitutions, that the federation admit no more discriminatory affiliates, and that it begin an educational campaign to teach white workers the value of fairness. Green withheld the committee's report and substituted a milder one written by George Harrison, the president of the white-only Railway Clerks Union. Even this he delayed until late in the evening of the last day of the convention. When A. Philip Randolph complained, Green responded that the federation could not dictate membership terms to affiliates. "I don't know why the AFL is repeatedly denounced by those who represent Negro academic organizations as standing in the way of colored workers when we have made our declaration, we stand up and defend it," he concluded. Harrison argued that his union treated black railway clerks with "complete economic equality" but that he did not want to recognize the "social equality" that admission would imply.[107]

This latest side-stepping of the race issue was overshadowed by the chief controversy at the 1935 convention, the fight between the advocates of industrial unionism and those of craft unionism. Led by John L. Lewis of the mine workers, the industrial unionists believed that the AFL had squandered the opportunity to organize the mass-production industries as its craftsmen squabbled over jurisdiction. The highlight of the Atlantic City convention came when carpenter union president William Hutcheson denounced Lewis with a vile imprecation and Lewis replied with a right fist to his jaw. The press reported that the "heads of the two largest and most powerful unions in the federation crashed to the floor pummeling at each other until separated by other delegates." Lewis, David Dubinsky, and Sidney Hillman of the garment workers, and Charles Howard of the typographers formed a Committee on Industrial Organization the day after the convention. This would soon break away as the Congress of Industrial Organizations, initiating the great schism of organized labor.[108]

107. Wolters, *Negroes and the Great Depression*, 179–81; Louis Stark, "AFL Warned on Bar to Negroes," *New York Times*, 10 Jul. 1935, p. 9; Edward Levinson, "AFL Ignores Data on Problems of Negro Bias," *New York Post*, 11 Oct. 1935 [SCCF 2719]; *Report of Proceedings of the 55th Annual Convention of the AFL* (Washington, 1935), 808–19, 827–29 [DH VI: 363]. Because of his education and elocution, and due to the fact that he had never actually worked as a porter, AFL members often depicted Randolph as an academic or political, rather than genuine trade union, figure.

108. Zieger, *John L. Lewis*, 82–84; Louis Stark, "Fist Fight Puts AFL in Uproar," *New York Times*, 20 Oct. 1935, p. 22.

Many had reason to hope that the Wagner Act and CIO could bring about a new deal in organized labor. Though Lewis had begun his rise to power as a defender of Samuel Gompers against black miners' complaints of racial discrimination in the AFL and had wrecked the miners union in the 1920s, the UMW's industrial organization had made room for blacks in the South and southern Appalachia and earned the reputation as among the most egalitarian of AFL unions. The needle trades were also prominent among black-friendly organizations. In the next decade, these breakaway organizations would provide the most important opening for black-union rapprochement in American history.[109]

109. Melvyn Dubofsky and Warren Van Tine, *John L. Lewis: A Biography* (New York, 1977), 25; Franklin, *The Negro Labor Unionist of New York,* 87.

5 / The New Deal and World War

The CIO's effort to organize mass-production industries compelled it to take black workers into account. But neither the leaders of the CIO nor their founding documents emphasized the principle of racial equality. The CIO constitution did declare its goal to organize "the working men and women of America regardless of race, creed, color, or nationality," but this was no more than the AFL's constitution held. The egalitarianism of the national unions that composed the congress held out promise, but their racial policies still had to be prudent. The CIO followed the example of the United Mine Workers in the South—black workers were simply too numerous in the steel, meatpacking, rubber, and auto industries to exclude. The federation tended from the outset to blame employers or rival unions for racial unrest and to overlook the problem among its own rank and file.[1]

Lewis made steel the focus of the CIO's first organizing drive. The open-shop citadel employed over eighty thousand blacks, whom many credited or blamed for the failure of the 1919 strike. The Steel Workers Organizing Committee (SWOC) took blacks into locals by the "UMW formula"—mixed locals with a white president and a black vice-president. This was one of the devices by which the UMW had appealed to blacks, but the SWOC and CIO in general were very reluctant to appear to be giving special recognition to blacks. The union adhered to a "color blind" racial policy and denied any desire for "social equality" or "reverse discrimination."[2]

The SWOC used black organizers to bring suspicious blacks into the union, and it was willing to use communists to do so. This was primarily a matter of necessity, for communists were among the few experienced black organizers. The Communist Party (CP) was more than willing to help, for coincident with the Wagner Act was the adoption of the Comintern's "Popular Front" policy, instructing communists to cooperate with nonfascist parties in democratic states. Although the party had opposed the Wagner Act and the New Deal, it now threw itself into the CIO effort, abandoning its separate unions and returning to a policy

1. August Meier and Eliot Rudwick, *Black Detroit and the Rise of the UAW* (New York, 1979), 24–28; Robert H. Zieger, *The CIO: 1935–55* (Chapel Hill, 1995), 82–84; Kenneth Robert Janken, *White: The Biography of Walter White, Mr. NAACP* (New York, 2003), 244.

2. Philip S. Foner, *Organized Labor and the Black Worker, 1619–1981* (New York, 1982), 218; Bruce Nelson, *Divided We Stand: American Workers and the Struggle for Black Equality* (Princeton, 2001), 190; Zieger, *The CIO,* 83–85.

of "boring from within." The Wagner Act and National Labor Relations Board helped communists to increase their influence in the American labor movement. Fearing that communists were using unionization as a way to bring blacks into the party and to take over American unions, American union leaders still knew that association with communism was an albatross—one that had helped to kill the 1919 steel campaign. National Urban League officials were careful to avoid communist takeover of the "workers councils" that it had established to educate black workers about the benefits of organization. Lewis had no illusions about communist participation in the CIO drive. He had used the accusation of communism in his rise to power in the UMW—John Brophy, the leader of the AFL Committee of Five, had been the target of his "red-baiting" in the previous decade but was now his lieutenant. But the canny Lewis believed that he could use and dispense with communists; as he confidently put it, "Who gets the bird: the hunter or the dog?" In the 1930s, the specter of fascism did more to promote new unionism than the fear of communism did to impede it. But in the long run, the taint of communism in the CIO meant that there were many birds that neither the hunter nor the dog would get.[3]

The violence of the CIO campaign posed a problem to many Americans, including many blacks. Despite the Wagner Act's emphasis on industrial peace, the number of strikes rose dramatically after it passed. Just as most black leaders did not want their race associated with alien ideologies like communism, so they also feared that the violence of strikes and picketing could turn into racial violence, as it had in the past. The AFL had used the instruments of coercion more cautiously, but they had always been part of organized labor's tool kit. The CIO was ready to use more and different kinds of force, and black workers faced intimidation from both union organizers and employers.[4]

3. Resolutions of the 7th World Congress of the Communist International, Aug. 1935, in Robert V. Daniels, ed., *A Documentary History of Communism*, 2 vols. (New York, 1960), II: 114–17; Theda Skocpol and Kenneth Finegold, "Explaining New Deal Labor Policy," *American Political Science Review* 84 (1990), 1303; T. Arnold Hill to Lester Granger, 7 Oct. 1935; Granger to Hill, 8 Oct. 1935 [NUL IV: 1]; Horace R. Cayton and George S. Mitchell, *Black Workers and the New Unions* (Chapel Hill, 1939), 118, 157; Nelson, *Divided We Stand*, 103, 193; Robert H. Zieger, *John L. Lewis: Labor Leader* (Boston, 1988), 42; Zieger, *The CIO*, 82; Jerold Auerbach, *Labor and Liberty: The La Follette Committee and the New Deal* (Indianapolis, 1966), 151.

4. George L. Schuyler, *Pittsburgh Courier*, 24 Jul. 1937 [DH VII: 51]; Sylvester Petro, "Injunctions and Labor Disputes: 1880–1932," *Wake Forest Law Review* 14 (1978), 402; Gwendolyn Mink, *Old Labor and New Immigrants in American Political Development: Union, Party, and State, 1875–1920* (Ithaca, NY, 1986), 25; Susan Olzak, "Labor Unrest, Immigration, and Ethnic Conflict in Urban America, 1880–

Just as the taint of communism mattered less in the 1930s than it had earlier (and would later), so union violence did not meet the reception that it formerly had. The Norris–La Guardia Act now prevented federal courts from enjoining picketing in labor disputes. Many states had adopted similar laws, and courts were willing to take a more liberal view of what constituted "violence, intimidation, or harm," which were still enjoinable. The Wagner Act's provision that labor unions should be free of employer interference gave unions a better defense for forceful tactics when employers resisted the act, as many of them did while it was challenged in the courts. Most important, state and local officials were less willing to use police to intervene in labor clashes. The first successful organization of a large meatpacking plant occurred in Minnesota in 1933, where Farmer-Labor authorities did not act against assaults and vandalism by Hormel workers.[5] Lewis acutely grasped the importance of state support for the success of industrial unionism, and went all out to reelect President Roosevelt in 1936 and to continue the replacement of Republican state and local officials.

Michigan governor Frank Murphy's decision not to intervene in the General Motors "sit-down strikes" in the winter of 1936–37 provided the most dramatic instance of the new position of the state in labor disputes. In a sit-down strike, used sporadically since 1933, the workers occupied and refused to vacate their place of employment, rather than patrol the establishment from the outside. Murphy declared in his January 1937 inaugural address that he would not use force to settle the strike, and the strikers were able to defy court injunctions that Murphy refused to enforce. The White House also pressured GM to negotiate with the union. Company officials realized that the 1936 election indicated public approval of the new regime, and they were also eager to avoid violence. One did not have to be a nineteenth-century proponent of laissez-faire to see the sit-down strike as a gross violation of property rights, and a public reaction to the tactic did set in, especially when it spread after GM settled with the UAW in February.[6]

1914," *American Journal of Sociology* 94 (1989), 1303–33; Carroll R. Daugherty et al., *The Economics of the Iron and Steel Industry*, 2 vols. (New York, 1937), II: 957; Nelson, *Divided We Stand*, 197.

5. David Plotke, "The Wagner Act, Again: Politics and Labor, 1935–37," *Studies in American Political Development* 3 (1989), 145; Roger Horowitz, *"Negro and White, Unite and Fight!" A Social History of Industrial Unionism in Meatpacking, 1930–90* (Urbana, 1997), 35.

6. Sidney Fine, "The General Motors Sit-Down Strike: A Re-Examination," *American Historical Review* 70 (1965), 691–713; Barbara S. Griffith, *The Crisis of American Labor: Operation Dixie and the Defeat of the CIO* (Philadelphia, 1988), 9.

At the same time that governments withdrew support for employer resistance to union organization, a public campaign to remove companies' private defense weapons got under way. Pennsylvania, which had permitted corporations to maintain private police forces—the notorious "coal and iron police"—now prohibited them. The overwhelmingly Democratic Congress elected in 1936 did its part to encourage labor organization. Congress outlawed the interstate transportation of strikebreakers and prohibited companies that did not bargain with unions from holding federal contracts.[7] The Senate Education and Labor Committee, under Robert M. La Follette Jr., began an investigation to expose the ways that employers foiled labor organization, particularly by the use of private detectives or "labor spies." "Labor wants this investigation pressed home and wants industry disarmed lest laboring men on their march to industrial democracy should have to take by storm the barbed-wire barricades and machine-gun emplacements maintained by the rapacious moguls of corporate industry," Lewis thundered.[8]

At the height of the New Deal, the old idea of liberty of contract was swept away by the idea of using government power to promote unionization, and "union" was increasingly used as a synonym for "labor." The chief architect of the La Follette investigation was Heber Blankenhorn, who had been the secretary to the Interchurch World Movement's Commission of Inquiry in the 1919 steel strike. He understood the value of propaganda and hoped that the La Follette committee would be more successful than the 1919 steel report had been. Others were communists. The influence of communists within the CIO and the committee was less of a problem, since in the 1930s the specter of fascism loomed larger than that of communism. "Once unionization came to be equated with freedom, the Left saw in every antilabor gesture the precursor of domestic fascism," observed one historian of the committee. "Antifascism, in the guise of a civil libertarian crusade, appealed to the Left, which often manipulated the Bill of Rights and labor organization for ends having little to do with civil liberties."[9]

The La Follette committee worked closely with the CIO, particularly to counter the bad publicity that the sit-down strikes were giving the organizers. It made no

7. William E. Leuchtenburg, *Franklin D. Roosevelt and the New Deal* (New York, 1963), 242; Philip Taft and Philip Ross, "American Labor Violence: Its Causes, Character, and Outcome," in Hugh Davis Graham and Ted Robert Gurr, eds., *The History of Violence in America* (New York, 1969), 317.

8. "Coal Pact Broken, J. L. Lewis Charges," *New York Times*, 1 Jan. 1937, p. 9.

9. Auerbach, *Labor and Liberty*, 166–69, 27.

pretence of objectivity. The committee's goal was to expose the grossest and most sensational examples of employer repression. It was not above using the methods of the agencies that it targeted, taking the advice of an NLRB lawyer to sift secretly through the wastebaskets of detective agencies. It helped to vindicate the Chicago demonstrators who were the victims of the 1937 "Memorial Day Massacre," in which ten strikers were killed by Chicago police outside the Republic Steel plant. President Roosevelt captured the public ambivalence about industrial violence when he pronounced "a plague on both your houses" after the incident, but it was the last large-scale bloodletting in an American labor dispute. Roosevelt continued to support the La Follette committee's work, which nearly brought to an end the ability of employers to protect themselves against union coercion. By the mid-1930s, the public had come to believe that such employer efforts were the chief cause of labor violence.[10]

It is notable that the La Follette committee did not consider the fomenting of racial hostility to be one of the devices used by strikebreaking organizations, particularly since this was a prominent element in communist theory. Communists believed that capitalists used racism in an effort to prevent the working class from developing class consciousness, in something like a "divide-and-conquer" tactic. The CIO provided most of the direction of the committee, so evidently it did not regard employer manipulation of racial differences as an important obstacle.[11]

Though Lewis had mixed feelings about the sit-down tactic, he took advantage of it and won the organization's first great victory in February 1937, when General Motors agreed to bargain with the UAW. Blacks played almost no role in these strikes. They did not compose a large part of any auto manufacturing work force outside of Ford, and those who worked for GM neither occupied nor tried to reopen the plants. Black workers did help Ford defeat a May 1937 UAW campaign, clashing with organizers in the "Battle of the Overpass," in which members of the

10. Ibid., 108, 93, 113–14, 120; Taft and Ross, "American Labor Violence," 361; Robert G. Anderson, "The Redistribution of Wealth—Labor Union Style," in Hans F. Sennholz, ed., *American Unionism: Fallacies and Follies* (Irvington, NY, 1994), 148; Walter Gordon Merritt, *Destination Unknown: Fifty Years of Labor Relations* (New York, 1951), 190.

11. James B. Carey, "Race Hate: Newest Union-Busting Weapon," *The Progressive* 22 (1958), 16; Walter Reuther to Lister Hill, 11 Feb. 1964, *Congressional Record*, 8 Apr. 1964, pp. 7206–07. Cf. Carey Speech to NAACP, 12 Jul. 1944 [NUL IV: 10].

company's notorious "service department" were photographed thrashing several UAW organizers, but the majority of the loyal workers at Ford were white.[12]

The steel campaign facilitated the forging of the black-CIO alliance, but the recruitment of black members was not a high priority for the SWOC.[13] In November 1936, Philip Murray expressed his disappointment at the black response to SWOC overtures and said that he expected that "the organization of the Negro steel worker will follow, rather than precede, the organization of white mill workers."[14] But the CIO did reach out to blacks, helping to finance the National Negro Congress (NNC), which John P. Davis formed as the radical successor to the Joint Committee on National Reconstruction. Black organizations remained cautious as the CIO campaign got under way. Claude Barnett, president of the Associated Negro Press, remained hostile to organized labor and tried to help U.S. Steel managers curry favor with their black workers. He advised them that black workers were usually loyal to business owners who had opened their doors to them, and suspicious of unions that had tried to exclude them. The CIO, he warned, presented a different prospect due to its roots in the egalitarian Mine Workers Union. The steel industry had not shown enough gratitude toward black loyalty, Barnett reported, and believed that they had not gotten adequate opportunity to advance out of hot-and-heavy jobs.[15]

Other black newspapers supported the steel campaign.[16] The national offices of the NAACP and Urban League began to take steps toward the CIO, while local branches often remained indifferent or positively hostile. The Urban League's director of industrial relations, Harold D. Gould, told Secretary of Labor Frances Perkins in 1934 that blacks had made progress in steel occupations and retained jobs during the depression. "We see then that although the open shop policy in the steel corporation may not on the whole be considered beneficial to labor, nevertheless it has offered substantial opportunities to Negroes . . . Departure from this

12. Lloyd H. Bailer, "The Automobile Unions and Negro Labor," *Political Science Quarterly* 59 (1944), 550–52; Bailer, "The Negro in the Automobile Industry" (Ph.D. diss., University of Michigan, 1943), 197–202; Herbert R. Northrup, *Organized Labor and the Negro* (New York, 1944), 191.

13. Nelson, *Divided We Stand*, 190.

14. Meier and Rudwick, *Black Detroit and the Rise of the UAW*, 25.

15. Ibid., 28; Nelson, *Divided We Stand*, 179; Claude Barnett to J. Carlisle MacDonald, 31 Oct. 1936 [CBP IX: 942]; "Special Memo to Mr. Barnett," c. 1936 [CBP X: 22].

16. "Negro Workers Face Big Opportunity to Better Conditions," *Chicago Defender*, 4 Jul. 1936, p. 1.

policy should be carefully examined to determine whether it would increase or decrease these benefits."[17] T. Arnold Hill assured Pittsburgh steelworkers that they had the league's support in their organizing effort.[18] At the end of 1935, *Crisis* editorialized that the leaders of the CIO offered "Some hope for Negro labor . . . The records of these men give assurance that they may be depended upon to see that the Negro worker does not receive the usual doublecross."[19]

The NAACP remained suspicious of the upstart and communist-influenced NNC. At its 1937 annual meeting in Detroit, despite conflict between the local branch and the UAW, UAW president Homer Martin addressed the convention and the convention endorsed the CIO.[20] The Urban League remained a step behind. In 1935, Lester Granger concluded, "Only continued stupidity on the part of white labor leadership can prevent black workers from lining up with the cause of organized labor." The next year he admitted that "It is hard not to see the advantage for black workers in the spread of the industrial union idea with its trends of inclusiveness instead of exclusiveness because of race, and its greater concern for the organization of unskilled workers," but he warned against "premature adulation." Conceding that "A more modern social intelligence has been shown by CIO leadership than that shown by the old time AFL leaders" and hailing the CIO as "a new champion to defend the rights of the underdog," he noted that there was no clear difference between craft and industrial unionism as far as race was concerned, and recommended that blacks not burn bridges to old friends in the AFL. The split between the federations probably would not last long, he surmised, and "For Negro leadership to move out on a racial limb in support of this group and against that group might easily mean that Negroes will be left on that limb when the two groups move together for compromise and understanding."[21]

17. Harold D. Gould to Frances Perkins, 23 Jun. 1934 [NUL IV: 2].

18. Cayton and Mitchell, *Black Workers and the New Unions,* 409–10.

19. "Some Hope for Negro Labor," *Crisis* 42 (1935), 369.

20. *Crisis* 43 (1936), 242; Meier and Rudwick, *Black Detroit and the Rise of the UAW,* 28; Homer Martin address to 1937 NAACP conference, 30 Jun. 1937 [NAACP 1, IX: 1177].

21. Lester Granger, "The Negro—Friend or Foe of Organized Labor," *Opportunity* 13 (1935), 142; Granger, "Industrial Unionism and the Negro," *Opportunity* 14 (1936), 29–30 [DH VI: 571]; "The Organization of Steel Workers and Its Importance to Negro Labor," Workers Council Bulletin No. 12, 7 Aug. 1936 [NAACP 13-A, XV: 206]; "New Trade Union Movements and the Negro Worker," Workers Council Bulletin No. 18, 23 Sep. 1937 [NAACP 13-A, XV: 141]; Robert C. Francis, "The Negro and Industrial Unionism," *Social Forces* 15 (1936), 273; Nancy J. Weiss, *The National Urban League: 1910–40* (New York, 1974), 292.

In one of the most shocking turns of American industrial history, the U.S. Steel Corporation agreed to recognize the SWOC in March 1937, weeks after the GM breakthrough. The process by which U.S. Steel president Myron Taylor came to this agreement remains unclear, but it appears that he recognized the force of public opinion expressed in the 1936 elections and saw the power of union pressure in the GM conflict. Roosevelt's personal influence may have weighed heavily, along with his subsequent appointment of Taylor as the president's personal representative at the Vatican. Pennsylvania, the heart of U.S. Steel operations, had been swept by Democrats and had enacted its own New Deal, including a "little Wagner Act." State legislator Homer S. Brown was among the black politicians who joined the Democrats, and he was able to secure a nondiscrimination provision in the act. The lieutenant governor of Pennsylvania was a UMW official and told steelworkers in Homestead that SWOC organizers were welcome in any town in the state, and he promised relief funds should the union call a strike. In April the Supreme Court, the last hope of liberty-of-contract and the open shop, upheld the Wagner Act. With large orders coming in as the European countries rearmed, Taylor believed that the SWOC could provide stability and order to his restive work force, and help restore U.S. Steel to the industry dominance that had eroded over the past decades. He may also have supposed that his competitors would follow (or be compelled to follow) his lead. It was not uncommon for the largest producers in an industry to accept "progressive" regulation that would impose costs that would burden their smaller competitors—the meatpackers' embrace of health and sanitary regulations being one example.[22]

Birmingham blacks had become more sympathetic to unionism as a protection against discriminatory layoffs in the 1930s, and many enrolled in the egalitarian Mine, Mill, and Smelter Workers Union, one of the charter members of the CIO. But resistance to unionism among most southerners, black and white, remained strong enough to forestall it before the enactment of the NLRA. U.S. Steel's decision to bargain with the SWOC brought the union into Birmingham, center of the

22. Leo Troy, "Twilight for Organized Labor," *Journal of Labor Research* 22 (2001), 253; "Myron Taylor," ANB; Dennis C. Dickerson, *Out of the Crucible: Black Steelworkers in Western Pennsylvania, 1875–1980* (Albany, NY, 1986), 139; Leuchtenburg, *Franklin D. Roosevelt and the New Deal,* 241; Zieger, *John L. Lewis,* 94; Donald R. Richberg, *Labor Union Monopoly: A Clear and Present Danger* (Chicago, 1957), 35; Morgan O. Reynolds, "An Economic Analysis of the Norris–LaGuardia Act, the Wagner Act, and the Labor Representation Industry," *Journal of Libertarian Studies* 6 (1982), 258; Gabriel Kolko, *The Triumph of Conservatism: A Reinterpretation of American History, 1900–16* (New York, 1963), 98–108.

Tennessee Coal and Iron Company, a U.S. Steel subsidiary, but white workers were able to maintain their privileges after organization. Black workers could no longer compete for better jobs by underbidding whites, the method by which they had ascended the occupational ladder in past decades. Thus blacks helped to establish union power that limited their opportunities. Indeed, the CIO's indifference to black welfare provided an opening for AFL competition, and an AFL union ousted the SWOC in a 1940 election.[23]

But some of the other steel firms—"Little Steel"—did not follow U.S. Steel's lead, and violent industrial conflict erupted in May 1937. Black participation in the Little Steel strike varied, generally greater in large urban centers like Cleveland, Chicago, and Gary than in the smaller and relatively isolated towns like Canton and Johnstown. "From the standpoint of union workers," T. Arnold Hill noted, "Negroes form . . . so small a percentage of the total that it makes very little difference whether Negroes go in or stay out of the unions."[24] George L. Schuyler, a reporter for the *Pittsburgh Courier,* provided an important voice for black unionism. Though already a staunch anticommunist who would later become a McCarthyite, Schuyler was unfazed by the communist role in the SWOC. Recent migrants in small steel towns had not developed the kind of class consciousness that longer-settled blacks had, and they responded to employer paternalism and repression that resembled "company town" domination in Appalachia. This had begun to change, however, as sympathetic officials took over state and local governments and state labor law followed the Wagner Act example. The governor of Ohio reacted ambivalently, with both the union and the owners complaining of his bias. The mayor of Dusquene was a SWOC official who ordered his firemen to turn their hoses on nonunion workers in order to help the SWOC collect dues. White worker

23. Douglas L. Smith, *The New Deal in the Urban South* (Baton Rouge, 1988), 190–99; Judith Stein, "Birmingham Steelworkers, 1936–51," in Robert Zieger, ed., *Organized Labor in the Twentieth-Century South* (Knoxville, 1991), 186–91; Herbert R. Northrup, "The Negro and Unionism in the Birmingham, Alabama, Iron and Steel Industry," *Southern Economic Journal* 10 (1943), 34, 39; Robert J. Norrell, "Caste in Steel: Jim Crow Careers in Birmingham, Alabama," *Journal of American History* 73 (1986), 672–79; Northrup, *Organized Labor and the Negro,* 180; Ray Marshall, *Organized Labor and the Negro* (New York, 1965), 45; "The Negro's War," *Fortune,* Jun. 1942, p. 157; Marshall, *Labor in the South* (Cambridge, 1967), 188; Ernest Obadele-Starks, *Black Unionism in the Industrial South* (College Station, TX, 2000), 120; Alan Draper, "The New Southern Labor History Revisited: The Success of the Mine, Mill, and Smelter Workers Union in Birmingham, 1934–38," *Journal of Southern History* 62 (1996), 87–108.

24. T. Arnold Hill, "The Negro and the CIO," *Opportunity* 15 (1937), 243.

hostility and the past record of discrimination by white unions contributed to the organizers' difficulties, and employers took full advantage of this animosity. The black middle class also discouraged blacks from associating with white unionists. Though some came around, the strike failed and most Little Steel firms remained unorganized until World War II.[25]

The *Courier* berated conservative black middle-class leaders and tried to prod black workers off the fence. "There must be a larger realization on the part of Negro leaders and educated folk that a revolution is taking place in American life; that labor is on the road to rule, and that the day of unrestricted individualism on the part of employers is ended."[26] Schuyler condemned the "desertion of the struggling Negro workers in this crisis" by the middle class as "one of the most shameful chapters in our recent history." Schuyler concluded that blacks were making progress, albeit slowly, into the labor movement. They were realizing that race relations improved when white and black workers came together. Though obstacles remained, "not in fifty years has America witnessed such interracial solidarity." Simply as a practical matter, Negro leaders should see that "under the recently enacted National Labor Relations Act workers had to be represented by *somebody,* and it were better to have a hand in choosing that representative."[27]

Claude Barnett's sources informed him that black steelworkers "point out the wisdom of being on the safe side if the union should win. They have reason to believe that the union will win, this time, because the white men are all signing up rapidly and because they feel that 'Roosevelt is behind them.'"[28] The NAACP tried to accelerate this trend, claiming that blacks in the Little Steel strike had contributed "blood for the cause." "They have everything to gain and nothing to lose by affiliation with the CIO and if they fight now, side by side with their white fellow workers, when the time comes to divide up the benefits they can demand their

---

25. Nelson, *Divided We Stand,* 197, 257; George S. Schuyler, "Schuyler Visits Steel Centers in Ohio and Pennsylvania," *Pittsburgh Courier,* 24 Jul. 1937 [DH VII: 51]; Schuyler, "Negro Workers Lead Great Lakes Steel Drive," ibid., 31 Jul. 1937 [DH VII: 58]; Romare Bearden, "The Negro in 'Little Steel,'" *Opportunity* 15 (1937), 362–65 [DH VII: 98]; Schuyler, *Black and Conservative* (New Rochelle, NY, 1966), 237–39; Cayton and Mitchell, *Black Workers and the New Unions,* 196–98; Dickerson, *Out of the Crucible,* 134–43; Mansel G. Blackford, *A Portrait Cast in Steel: Buckeye International and Columbus, Ohio, 1881–1980* (Westport, 1982), 127.

26. "Loose Talk about Labor," *Pittsburgh Courier,* 28 Aug. 1937.

27. George L. Schuyler, "Reflections on Negro Leadership," *Crisis* 44 (1937), 327.

28. "Special Memo to Mr. Barnett"; Catyon and Mitchell, *Black Workers and the New Unions,* 202.

share."[29] Though black workers had responded less enthusiastically than other ethnic groups, they were not perceived as an important obstacle to unionization. As sociologists Horace Cayton and George S. Mitchell put it in 1939, "The entire country had undergone a liberal education with respect for trade union organization since the passage of the NRA and this had reached certain sections of the Negro public . . . One of the most striking phases in the entire SWOC campaign was the extent to which the union had been able to modify racial prejudice within the ranks of white laborers."[30] Sometimes white unionists exaggerated their overtures to, and black organizations exaggerated the receptiveness of, black workers. Lester Granger, noting the remarkable transformation among black workers' attitude toward organized labor in a five-year period, warned, "It is an ironical paradox that in our new acceptance of the philosophy of trade unions there may lie a serious danger to the future of Negro workers."[31]

THE UNITED AUTO WORKERS

Black workers also adopted a wait-and-see attitude and played a marginal role in the organization of the auto industry which, like steel, was not fully organized until the eve of World War II. They did become involved in some moments of crisis in the last years before the war. Ford steadfastly held out, and the loyalty of his black employees was an important source of antiunion strength. Black workers feared that unionization would undermine the position they had gained in the industry and fought to protect themselves. Claude Barnett told a Ford executive, "If I felt the CIO could deliver on its claims, I would be in favor of Negroes' joining it. My observation of union treatment of Negroes, however, convinces me that once the CIO is in power, there will be absolutely no way for Negroes, who now furnish so great a measure of the unemployed, to get into the industry or even back into the jobs for which they have been furloughed."[32] Before the Wagner Act was passed, as the president was attempting to settle a threatened strike in the industry, Walter White urged him to secure a nondiscrimination commitment from the

---

29. "Blood for the Cause," *Crisis* 44 (1937), 209 [DH VII: 51].

30. Catyon and Mitchell, *Black Workers and the New Unions*, 204–16.

31. Lester Granger, "The Negro in Labor Unions," address to 1938 NAACP conference, 30 Jun. 1938 [NAACP 1, X: 187]; Meier and Rudwick, *Black Detroit and the Rise of the UAW*, 3; Janken, *White*, 251.

32. Claude Barnett to W. J. Cameron, 14 Jul. 1937 [CBP X: 612].

union. Blacks had won greater opportunities in autos than in any other open shop industry, he said. "Unhappily, [the] Negro in some industries has joined unions and then after going on strike has been replaced with white unionists."[33] In 1937 the NAACP asked UAW president Homer Martin about rumors that blacks were going to be excluded from seniority provisions in the Dodge contract and put into a segregated local at Ford. Martin denied the claims and blamed the company for spreading the rumor to divide black and white workers. But black workers themselves sometimes sought departmental rather than plant seniority, seeking security in the jobs that they already had, even if they were less able to transfer to better jobs.[34]

The black Detroit establishment particularly disdained the UAW, and national black leaders took the side of the union cautiously. The June 1937 NAACP convention held in Detroit condemned discrimination in organized labor and offered less praise to the CIO than the previous year's convention. William Pickens, the director of the New York NAACP branch, made a spirited defense of Henry Ford, and Homer Martin exposed himself to ridicule by comparing himself to Jesus Christ.[35]

The UAW remained deeply divided in these years between a communist-leaning "unity" caucus and a less radical and usually dominant "progressive" caucus. Both sides appealed to black workers as they vied to control the union, and blacks attempted to use their influence to get the union to act more forcefully against discrimination and to secure greater representation in union leadership offices. Thus in 1939 President Martin proposed to set aside an at-large seat on the executive board for a black representative, but new president R. J. Thomas, selected by CIO leaders who feared that the UAW was out of control, blocked the move. The idea of race-based board representation continued to roil the UAW for decades. Industrial unionism exacerbated the issue: whereas blacks had more op-

33. Walter White to Franklin D. Roosevelt, 21 Mar. 1934 [NAACP 10, IV: 971]; Bailer, "The Negro in the Automobile Industry," 197.

34. Walter White to Homer Martin, 1 Apr. 1937 [NAACP 10, XII: 511]; Meier and Rudwick, *Black Detroit and the Rise of the UAW*, 51–52; Robert C. Weaver, *Negro Labor: A National Problem* (New York, 1946), 66; Weaver, "Recent Events in Negro-Union Relationships," *Journal of Political Economy* 52 (1944), 234–49 [SCCF 2713].

35. Meier and Rudwick, *Black Detroit and the Rise of the UAW*, 57; Richard W. Thomas, *Life for Us Is What We Make It: Building Black Community in Detroit, 1915–45* (Bloomington, 1992), 287; Homer Martin address to 1937 NAACP conference, 30 Jun. 1937 [NAACP 1, IX: 1177]; Janken, *White*, 244.

portunities to control segregated locals or craft union auxiliaries, they were almost always a minority in the large units of industrial unions.[36]

Though blacks played only a limited role in auto strikes, the competition among various groups for black support came to a dangerous head in the 1939 Chrysler strike. After its flush of victory in 1936–37, the UAW had been weakened by internal division, the 1937–38 recession (itself partly due to CIO success), and Governor Frank Murphy's reelection defeat and the fall of many other liberal Democrats in 1938.[37] Homer Martin, ousted as UAW president, encouraged blacks to break the strike at the Dodge Main plant in Highland Park, and the company was accused of promoting a "back to work" campaign among black workers. The company denied that it was attempting to break the strike but said that it would give employment to anyone willing to work and "will not discriminate against our colored employees by closing our plants to them." Though they faulted the company for their low occupational status, the black strikebreakers "said they had been promised better jobs by the company and felt the wisest policy to pursue was one of playing management against the union," one observer said.[38] UAW president R. J. Thomas charged that, since the numbers of returning workers were far too few to reopen the plant, the company's goal was to foment a race riot, which would induce the governor to bring in troops to break the strike. Some interpreted Thomas's statement as a threat to attack blacks who crossed the picket line. Local black leaders lined up decisively behind the UAW, violence was averted, and the company soon came to terms.[39]

Blacks now had more to fear from defying the UAW than they had to gain by loyalty to the auto companies. The charge that Chrysler sought to foment a race

36. Meier and Rudwick, *Black Detroit and the Rise of the UAW*, 45, 62–65; Scott Greer, *Last Man In: Racial Access to Union Power* (Glencoe, IL, 1959), 63; Paul H. Norgren and Samuel E. Hill, *Toward Fair Employment* (New York, 1964), 44–45.

37. Nelson Lichtenstein, *The Most Dangerous Man in Detroit: Walter Reuther and the Fate of American Labor* (New York, 1995), 111; Benjamin M. Anderson, *Economics and the Public Welfare: Financial and Economic History of the United States, 1914–46* (New York, 1949), 444–46; Gene Smiley, *Rethinking the Great Depression* (Chicago, 2002), 118.

38. *Detroit Free Press*, 26 Nov. 1939, p. 1; 28 Nov. 1939, p. 2; Lloyd H. Bailer, "The Automobile Unions and Negro Labor," *Political Science Quarterly* 59 (1944), 553.

39. Meier and Rudwick, *Black Detroit and the Rise of the UAW*, 62, 68–70; Northrup, *Organized Labor and the Negro*, 191; Thomas, *Life for Us Is What We Make It*, 299; Paul Norgren et al., "Negro Labor and Its Problems" (unpublished ms. for the Carnegie-Myrdal Study, 1940), 633–34.

riot is open to question. The corporation had become more assertive in light of the Progressive-Unity fragmentation of the UAW and the presence of a more supportive governor, Luren D. Dickinson, who had promised police protection for workers who wanted to return to the plant.[40] Government intervention after a race riot would probably have resulted in a neutral or even pro-striker effort to maintain order. If the number of strike breakers was too few to resume plant operations, why should the strikers have even attempted to stop them? The accusation that Chrysler rather than the union was a threat to black workers was part of the union's assertion that rival unions and owners, never the UAW itself, were responsible for racial problems.[41] The most likely explanation for the outcome of the strike is that black leaders could see the shift to union predominance and followed it.[42]

This shift was clearly visible in the culmination of the UAW campaign, the Ford strike of 1941. Homer Martin had joined the AFL and headed its rival UAW, but both unions had difficulty recruiting members at Ford due to the company's paternalism and intimidation. Black workers were especially difficult to attract, and Ford redoubled his solicitude toward blacks to keep the UAWs at bay, but the majority of anti-union employees at Ford were white. When the strike began, UAW leaders again exploited Negro leaders' fears of a race riot against black strike breakers. Though several hundred black workers remained inside the Rouge plant, "guarding" it, black leaders, including NAACP secretary Walter White, appealed to them to leave. In most cases, black strikebreakers had to force their way *into* plants through white picket lines; here black workers served as "sit-down strike breakers," who claimed that they feared to cross a picket line to get *out*. The UAW charge that Harry Bennett, Ford's enforcer, was trying to foment a race riot was more plausible in the Ford than in the Chrysler strike. Bennett was able to appeal to both the loyalty of the company's black workers, and to claim that the strike was a communist attempt to disrupt war production (as the simultaneous strike at Milwaukee's Allis-Chalmers plant was). Ford was as staunchly antiunion as the Al-

---

40. Norgren et al., "Negro Labor and Its Problems," 633; Willis F. Dunbar and George S. May, *Michigan: A History of the Wolverine State,* 3d ed. (Grand Rapids, 1995), 531. In counterpoise to Homer Martin's Christian claims, Dickinson was "an octogenarian who was completely out of touch with the times and who had been an easy mark for ridicule when he was quoted as saying he had a 'pipeline to God.'"

41. Northrup, *Organized Labor and the Negro,* 192.

42. Thomas, *Life for Us Is What We Make It,* 294.

abama coal operators, and strikes tended to be more intensely fought in family-owned companies than in large, managerial-oriented ones like U.S. Steel.[43]

Bennett's stratagem failed. It caused a deep conflict among the Fords, with Henry's wife Clara and son Edsel urging the patriarch to come to terms with the union while Bennett stoked the founder's instinct to fight it out. Black leaders and workers surmised that this lone open-shop holdout could not prevail, and that the CIO was bound to win. The governor and company urged the black loyalists not to resist and violence was again averted. Most blacks ended up voting for the AFL union in the NLRB election, while the CIO won 70 percent of the overall vote. The UAW-CIO bent over backward to avoid any recriminations from its white members and placed the blame for black aversion entirely on the company.[44]

Detroit showed the persistence of pro-employer sentiment among black workers and middle-class leaders, but the Ford strike of 1941 proved that it was waning. Some observers counseled blacks to continue to bargain between white unions if black workers would no longer be bargaining between white workers and white owners. Negro labor had benefited from the AFL-CIO schism, Horace Cayton argued. "Still later, with the growth of the 'right' and 'left' wing factions in the CIO, the Negro laborer's bargaining position was again enhanced." Black leaders should recognize "the necessity of exploiting the situation for further gains . . . In this situation Negro labor, if organized into a block, could play a shrewd game of 'power politics,' a game of making each side and faction bid against one another for his support, until he is given every right, privilege, and prerogative of white labor."[45]

OTHER CIO CAMPAIGNS

Organization of the meatpacking industry, about one-third black, proceeded slowly before the war. Though a skilled craft union, the Amalgamated Meat Cut-

43. Stephen H. Norwood, *Strikebreaking and Intimidation: Mercenaries and Masculinity in Twentieth-Century America* (Chapel Hill, 2002), 189–90; Robert H. Zieger, *American Workers, American Unions, 1920–85* (Baltimore, 1986), 73; Taft and Ross, "American Labor Violence," 386; Robert G. Anderson, "The Redistribution of Wealth," 150.

44. Meier and Rudwick, *Black Detroit and the Rise of the UAW*, 83–101; Bailer, "The Automobile Unions and Negro Labor," 552; Bailer, "The Negro in the Automobile Industry," 210–27; Benjamin Gitlow, *The Whole of Their Lives* (New York, 1948), 322; Northrup, *Organized Labor and the Negro*, 195; Norwood, *Strikebreaking and Intimidation*, 190; Cayton and Mitchell, *Black Workers and the New Unions*, 202.

45. Horace R. Cayton, "A Strategy for Negro Labor," address to 1941 NAACP convention, 24 Jun. 1941 [NAACP 1, X: 1191].

ters had been on friendly terms with John L. Lewis, and he was careful not to alienate them. Like the UAW, the packinghouse workers were diverse and hard to control, and among them was a significant communist constituency. Black loyalty to their employers and suspicion of unions had eroded in the 1930s, particularly due to discriminatory layoffs during the depression. The Packinghouse Workers Organizing Committee brought together several unions in 1937 and made an effort to appeal to blacks, including making a promise of racially designated seats on the executive board; it even negotiated an agreement with Swift to hire blacks by local population quota.[46] Independent black organization and then CIO competition forced the dormant AFL tobacco workers union to pay more attention to black workers, who composed over half of the labor force in this south Atlantic industry. Though it continued to favor segregated locals, the AFL union was able narrowly to defeat a largely black-supported CIO rival in a 1937 election.[47] But most black workers remained untouched by organized labor because they lived in the South and worked in parts of the economy that were not targeted by the CIO. The CIO's failure to organize the nearly all-white textile industry impeded its efforts throughout the region. Many southern black middle-class leaders remained hostile to all labor unions, and many black unionists remained committed to separate black organization.[48]

The Railway Labor Act amendments of 1934 accelerated the expulsion of black workers from the railroad crafts. At its 1937 convention the Brotherhood of Locomotive Firemen reaffirmed its commitment to the complete elimination of blacks from the trade. The union was able to make sure that job-threatening technological changes removed only black firemen. When the Interstate Commerce Com-

46. David Brody, *The Butcher Workmen: A Study of Unionization* (Cambridge, 1964), 176; Horowitz, *"Black and White,"* 69–71; Rick Halpern, *Down on the Killing Floor: Black and White Workers in Chicago's Packinghouses, 1904–54* (Urbana, 1997), 128–69; Paul Street, "The Logic and Limits of 'Plant Loyalty': Black Workers, White Labor, and Corporate Racial Paternalism in Chicago's Stockyards, 1916–40," *Journal of Social History* 29 (1996), 671; Cayton and Mitchell, *Black Workers and the New Unions,* 260–77.

47. Smith, *The New Deal in the Urban South,* 202; A. V. Jackson, "A New Deal for Tobacco Workers," *Crisis* 45 (1938), 323; Herbert R. Northrup, "The Tobacco Workers International Union," *Quarterly Journal of Economics* 56 (1942), 606–18; Norgren et al., "Negro Labor and Its Problems," 756–65; Marshall, *Labor in the South,* 215.

48. Zieger, *The CIO,* 74–77; Zieger, "Textile Workers and Historians," in Zieger, ed., *Organized Labor in the Twentieth-Century South;* Ernest Obadele-Starks, *Black Unionism in the Industrial South* (College Station, TX, 2000), 27–31.

mission required all high-speed locomotives to use mechanical stokers by 1943, the Brotherhood secretly negotiated to waive higher wages in exchange for racial preference on stokers. When diesel engines made firemen redundant, the Brotherhood negotiated "featherbed" protection for "promotable" (i.e., white) firemen only. The campaign reached its climax in the 1941 Southeastern Carriers Agreement, which imposed a 50 percent maximum quota for black firemen (lower quotas were negotiated, secretly, on individual roads). When railroad employment began to increase as the war economy geared up, black railroad employment continued to decline. Most black railroaders "found not salvation in New Deal labor legislation, which for them represented not labor's Magna Carta but rather a major setback to their organizational aspirations and even their livelihoods," a historian observes.[49]

The Railway Labor Act also enabled A. Philip Randolph's Brotherhood of Sleeping Car Porters to win recognition from the Pullman Company and an international charter from the AFL. During the depths of the depression, Randolph began slowly rebuilding the union and challenging Pullman's Employee Representation Plan. The revised Railway Labor Act outlawed company unions and covered porters, removing two elements of ambiguity in earlier railroad legislation. When the Pullman Company threatened to replace black unionists with Chinese or Japanese porters, Randolph denounced the move as "a threat to American standards of health and decency," and the black press began an "Employ Americans First" campaign. The *Pittsburgh Courier* claimed that the Japanese were too short to be porters. Finally, a U.S. senator threatened to introduce legislation to prohibit the employment of foreigners on railroads. As the porters approached victory, the white-only Order of Sleeping Car Conductors attempted to assert jurisdiction over the porters, and the AFL sustained their claim. Randolph refused to give up his organization's independence, and in 1935 the AFL agreed to grant an international charter, though this breakthrough was overshadowed by the convention's battle between craft and industry and the spiking of the Committee of Five's report on racial discrimination. The Pullman Company finally agreed to recognize the brotherhood when the Supreme Court upheld the Railway Labor Act, along with the Wagner Act, in 1937. Despite the CIO's egalitarian reputation, Randolph kept

49. Northrup, *Organized Labor and the Negro*, 62–66, 100; Eric Arnesen, *Brotherhoods of Color: Black Railroad Workers and the Struggle for Equality* (Cambridge, 2001), 116, 126, 138; David Bernstein, "Racism, Railroad Unions, and Labor Regulations," *Independent Review* 5 (2000), 242–44.

the porters in the AFL, where he continued to act as a kind of watchdog on racial discrimination.[50]

The CIO had made impressive progress toward reconciling black Americans and organized labor. With due allowance for its manifold limitations, it seems fair to conclude that "It would be a serious error to underestimate the extent to which the CIO improved the economic position of Negro workers and educated white workers on the color problem."[51] Just as there was considerable truth in the claim that the United Mine Workers had been the most racially progressive institution in turn-of-the-century Alabama, so there was substantial merit in the claim that the CIO had done more to improve American race relations than any other organization.[52] By 1940 the stage had been set for a honeymoon between blacks and organized labor that would last a generation. In 1940 Jimmy Rushing of the Count Basie orchestra, as apolitical as any of the swing bands, sang out the concluding lines from "It's the Same Old South," a song from one of that year's minor Broadway hits, "Meet the People":

> Honey hush my mouth
> When the bloodhounds that once chased Liza
> Chase the poor CIO organizer
> It's the same old South

As an indication of the difficulty that the CIO faced in organizing the South, and the esteem in which blacks held it, it was something of an exaggeration, but it was a sign of the times.[53]

50. Arnold Shankman, *Ambivalent Friends: Afro-Americans View the Immigrant* (Westport, 1982), 19, 49; William H. Harris, *Keeping the Faith: A. Philip Randolph, Milton P. Webster, and the Brotherhood of Sleeping Car Porters, 1925–37* (Urbana, 1977), 170–201; Arnesen, *Brotherhoods of Color,* 86–115; Northrup, *Organized Labor and the Negro,* 76.

51. Raymond Wolters, *Negroes and the Great Depression: The Problem of Recovery* (Westport, 1970), 308.

52. Lizabeth Cohen, *Making a New Deal: Industrial Workers in Chicago, 1919–39* (Cambridge, 1990), 337; Ronald L. Lewis, *Black Coal Miners in America: Race, Class, and Community Conflict, 1780–1980* (Lexington, KY, 1987), 64.

53. Gerald M. Bordman, *American Musical Theatre: A Chronicle,* 3d ed. (New York, 2001), 575. The play was among the last "socialist realist" productions that marked the 1930s.

Black leaders like Lester Granger, who had warned blacks not to be seduced by the initial openness of the CIO, were prescient.[54] For the most part, issues of racial discrimination would move from admission to the work force to equal treatment within it. The CIO's success and structure aggravated some problems. Since unionization raised labor costs and made jobs scarcer, the issue of seniority would be exacerbated. The larger bargaining units of industrial unions would make election of black officials more difficult. Above all, however, the CIO unions were not fundamentally different from the AFL. The basic principle of job protection, and thus the incentive for exclusion of unpopular minorities, remained. As Selig Perlman put it, "The art of building fortifications and their defense offers a good analogy of how change in basic circumstances compels change in strategy, even if the objective remains unaltered. Prior to the airplane, it was enough to fortify a limited area, to garrison it adequately, and to await confidently the assault. Today, to be impregnable, a fortress must control an area with a radius of many hundreds of miles, even aside from the consideration of the wider strategy of protecting the whole country. The mere 'nuclear' interest, the holding of the fortress, has thus compelled the erection of outlying strongpoints to keep away enemy bombers." [55]

In other words, the industrial unions were still concerned primarily with "controlling the labor supply," and while the scope of that control had widened, it remained limited. The fortress might be more commodious, but it was not coeval with the American work force. The CIO organized the "core" industries while those in the "periphery" remained unorganized—and most blacks continued to work in the periphery. Moreover, entry into the core industrial labor market would be impeded by higher labor costs that reduced overall employment.[56] Blacks bore a disproportionate brunt of New Deal policies that depressed total employ-

54. Weaver, "Recent Events in Negro-Union Relationships."

55. Selig Perlman, "The Basic Philosophy of the American Labor Movement," *Annals of the American Academy of Political and Social Science* 274 (1951), 59.

56. Foster Rhea Dulles, *Labor in America, 1900–70,* 3d ed. (New York, 1966), 298; Sumner M. Rosen, "The CIO Era," in Julius Jacobson, ed., *The Negro and the American Labor Movement* (Garden City, NY, 1968), 190; Zieger, *The CIO,* 68–70, 305, 348; Northrup, *Organized Labor and the Negro,* 234; Herbert Hill, "Black Labor and Affirmative Action: An Historical Perspective," in Steven Shulman and William Darity Jr., eds., *The Question of Discrimination: Racial Inequality in the United States Labor Market* (Middletown, CT, 1989), 191; Richard Vedder and Lowell Gallaway, "The Economic Effects of Labor Unions Revisited," *Journal of Labor Research* 23 (2002), 105.

ment—its union policy as well as others, such as the Fair Labor Standards Act, which established a national minimum wage. "Just as an economist would predict," an economic historian notes, "when jobs were made scarce by upward pressure on wages, racism became easier to indulge, and blacks were the first to be laid off." [57]

This problem was perhaps most obvious in John L. Lewis's own United Mine Workers. Lewis's strategy was to improve miners' jobs by cooperating with owners to cartelize the industry and to augment safety and mechanization, and he knew full well that this would reduce overall employment in the industry. When jobs became scarcer, blacks were the most likely to be shed. Between 1930 and 1950, black coal employment fell from 55,000 to 30,000 and would be almost wiped out in southern Appalachia by 1970. "If Negroes continue to bear the brunt of technological unemployment," Herbert Northrup noted in 1944, "the UMW will no longer be able to claim that it adheres to a policy of racial equality as steadfastly as any other American labor union." [58]

The Democratic Party would chaperon this honeymoon between blacks and organized labor. Nearly all the power of organized labor apart from specialized, skilled workers derived from government support, which had been growing since the turn of the century. Only the National Labor Relations Act made industrial unionism possible. But even in the palmy days of the late 1930s, the CIO had not attained carte blanche. Not only did the CIO follow the steps of the AFL, but the AFL, far from being wiped out by the wave of industrial unionism, remained vigorous, always maintaining more members than the CIO and holding "senior circuit" status in terms of political power. Although organized labor became among the most powerful interest groups in Washington, the Roosevelt administration maintained ultimate control over the American labor movement, keeping it divided and dependent. This competition probably helped black workers by making the rival federations more solicitous of their support. As Swedish sociologist Gun-

57. Gavin Wright, *Old South, New South: Revolutions in the Southern Economy since the Civil War* (New York, 1986), 223; Elmer F. Andrews, "A New Deal for Negro Workers," *Opportunity* 17 (1939), 166; Paul Moreno, "An Ambivalent Legacy: Black Americans and the Political Economy of the New Deal," *Independent Review* 6 (2002), 526–28.

58. Lewis, *Black Coal Miners in America*, 167–83; Zieger, *John L. Lewis*, 66–71; James C. Cobb, *Industrialization and Southern Society, 1877–1984* (Lexington, KY, 1984), 85; Northrup, *Organized Labor and the Negro*, 171.

nar Myrdal concluded, "This split cannot last forever. Unity, when it comes, may be gained at the expense of the Negro."[59]

THE SECOND WORLD WAR

As the United States began to prepare for war, employment returned to pre-depression levels. As during World War I, the organization of a wartime command economy both augmented and reduced union power. Labor leader Sidney Hillman was very close to the centers of power in Washington, and in 1942 unions won the "maintenance of membership" principle from the National War Labor Board. In what amounted to a virtual union-shop order, it compelled war workers to pay union dues or lose their jobs. Membership in unions doubled from 1940 to 1945, reaching 15 million members.[60] But many workers complained that the government allowed prices to rise faster than wages. The AFL and CIO swore a "no strike pledge" for the war, a surrender of what many unionists considered to be their chief means of self-protection. John L. Lewis had broken with FDR in 1940 for fear that war statism would destroy organized labor's independence. "Labor today seems to be at the crossroads," the *Pittsburgh Courier* noted in 1942, "faced with the momentous problem of deciding whether or not it will accept government dictation and control." But labor really had little choice in the matter. When significant work stoppages erupted in 1943 despite the no-strike pledge, Congress enacted (over FDR's veto) the War Labor Disputes Act, virtually outlawing strikes. On the whole, however, the war strengthened organized labor. The war increased central government power, and this was the source of organized labor's own power. Added to the interventions of the New Deal, federal regulation of the economy increased with the war and continued through decades of cold war.[61]

59. *Crisis* 40 (1933), 292 [DH VI: 338]; Robert C. Francis, "The Negro and Industrial Unionism," *Social Forces* 15 (1936), 273; John A. Wettergreen, "The Regulatory Policy of the New Deal," in Robert Eden, ed., *The New Deal Legacy: Critique and Reappraisal* (Westport, 1989), 199–213; George I. Lovell, *Legislative Deferrals: Statutory Ambiguity, Judicial Power, and American Democracy* (Cambridge, 2002), 218; Gunnar Myrdal, *An American Dilemma* (New York, 1944), 403; Daniel Nelson, "The Other New Deal and Labor: The Regulatory State and the Unions, 1933–40," *Journal of Policy History* 13 (2001), 367–90.

60. Sumner H. Slichter, "The Taft-Hartley Act," *Quarterly Journal of Economics* 63 (1949), 7.

61. Steven Fraser, *Labor Will Rule: Sidney Hillman and the Rise of American Labor* (Ithaca, NY, 1991), 452; Dulles, *Labor in America*, 335–42; "Labor at the Crossroads," *Pittsburgh Courier*, 1 Aug. 1942 [DH VII: 230]; Zieger, *The CIO*, 121–55; Daniel Nelson, "The Other New Deal and Labor: The Regulatory State and the Unions, 1933–40," *Journal of Policy History* 13 (2001), 367–90.

Black workers, however, found themselves excluded from many new war industries. In some cases, like the auto industry, black workers actually lost jobs as the automakers shut down civilian production and converted to defense work. President Roosevelt had begun to establish tripartite government-business-labor coordination of defense production, first in the National Defense Advisory Committee and then, after the 1940 election, in the Office of Production Management (OPM). The OPM was co-chaired by former General Motors president William Knudsen and Sidney Hillman, head of the Amalgamated Clothing Workers. Although black economist Robert C. Weaver served on its staff and Hillman directed defense contractors to make use of the entire labor supply without discrimination, the OPM did little to address black concerns.[62]

The opening of World War II marked perhaps the high point of union power in American history. Organized labor was the most powerful interest group in the Democratic Party, which continued to control the legislative and executive branches. The judiciary, once the greatest obstacle to union power, now moved ahead of the elected branches in extending privileges to organized labor. In 1940 the Court, in an opinion by Frank Murphy, declared that picketing was a form of free speech protected by the First Amendment.[63] When the antitrust division of the Justice Department tried to use the Sherman Act to prosecute the carpenters union, the Court held that unions were exempt from such prosecutions. Justice Owen Roberts's dissent noted that "no court has ever undertaken so radically to legislate what Congress has refused to do."[64] This same year Congress gave to the AFL construction trades a virtual monopoly on defense building through its "stabilization agreements." Walter White sought Justice Department protection against the abuse of these monopolies, but the Supreme Court had obviated such action. At the AFL's 1941 convention, carpenter union chief William Hutcheson tried to

62. Robert C. Weaver, "Negro Labor since 1929," *Journal of Negro History* 35 (1950), 25; Northrup, *Organized Labor and the Negro*, 200; Fraser, *Labor Will Rule*, 478; Weaver, *Negro Labor*, ch. 2; "A Word from OPM," *Crisis* 48 (1941), 151 [DH VII: 212]; NDAC Press Release, 23 Oct. 1940 [NAACP 13-B, X: 923].

63. *Thornhill v. Alabama*, 310 U.S. 88 (1940). The Court soon began to retreat from this position and largely abandoned it by 1949. Hugh Douglas Price, "Picketing—A Legal Cinderella," *University of Florida Law Review* 7 (1954), 143–77; Sidney Fine, "Frank Murphy, The Thornhill Decision, and Picketing as Free Speech," *Labor History* 6 (1965), 99–120.

64. *U.S. v. Hutcheson*, 312 U.S. 219 (1941); Lawrence E. Davis, "AFL Hits Arnold and Asks for Ouster," *New York Times*, 15 Oct. 1941, p. 11. Hutcheson's attorney in this case was Charles H. Tuttle, who was widely credited with drafting New York's pioneer fair employment practice statute.

assuage A. Philip Randolph's concerns about craft-union discrimination by telling him, "In our union, we don't care whether you're an Irishman, a Jew, or a nigger." But the NAACP concluded that the upshot was that "the government has handed a monopoly to unions whose policies, with few exceptions, exclude Negro workers from full-fledged membership."[65]

Black protest organizations called for government action against discrimination by defense contractors. A. Philip Randolph took the most dramatic step, threatening to lead a hundred thousand black workers in a march on the capital to protest discrimination in industry and segregation in the armed forces. Randolph had resigned from the National Negro Congress in 1940 when the organization, captured by Communists, became an organ of opposition to American defense preparations and intervention in the European war. Randolph made the March on Washington Movement a black-only organization to prevent another Communist Party takeover. When Stalin signed a nonaggression pact with Hitler in August 1939, the Popular Front period of CP cooperation with all "antifascist" organizations ended, and the party now exhorted blacks to oppose President Roosevelt's steps to involve the nation in an "imperialist" war. The party attacked organizations that attempted to gain black jobs in defense work and encouraged blacks in Communist-dominated unions to go on strike to disrupt war preparations. The disruptive potential of the March on Washington Movement appealed to the Communists but, though they objected to racial discrimination in the defense industry, the party's pro-Hitler policy benefited from it.[66]

---

65. Andrew E. Kersten, *Race, Jobs, and the War: The FEPC in the Midwest, 1941–46* (Urbana, 2000), 32–33; "The AFL Slams the Door Again," *Crisis* 48 (1941), 343 [DH VII: 411]. The carpenters were, in fact, among the less exclusive of the building trades unions. Walter Galenson, *The United Brotherhood of Carpenters: The First Hundred Years* (Cambridge, 1983), 379.

66. Lester Granger, "The Negro Congress—Its Future," *Opportunity* 18 (1940), 164–66 [DH VII: 165]; Paula F. Pfeffer, *A. Philip Randolph, Pioneer of the Civil Rights Movement* (Baton Rouge, 1990), ch. 2; Herbert Garfinkel, *When Negroes March: The March on Washington Movement in the Organizational Politics for FEPC* (New York, 1958), chs. 1–2; Louis Ruchames, *Race, Jobs, and Politics: The Story of FEPC* (New York, 1952), 3–21; Merl E. Reed, *Seedtime for the Modern Civil Rights Movement: The President's Committee on Fair Employment Practice, 1941–46* (Baton Rouge, 1991), 1–17; Wilson Record, *The Negro and the Communist Party* (Chapel Hill, 1951), 186–204; Record, *Race and Radicalism: The NAACP and the Communist Party in Conflict* (Ithaca, NY, 1964), 114; William A. Nolan, *Communism versus the Negro* (Chicago, 1951), 146–49, 160; Zieger, *The CIO*, 103. These works suggest the opposite of the claim that "The Communists opposed Randolph's tactics, not his objectives." Roger Keenan, *The Communist Party and the Auto Workers Unions* (Bloomington, 1980), 231.

The NAACP and Urban League were late in supporting the March on Washington Movement, and some black voices, like the *Pittsburgh Courier,* opposed it. As the July deadline approached, FDR met with Randolph and representatives of the government and the movement worked out a compromise. Randolph called off the march in exchange for an executive order that declared, "It is the duty of employers and labor organizations . . . to provide free and equitable participation of all workers in defense industries, without discrimination because of race, creed, color, or national origin." The order established a five-man Fair Employment Practice Committee (FEPC) in the Office of Production Management to hear complaints of discrimination and to "take appropriate steps to redress grievances which it finds to be valid" and to "recommend to the several departments and agencies of the Government of the United States and to the President all measures which may be deemed by it necessary or proper to effectuate the provisions of this order."[67]

Randolph had won an impressive victory, a clear breakthrough toward a public policy of nondiscrimination. The majority of the black public responded enthusiastically, often comparing the order to the Emancipation Proclamation.[68] But its limits were clear enough. Randolph agreed to put off the question of military integration and maintained that the march had only been "postponed" and that his movement would remain a permanent organization. The president's committee had no legislative warrant and was established and financed out of the president's pocket in unusual wartime circumstances. The justification for the order was manpower efficiency—discrimination was undermining the nation's defense preparation efforts. It also appeared to lack any enforcement powers.

Mark Ethridge, a liberal white Mississippian, chaired the committee. David Sarnoff, president of the Radio Corporation of America, represented business and the Jewish community. Milton Webster of the Brotherhood of Sleeping Car Porters and Earl Dickerson, a Chicago politician, were the black members. AFL president William Green and CIO president Philip Murray sat for organized labor. The committee began to investigate complaints and hold hearings in Los Angeles in the fall of 1941. More hearings were held in Chicago and New York in the winter of 1942, and the committee came to Birmingham in June 1942. Its chief goal in these first months was to publicize the problem of discrimination.

67. Executive Order 8802, 25 Jun. 1941, CFR 3 (1938–43), 957. In July the president added a sixth member to the committee.

68. Ruchames, *Race, Jobs, and Politics,* 23.

The majority of complaints were against employers rather than unions, and in many cases management used employee prejudice as a pretext for inaction. Often, though, this claim was justified, and the committee's most difficult cases involved union resistance.[69] Competitive market forces were largely absent for defense producers with cost-plus contracts. They could discriminate without having to pay for it, passing on the cost of a less efficient all-white work force to their customer, the government. But they were susceptible to the demands of that customer, which now insisted on a nondiscrimination requirement. Employers also responded to adverse publicity more than unions did.[70] Fair employment advocates often noted that job integration could be accomplished when employers communicated a firm policy to their workers, but the executive order called for managerial firmness at the moment when organized employee power was at its height.

The committee was packed with union personnel and was often biased toward organized labor because the government applied pressure more directly to employers than to unions.[71] The AFL and CIO each had a representative on the committee throughout its life, the black members were often also unionists, and its last two chairmen were former NLRB members. The last chairman, Malcolm Ross, claimed in his memoir that "Most employers are apathetic. The union line is the firmest, because self-interest and the democratic principle of equal opportunity must always be for trade unions one and the same thing."[72] The former point rings true; the latter was wishful thinking.

Although AFL and CIO leaders repeatedly expressed their support for the FEPC, they often had difficulty controlling their member unions. This was partic-

69. American Management Association, *The Negro Worker* (New York, 1942), 9, 15; Cecilia A. Conrad and George Sherer, "From the New Deal to the Great Society: The Economic Activism of Robert C. Weaver," in Thomas D. Boston, ed., *A Different Vision: African-American Economic Thought*, 2 vols. (New York, 1997), I: 292; "The Negro's War," *Fortune*, Jun. 1942, p. 157; Kersten, *Race, Jobs, and the War*, 4, 11, 90; Ruchames, *Race, Jobs, and Politics*, 36; Ray Marshall, "The Negro and Organized Labor," *Journal of Negro Education* 32 (1963), 381.

70. John F. Cushman, "Mediation and Education for Equal Economic Opportunity," in Milton R. Konvitz and Clinton Rossiter, eds., *Aspects of Liberty: Essays Presented to Robert E. Cushman* (Ithaca, 1958), 124; Thomas Sowell, "Ethnicity in a Changing America," *Daedalus* 107 (1978), 230; Sowell, *Markets and Minorities* (New York, 1981), 26, 50; Walter Williams, *The State against Blacks* (New York, 1982); Reed, *Seedtime for the Modern Civil Rights Movement*, 46.

71. Charles W. Baird, "A Tale of Infamy: The Air Associates Strikes of 1941," in Sennholz, ed., *American Unionism*, 100–15.

72. Malcolm Ross, *All Manner of Men* (New York, 1948), 169.

ularly true of the AFL. The CIO was more centrally controlled, was founded by less discriminatory unions, and in 1942 established its own Committee to Abolish Racism and Discrimination, but it still faced rank-and-file problems. Worst of all were the independent railroad brotherhoods.[73]

As railroad employment increased during the defense buildup, black employment continued to fall due to union contracts that limited the geographic area and percentage of jobs black workers could hold. The Brotherhood of Locomotive Firemen used the National Mediation Board to force reluctant shippers to meet their demand for an accelerated program of black elimination. Just months before the president issued his nondiscrimination order, the union won the Southeastern Carriers (or Washington) agreement. The black press dubbed it the "Hitler Agreement." It limited employment of "unpromotable" (i.e., black) firemen to 50 percent, ended the hiring of blacks, and stripped black employees of all seniority rights until this quota was attained. It also permitted secret side-agreements with individual roads to set lower quotas. Here was an obvious case of unfair employment practice.[74]

Facing the 1942 elections, the Roosevelt administration feared alienating southern Democrats, who became increasingly vocal in their opposition to the FEPC after its Birmingham hearings. In the summer of 1942 FDR transferred the FEPC to the War Manpower Commission under Paul V. McNutt, which subjected the committee to congressional oversight. When Roosevelt instructed McNutt to cancel planned hearings on the railroad problem, he confirmed suspicions that this reorganization was part of an effort to rein in the committee, the committee rose from its deathbed and won a new executive order in May 1943 that augmented its membership and powers. The new FEPC regained its place in the president's Office of Emergency Management, acquired explicit power to conduct hearings, and secured a larger budget that enabled it to open twelve regional offices.[75]

73. *Proceedings, 61st Annual Convention of the AFL* (1941), 536–39 [DH VII: 440]; Emma Lou Thornbrough, *Indiana Blacks in the Twentieth Century* (Bloomington, 2000), 109; Zieger, *The CIO,* 155–58.

74. Bernstein, "Racism, Railroad Unions, and Labor Regulations," 244–45; Northrup, *Organized Labor and the Negro,* 62–67; Ross, *All Manner of Men;* Alexa B. Henderson, "FEPC and the Southern Railway Case: An Investigation into the Discriminatory Practices of Railroads during World War II," *Journal of Negro History* 61 (1976), 177.

75. Ruchames, *Race, Jobs, and Politics,* 46–52; Reed, *Seedtime for the Modern Civil Rights Movement,* 91; James A. Neuchterlein, "The Politics of Civil Rights: The FEPC, 1941–46," *Prologue* 10 (1978),

The new committee held its railroad hearings in September 1943, focusing on the Southeast Carriers agreement. It summoned twenty-two railroads and fourteen unions. All of the unions refused to appear, though seven sent written responses, while twenty-one of the railroads showed up. The Union Pacific agreed to alter its discriminatory practices immediately. The others attempted to give the hearings as little attention and publicity as possible, arguing simply that they were bound by collective bargaining agreements and had to defer to regional mores. In December, the committee issued its findings and directives to end discrimination. The Pennsylvania and New York Central acceded, but the southern carriers refused. The committee referred the matter to the president, who put together another committee to study the problem, which did nothing. The FEPC chairman called the railroad cases "among the Committee's outstanding failures." [76]

The committee met equal resistance on the West Coast from the International Brotherhood of Boilermakers (IBB), which it began to investigate in the fall of 1943. The IBB enjoyed a closed shop under an agreement with the Pacific Coast shipbuilders, which became a bonanza when the war began. The union allowed blacks to join separate "subordinate lodges" in 1937. Black workers paid dues to the IBB but were denied membership in the international union; were not permitted to have their own business agents, grievance committees, or apprentices; were not permitted to transfer from one local to another; and were subject to discipline that whites were exempted from. Black workers protested this unfair treatment and stopped paying dues, whereupon the IBB forced the shipyards to discharge them under the terms of the master agreement. [77]

As in the railroad case, the union had forced the employers to accept a discriminatory labor agreement. The shipbuilders cooperated more than the southern railroads, but the FEPC insisted that they be cited as violators of the executive

---

177–79; "Post-Mortem on FEPC," *Pittsburgh Courier*, 23 Jan. 1943 [DH VII: 275]; Executive Order 9346, 3 CFR 1280 (1938–43).

76. U.S. Committee on Fair Employment Practice, *Final Report* (Washington, 1947), 12–14; Ruchames, *Race, Jobs, and Politics*, 59–64; Henderson, "FEPC and the Southern Railway Case," 184–85; Reed, *Seedtime for the Modern Civil Rights Movement*, 127–39; "Railroads Plead Guilty," *Crisis* 50 (1943), 295 [DH VII: 282]; Herbert R. Northrup, "Race Discrimination in Unions," *American Mercury*, Jul. 1945, p. 94.

77. Reed, *Seedtime for the Modern Civil Rights Movement*, 268; William H. Harris, "Federal Intervention in Union Discrimination: FEPC and West Coast Shipyards during World War II," *Labor History* 22 (1981), 325–47; Charles Wollenberg, "*James v. Marinship*: Trouble on the New Black Frontier," *California History* 60 (1981), 262–79.

order. This decision angered builders like the Kaisers, who had cooperated with the committee's regional office, and suggested a pro-union bias.[78] After hearings (boycotted by the IBB) the committee told the companies and union to end the subordinate lodge system. The committee said that it understood the "reluctance of the companies to involve themselves in a violation of the National Labor Relations Act" but argued that the act did not sanction closed shops being used to discriminate on the basis of race—a dubious assertion at this point. The committee concluded that the shipyards, "by assisting the union through complying with its discharge demands, were likewise guilty of discrimination." It told three of the five accused employers, "Regardless of the measure of the union's responsibility in this case, the power to hire and fire remains with the companies, and their obligation to eliminate the obvious and admitted discrimination because of race or color in hiring or firing is primary and fundamental."[79] The IBB angrily denounced the FEPC's findings and directives and warned shipyards to ignore it. Two of five shipyards complied with the committee, but the others refused and met IBB demands to fire blacks who did not pay dues. They were able to defy the committee and run out the clock. By the time that the war ended and the committee expired, the union had still not come to terms, although, as in the railroad case, court decisions in independent suits had reinforced the committee's position.

In several cases, employers were accused of manipulating worker prejudice as a way to weaken or defeat labor organizations, a charge union advocates often made.[80] The Sun Shipbuilding Company in Chester, Pennsylvania, established an all-black shipyard in 1942. Some saw this as an attempt to build an economically and politically dependent black work force, akin to Ford's River Rouge plant, that would support a company union over the CIO's Industrial Union of Marine and Shipbuilding Workers. But the local Urban League supported the plan, as did the local NAACP (until forced to recant by the national office), the *Pittsburgh Courier*, and FEPC member Earl Dickerson, who was widely regarded as the committee's most militant member.[81] Dickerson's position, that segregation was not necessar-

78. Reed, *Seedtime for the Modern Civil Rights Movement*, 277; Weaver, *Negro Labor*, 143.

79. FEPC, *First Report*, 49, 59; "Summary, Findings, and Directives," 9 Dec. 1943 [NAACP 13-B, XII: 483, 506]; FEPC, *Final Report*, 19–21.

80. Ross, *All Manner of Men*, 232; Reed, *Seedtime for the Modern Civil Rights Movement*, 37; "Conference on the Scope and Powers of the Committee on Fair Employment Practice," 19 Feb. 1943 [NAACP 13-B, XII: 417].

81. Northrup, *Organized Labor and the Negro*, 221–24; Reed, *Seedtime for the Modern Civil Rights Movement*, 121; John M. McLarnon, "Pie in the Sky vs. Meat and Potatoes: The Case of Sun Ship's Yard

ily discrimination, met a more difficult test in the Alabama Shipbuilding and Dry-dock Company case in Mobile. AFL unions had driven blacks out of jobs that they held in southern ports before the Wagner Act. The FEPC pressed for the upgrading of black workers, but both the company and unions resisted. The CIO union feared that it would lose white support to its AFL rival if it called for black promotions. The situation was complicated by a feud between the local NAACP and the CIO and by the bid of John L. Lewis's independent union for support. The company suddenly put twelve blacks in skilled jobs, causing a riot that required federal troops to quell. Though the company had done what the committee asked, it was accused of having done so carelessly in order to embarrass the FEPC and the CIO. The committee eventually agreed to a settlement that set aside four shipways in which blacks would have access to some (but not all) skilled jobs.[82]

Labor organization rivalry figured prominently in another of the committee's difficult cases, that of the Philadelphia Rapid Transit Company. Increased demand for skilled workers in urban transportation systems, combined with the non-discrimination policy, led black workers and the FEPC to seek upgrading of blacks to "platform" jobs traditionally reserved for whites. Some cities like Chicago accomplished this easily. Others, like Los Angeles, did it with difficulty. Southern cities never attempted it. The Philadelphia case involved a bafflingly complex situation in which an independent union, the Philadelphia Rapid Transit Employees Union (PRTEU), successor to a company union that had bilked its employee-stockholders out of millions of dollars in its wage fund, was fighting for its survival against the Communist-dominated Transport Workers Union (TWU) of the CIO. The TWU, which favored promotion for blacks, won a 1944 election. Partisans in the PRTEU argued that upgrading blacks would deprive white workers of their accrued seniority.[83] The War Manpower Commission ordered the company to pro-

No. 4," *Journal of American Studies* 34 (2000), 67–88; Reed, "Black Workers, Defense Industries, and Federal Agencies in Pennsylvania, 1941–45," *Labor History* 27 (1986), 367–68; excerpt from speech by A. Philip Randolph, 26 Jun. 1942 [NAACP 13-B, XXIII: 827].

82. Reed, "The FEPC, the Black Worker, and the Southern Shipyards," *South Atlantic Quarterly* 74 (1973), 446–67; "Lily White Unions Steal Negro Jobs," *Crisis* 46 (1939), 273 [DH VII: 411]; Reed, *Seedtime for the Modern Civil Rights Movement*, 117–21; Bruce Nelson, "Organized Labor and the Struggle for Black Equality in Mobile during World War II," *Journal of American History* 80 (1993), 952–88; John P. Davis, "Haas Compromise Bitterly Scored," *Pittsburgh Courier*, 12 Jun. 1943 [DH VII: 279]; Weaver, *Negro Labor*, 37.

83. Whatever the truth of the claim in this case, Communist unionists did embrace the principle of "superseniority" for blacks at the end of the war.

mote blacks in July 1944, and a small group of white workers led a strike that required the War Department to take over the system. Hearings by the FEPC and a grand jury investigation blamed the company for its lax response to the crisis, but they did not find that an attempt to destroy the TWU was the chief source of the strike. Rather, the machinations of a small group of white agitators, and the majority of white workers' fear of acting as "scabs," brought it about. A TWU vice-president complained that the grand jury was "dominated by reactionary, partisan, Republican thinking."[84]

In Texas, the Humble Oil Company, a Standard Oil subsidiary, did use the racial egalitarianism of the CIO's Oil Workers International Union to defeat its attempt to organize its refinery. The company hired a propagandist to promote white fears of black job competition, and the FEPC told the company that its anti-union campaign was "an incitement to violence against Negro workers . . . an act of gross irresponsibility creating disunity among workers and retarding the war effort." The National Labor Relations Board, by contrast, did not see the company's campaign as an unfair labor practice. Though the Oil Workers Union lost the election at Humble, it succeeded in organizing eleven of the twelve refineries in southeast Texas.[85]

The racial policies of labor organizations during the war largely confirmed their prewar reputations: The railroad brotherhoods were the worst, AFL unions varied, and CIO unions were the most open. The AFL members of the FEPC often attempted to divert attention from their affiliates' abuses or to excuse them. This was particularly true of Frank Fenton, the first AFL member. His successor, Boris Shishkin, who would later become the director of the AFL-CIO Civil Rights Committee, also tried to delay or deflect hearings into union violations of the executive

84. FEPC, *Final Report*, 14–17; Ruchames, *Race, Jobs, and Politics*, 100–120; Allan M. Winkler, "The Philadelphia Transit Strike of 1944," *Journal of American History* 59 (1972), 73–89; August Meier and Elliott Rudwick, "Communist Unions and the Black Community: The Case of the Transport Workers Union, 1934–44," *Labor History* 23 (1982), 187–94; Joseph E. Weckler, "Prejudice Is Not the Whole Story," *Public Opinion Quarterly* 9 (1945), 126–39; Ross, *All Manner of Men*, 87–96; "The Philadelphia Strike," *The Nation* 159 (1944), 172–73; "Wasted Manpower," *Philadelphia Tribune*, 12 Aug. 1944; "Where the Blame Rests," *Philadelphia Daily News*, 5 Oct. 1944 [DH VII: 315–18]; "Indict 30 Strikers in Philadelphia," *New York Times*, 5 Oct. 1944, p. 1.

85. Clyde Johnson, "CIO Oil Workers' Organizing Campaign in Texas, 1942–43," Gary M. Fink and Merl E. Reed, eds., *Essays in Southern Labor History: Selected Papers, Southern Labor History Conference, 1976* (Westport, 1977), 180–86; Lawrence W. Cramer to Edwin D. Smith [NAACP 13-A, XV: 414]; Obadele-Starks, *Black Unionism in the Industrial South*, 78.

order. The black unionists and CIO representatives evinced no such ambivalence about the committee's work, and leaders of major CIO unions like the autoworkers, often despite local opposition, championed civil rights and strengthened black-union ties.[86]

The CIO unions could promote discrimination, as the Industrial Union of Marine and Shipbuilding Workers case in Mobile showed. While the Oil Workers Union lost to an employer race-hate campaign at Humble, a successful Oil Workers local signed a contract that left black and Mexican-American workers out of skilled jobs elsewhere in Texas. A New York local of the United Electrical, Radio and Machine Workers established a vigorous fair employment committee, while fifty workers in a St. Louis United Electrical local left their jobs when their employer upgraded black workers. The CIO was relatively more open than the AFL.[87] Julian Thomas of the National Urban League later wrote, "I always recall a statement made by the former president of the American Management Association: 'For heaven's sake, never let the CIO stop pressing for equality of opportunity. It has done more to needle management than any single thing I know of.'"[88]

The FEPC suffered from a number of hindrances. Perhaps most important, it lacked a legislative mandate and existed as a temporary wartime agency. This limited its budget and made it dependent on FDR's support, which vacillated. It remained vulnerable to harassment by southern Democrats, especially Virginia representative Howard Smith's Special Committee to Investigate Executive Agencies. The very war emergency that created the committee also limited its effectiveness— if enforcement of nondiscrimination threatened to disrupt vital war production, fair employment would be sacrificed. The political power of organized labor, particularly the AFL, also limited the committee's effectiveness. In addition to Fenton and Shishkin's caviling at discriminatory practices of AFL unions in the FEPC, the federation was a lukewarm supporter of the effort to enact a permanent, postwar

86. Reed, *Seedtime for the Modern Civil Rights Movement*, 38, 42–43, 150; Robert D. Reynolds Jr., "A Career at Labor Headquarters: The Papers of Boris Shishkin," *Labor's Heritage* 1 (1989), 58–75; Thomas L. Griffith Jr. to Walter White, 23 Oct. 1941 [NAACP 13-B, XII: 967]; Meier and Rudwick, *Black Detroit and the Rise of the UAW*, 132, 194, 218.

87. FEPC, *Final Report*, 23; Ross, *All Manner of Men*, 296; Weaver, *Negro Labor*, 219–20; Kersten, *Race, Jobs, and the War*, 123; Reed, "The FEPC, the Black Worker, and the Southern Shipyards," 466; Zieger, *The CIO*, 160; James B. Atleson, *Labor and the Wartime State: Labor Relations and Law during World War II* (Chicago, 1998), 169; Weaver, "Recent Events in Negro-Union Relationships," 234–49.

88. Julian Thomas to Boyd Wilson, 25 Jun. 1956 [NUL IV: 19].

fair employment law. The AFL had endorsed the general principle of fair employment from the very first but was unhappy about the application of a permanent law to unions, and it abstained only from any open, "official" opposition.[89] The committee noted that the reluctance of courts and legislatures to interfere with the internal practices of labor unions abetted their power to discriminate.[90] Robert C. Weaver, who spent the war in various federal agencies, understood this. "Government had secured recognition for unions which had always violated the spirit of nondiscrimination in employment," he wrote shortly after the war, "at the same time government was committed to a nondiscriminatory employment policy. As between the two inconsistent approaches, government decided to support the stronger and, consequently, took no aggressive steps to secure job opportunities for Negroes in skilled capacities at shipyards which had contracts with AFL unions." Though Weaver muted his criticism of unions in his government work and writings, he later confessed that unions were greater obstacles to job integration than employers.[91]

Faced with all these problems, one could conclude that the committee succeeded remarkably.[92] Southern segregationists harassed the FEPC throughout its last years. Richard Russell took advantage of rising congressional concern over the expansion of unaccountable executive power to finish off the FEPC. In 1944 Congress required all emergency executive agencies to get specific appropriations within one year of their creation. The FEPC narrowly won an appropriation for 1945 but

89. *Proceedings, 61st Annual Convention of the AFL* (1941), 536–39 [DH VII: 440]; John T. Montoux, "AFL Backs FEPC in First Step," *PM,* 30 Nov. 1944 [SCCF 247]; "AFL Backs Permanent FEPC in Historic Convention Move," Associated Negro Press, 4 Dec. 1944 [CBP X: 394]; Louis C. Kesselman, *The Social Politics of FEPC: A Study in Reform Pressure Movements* (Chapel Hill, 1948), 145–47. Cf. Herbert Hill, "Black Workers, Organized Labor, and Title VII of the Civil Rights Act of 1964: Legislative History and Litigation Record," in Herbert Hill and James E. Jones Jr., eds., *Race in America: The Struggle for Equality* (Madison, 1993), 266.

90. FEPC, *First Report,* 49.

91. Weaver, *Negro Labor,* 13, 36; Conrad and Sherer, "From the New Deal to the Great Society," in Boston, ed., *A Different Vision,* I: 292; Herbert Hill, *Black Labor and the American Legal System: Race, Work, and the Law* (Washington, 1977), 183.

92. Historians and economists have given the committee a more favorable appraisal recently. Reed, *Seedtime for the Modern Civil Rights Movement,* 347–57; Kersten, *Race, Jobs, and the War,* 2–4; William J. Collins, "Race, Roosevelt, and Wartime Production: Fair Employment in World War II Labor Markets," *American Economic Review* 91 (2001), 272–86; Paul Moreno, *From Direct Action to Affirmative Action: Fair Employment Law and Policy in America, 1933–72* (Baton Rouge, 1997), 72.

was cut off after the first half of 1946 by a threatened filibuster. Legislative efforts to enact a peacetime fair employment act would fail until 1964.[93]

POSTWAR ADJUSTMENT

In the postwar years, Congress and the courts took action that limited the power of labor unions and expanded the rights of minorities in them. Two important court cases grew out of FEPC investigations and established a principle of "fair representation" for unions. Congress amended the National Labor Relations Act in 1947 and for the first time established that unions were prohibited from engaging in "unfair labor practices." Finally, Congress and the unions themselves crippled the influence of the Communist Party in the American labor movement.

Several black firemen brought suit against the southern railroads and unions when they ignored or defied the FEPC. Federal courts in Virginia dismissed their argument that the Railway Labor Act required the unions to represent the interests of all railway workers. The Fourth Circuit Court of Appeals decided that the act did not permit the government to interfere in the membership requirements or bargaining tactics of the unions.[94] The Alabama Supreme Court reached a similar decision, ruling that the act intended only to ensure orderly collective bargaining, not to reform job discrimination or segregation.[95] The U.S. Supreme Court reversed both decisions in December 1944. The Court held that the Railway Labor Act had given the railroad unions virtually sovereign power, and therefore it required them to represent minority group members fairly. The Court did not go so far as to require the unions to admit blacks as members, a fact that stirred Justice Frank Murphy to object that "The cloak of racism surrounding the actions of the Brotherhood in refusing membership to Negroes and in entering into and enforcing agreements discriminating against them, all under the guise of congressional authority, still remains." While the Court attempted to balance the interests of labor unions and racial minorities, Murphy wanted it to go further and hold that "the Constitution voices its disapproval whenever economic discrimination is applied under authority of law against any race, creed, or color."[96] In a sense, however, the

---

93. Neuchterlein, "Politics of Civil Rights," 180–91; Reed, *Seedtime for the Modern Civil Rights Movement*, 157–72, 338–43; Ross, *All Manner of Men*, 249.

94. *Tunstall v. Brotherhood of Locomotive Firemen & Enginemen*, 140 F. 2d 35 (1944). John J. Parker was one of the three justices who decided the case.

95. *Steele v. Louisville & Nashville Railroad*, 16 So. 2d 416 (1944).

96. *Steele v. Louisville & Nashville Railroad*, 323 U.S. 192; *Tunstall v. Brotherhood of Locomotive Firemen & Enginemen*, 323 U.S. 210 (1944); George Louis Creamer, "Collective Bargaining and Racial Dis-

Court had provided special protection to blacks—faced with the general problem of the rights of minorities in the majority-rule system established by the Wagner Act, it singled out blacks as an easily identified group that needed protection.[97] Individual suits against the IBB attained further results in the California courts. Racial discrimination violated public policy, as expressed in the fair employment executive orders and state civil rights laws, the California Supreme Court held, and thus a union could not use a closed shop for an illegal purpose.[98]

These cases were pathbreaking, if not quite the *"Dred Scott* decision in reverse" that former FEPC chairman Malcolm Ross depicted. Without an administrative agency like the FEPC to pursue them, the principles would have to be vindicated by individual litigants. Arthur Fletcher, assistant secretary of labor under President Nixon, later claimed that if these decisions had been implemented, no Civil Rights Act would have been necessary. The Court held only railroad unions under the Railway Labor Act, not all unions under the Wagner Act, to a duty of fair representation. The National Labor Relations Board had not acted so boldly. It could refuse to certify discriminatory unions; as early as 1938 the board had denied recognition to a white-only tobacco workers union where black employees in the plant performed the same work. In 1943, the NLRB expressed "grave doubt" that a racially closed union could serve as the bargaining agent in a closed shop. Consistent with the Supreme Court, the board held that segregated locals were not inherently discriminatory. "Neither exclusion from membership nor segregated membership *per se* represents evasion on the part of a labor organization of its statutory duty of 'equal representation,'" the NLRB stated in 1945. "But in each case where the issue is presented the Board will scrutinize the contract and conduct of a representative organization and withdraw certification if it finds the organization has discriminated against employees in the bargaining units through its membership restrictions or otherwise."[99]

crimination," *Rocky Mountain Law Review* 17 (1945), 163–96; Richard Epstein, *Forbidden Grounds: The Case against Employment Discrimination Laws* (Cambridge, 1992), 118–23.

97. Norman Thomas, "How Democratic Are Labor Unions?" *Harper's Magazine,* May 1942, pp. 655–62 [SCCF 2712]; Philip D. Bradley, "Involuntary Participation in Unionism," in Edward H. Chamberlin et al., *Labor Unions and Public Policy* (Washington, 1958), 78; Reuel E. Schiller, "From Group Rights to Individual Liberties: Postwar Labor Law, Liberalism, and the Waning of Union Strength," *Berkeley Journal of Employment and Labor Law* 20 (1999), 3–73.

98. *James v. Marinship Corp.,* 155 P. 2d 329 (1945); Wollenberg, *"James v. Marinship."*

99. Ross, *All Manner of Men,* 135; Arthur Fletcher, *The Silent Sell-Out: Government Betrayal of Blacks to the Craft Unions* (New York, 1973), 26; FEPC, *Final Report,* 14; Ray Marshall, "The Negro and

Judicial support for the power of organized labor abated by the end of the war, presaging the general public sense that unions had acquired too much power since the New Deal and were harming the public interest and the rights of minorities— racial and other. The Court began to retreat from its picketing-as-free-speech position. In 1945, the Court narrowly upheld the power of a labor union to use its closed shop contracts with Philadelphia companies to force out of business a trucking company that had resisted its demands. The decision evoked a caustic dissent from Justice Robert Jackson: "With this decision, the labor movement has come full circle. The working man has struggled long, the fight has been filled with hatred, and conflict has been dangerous, but now workers may not be deprived of their livelihood merely because their employers opposed and they favor unions. Labor has won other rights as well . . . This Court now sustains the claim of a union to the right to deny participation in the economic world to an employer simply because the union dislikes him. This Court permits to employees the same arbitrary dominance over the economic sphere which they control that labor so long, so bitterly and so rightly asserted should belong to no man."[100]

In 1947 the Republicans regained control of Congress and amended the Wagner Act. The Labor-Management Relations Act, known as the Taft-Hartley Act, resulted from the growth of union power and particularly the wave of strikes that followed the end of the war. Fully 113 million man-hours were lost to strikes in 1946, three times as many as in any year of American history. Many advocates of racial equality and union democracy hoped that amendments to the Wagner Act might improve the unions' racial performance. The act was a compromise between an extremely anti-union House bill and the desires of organized labor, which labeled it a "slave labor act" and claimed that it would help the Soviets. It accepted the premises of the NLRA but tried to balance the power of unions and employers.

Organized Labor," *Journal of Negro Education* 32 (1963), 386; Michael Jordan, "The NLRB Racial Discrimination Decisions, 1935–41: The Empiric Process of Administration and the Inner Eye of Racism," *Connecticut Law Review* 24 (1991), 55–96; Paul L. Styles, "Handling Race Relations through Collective Bargaining," speech at Fisk University Institute on Race Relations, 29 Jun. 1950, Box 1, RG 9-001, George Meany Memorial Archives, Silver Spring; *Larus & Brother Co.,* 62 NLRB 1075 (1945); NLRB, *Tenth Annual Report* (Washington, 1945), 18. For an early observation of the idea that the legal empowerment of unions could bring in its train legal protection for blacks, see Joseph R. Houchins, "Racial Minorities and Organized Labor," *Opportunity* 13 (1935), 109.

100. Price, "Picketing"; *Hunt v. Crumboch,* 325 U.S. 821 (1945); Morgan O. Reynolds, *Making America Poorer: The Cost of Labor Law* (Washington, 1987), 22.

The act outlawed the closed shop, and more explicitly allowed states to prohibit the union shop—an option many southern states quickly exercised by "right to work" laws.[101] It denied the privileges of the NLRB to unions whose officers did not sign affidavits swearing that they were not Communist Party members. For the first time, it allowed the NLRB to issue orders against unfair labor practices by unions.

It seems unlikely that the Taft-Hartley Act intended to interfere in the discriminatory practices of unions. Principally concerned with the right not to join a union, its protections of the right to union membership were poorly drafted.[102] Most black newspapers regarded the act as a boon to black workers, hailing it as a "little FEPC."[103] Allowing employers to hire workers who were barred from regular union membership gave minority workers some protection against union discrimination. Senator Robert Taft said in congressional debate, "Let us take the case of unions which prohibit the admission of Negroes to membership, they may continue to do so; but representatives of the union cannot go to the employer and say,

101. Slichter, "The Taft-Hartley Act," 7; Ralph A. Newman, "The Closed Union and the Right to Work," *Columbia Law Review* 43 (1943), 42–57 [SCCF 2713]; Thomas, "How Democratic Are Labor Unions?"; Charles W. Baird, "Right to Work Before and After 14(b)," *Journal of Labor Research* 19 (1998), 471–93.

102. Slichter, "The Taft-Hartley Act," 23; Anders Lewis and John Braeman, "The American Federation of Labor and Cold War Anti-Communism," *Continuity* 26 (2003), 108–9.

103. Donald R. McCoy and Richard T. Ruetten, *Quest and Response: Minority Rights and the Truman Administration* (Lawrence, KS, 1973), 145; Proceedings, Civil Rights Staff Conference, National CIO Committee to Abolish Discrimination, 24 May 1950, p. 208, Box 7, RG 9-001, George Meany Memorial Archives, Silver Spring. As businessmen and employers, the black press often took an antiunion position, and their marginal profitability made it unlikely that they could survive increased labor costs that came with unionization. Civil rights groups feared the loss of Negro newspaper support on other issues. The widow of the founder of the *New York Amsterdam News* explained the problem to W. E. B. Du Bois in 1935. Sadie Warren-Davis to W. E. B. Du Bois, 26 Nov. 1935, in Herbert Aptheker, ed., *The Correspondence of W. E. B. Du Bois*, 3 vols. (Amherst, MA, 1973–78), II: 115. When the *Norfolk Journal and Guide* was resisting organization in 1950, Edna Berger of the American Newspaper Guild told the CIO Civil Rights Committee that the owners could continue to publish through a strike by using "their daughters, sons-in-law, nieces and nephews." Committee member Boyd L. Wilson suggested that "A daughter's head will bleed just like a head that isn't a daughter's. You simply have to apply that kind of tactics." George L.-P. Weaver, chairman of the committee, objected, but Wilson replied, "We put a picket line out there and that daughter, mama or nobody else is going in." Proceedings of Civil Rights Staff Conference, National CIO Committee to Abolish Discrimination, 24 May 1950, pp. 205–6, 234, RG 9-001, Box 7, George Meany Memorial Archives, Silver Spring.

'You have got to fire this man because he is not a member of our union.'"[104] Leaders of the machinists union used the new law to convince reluctant members that they must drop their white-only ritual.[105] The act may have helped black workers by weakening unions in general. Clarence Mitchell, NAACP labor secretary, complained that "The framers of the Taft-Hartley Act, while publicly announcing that they intended to prevent discrimination against colored persons in labor unions, actually made it clear that the doctrine of the *Larus* case [which permitted segregated locals] should be followed by the Board in matters of this kind."[106] Mitchell claimed, "The authors of the Taft-Hartley Act pretended to be giving minorities a pat on the back, but were really pinning a donkey's tail of second-class citizenship on all the colored people in the labor movement."[107]

The NLRB, already retreating from some indications that it might undermine union discrimination even under the Wagner Act, did not take the Taft-Hartley Act as an invitation to exercise more power in racial discrimination cases, though it did in nonracial cases, evincing its overall selectivity about which parts of the act it enforced. *Pittsburgh Courier* editors rebuked the NAACP for opposing the act rather than pressuring the NLRB to interpret it correctly.[108] As late as 1959, NAACP attorney Jack Greenberg claimed that sections of the act "specifically forbid racial discrimination in some situations."[109]

The Taft-Hartley requirement of noncommunist affidavits and the general na-

104. *Congressional Record,* 29 Apr. 1947, pp. 4317–18, in National Labor Relations Board, *Legislative History of the Labor-Management Relations Act, 1947,* 2 vols. (Washington, 1985), II: 1096.

105. Mark Perlman, *The Machinists: A New Study in American Trade Unionism* (Cambridge, 1961), 279; Lloyd H. Bailer, "Organized Labor and Racial Minorities," *Annals of the American Academy of Political and Social Science* 274 (1951), 102.

106. Statement of Clarence Mitchell before Senate Committee on Labor and Public Welfare, 10 Feb. 1949 [NAACP 13-A, I: 751]; Clarence Mitchell, "Notes on Taft-Hartley," *Crisis* 55 (1948), 300–01; Clarence Mitchell to All Chairmen of Labor Committees, 2 Jul. 1947 [NAACP 13-A, VI: 704]; Conference Report, "Labor-Management Relations Act, 1947," House Report 510, 80th Cong., 1st Sess. (1947), 41, in National Labor Relations Board, *Legislative History,* I: 505; Robert F. Drinan, "Negroes Oppose Taft-Hartley," *Interracial Review* (Mar. 1950), 41–43 [NAACP 13-A, VI: 933].

107. NAACP Press Release, 17 Mar. 1949 [NAACP 13-A, IV: 901]. For a broader interpretation of the act's potential for fair representation, see Michael I. Sovern, "The National Labor Relations Act and Racial Discrimination," *Columbia Law Review* 62 (1962), 603.

108. Jordan, "The NLRB and Racial Discrimination Decisions," 87; Sylvester Petro, *How the NLRB Repealed Taft-Hartley* (Washington, 1958); "FEPC in the New Labor Bill," Pittsburgh *Courier,* 5 Mar. 1949, p. 14.

109. Jack Greenberg, *Race Relations and American Law* (New York, 1959), 178.

tional awakening to the Soviet threat brought the issue of communist influence in organized labor to the crisis point. It culminated in the expulsion of eleven Communist-dominated unions from the CIO in 1949–50. The impact of this "purge" on the matter of racial discrimination has been a subject of intense controversy, related to the general question of the nature and aims of the American Communist Party. Early scholars argued that American Communists always subordinated civil rights issues to Moscow's dictates. A later group lamented the loss of the greatest force for racial equality in the American labor movement. A number of studies have shown that the behavior of CP unions varied one from another and that union leaders often mediated Soviet policy with rank-and-file interests. Leaving aside the fact that these unionists usually acted to promote the aims of aggressive, totalitarian mass murderers, and taking into account the substantial independent commitment of many Communist unionists to racial fairness, their mixed record and manipulation of the race issue was such as to make their elimination no great loss to the movement for economic equality; moreover, the removal of communist association helped the success of the later civil rights movement.[110]

The party's ambivalence about the fair employment issue during the Hitler-Stalin pact period became even more of a problem after Hitler invaded the Soviet Union on June 22, 1941. Moscow compelled American Communists to return to the Popular Front position of cooperation with the government, indeed to do everything necessary to help win the war. The party shelved its "Black Belt" thesis, began to say that bourgeois America could reform its class and race problems, and finally voted itself out of existence in 1944. Communist unions enthusiastically supported the wartime "no strike" pledge. Even recent communist apologists recognize that probably nothing did more to confirm black suspicions about the motives of the party than its subordination of racial equality to the defense-production effort.[111]

110. Zieger, *The CIO,* 253; John Earl Haynes, "The Cold War Debate Continues: A Traditionalist View of Historical Writing on Domestic Communism and Anti-Communism," *Cold War Studies* 2 (2000), 86–89, 114; John Braeman, "The New Deal Revisited," *Continuity* 23 (1999), 26; Robert H. Zieger, "A Venture into Unplowed Fields: Daniel Powell and CIO Political Action in the Postwar South," in Glenn T. Eskew, ed., *Labor in the Modern South* (Athens, GA, 2001), 174; Lewis and Braeman, "The American Federation of Labor and Cold War Anti-Communism," 106–07; Michael S. Sherry, *In the Shadow of War: The United States since the 1930s* (New Haven, 1995), 148.

111. John W. Van Zanten, "Communist Theory and the American Negro Question," *Review of Politics* 29 (1967), 438–39; James R. Barrett, *William Z. Foster and the Tragedy of American Radicalism* (Ur-

When A. Philip Randolph maintained the March on Washington Movement to monitor discrimination in defense industries, the Communists denounced him as subversive and pro-Axis. Nor did the Communist Party assist the fair employment effort when the president nearly spiked the FEPC in 1942. The party similarly belabored John L. Lewis and Adam Clayton Powell for bringing up racial grievances during the war.[112] A *Negro Digest* poll in 1944 found that more black Americans believed that the Communists were still fighting for Negro rights but that most of them believed that an American victory would best encourage democracy and equality. Journalist George L. Schuyler commented that, "Communists have not quit fighting for Negro rights because they never began." Ever since coming to power in 1917, "the Communists have fought for nobody's rights except their own." Sociologist Horace R. Cayton noted that communist unions had been fairest to Negroes but that blacks were becoming disillusioned about their commitment to equality.[113] "There was a time in the war years when Communists sought to sabotage every move toward integration of Negro workers if they thought it would hamper production," George L.-P. Weaver, the director of the CIO's Committee to Abolish Racism and Discrimination, said in 1947.[114] Herbert Hill, future labor secretary of the NAACP, was equally scathing, arguing that the Communist Party was the tool of Soviet foreign policy. "It is therefore inevitable that American Communist party interest in the Negro can be neither genuine nor sincere . . . If Communists gained influence among Negroes they would not hesitate for a moment to foment racial strife and dissension, and all in the interests of the Soviet Union."[115] Indeed, Communist unionists had manipulated racial and ethnic divisions when it was expedient, and who was to say in the postwar years that black Americans, like Israel, might be but a temporary CP pet?[116]

---

bana, 1999), 243; Zieger, *The CIO*, 172; Foner, *Organized Labor and the Black Worker*, 279; Steven Rosswurm, ed., *The CIO's Left-Led Unions* (New Brunswick, 1992), 10.

112. Record, *The Negro and the Communist Party*, 219; Record, *Race and Radicalism*, 120; Sumner Rosen, "The CIO Era, 1935–55," in Julius Jacobson, ed., *The Negro and the American Labor Movement* (Garden City, NY, 1968), 196.

113. "Have the Communists Quit Fighting for Negro Rights," *Negro Digest* 3 (Dec. 1944), 56–68; Horace Catyon, *Long Old Road* (New York, 1965), 253; Richard S. Hobbs, *Cayton Legacy: An African American Family* (Pullman, WA, 2002), 159.

114. Donald T. Critchlow, "Communist Unions and Racism," *Labor History* 17 (1976), 230.

115. Herbert Hill, "The Communist Party—Enemy of Negro Equality," *Crisis* 58 (1951), 365–71, 421–24.

116. Fraser, *Labor Will Rule*, 204.

In 1945, the anti-Nazi alliance fell apart and American Communists again shifted gears. They resurrected the party and pinned the errors of their wartime "revisionism" on Earl Browder, whom William Z. Foster replaced as chairman. The Communists confessed their errors on many questions, including their handling of the race issue. James W. Ford apologized for "the opportunistic line which has led our organization into the swamp of revisionism" but explained that he had believed that "the bourgeoisie would industrialize the South and itself open up the path of bourgeois-democratic development."[117] Benjamin J. Davis also noted that the wartime gains of black workers had misled him. As the war neared its end, the Communists began to pay more attention to the race question. The party claimed that it had never abandoned Negro rights but had merely shifted emphasis.[118]

While the Communists did not completely abandon the racial equality issue during the war, they often promoted it in dubious ways. In 1943 the Communist faction in the UAW pressed for a special seat on the union's executive board reserved for a Negro. Though local blacks endorsed the idea, mainstream civil rights organizations and the FEPC usually abjured racial quotas or preferential treatment.[119] Many believed that the Communists were exploiting the issue to get black votes. Walter Reuther excoriated the Communists for hypocrisy and opportunism, and Victor Reuther argued, "We must not establish the practice of giving special privileges to special groups, because that is a Jim Crow privilege, and will . . . kick in the teeth the very people it is trying to help. If there is a special post for Negroes, then in all justice there should be a post at large for the Catholics, the women, the Jews, the Poles, and the rest." George L.-P. Weaver added that "that same argument could be used to justify segregation on a streetcar, in a hotel, and in a restaurant."[120]

As the war neared its end, Communists led a movement to protect black job

---

117. James W. Ford, "Revisionist Policies Weakened Struggle for Negro Rights," *Daily Worker,* 25 Jun. 1945, p. 7.

118. Benjamin J. Davis Jr., "Calls for Examination of Negro Work," *Daily Worker,* 22 Jul. 1945, p. 8; Record, *Race and Radicalism,* 120. This plea is sustained by Maurice Isserman, *Which Side Were You On? The American Communist Party during the Second World War* (Middletown, CT, 1982), 141.

119. Moreno, *From Direct Action to Affirmative Action,* 68–71; Kersten, *Race, Jobs, and the War,* 2.

120. Meier and Rudwick, *Black Detroit and the Rise of the UAW,* 210; Lichtenstein, *The Most Dangerous Man in Detroit,* 211; George L.-P. Weaver, "Pitfalls that Beset Negro Trade Unionists," *Opportunity* 22 (1944), 12–13 [DH VII: 387]. Keenan, *The Communist Party and the Auto Workers Unions,* 234, and Bert Cochran, *Labor and Communism: The Conflict that Shaped American Unions* (Princeton, 1977), 225, defend the Communists.

gains through a system of race-based "superseniority."[121] Under ordinary conditions, workers would be laid off according to their time on the job and thus blacks and women, usually the most recently hired, would be the first to be fired. Communists proposed that unions press employers to lay off workers with an eye toward maintaining the current racial proportions of their work force instead. They denied that this implied any preferential treatment but would ensure fair treatment for black workers, who were being purged from industrial work forces as the fascist plutocrats prepared for war.[122] Organized labor rejected the idea. Philip Murray called seniority "a safeguard against discrimination and favoritism" and claimed that alteration of seniority would make white men "become not only anti-Negro and anti-woman, but also anti-union." George L.-P. Weaver warned that "One of the most dangerous pitfalls that Negroes in the labor movement can fall into is that of allowing themselves to be maneuvered into a position of demanding special racial rights and consideration." Robert C. Weaver noted, "As a general rule, group-adjusted seniority is like hot ice cream; it is not consistent with the basic principles of the concept."[123] Communists labeled as race traitors black leaders who opposed the idea.[124]

The United Electrical Workers were among the first to push for "superseniority." Communists had captured the NAACP local in Bridgeport, Connecticut, and tried to use the association to endorse the union's idea. The national office of the NAACP denounced the proposal, saying that it never endorsed "asking for special consideration because we happen to be Negroes." Special counsel Thurgood Marshall noted, "It has long been a cardinal point in the program of the Association to strongly oppose any idea that would distinguish colored citizens as a unique or separate group apart from the rest of the American people." Labor secretary Herbert Hill called the idea "a sugar-coated form of segregation."[125] It turned out to

121. The party also revived the prewar tactic of picketing white businesses for racial job quotas. Paul Moreno, "Direct Action and Fair Employment: The *Hughes* Case," *Western Legal History* 8 (1995), 1–34.

122. Hal Simon, "The Struggle for Jobs and Negro Rights in the Trade Unions," *Political Affairs* 29 (Feb. 1950), 33–48.

123. Philip Murray, "CIO Head Opposes Seniority Revision," *Chicago Defender*, 27 Jan. 1945; Weaver, "Pitfalls That Beset Negro Trade Unionists"; Weaver, *Negro Labor*, 301; Ernest E. Johnson, "CIO National Convention to Consider Negro Cutbacks," Associated Negro Press, 22 Nov. 1944 [CBP X: 537].

124. Foner, *Organized Labor and the Black Worker*, 289.

125. Zieger, *The CIO*, 159; Barrett, *William Z. Foster and the Tragedy of American Radicalism*, 244; Robert Korstad and Nelson Lichtenstein, "Opportunities Found and Lost: Labor, Radicals, and the

be unnecessary in any event. Although the FEPC warned that "wartime gains of Negro, Mexican-American, and Jewish workers are being lost through an unchecked revival of discriminatory practices," in fact reconversion did not produce a major setback for black workers.[126]

Communists also posed problems in the effort to get Congress to enact a permanent, peacetime FEPC. The party may have wanted to prevent the passage of fair employment legislation without appearing to do so, knowing that its endorsement would undermine support for it. It is more likely that the CP wanted to get the credit for any legislation that was enacted, working through the CIO to wrest control of the effort from A. Philip Randolph's National Council for a Permanent FEPC. Randolph was especially determined to keep the FEPC effort from being linked to communism. His own maladroit lobbying impeded the task in the late 1940s. Though it took twenty years for Congress to enact a fair employment law, and the ultimate success was due to a number of changed circumstances, the fading away of Communist connection helped it.[127]

As the CIO expelled party-dominated unions, Communists appealed for black support, charging that their opponents were racists and that discrimination would increase without Communist influence. That anticommunist unionists had equal or better reputations on civil rights undermined these Stalinist accusations.[128] The International Union of Mine, Mill, and Smelter Workers accused the United Steelworkers of collaborating with racist white workers and owners to oust it in the Alabama iron country. The CIO replied in kind, accusing the union of attempting "to split the white and Negro workers, using the Communist weapons of fear, intolerance, racial hatred."[129] Though many black workers lamented the loss of their union, the Steelworkers and NAACP took steps to heal the rift. The International

---

Early Civil Rights Movement," *Journal of American History* 75 (1988), 792; "NAACP Fights 'Super-Seniority,'" *Crisis* 56 (1949), 250–51; Moreno, *From Direct Action to Affirmative Action*, 82–83.

126. FEPC, *Final Report*, viii; Weaver, "Negro Labor since 1929," 33.

127. Pfeffer, *A. Philip Randolph*, 90, 118; Nolan, *Communism versus the Negro*, 181; Kesselman, *Social Politics of FEPC*, 156–58; Walter White to Leslie Perry, 23 Nov. 1945; Perry to White, 20 Nov. 1945 [NAACP 13-B, XVIII: 863, 866].

128. Record, *Race and Radicalism*, 165.

129. Vernon H. Jensen, *Nonferrous Metals Industry Unionism, 1932–54: A Study of Leadership Controversy* (Ithaca, NY, 1954), 239–41; Norrell, "Caste in Steel," 684–85; Horace Huntley, "The Red Scare and Black Workers in Alabama: The International Union of Mine, Mill, and Smelter Workers, 1945–53," in Robert Asher and Charles Stephenson, eds., *Labor Divided: Race and Ethnicity in U.S. Labor Struggles, 1835–1960* (Albany, NY, 1990); Zieger, *The CIO*, 282; "Leftists Warned: Follow CIO Policy or Quit Board" and Arthur Riordan, "Mine, Mill Smear of Murray Carried Even to His Faith," *CIO News*,

Union of Electrical Workers, which replaced the Communist United Electrical Workers, was similarly attentive to civil rights issues. Indeed, the communist union became more concerned about black issues *after* its ouster.[130] These unions would continue to face black complaints, but probably no more than they would have under Communist control. In his 1955 memoir, Walter White praised the CIO for the expulsions, though his biographer argues that this was more of a "genuflection at the Cold War altar than an honest rendering of his and the NAACP's differences with the CP over time."[131] Herbert Hill concluded, "Those unions with a predominantly white membership that were controlled for years by leaders loyal to the Communist party were substantively no different in their racial practices than other labor organizations."[132]

In those unions that were Communist-led but predominantly black, racial fairness continued to be a problem. The United Packinghouse Workers (UPW) evaded the CIO purge and became increasingly black-dominated. Herbert March, the UPW official, had promoted interracial slates for union offices, but black Communists demanded an all-black slate and charged March with "white chauvinism," prompting him to leave the party and the union. The UPW moved its offices to the former Communist International Workers Order building in Chicago in 1949, despite its distance from the stockyards where most members worked, more effectively to recruit black party members. One observer wrote, "The Communist Party in its efforts to win the Negro packinghouse workers, was willing to sacrifice biracial participation in the Chicago locals."[133]

The communist tobacco workers union was expelled from the CIO and chased

---

23 May, 1949, pp. 3, 6; Michael Goldfield, *The Color of Politics: Race, Class, and the Mainsprings of American Politics* (New York, 1997), 223.

130. Nelson, *Divided We Stand*, 202–15. For a revisionist view of this union, see Draper, "The New Southern Labor History Revisited," 87–108; Critchlow, "Communist Unions and Racism," 234; Gerald Zahavi, "Passionate Commitments: Race, Sex, and Communism at Schenectady General Electric, 1932–54," *Journal of American History* 83 (1996), 525.

131. Janken, *White*, 364.

132. Herbert Hill, "Black Labor and Affirmative Action: An Historical Perspective," in Shulman and Darity, eds., *The Question of Discrimination*, 245. For a contrary view, see Michael Goldfield, "Race and the CIO: The Possibilities for Racial Egalitarianism during the 1930s and 1940s," *International Labor and Working Class History* 44 (1993), 1–32.

133. Halpern, *Down on the Killing Floor*, 243; Jack Barbash, *The Practice of Unionism* (New York, 1956), 354; Theodore V. Purcell, *The Worker Speaks His Mind on Company and Union* (Cambridge, 1953), 71.

out of the Virginia cigarette factories, usually giving way to the AFL's tobacco workers union. While communist competition did provoke the AFL to liberalize its racial policies, the Communist unionists sacrificed the fundamental economic interests of their black members for the sake of Stalin's foreign policy goals. However, the fight between the Communists, the AFL, and a noncommunist CIO union left the R. J. Reynolds plant an open shop, one that paid higher wages and made the first steps toward integration of skilled jobs.[134] The open shop continued to rival the union shop, Communist or not.

By midcentury, organized labor appeared to enjoy a secure place in the American economy, with the Wagner Act modified but basically ratified by the Taft-Hartley amendments. The executive branch and the courts had begun to devise the doctrines of "fair employment" and "fair representation" to safeguard the rights of blacks within the economy. Blacks and unions, antagonists for decades, seemed to be solid allies, but the next fifteen years would show the strengths and weaknesses of this coalition.

134. Herbert R. Northrup, *The Negro in the Tobacco Industry* (Philadelphia, 1970), 37–39, 61; Norgren et al., "Negro Labor and Its Problems," 756; William Smith to Walter White, 6 Apr. 1949 [NAACP 13-A, XIV: 487]; Henry Lee Moon to William Smith, 19 Apr. 1949 [NAACP 13-A, XIV: 547]; Judith Stein, "The Ins and Outs of the CIO," *International Labor and Working Class History* 44 (1993), 62.

6 / The Civil Rights Era, 1950–1965

The generation after World War II witnessed a revolution in American race relations, often called the "Second Reconstruction." The war undermined the ideology of white supremacy. As *Fortune* magazine put it in 1942, "In the consciousness of all peoples in the world, this war is being fought for and against the idea of racial superiority. America's Constitution, like Christianity, is based on the principle that every man is born with the inalienable right to equality of opportunity."[1] The emerging liberal nationalist view of the race problem was captured in Gunnar Myrdal's *An American Dilemma,* published in 1944, which documented the gap between America's principles of equality and its treatment of blacks.[2] A "quiet revolution" was taking place in the racial attitudes of white Americans in the 1940s and 1950s.[3] As the economic effects of continued war spending propelled black economic progress, so American defense of liberal democratic principles in the cold war augmented the civil rights movement. "The cold war has taken the matter of racial discrimination in all its forms out of the realm of a national issue to make it a problem of international importance and implications," Robert C. Weaver observed in 1950. "This fact, perhaps more than any other, is responsible for the concern with which Americans are viewing Negro-white relations."[4]

The New Deal accelerated the integration of the South into the national econ-

1. "The Negro's War," *Fortune,* Jun. 1942, p. 164.

2. Paul Sniderman and Thomas Piazza, *The Scar of Race* (Cambridge, 1993), 4.

3. J. Milton Yinger and George E. Simpson, "Can Segregation Survive in an Industrial Society?" *Antioch Review* 28 (1958), 16; Stephan and Abigail Thernstrom, *America in Black and White: One Nation, Indivisible* (New York, 1997), 103; Steven M. Gelber, *Black Men and Businessmen: The Growing Awareness of a Social Responsibility* (Port Washington, NY, 1974), ch. 6.

4. Robert C. Weaver, "Negro Labor since 1929," *Journal of Negro History* 35 (1950), 37; Mary L. Dudziak, *Cold War Civil Rights: Race and the Image of American Democracy* (Princeton, 2000), 11–12; Azza Salama Layton, *International Politics and Civil Rights Policies in the United States, 1941–60* (New York, 2000); Thomas Borstelmann, *The Cold War and the Color Line: American Race Relations in the Global Arena* (Cambridge, 2001); Donald R. McCoy and Richard T. Ruetten, *Quest and Response: Minority Rights and the Truman Administration* (Lawrence, KS, 1973), 180, 199; Carl M. Brauer, *John F. Kennedy and the Second Reconstruction* (New York, 1977), 76; Gelber, *Black Men and Businessmen,* 89. Cf. Richard Polenberg's conclusion that the attempt to use the cold war to promote civil rights was a "boomerang"; *One Nation Divisible: Class, Race, and Ethnicity in the United States since 1938* (New York, 1980), 108–15.

omy, and the war added to the momentum. While the New Deal Democratic coalition shaped the region's development in the so-called welfare and warfare states, private development of things like air conditioning and the mechanical cotton picker also shaped its evolution. Southern per capita income rose from 47 to 64 percent of the North's between 1928 and 1948. Cold war spending, particularly the Korean War, continued the economic gains that blacks made during the 1940s. The 1950s saw some of the greatest progress for blacks in terms of income relative to white Americans. One million blacks left southern farms in the 1940s; by 1960, black Americans had become more urban than whites.[5] The urbanization and industrialization of the South, as in the North, began to alter race relations, increasing the pressure of black protest and presenting white southerners with a crisis.

In addition to the religious and political forces behind the civil rights movement, black Americans began to turn their increased economic power toward an attack on segregation. This tactic had a long history, most prominent in the "Don't Buy Where You Can't Work" campaigns of the depression period. After World War II, however, black activists began to use their power as consumers to get white businessmen to provide jobs and better service, rather than patronizing black businesses, which often had a stake in segregation and stood to lose by integration.[6]

An increasing number of businessmen began to respond to the pressure and appeal of black consumers after World War II. Most northern businesses that moved South before the war easily accommodated themselves to southern racial patterns.[7] The change during and after the war years was most notable in International Harvester, which acquired a reputation as a leader in equal opportunity, aided by the cooperation of its union leaders.[8] While many older, smaller, locally

5. James C. Cobb, *Industrialization and Southern Society, 1877–1984* (Lexington, KY, 1984), 52; U.S. Department of Commerce, Bureau of the Census, *Historical Statistics of the United States: Colonial Times to 1970*, 2 vols. (Washington, 1975), I: 303; James P. Smith, "Race and Human Capital," *American Economic Review* 74 (1984), 695; William H. Harris, *The Harder We Run: Black Workers since the Civil War* (New York, 1982), 128; Yinger and Simpson, "Can Segregation Survive," 17.

6. Robert E. Weems Jr., *Desegregating the Dollar: African American Consumerism in the Twentieth Century* (New York, 1998), 4, 54–70; Gunnar Myrdal, *An American Dilemma: The Negro Problem and Modern Democracy* (New York, 1944), 305; Thernstrom and Thernstrom, *America in Black and White*, 186.

7. James C. Cobb, *The Selling of the South: The Southern Crusade for Industrial Development, 1936–90*, 2d ed. (Urbana, 1993), 122; Cobb, *Industrialization and Southern Society*, 109; Thomas V. Purcell and Daniel P. Mulvey, *The Negro in the Electrical Manufacturing Industry* (Philadelphia, 1971), 111.

8. Robert Ozanne, *A Century of Labor-Management Relations at McCormick and International Harvester* (Madison, 1967), 183–93; John Hope, *Equality of Opportunity: A Union Approach to Fair Em-*

oriented southern enterprises remained committed to white supremacy, a new generation of southern business leaders put economic rationality ahead of racial order.[9] It was becoming increasingly clear that the South could not have both economic development and segregation, and an increasing number of business and political leaders opted for economic development.[10] The process was often reluctant and halting and marked no sudden, seismic shift in racial attitudes, but it was a significant change. "At both the state and local level southern business leaders and other proponents of industrial growth often played crucial roles in engineering peaceful transitions to token desegregation," one historian notes. "The desire for industry was on occasion a potent force for moderation during the civil rights era."[11]

The quickening of the civil rights movement in the mid-1950s made it more difficult for southerners to avoid the choice between tradition and progress. The *Brown* decision of 1954 was the first indication of the crisis of segregation, followed by the Montgomery bus boycott and anger over the exoneration of the murderers of Emmett Till. The reaction of southern businessmen and communities varied. A 1963 study showed that the overwhelming majority of southern businessmen favored segregation.[12] But as protest grew, the business elite sought accommodation, peaceful compliance, and at least a modicum of desegregation. Little Rock provided the object lesson. Arkansas, which had a reputation for "progressivism," good race relations, and attracting outside investment, saw its image sullied as a result of Governor Orval Faubus's intransigence. Little Rock had opened five indus-

---

ployment (Washington, 1956); Yinger and Simpson, "Can Segregation Survive," 17; "Racial Dispute Irks Reuther," *New York Times*, 2 May 1953, p. 11.

9. Elizabeth Jacoway and David R. Colburn, eds., *Southern Businessmen and Desegregation* (Baton Rouge, 1982), 1–13; Cobb, *Industrialization and Southern Society*, 151–53; Numan V. Bartley, *The Rise of Massive Resistance: Race and Politics in the South during the 1950s* (Baton Rouge, 1969), 26–27, 313–14.

10. Ray Marshall, "Industrialization and Race Relations in the Southern United States," in Guy Hunter, ed., *Industrialisation and Race Relations: A Symposium* (New York, 1965), 79–80; William H. Nicholls, *Southern Tradition and Regional Progress* (Westport, 1976 [1960]), 68, 185; Nicholls, "Southern Tradition and Regional Economic Progress," *Southern Economic Journal* 26 (1960), 193–95; Thernstrom and Thernstrom, *America in Black and White*, 110, 117

11. Cobb, *Industrialization and Southern Society*, 111–15.

12. M. Richard Cramer, "School Desegregation and New Industry: The Southern Community Leaders' Viewpoint," *Social Forces* 41 (1963), 385–86; Charles Sallis and John Quincy Adams, "Desegregation in Jackson, Mississippi," in Jacoway and Colburn, *Southern Businessmen and Desegregation*, 248.

trial plants per year before 1957, but none in the four years after the crisis at Central High School. The economic cost of defending segregation brought business and civic leaders to push for compliance.[13]

Southern cities with less concern for economic development were often the ones that witnessed the bitterest resistance to desegregation. Businessmen in Atlanta and other cities took the lesson of Little Rock and avoided conflict.[14] Birmingham's business elite began a pro-desegregation movement after the *Brown* decision but was overwhelmed by segregationist resistance until the next phase of the civil rights movement—sit-ins, freedom rides, and finally the Birmingham crisis of 1963—revived their interest. The local leaders of Vicksburg, Mississippi, responded to a Westinghouse threat to relocate after the introduction of black workers led its plant to be bombed in 1965.[15] "Industrialization was a particularly important factor in the undermining of segregation and discrimination in the South," economist and future labor secretary Ray Marshall observed in 1967, "because it brought Negroes and whites into close contact on the job, intensified competition between Negroes and whites for jobs, and made Negroes aware of their need for better education and equal rights, and exposed the South's racial practices to worldwide scrutiny."[16] Industrialization certainly provided no panacea, but it did weaken militant segregationism and laid the groundwork for further civil rights advances.[17]

Ironically, the most important predominantly black union in the country did

13. Herbert Hill, "Recent Effects of Racial Conflict on Southern Industrial Development," *Phylon* 20 (1959), 319–26; Cramer, "School Desegregation and New Industry," 384; Elizabeth Jacoway, "Taken by Surprise: Little Rock Business Leaders and Desegregation," in Jacoway and Colburn, eds., *Southern Businessmen and Desegregation,* 15–41.

14. Bartley, *Rise of Massive Resistance,* 315; Alton Hornsby Jr., "A City That Was Too Busy to Hate: Atlanta Businessmen and Desegregation," in Jacoway and Colburn, *Southern Businessmen and Desegregation,* 120; Steven F. Lawson, "From Sit-In to Race Riot: Businessmen, Blacks, and the Pursuit of Moderation in Tampa, 1960–67," ibid., 258; Anne Trotter, "The Memphis Business Community and Integration," ibid., 282.

15. Robert Corley, "In Search of Racial Harmony: Birmingham Business Leaders and Desegregation, 1950–63," in Jacoway and Colburn, *Southern Businessmen and Desegregation,* 179; Weems, *Desegregating the Dollar,* 66; Purcell and Mulvey, *The Negro in the Electrical Manufacturing Industry,* 102.

16. Ray Marshall, *The Negro Worker* (New York, 1967), 44.

17. Cramer, "School Desegregation and New Industry," 389; Jack Paterson, "Business Response to the Negro Movement," *New South* 21 (1966), 67–74.

not recognize the effects of southern industrialization. The leaders of the United Packinghouse Workers, applying the communist theory that industrialists favor segregation because it enables them to lower wages for all workers and reap "super-profits" from the depressed wages of minorities, believed that northern investors would want to preserve segregation.[18] But in 1957, Martin Luther King Jr. told the union that segregation was waning because of industrialization. "Day after day the South is receiving new multimillion dollar industries. With this growth of industry the folkways of white supremacy will necessarily pass away. Moreover, southerners are learning to be good businessmen, and as such realize that bigotry is costly and bad for business."[19] Though King was essentially a socialist, he understood the economic forces behind desegregation better than the UPWA leaders. Few black members of the UPWA paid any attention to the union's social and macroeconomic ideas anyway.[20]

The business response to black consumer and government pressure also affected the North. In 1947, major league baseball made perhaps the most dramatic break with racial exclusion when the Brooklyn Dodgers signed Jackie Robinson. Blacks had been excluded from the game in the 1880s at the behest of the players—customers, if the press is any indication, opposed the move. By the 1940s, player opposition had almost disappeared; a 1938 survey indicated that four out of five major leaguers did not oppose integration. Pressures for racial fairness increased during World War II, and the death of Commissioner Kenesaw Mountain Landis in 1944 removed an important obstacle to integration. While every major league owner except the Dodgers' Branch Rickey opposed integration in 1946, none of them could legally prevent Rickey from breaking the color line. Rickey claimed to have been acting on the impulse of Christianity; most observers attributed his action to desire to get black talent that would turn the Dodgers into pennant contenders, as well as to take advantage of the increased fan base that black spectators

18. United Packinghouse Workers of America, Third Biennial Wage and Contract Conference, 9–13 May 1955, pp. 255, 332, Box 525; Resolutions Adopted at District 4 Antidiscrimination Conference, 25–26 Jul. 1953, Box 342, UPWA Papers, Wisconsin Historical Society.

19. United Packinghouse Workers of America, Fourth Biennial Wage and Contract Conference, 30 Sep.–4 Oct. 1957, p. 219, UPWA Papers, Wisconsin Historical Society.

20. "Notes on American Capitalism" (1951), *The Papers of Martin Luther King, Jr.*, 4 vols. to date (Berkeley, 1992–), I: 435; "A Look to the Future," 2 Sep. 1957, ibid., IV: 269; Raymond H. Anderson, "Randolph Fears Crisis on Rights," *New York Times*, 29 May 1965, p. 11 [DH VIII: 317]; Alan Draper, *Conflict of Interest: Organized Labor and the Civil Rights Movement, 1954–68* (Ithaca, NY, 1994), 12.

would provide. In addition, New York had enacted a fair employment practice law in 1945, and members of the state's Commission against Discrimination helped to push Rickey to act.[21]

There remained a significant kernel of player resistance to Robinson's signing, led by Fred "Dixie" Walker, a Dodger outfielder and Georgia native. Walker, also known as "The People's Choice," had been chosen as the National League player representative to baseball's Executive Committee, a sort of company union formed in 1946 after an abortive effort to establish a Baseball Players Guild. The commissioner, league president Ford Frick, and several owners were able to quell attempted strikes by Walker's confederates, who saw blacks as a job threat. Black players and white owners gained by the reintegration of major league baseball; marginal white players and, most of all, Negro League owners lost by it.[22]

The labor movement in the South evinced a similar ambivalence toward the civil rights movement, and here, too, national leaders were more sympathetic than local ones. Many historians observe that the AFL and CIO became less concerned about racial equality after World War II, especially after the merger of the federations in 1955. This view exaggerates the commitment of the federations to fair employment before the 1950s and understates it afterward.[23]

Philip Murray died in 1952 and was succeeded by Walter Reuther of the United Auto Workers. Reuther was at least as committed to civil rights as Murray had

21. Jules Tygiel, *Baseball's Great Experiment: Jackie Robinson and His Legacy* (New York, 1983), 54; Bill L. Weaver, "The Black Press and the Assault on Professional Baseball's 'Color Line,'" October, 1945 – April, 1947," *Phylon* 40 (1979), 304; Robert F. Burk, *Much More Than a Game: Players, Owners, and American Baseball Since 1921* (Chapel Hill, 2001), 61–98; Elmer A. Carter, "Practical Considerations of Antidiscrimination Legislation—Experience under the New York Law against Discrimination," *Cornell Law Quarterly* 40 (1954), 44; Sam Roberts, "Faster Than Jackie Robinson: Branch Rickey's Sermons on the Mound," *New York Times,* 13 Apr. 1997, p. E7.

22. Burk, *Much More Than a Game,* 87–93, 99–103; Dan W. Dodson, "The Integration of Negroes in Baseball," *Journal of Educational Sociology* 28 (1954), 73–75; James B. Dworkin, *Owners versus Players: Baseball and Collective Bargaining* (Boston, 1981), 26; Weems, *Desegregating the Dollar,* 38 – 41; James Gwartney and Charles Haworth, "Employer Costs and Discrimination: The Case of Baseball," *Journal of Political Economy* 82 (1974), 873–81. While some CIO officers urged Landis to open major league baseball to blacks in 1942, there is no evidence for Bill Veeck's claim that the CIO was prepared to finance his purchase of the Philadelphia Phillies in order to stock the team with black players. David M. Jordan, Larry R. Gerlach, and John P. Rossi, "A Baseball Myth Exploded," *The National Pastime* 17 (1998), 3–13.

23. Robert Zieger, *The CIO: 1935–55* (Chapel Hill, 1995), 345.

been, and he reduced the CIO's antagonism toward Communist-led and predominantly black unions like the United Packinghouse Workers and Detroit's UAW Local 600. Reuther helped the International Harvester Company to promote fair employment over the objections of a Memphis UAW local. But until 1961 he continued to oppose black demands for an executive board seat.[24] While the UAW and CIO's antidiscrimination efforts should not be overlooked, the organizations did more to support the broader civil rights movement than they did to address discrimination in the workplace. Even the most racially liberal unions found it easier to support "civil rights causes far removed from the factories where its members worked and far from the union itself," recalled Herbert Hill.[25]

The AFL became much more committed to racial equality in the postwar years. Unions in the AFL had twice as many members as those in the CIO in 1950, and many more black members. Indeed, the Communists noted that the AFL was more successful in organizing southern blacks. Ironically, the AFL's policy of segregation did provide some room for black organization, and particularly for black local control and leadership, the lack of which was one of the chief complaints against CIO unions.[26]

William Green died less than two weeks after Philip Murray and was succeeded by George Meany. Despite his persistent criticism of AFL racial policy, A. Philip Randolph had presented Green with an award "for distinguished service in the fight for the abolition of racial discrimination in the labor movement" in 1949.[27] Whereas Green had been a member of the relatively egalitarian United Mine Workers, Meany rose from the ranks of the plumbers, among the most discriminatory of the craft unions. Meany himself had a reputation for personal fairness and had worked with civil rights groups while president of the New York Federation of Labor.[28] But when the New York legislature investigated union discrimination in

24. Nelson Lichtenstein, *The Most Dangerous Man in Detroit: Walter Reuther and the Fate of American Labor* (New York, 1995), 317–79.

25. Herbert Hill, "Lichtenstein's Fictions: Meany, Reuther and the 1964 Civil Rights Act," *New Politics* 7 (1998), 102. Lichtenstein defends his work in "Walter Reuther in Black and White: A Rejoinder to Herbert Hill," *New Politics* 7 (1999), 133–47, followed by Hill's final riposte.

26. Zieger, *The CIO,* 359; John Williamson, "The Situation in the Trade Unions," *Political Affairs* 26 (1947), 34; Ray Marshall, "The Negro and Organized Labor," *Journal of Negro Education* 32 (1963), 379; Scott Greer, *Last Man In: Racial Access to Union Power* (Glencoe, IL, 1959), 63.

27. *Proceedings,* 69th Annual AFL Convention (Washington, 1949), 328–31 [DH VII: 526].

28. Herbert Northrup, *Organized Labor and the Negro* (New York, 1944), 23–24; Joseph C. Goulden, *Meany* (New York, 1972), 306; Robert H. Zieger, "George Meany: Labor's Organization Man," in Melvyn Dubofsky and Warren Van Tine, eds., *Labor Leaders in America* (Urbana, 1986), 342.

1938, he testified that the only discrimination that he was aware of was against white workers. In the Rock Drillers union, he said, "the white men could not secure employment because of the fact that the secretary was a Negro and was discriminating against white men."[29]

While Reuther and Meany were preoccupied with planning a merger of the CIO and AFL, the *Brown* decision brought the civil rights issue to the fore. The federations endorsed the decision, which opened a chasm between union leadership and the southern white rank and file. For decades southern labor organizers had denied that they sought anything more than job equality. Now organized labor was committed to "social equality." Meany and Reuther underestimated southern white opposition to desegregation, primarily because they believed that racial antagonism was the tool of "antilabor" forces in the South.[30]

The failure of the postwar effort to unionize the South up to levels in the North showed the problem. "Simply put, the CIO faced the central organizing dilemma: one cannot want for people what circumstances do not encourage them to want for themselves," a historian concludes. Racial divisions were but one of the many reasons for the failure of "Operation Dixie," the CIO's southern campaign.[31] The leading industry in the South, textiles, remained almost entirely white, so racial antagonism among the workers was not a problem. There were enough other reasons for southern workers to resist organization so that employers did not have to "play the race card" and, when they did, it was often not an effective tactic.[32] Odd crosscurrents and strange bedfellows marked the campaign—one antiunion Georgian compared the CIO to the Ku Klux Klan, both being "extralegal, totalitarian organizations that sowed 'hatred, violence, and anarchy.'" On the other hand, a Textile Workers Union organizer asked his congressman to have the House Un-American Activities Committee investigate employer antiunion tactics. The AFL

---

29. "Report to the Legislature of the State of New York by the New York State Temporary Commission on the Condition of the Urban Colored Population" (mimeograph copy, 1938), 1403–9.

30. Draper, *Conflict of Interest,* 20; "Jim Crow Whispers Hit Unions in South," *PM,* 28 Dec. 1945 [SCCF 2712].

31. Leo Troy, "The Growth of Union Membership in the South, 1939–53," *Southern Economic Journal* 24 (1958), 416–20; Frank T. De Vyver, "The Present Status of Labor Unions in the South—1948," *Southern Economic Journal* 16 (1949), 16–22.

32. "Labor Drives South," *Fortune,* Nov. 1946, pp. 134–41, 230–37; Ray Marshall, "Union Racial Problems in the South," *Industrial Relations* 1 (1962), 117–21; George Morris, "How Racism and Red-baiting Boomeranged in Ecorse," *Daily Worker,* 3 Jun. 1953, p. 4 [SCCF 2712]; Michelle Brattain, *The Politics of Whiteness: Race, Workers, and Culture in the Modern South* (Princeton, 2001), 128–30.

was more successful in its southern campaign than the CIO and attempted to cap-
italize on anticommunist sentiment against its rival, but also to little effect.[33] The
federation turned the communist issue against the right, claiming that the Taft-
Hartley Act would hinder American efforts in the cold war. The CIO went out of
its way to neutralize the race issue, again disclaiming any commitment to "social equality."[34] Nor did black workers lose by the failure of Operation Dixie. "So
far, then, as Negro prospects are concerned," an economist observed, "the union
casts an ominous shadow in the South . . . A really successful organizational drive
would write *finis* to Negro prospects in southern manufacturing for many years to
come."[35]

Brown and the AFL and CIO support for it gave employers the opportunity to
exploit racial tensions as never before. "Social equality" was the decision's main
thrust, and employers knew that many workers would reject such a notion. They
were aided by the employer "free speech" provisions of the Taft-Hartley Act.[36] Under the Wagner Act, employers were forbidden to tell the truth about union racial
policies while unions were free to lie about the employer's position. Under the
Wagner Act the NLRB had overturned elections not only when employers appealed to the racial prejudices of their white workers but also when an employer
warned black workers of discriminatory union practices. Employers were not permitted to participate at all in union election campaigns.[37] After the Taft-Hartley

33. Brattain, *The Politics of Whiteness*, 145, 148; Bob Kiney to Julian Thomas, 26 Nov. 1946 [NUL
IV: 10]; John Williamson, "The Situation in the Trade Unions," *Political Affairs* 26 (1947), 34.

34. Anders Lewis and John Braeman, "The American Federation of Labor and Cold War Anti-
Communism," *Continuity* 26 (2003), 108–9; Barbara S. Griffith, *The Crisis of American Labor: Operation Dixie and the Defeat of the CIO* (Philadelphia, 1988), 76, 171; Milton MacKaye, "The CIO Invades
Dixie," *Readers Digest*, Oct. 1946, pp. 91–95; A. G. Mezerik, "The CIO Southern Drive," *The Nation*,
11 Jan. 1947 [SCCF 1194].

35. Donald Dewey, "Negro Employment in Southern Industry," *Journal of Political Economy* 60
(1952), 290; Dewey, "Four Studies of Negro Employment in the Upper South," in National Planning
Association, *Selected Studies of Negro Employment in the South* (Washington, 1955), 167, 211; Paul H.
Norgren and Samuel E. Hill, *Toward Fair Employment* (New York, 1964), 52.

36. Sumner H. Slichter, "The Taft-Hartley Act," *Quarterly Journal of Economics* 63 (1949), 13;
Daniel H. Pollitt, "The NLRB and Race Hate Propaganda in Union Organization Drives," *Stanford Law
Review* 17 (1965), 380; Sidney Fine, "Frank Murphy, The *Thornhill* Decision, and Picketing as Free
Speech," *Labor History* 6 (1965), 115.

37. Pollitt, "The NLRB and Race Hate Propaganda," 380; John E. Drotning, "Race Propaganda:
The NLRB's Impact on Employer Subtlety and the Effect of This Propaganda on Voting," *Labor Law
Journal* (1967), 173; *Arcade-Sunshine Co., Inc.*, 12 NLRB 259 (1939).

Act, the board allowed employers to address racial issues in union election campaigns so long as the appeals did not "interfere, restrain, or coerce" employees. If no promises or threats were made, employers could make "temperate and factually correct" statements about race. Thus Jackie Robinson, retired from baseball and a vice-president at the Chock Full O' Nuts company in New Jersey, could claim that a union attempting to organize one of the company's plants was jealous of his position and would oust the black employees if it won. The board permitted a textile manufacturer to dispassionately inform his employees that the Textile Workers Union supported integration.[38]

In the mid-1950s, southern employers began to use the issue of racial equality to divide black and white workers to prevent unionization.[39] They highlighted union support for the NAACP, depicted integrated union social events, and generally denounced northern or "foreign" interference in the South. A Mississippi electric manufacturer circulated a photograph of James B. Carey, electrical workers president and AFL-CIO civil rights department head, dancing with a black woman. Carey noted that unions were "confronted for the first time, with calculated, correlated campaigns waged by large and small employers to exploit prejudice and bigotry in order to forestall organization of their employees."[40] Sometimes rival unions made racial appeals in election campaigns. An independent union had five blacks pass out leaflets supporting the UAW in an attempt to make it appear to be a predominantly black union, but the board ordered a new election after this deceptive stunt.[41] A union that won an election that included an anti-Semitic comment about an employer was sustained, the board concluding that "incidental ugliness that probably did not affect the outcome of the election should not invalidate it."[42]

38. *Chock Full O' Nuts*, 120 NLRB 1296 (1958); *Sharnay Hosiery Mills, Inc.*, 120 NLRB 750 (1958); Michael I. Sovern, "The National Labor Relations Act and Racial Discrimination," *Columbia Law Review* 62 (1962), 623–24; "NLRB Decides on Racial Issue," *New York Times*, 6 May 1958, p. 25.

39. Two-thirds of the sixty race-hate cases took place in the South, and one-third in the South in the decade after *Brown*.

40. James B. Carey, "Race Hate: Newest Union-Busting Weapon," *The Progressive* 22 (1958), 16; Walter Reuther to Lister Hill, 11 Feb. 1964, *Congressional Record*, 8 Apr. 1964, pp. 7206–7. But cf. Carey, speech to NAACP, 12 Jul. 1944 [NUL IV: 10]. James E. Youngdahl, "Unions and Segregation," *New Republic*, 9 Jul. 1956, pp. 14–15; Warner Bloomberg Jr., Joel Seidman, and Victor Hoffmann, "New Members, New Goals," *New Republic*, 6 Jul. 1959, pp. 9–15 [SCCF 2713]; Benjamin D. Segal, "Racism Stymies Unions in the South," *New Leader*, 11 Nov. 1957 [SCCF 1194].

41. *Heintz Division, Kelsey-Hayes Co.*, 126 NLRB 151 (1960).

42. Sovern, "The National Labor Relations Act and Racial Discrimination," 626.

The AFL-CIO pressed the NLRB to adopt a more stringent standard.[43] The board was in a difficult position on both constitutional, free speech, grounds and policy grounds. "Surely no one would suggest that Negro workers are not entitled to know that the union seeking to represent them engages in racial discrimination," one law professor commented. "Can we treat differently the freedom to inform white workers who benefit from their employer's discrimination that the union seeking their support has elsewhere insisted upon equal rights for Negroes?" While the board generally frowned on race-based appeals in union elections, it more often "relied on the good sense of the voters to evaluate the statements of the parties."[44] Race-based blandishments were treated like any other blandishments and did not constitute a particularly effective antiunion device.[45]

AFL-CIO leaders often exaggerated the impact of these tactics, reinforcing their tendency to overlook civil rights resistance in their own ranks. Claims that the white citizens councils were organized by business as part of an antiunion campaign were wide of the mark.[46] James B. Carey, first head of the AFL-CIO civil rights department, claimed that "There is substantial evidence that the movement is directed at trade unions . . . Among the leaders of this new subversive movement are a number of individuals active in the anti-labor organizations."[47] In fact, the councils drew considerable support from southern unionists, as AFL-CIO and Jewish Labor Committee surveys showed. Nor did they officially endorse antiunion positions. "The voice of the union member, although it may not be the most articulate among the segregationists, is already one of the loudest," a reporter ob-

43. Pollitt, "NLRB and Race Hate Propaganda," 373–408; James A. Gross, *Broken Promise: The Subversion of U.S. Labor Relations Policy, 1947–94* (Philadelphia, 1995), 155–62; A. H. Raskin, "Union Is Fighting 'Race Hate' Tactic," *New York Times,* 15 Sep. 1957, p. 57.

44. *Sharnay Hosiery Mills, Inc.,* 120 NLRB 750 (1958); Sovern, "The NLRB and Racial Discrimination," 626, 618; "NLRB Bars Inflammatory Use of Race Issue by Firm to Block Organizing Effort of Union," *Wall Street Journal,* 13 Aug. 1962, p. 7.

45. Drotning, "Race Propaganda," 181–85; Draper, *Conflict of Interest,* 165.

46. Marshall, "Union Racial Problems," 117; Marshall, *The Negro Worker* (New York, 1967), 51; M. Richard Cramer, "Race and Southern White Workers' Support for Unions," *Phylon* 39 (1978), 319–21; Draper, *Conflict of Interest,* 20, 60; Henry L. Trewhitt, "Southern Unions and the Integration Issue," *The Reporter,* 4 Oct. 1956 [SCCF 2708]; "Southern Labor and Desegregation," *Jewish Life,* Oct. 1956, pp. 22–25 [SCCF 1194]; "Progress Report on the Work of the Civil Rights Department," 1956, Box 13, RG 9-001, George Meany Memorial Archives, Silver Spring; Paula Pfeffer, *A. Philip Randolph: Pioneer of the Civil Rights Movement* (Baton Rouge, 1990), 207.

47. *Proceedings,* 1st Annual Convention of the AFL-CIO (Washington, 1955), 109–13 [DH VIII: 51].

served.[48] An Alabama council leader noted, "The labor boys played a big part in the segregation effort. The business people would give lip service, but the labor people would get out and work."[49]

When the AFL-CIO endorsed the *Brown* decision, angry letters from southern members inundated Meany's office. Several local unions seceded from the federation and attempted to form a Southern Federation of Labor. Though secessionist attempts to establish pro-segregation labor federations in the South fizzled, the Alabama AFL-CIO lost half its members in the ten years after *Brown*. One of the chief faces of segregation was George Wallace, who had a strong pro-union record and was endorsed by the AFL-CIO in the gubernatorial election of 1962.[50] Nor did the federation's stand, and the reaction to it by southern employers and members, hinder its organizing efforts in the South; the national exposé of union racketeering by the McClellan committee or the mayhem of the Kohler strike were perhaps more important.[51] The AFL-CIO gained 142,000 members in the South between 1953 and 1966, while losing 815,000 in the rest of the country.[52]

Despite these tensions, civil rights groups and organized labor maintained the alliance that was forged in the 1930s. Communists attempted to recoup their losses from the 1949–50 CIO expulsions via the National Negro Labor Council. The group had little success, was condemned by black civil rights groups and black unionists, and was finally curbed by the Subversive Activities Control Board in

48. Trewhitt, "Southern Unions and the Integration Issue," 25; "Race Troubles Hurt Unions, Too," *U.S. News and World Report*, 6 Apr. 1956, p. 95; Irving Spiegel, "Race Issue Splits Southern Unions," *New York Times*, 13 May 1957, p. 23; Brattain, *The Politics of Whiteness*, 199, 225–29.

49. Neil R. McMillen, *The Citizens' Council: Organized Resistance to the Second Reconstruction, 1954–64* (Urbana, 1994), 202–3; Bartley, *Rise of Massive Resistance*, 308–9; Draper, *Conflict of Interest*, 24.

50. Goulden, *Meany*, 309; Bartley, *Rise of Massive Resistance*, 308–9; Draper, *Conflict of Interest*, 113, 108, 120; "Lucy Case Splits Alabama Unions," *New York Times*, 26 Feb. 1956, p. 48; "Threat to Unions in South Depicted," *New York Times*, 7 May 1956, p. 25; Marshall, *The Negro Worker*, 46; Brattain, *The Politics of Whiteness*, 255. Zieger, *American Workers*, 189, disputes Wallace's pro-union record. Cf. Dan T. Carter, *The Politics of Rage: George Wallace, the Origins of the New Conservatism, and the Transformation of American Politics* (New York, 1995), 352.

51. Gross, *Broken Promise*, 138; Morgan O. Reynolds, *Making America Poorer: The Cost of Labor Law* (Washington, 1987), 10, 24; Sylvester Petro, *The Kohler Strike: Union Violence and Administrative Law* (Chicago, 1961).

52. Draper, *Conflict of Interest*, 165. This was mostly due to the rapid increase in industrial employment in the South, which actually caused the *percentage* of southern workers who were union members to decline.

1956.[53] Mainstream civil rights groups, while grateful to the AFL and CIO for their support on civil rights issues, complained about the federations' unwillingness to compel local unions to open their ranks to blacks.

The demise of Murray and Green helped to facilitate the long-anticipated merger of the AFL and CIO. Though the NAACP hailed the merger, the association and black unionists were concerned that the AFL-CIO would neglect black civil rights matters, especially since the AFL would be the senior partner with two-thirds of the seats on the executive board. Black workers were also likely to lose the benefits of competition between the federations.[54] Two black unionists, A. Philip Randolph and Willard Townsend of the Transport Service Employees Union, were named to the merged executive board, which some white unionists regarded as an unfair racial preference.[55] The merger agreement contained a statement that the AFL-CIO "shall constitutionally recognize the right of all workers, without regard to race, creed, color, or national origin, to share in the full benefits of trade union organization" and "shall establish appropriate internal machinery to bring about, at the earliest possible date, the effective implementation of this principle of nondiscrimination."[56] James B. Carey, the tempestuous head of the International Union of Electrical Workers known as the "bantam rooster of organized labor" and a longtime civil rights supporter, was made chairman of the civil rights department. Mike Quill, president of the CIO Transport Workers Union, refused to serve on the board because the resolution was not strong enough. "This is a license for discrimination against minority groups," he told the last CIO convention.[57]

53. "New Council Maps Negro Job Battle," New York Times, 29 Oct. 1951, p. 12 [DH VII: 559]; "Labor Unit Set Up for Negro Rights," ibid., 2 Mar. 1952, p. 41 [DH VII: 580]; "Negro Labor Committee, USA," ibid., 24 Mar. 1952, p. 24; John N. Popham, "NAACP Demands Curb on Red Aims," ibid., 4 Jul. 1954, p. 16 [DH VII: 586]; Mindy Thompson, The National Negro Labor Council: A History (New York, 1978).

54. "The NAACP Hails the AFL-CIO Merger," Crisis 63 (1956), 35 [DH VIII: 162]; "Labor Leaders Express Views on Proposed Merger," Chicago Defender, 24 Nov. 1951 [DH VII: 613]; "What Goes on Here?" Pittsburgh Courier, 3 Dec. 1955 [DH VIII: 56].

55. "Solidarity Forever," New York Age-Defender, 17 Dec. 1955 [DH VIII: 59]; Goulden, Meany, 205.

56. "Agreement for the Merger of the AFL and CIO," 9 Feb. 1955, Proceedings, 1st Annual Convention of the AFL-CIO (Washington, 1955), liv, 26 [DH VIII: 49]; Goulden, Meany, 202.

57. Stanley Levey, "Quill Balks at Labor Unity Plan; Seeks Pledge of 'Fighting' Policy," New York Times, 14 Feb. 1955, p. 1; Levey, "Meany Vows Fight on Bias When Labor's Ranks Unite," ibid., 27 Feb. 1955, p. 1 [DH VII: 615]; Pittsburgh Courier, 5 Dec. 1955 [DH VIII: 123]; Herbert Hill, "The AFL-CIO and the Black Worker: Twenty-Five Years after the Merger," Journal of Intergroup Relations 10 (1982), 15.

At times, AFL-CIO statements on racial discrimination were little short of delusional. United Steelworkers general counsel Arthur Goldberg wrote shortly after the merger that "It may seem surprising that racial discrimination . . . has ever been an issue in unions. Racial discrimination is morally wrong and unions are formed to achieve moral and ethical goals, and, of course, racial discrimination has no rational justification."[58] A few years earlier an Inter-Union Institute study had claimed that "The ethnic group patterns in most industries and trades were set by employer decisions, not by the unions" and cited the exclusion of blacks from skilled railroad jobs as an example. Walter White echoed this story in his 1955 memoir; his chapter on organized labor has been described as "eyewash," and his "new spin reflected the NAACP's cozy post-1948 relationship with the AFL and CIO (and their financial contributions) rather than the actual historical or contemporary labor movement."[59]

Trouble in the merged federation's civil rights unit surfaced almost immediately. James Carey resigned as head of the civil rights department, claiming that AFL elements had too much control over it, particularly after Boris Shishkin was made committee's director. "I'd like to see the committee taken out of Meany's vest pocket and Boris Shishkin's briefcase," Carey said. The conflict was also said to have derived from Carey's irascible temper and the obduracy of the Cleveland local of his own electrical workers union.[60]

But rarely did the racial discrimination of organized labor lead blacks to consider a divorce. Advocates of "right to work" legislation used the issue of union discrimination to appeal to black voters. Black voters supported right-to-work legislation in Florida, and delegates to the 1958 NAACP convention proposed that the association endorse an upcoming referendum to make Ohio a right-to-work state.[61] The AFL-CIO's Committee on Political Education noted that, facing a 1958

58. Arthur Goldberg, *AFL-CIO: Labor United* (New York, 1956), 195.

59. J.B.S. Hardman and Maurice Neufeld, eds., *The House of Labor: Internal Operations of American Unions* (Westport, CT, 1951), 346; Marshall, *The Negro Worker*, 60; Kenneth Robert Janken, *White: The Biography of Walter White, Mr. NAACP* (New York, 2003), 364.

60. Ethel L. Payne, "Force AFL-CIO Bias Showdown," *Chicago Defender*, 27 Apr. 1957, p. 1; Adolph J. Slaughter, "Carey Resignation Called Blow to Labor Bias Fight," ibid., 27 Apr. 1957, p. 3; Payne, "Organized Labor and the Negro," ibid., 11 May 1957, p. 11; Payne, "Why Jim Carey Quit," ibid., 1 Jun. 1957, p. 11; "Union Bids Local End Bias Policy," *New York Times*, 20 Apr. 1957, p. 8; A. H. Raskin, "Carey Quits Post on AFL-CIO Unit," ibid., 12 Apr. 1957, p. 52.

61. Dick Bruner, "The Negro Bids for Union Power," *The Nation* 190 (1960), 207; "Prejudice a Big Factor in South's Union Picture," *New York Voice*, 12 Mar. 1955 [SCCF 2719].

right-to-work referendum election in Ohio, "our biggest obstacle to offset was the matter of discrimination within some of the unions." The NAACP actively disputed claims that right-to-work laws were really "little Fair Employment Practice acts." [62] Some black leaders objected to the unwillingness of the NAACP to discuss the merits of the issue, and Executive Secretary Roy Wilkins noted that "certain elements in the Negro population were vigorous in their denunciation of the NAACP for taking such a stand, holding that the issue was outside of the area of civil rights." [63] After seeing that right-to-work supporters also opposed fair employment legislation, 85 percent of blacks Ohioans voted against the referendum, and a California initiative also failed. [64] However, the federation's unwillingness to take on discriminatory locals continued to unsettle the black-union alliance. [65]

By 1958, perhaps responding to the increase in popular action by groups like Martin Luther King's Southern Christian Leadership Conference and the Congress of Racial Equality (CORE), the NAACP began to press organized labor for more forceful action on job discrimination. The principal voice in this campaign was Labor Secretary Herbert Hill. Hill had joined the association ten years earlier, an anti-Stalinist socialist who had worked for the United Steelworkers. He had helped to bring the labor–civil rights coalition together, but after the AFL-CIO merger he became the principal source of contention in the conflict between them. "Labor's democratic ideals are in serious conflict with a tradition of racial discrimination in the unions that is currently very much alive," he wrote in *Commentary*, the organ of the American Jewish Committee, in 1959. [66]

62. Herbert Hill, "'Right to Work' Laws and the Negro Worker," *Crisis* 65 (1958), 327–32 [SCCF 2712]; "NAACP Opposes Right to Work Referendum," Apr. 1958 [NAACP 13-S, XIV: 5].

63. James E. McCann to Roy Wilkins, 25 Jun. 1958 [NAACP 13-S, XIV: 27]; Roy Wilkins to James L. McDevitt, 16 Dec. 1958 [NAACP 13-S, XIV: 76].

64. Gilbert J. Gall, *The Politics of Right to Work: The Labor Federations as Special Interests, 1943–79* (New York, 1988), 142; Gall, "Thoughts on Defeating Right-to-Work: Reflections on Two Referendum Campaigns," in Kevin Boyle, ed., *Organized Labor and American Politics, 1894–1994: The Labor-Liberal Alliance* (Albany, NY, 1998), 195–215; Robert H. Zieger, *American Workers, American Unions, 1920–85* (Baltimore, 1986), 176; Elizabeth A. Fones-Wolf, *Selling Free Enterprise: The Business Assault on Labor and Liberalism, 1945–60* (Urbana, 1994), 273.

65. Bartley, *Rise of Massive Resistance*, 310; A. H. Raskin, "Meany, in Fiery Debate, Denounces Negro Unionist," *New York Times*, 24 Sep. 1959, p. 1.

66. Judith Stein, *Running Steel, Running America: Race, Economic Policy, and the Decline of Liberalism* (Chapel Hill, 1998), 106; Nelson, *Divided We Stand*, 215; Herbert Hill, "Labor Unions and the Negro: The Record of Discrimination," *Commentary* 28 (1959), 479–88.

The inability of the merged federation to change the behavior of its affiliates brought increased disillusionment among civil rights advocates. *Fortune* magazine concluded that "it is apparent that the federation's ambitious plans for improving the lot of Negro workers have been a dismal failure—and not only in the South."[67] A. Philip Randolph felt frustrated that George Harrison, president of the segregationist Brotherhood of Railway Clerks, who had helped to spike the AFL's 1935 report on racial discrimination, was a member of the civil rights committee and the head of the federation's resolutions committee.[68]

Blacks were not the only ones becoming skeptical about organized labor. Exposés of union corruption in the late 1950s culminated in the dramatic hearings before a Senate Select Committee on Improper Activities in the Labor-Management Field, known as the "McClellan committee," after its chairman, Senator John McClellan of Arkansas. The hearings resulted in stricter union accountability under the 1959 Landrum-Griffin Act and, more important, permanently damaged the public image of the labor movement.[69] Roscoe Pound, erstwhile Harvard Law School dean and the legal philosopher who did more than anyone else to undermine nineteenth-century "liberty of contract" doctrine, concluded that New Deal labor law had overreacted and established a countervailing tyranny. Unions, he said, were free to commit torts against persons and property, interfere with the use of transportation, break contracts, deprive people of the means of livelihood, and misuse trust funds, "things no one else can do with impunity. The labor leader and labor union now stand where the king and government . . . stood at common law." In addition, its ability to exclude minorities from membership was only slightly inhibited by the law. "A potent stabilizing force may be a despotic centralized control. As Mr. Justice Brandeis put the matter, it may substitute tyranny of centralized employee oligarchies for tyranny of the employers."[70] Intellectuals on the left and the right were coming to regard organized labor as a narrow interest group.[71]

The conflict reached a dramatic climax at the 1959 AFL-CIO convention. Ran-

67. "Labor's 'Race Problem,'" *Fortune,* Mar. 1959, p. 191.

68. A. H. Raskin, "AFL-CIO Faces 'Jim Crow' Fight," *New York Times,* 20 Sep. 1959, p. 1.

69. Gross, *Broken Promise,* 138, 191.

70. Roscoe Pound, "Legal Immunities of Labor Unions," in Edward H. Chamberlin et al., *Labor Unions and Public Policy* (Washington, 1958), 145–63; "Labor Rein Urged by Roscoe Pound," *New York Times,* 20 May 1957, p. 12; For Pound's earlier views, see "Liberty of Contract," *Yale Law Journal* 18 (1909), 454–87.

71. Zieger, *American Workers,* 145; Morgan O. Reynolds, *Making America Poorer: The Cost of Labor Law* (Washington, 1987), 10, 24; Gross, *Broken Promise,* 145, 191.

dolph had long considered himself the conscience of organized labor on the race question, but most members simply ignored him. "For years the opening words of a Randolph speech were a signal for the delegates to begin a mass exodus from the convention floor to the nearest bar," a journalist wrote, and the stentorian orator could rarely be heard on the floor.[72] Randolph continued to press the federation to oust any affiliate that maintained a constitutional color bar or segregated locals. (The two railway brotherhoods that had been admitted to the merged federation still retained their white-only constitutional provisions.) Some delegates pointed out that black members often wanted to keep segregated locals. Randolph argued that such a desire was no more defensible than a local's desire to have communist or racketeer leaders. Meany, who felt that Randolph was grandstanding, shouted at him, "Who the hell appointed you as the guardian of all the Negroes in America?"[73] Meany had a point. Some black workers had made the best they could out of segregation and had a vested interest in its continuation. But Randolph's argument, striking at the principle of segregation itself, was stronger. Just as black businessmen who benefited from segregation would not pose a significant obstacle to desegregation, neither would black-controlled unions. Randolph added that the federation had acted vigorously against unions controlled by racketeers and communists, regardless of the sentiments of their members. Meany rejected this analogy. "I do not equate the problem of racial discrimination with the problem of corruption any more than I equate Hungary with Little Rock," he later said.[74]

The Meany-Randolph imbroglio was one of several unpleasant altercations between civil rights and union leaders in the early 1960s. In January 1960, Herbert Hill delivered a report, "Racism within Organized Labor," that detailed the failure of the AFL-CIO to curb discrimination in the five years since the merger. This salvo opened a campaign that increasingly irritated union leaders, and leaders of reputedly progressive and Jewish unions in particular. A contemporaneous Jewish Labor Committee report claimed to demonstrate progress in the elimination of union discrimination.[75] Charles Zimmerman, a garment workers union vice-

72. Goulden, *Meany*, 308.

73. Marshall, *The Negro Worker*, 83; A. H. Raskin, "NAACP Accuses Labor of Bias Lag," *New York Times*, 5 Jan. 1959, p. 29; Raskin, "Meany, in Fiery Debate, Denounces Negro Unionist"; Goulden, *Meany*, 312.

74. Stanley Levey, "AFL-CIO Chiefs Score Randolph," *New York Times*, 13 Oct. 1961, p. 1.

75. "Racism within Organized Labor: A Report of Five Years of the AFL-CIO," [SCCF 719]; "Labor-Negro Division Widens," *Business Week*, 9 Jul. 1960, pp. 79–80; Philip Benjamin, "NAACP Charges Unions with Bias," *New York Times*, 4 Jan. 1961, p. 18.

president and chairman of the federation's civil rights committee, claimed, "Herb Hill's statements are creating an entirely wrong picture of what the labor movement does to eliminate segregation and he is doing a great deal of damage to all the forces fighting segregation."[76] But Hill regarded the AFL-CIO civil rights department as "a public relations department. It's a hollow ritual and a cover-up. It's a complete fraud."[77]

In October 1961 the AFL-CIO executive committee voted to censure A. Philip Randolph, blaming him for fomenting division between blacks and organized labor. Randolph had "gotten close to these militant groups and he's given up on cooperation for propaganda," Meany said. By the end of the year the council had buried the censure report, and Randolph agreed to retract his criticism of it. The federation again revised its antidiscrimination apparatus, making William F. Schnitzler the new civil rights department head, but the Hill attacks continued.[78]

Hill worked with Harlem representative Adam Clayton Powell Jr., who became chairman of the House Committee on Education and Labor in 1961. George Meany said that Powell would be a terrible chairman, and Powell in turn called for Meany's ouster as AFL-CIO head, referring to him as "stupid" and "absolute zero as a lobbyist." Powell charged that organized labor had "degenerated into the cocktail, black tie, Milquetoast diplomatic set." His committee concentrated on the International Ladies Garment Workers Union, one of the founding unions of the CIO that had prided itself on its progressivism and egalitarianism, and the United Steelworkers, which had a similarly proud reputation on civil rights. In September 1962 it was revealed that Hill was being paid $10,000 a year as a consultant to Powell's committee while also testifying before it. Hill resigned the consultantship, and the House of Representatives reprimanded Powell. Zimmerman quit his position in the NAACP, denouncing Hill as an anti-Semite, and Walter Reuther was said to be thinking about doing the same.[79]

76. "Union Aides Rebut Bias Accusation," *New York Times*, 5 Jan. 1961, p. 51.

77. Joseph Wershba, "Daily Closeup: Herbert Hill," *New York Post*, 14 Oct. 1959 [SCCF 2719].

78. Marshall, *The Negro Worker*, 37; Levey, "AFL-CIO Chiefs Score Randolph"; Goulden, *Meany*, 314–18; Levey, "Peace Formula Voted by Labor," *New York Times*, 14 Dec. 1961, p. 39; Levey, "Labor Recasts Civil Rights Unit," Ibid., 15 Dec. 1961, p. 1.

79. J. C. Rich, "The NAACP v. Labor," *New Leader*, 26 Nov. 1962, p. 2 [DH VIII: 169]; Charles V. Hamilton, *Adam Clayton Powell, Jr.: The Political Biography of an American Dilemma* (New York, 1991), 330; Wil Haygood, *King of the Cats: The Life and Times of Adam Clayton Powell, Jr.* (Boston, 1993), 257, 283; "Powell Bids Labor Oust Meany as Head," *New York Times*, 23 Jun. 1961, p. 27; "US Reports 14% of Negroes Idle," ibid., 18 Feb. 1961, p. 7; Alfred E. Clark, "House Aide Quits in Garment Fight," ibid.,

Though Randolph established a Negro American Labor Council to press his agenda within the AFL-CIO, he and Meany smoothed over their differences and the federation strengthened its civil rights efforts.[80] Observers noted how ironic it was that organized labor and civil rights groups were working so closely together on civil rights legislation in the midst of these conflicts.[81] Others commented that the labor–civil rights conflict had more fundamental causes and was likely to persist. Organized labor was weakening as a political force, the *Detroit Free Press* observed, and the civil rights movement was becoming more militant. "A falling out of the NAACP and the AFL-CIO may have been inevitable from the beginning," it noted. The claim that "the destiny of the Negro is linked with the destiny of labor and liberalism" was "another of those old-fashioned labor chants that ring hollow . . . The end may be approaching for a romance that probably was unhappy because it was based on mutual fear that without each other's good will neither could advance its own cause, even though the causes were at best no more than parallel and often—as it now is charged—even at odds."[82] Many who expressed surprise at the falling out between organized labor and black organizations failed to recognize how recent and tenuous the relationship was.[83] Not surprisingly, black groups turned increasingly toward the federal government, which had been the principal force in the empowerment of organized labor, to strengthen their own hand.

FAIR EMPLOYMENT AND FAIR REPRESENTATION

Mounting government pressure provided a secondary but significant force altering racial employment patterns after World War II. Civil rights groups and black workers pursued remedies against employer and union discrimination in a number of venues. The federal courts extended the "fair representation" doctrine, but its limits appeared in sight by the end of the 1950s. The National Labor Relations Board responded less vigorously to complaints about union discrimination. Presidential executive orders required nondiscrimination by government contractors

---

20 Sep. 1962, p. 23; Stanley Levey, "Zimmerman Quits Post in NAACP Over Bias Charges," ibid., 12 Oct. 1962, p. 20.

80. "A Breach Is Closed," *New York Times*, 21 Mar. 1959, p. 42; A. H. Raskin, "Labor to Tighten Racial Bias Curb," ibid., 25 Sep. 1959, p. 12; "Split with Negro Denied by Meany," ibid., 6 Oct. 1959, p. 33.

81. John D. Pomfret, "Labor-Negro Rift Expected to Last," *New York Times*, 17 Aug. 1963, p. 8.

82. "Frost upon a Friendship," *Detroit Free Press*, 10 Sep. 1959.

83. Dick Brumer, "The Negro Bids for Union Power," *The Nation* 190 (1960), 207.

continuously after 1951, but these were even weaker than the World War II Fair Employment Practice Committee, particularly when union discrimination was concerned. The most powerful agencies on paper were the state FEPCs, which covered nearly all employers and unions in fifteen states by 1960. They achieved some notable results in the postwar decade, but found themselves less able to deal with more difficult economic problems and increased black demands thereafter.

The "fair representation" doctrine offered the most direct means of combating union discrimination. The National Labor Relations Board did not hold discrimination to be an unfair labor practice until 1962, so aggrieved union members had to proceed through the courts, at their own expense. The Supreme Court extended the doctrine, devised under the Railway Labor Act, to the National Labor Relations Act in 1953. The doctrine continued to have its greatest impact on the most discriminatory unions, the railroad brotherhoods. Courts overturned racially discriminatory job classifications and schemes to eliminate blacks, but in 1958 the Supreme Court reiterated its belief that fair representation did not require white unions to admit blacks.[84] While the courts usually applied the doctrine more forcefully than the NLRB, sometimes they restrained the board. In 1958, the NLRB prohibited contracts in which employers agreed to hire only through union hiring halls, a system that effectively evaded the Taft-Hartley Act's ban on closed-shop agreements, but the Supreme Court overruled the board, holding that it could act against hiring halls only after they had been shown to discriminate against nonunion members.[85]

Ironically, blacks sometimes fared worse in unions that *did* admit them. When black members of a Pittsburgh teamsters union sued to enjoin a discriminatory contract with a taxicab company, the federal courts dismissed their complaint. By joining the union the black drivers implicitly had consented to its policies. The federal appeals court pointed out that industrial peace and collective bargaining were the primary goals of the National Labor Relations Act, which was less concerned with post-organization questions than the Railway Labor Act. This ruling

84. Herbert Hill, *Black Labor and the American Legal System: Race, Work, and the Law* (Washington, 1977), 106–21; Eric Arnesen, *Brotherhoods of Color: Black Railroad Workers and the Struggle for Equality* (Cambridge, 2001), 203–29.

85. Sovern, "The NLRA and Racial Discrimination," 574; "Supreme Court Calls Union-Run Hiring Halls Legal," *Wall Street Journal,* 18 Apr. 1961, p. 24; William B. Gould, *Black Workers in White Unions: Job Discrimination in the United States* (Ithaca, 1977), 295.

reflected the fundamental problem of the "fair representation" doctrine—some interests were bound to be sacrificed under the system of "majority rule" that undergirded national labor policy.[86]

Black workers also sued to amend their seniority status when employers and unions opened previously all-white job lines to them. The problem was that blacks who had accumulated seniority in one department would have to start at the bottom of the line in newly opened jobs—as white workers always had, though whites usually stepped quickly off the bottom-rung jobs to which blacks were confined. They would have to sacrifice the security that they had acquired under segregation in order to break into better jobs. Past discrimination thus limited black workers' willingness to explore new opportunities and acted as a sort of "grandfather clause" for white workers. Civil rights groups proposed to allow blacks to bring the seniority they had accrued for their entire career in the plant ("plant seniority") into their new job lines, but this proposal aroused the opposition of management, as well as of white workers. Besides being generally suspicious of seniority, employers were concerned about the preparation of black workers for new jobs, particularly when many of them had been hired under the assumption that they would not be promoted. The New York State Commission against Discrimination had attempted to make adjustments to unions' seniority systems to deal with this situation, and some unions had responded. The President's Committee on Government Contracts addressed this problem in the South in its efforts to integrate job lines in the oil industry. It faced resistance not only from white workers, who defied the national oil workers union, but also from some black unionists who wanted to preserve control of their own locals or who held out for cash back-pay awards. The reaction of the oil companies varied. Some employers dragged their feet and used union discrimination as a pretext for their own bias; others welcomed government pressure as an opportunity to tap a wider labor pool.[87]

Black workers encountered the limits of judicial enforcement of fair represen-

86. *Williams v. Yellow Cab Co.*, 200 F. 2d 302 (1952); Dan C. Heldman et al., *Deregulating Labor Relations* (Dallas, 1981), 64–68; Philip D. Bradley, "Involuntary Participation in Unionism," in Chamberlin et al., *Labor Unions and Public Policy,* 78; Reuel E. Schiller, "From Group Rights to Individual Liberties: Postwar Labor Law, Liberalism, and the Waning of Union Strength," *Berkeley Journal of Employment and Labor Law* 20 (1999), 1–73.

87. Paul Moreno, *From Direct Action to Affirmative Action: Fair Employment Law and Policy in America, 1933–72* (Baton Rouge, 1997), 117, 130; Ray Marshall, "Some Factors Influencing the Upgrading of Negroes in the Southern Petroleum Refining Industry," *Social Forces* 42 (1963), 186–95; Carl B. King and Howard W. Risher Jr., *The Negro in the Petroleum Industry* (Philadelphia, 1969), 36–38.

tation in a 1959 suit against the United Steelworkers. The Armco Steel Company and the union agreed to merge job lines in 1956. Black workers were given preference to move into jobs in the formerly white-only line but had to pass a qualifying test in order to do so. Some black workers argued that it was unfair for them to have to pass an exam that previously hired whites did not have to take, and they objected to the use of departmental rather than plant seniority in the new system. The Fifth Circuit Court of Appeals rejected their claim that the new contract discriminated against black workers. "If there is racial discrimination," the court held, "it is discrimination in favor of Negroes." The company had legitimate business reasons for requiring the tests, and the union had the right to preserve the expectations of white incumbents. "We cannot turn back the clock," the court declared. "Unfair treatment to their detriment in the past" gave black workers "no claim now to be paid back by unfair treatment in their favor." The problem of the present effects of past discrimination was "bound to come up every time a large company substitutes a program of equal job opportunity for previous discriminatory practices . . . In this situation time and tolerance, patience and forbearance, compromise and accommodation are needed in solving a problem rooted deeply in custom . . . The union and the company made a fresh start for the future. We might not agree with every provision, but they have a contract that from now on is free from any discrimination based on race. Angels could do no more." [88]

The NAACP hoped to have the decision overturned, seeing it as providing unions with an "all deliberate speed" loophole similar to that in *Brown*. The steelworkers union found itself in a difficult position in this case. Armco management believed that the integration plan went too far, and disgruntled black workers felt that it did not go far enough. Since southern employers were legally free to discriminate while unions faced at least some obligation of fair representation, the union found itself the object of this lawsuit, which was one of the reasons that national union leaders supported a national fair employment practice act, one that would make employers equally responsible for nondiscrimination. [89]

THE PRESIDENTIAL ANTIDISCRIMINATION CAMPAIGNS

After Congress cut off funding for the wartime FEPC in 1945, civil rights groups pressed for congressional enactment of a permanent commission. House and Sen-

---

88. *Whitfield v. United Steelworkers*, 263 F. 2d 546 (1959).

89. Moreno, *From Direct Action to Affirmative Action*, 242; Arthur Fletcher, *The Silent Sell-Out: Government Betrayal of Blacks to the Craft Unions* (New York, 1973), 26; Stein, *Running Steel*, 110.

ate committees considered dozens of bills, but only one, a 1950 House proposal creating an agency that was considerably weaker than the wartime one, passed either chamber. President Truman was pressed to create a committee by executive order when the Korean War broke out. Truman had ordered the integration of the military and created a fair employment board to monitor minority employment in the civil service in 1948, but he waited until December 1951 to create a Government Contracts Compliance Committee.[90] It received about a hundred complaints but did little more than explore the problem of discrimination before the administration came to an end.

President Eisenhower established the President's Committee on Government Contracts in the summer of 1953.[91] The committee, headed by Vice-President Nixon and with Labor Secretary James P. Mitchell as vice-chairman, would receive complaints and work with government contracting agencies and state and local fair employment commissions to promote equal opportunity. The "Nixon committee" faced many limitations—lack of statutory authority, economic torpor that followed the Korean War, increasing demand for skilled labor, and the ease with which noncompetitive government contractors could discriminate. One of its most severe limitations was that it possessed no power to eradicate labor union discrimination. "A contractor cannot be held responsible for discrimination over which he has no control," John F. Cushman of the Justice Department explained, such as "when a contractor must look to organized labor for his employees."[92] Roy Wilkins complained, "If the committee continues to maintain that it can deal only with violations by employer-signatories to a contract, every employer is thus presented with a loop-hole through which he can escape attention."[93]

The Nixon committee did work informally to overcome labor union opposition to fair employment. In the Gulf Coast oil refineries, where hiring had virtually ceased in the 1950s, the committee induced refiners and the international

90. Moreno, *From Direct Action to Affirmative Action*, 162–77; Ex. Ord. 10308, 16 Fed. Reg. 12303 (1951).

91. Ex. Ord. 10479, 18 Fed. Reg. 4899 (1953); amended by Ex. Ord. 10590, 20 Fed. Reg. 409 (1955).

92. John F. Cushman, "Mediation and Education for Equal Economic Opportunity," in Milton R. Konvitz and Clinton Rossiter, eds., *Aspects of Liberty: Essays Presented to Robert E. Cushman* (Ithaca, NY, 1958), 125; U.S. Commission on Civil Rights, *1961 Report, Part III: Employment* (Washington, 1961), 68; Gould, *Black Workers in White Unions*, 298.

93. Roy Wilkins to Jacob Seidenberg, 2 Nov. 1956 [NAACP III, A: 192]; Lawrence Stessin, "Labor's Color Line," *Forbes*, 15 Feb. 1955; Marshall, *The Negro Worker*.

union to upgrade blacks over the objections of local white workers.[94] Near the end of its term, the committee began to lean more heavily on construction trade unions, particularly the electrical workers in Washington, DC. In 1960 it required the contractors to furnish statistical data on minority hiring and plans for increasing the number of minority workers. If the union would not provide them, the contractors were urged to hire minorities on a "limited preferential basis."[95] Its own fundamental weakness and the recalcitrance of the building trades drove the committee to propose this remarkable expedient. The idea of racial preferences and quotas was associated almost exclusively with communists in previous decades, but it was also an old method that AFL locals used in the South. Vice-President Nixon was also trying to appeal to black voters for the 1960 election, and his committee did receive some compliments from civil rights organizations that more often criticized the Eisenhower administration.[96]

The Kennedy administration attempted to strengthen the federal contract program rather than battle southern Democrats for a fair employment statute. Kennedy's executive order created a new committee with more explicit powers, including the exhortation to take "affirmative action" to promote minority employment, but it did not extend its jurisdiction to labor unions. The Democratic administration was even less inclined than its predecessor to annoy organized labor.[97]

The centerpiece of the Kennedy administration effort was "Plans for Progress," in which businesses voluntarily agreed to try to employ more minorities, a de facto program of racial preferences. The program made modest gains—winning praise from many civil rights leaders and drawing fire from southern Democrats. When

94. King and Risher, *The Negro in the Petroleum Industry,* 36–38; Ed Cony, "Industry Integration," *Wall Street Journal,* 29 Sep. 1958; Jacob Seidenberg, "The President's Committee on Government Contracts, 1953–60—An Appraisal" (unpublished ms., Columbia University Law School, 1961), ch. 5.

95. Herman Belz, *Equality Transformed: A Quarter-Century of Affirmative Action* (New Brunswick, 1991), 15; U.S. Commission on Civil Rights, *1961 Report, Part III,* 68; Ray Marshall, "Equal Employment Opportunities: Problems and Prospects," *Labor Law Journal* 16 (1965), 464.

96. Hugh Davis Graham, *The Civil Rights Era: Origins and Development of National Policy* (New York, 1990), 18; Marshall, "The Negro and Organized Labor," 387; August Meier and John H. Bracey Jr., "The NAACP as a Reform Movement: 'To Reach the Conscience of America,'" *Journal of Southern History* 59 (1993), 25–26; Jesse Thomas Moore Jr., *A Search for Equality: The National Urban League, 1910–61* (University Park, PA, 1981), 185; Robert F. Burk, *The Eisenhower Administration and Black Civil Rights* (Knoxville, 1984), 107.

97. Ex. Ord. 10925, 3 CFR 448 (1961); Graham, *Civil Rights Era,* 38; Belz, *Equality Transformed,* 18; Marshall, *The Negro Worker,* 127.

NAACP labor secretary Herbert Hill derided the program as symbolic tokenism, Roy Wilkins scolded him for giving aid and comfort to segregationists.[98]

One area of union discrimination that the committee took up was that of apprenticeship training. Following the lead of the New York State Commission Against Discrimination, it tried to reform the system by which construction contractors and unions admitted young men into the building trades. Few unions guarded their jobs more jealously than the AFL construction tradesmen. These unions suspected that antidiscrimination efforts veiled attempts to introduce "cheap labor."[99] When the Connecticut Civil Rights Commission tried to get the electricians union to abide by the state antidiscrimination law, the union replied that it had not violated the law because it discriminated against all races.[100] Strong sociocultural forces augmented the usual job-control motives to discriminate. Blacks were among the many groups excluded from the insular world of nepotism through which apprentices were screened into the trades. As two economists noted, "The building trades form a tight-knit social group. They have a strong sense of pride and identification with their craft and with the construction industry as a whole. The rough, dirty, dangerous nature of their job tends to draw them together and, in a way, to isolate them from the rest of the community. They have a sense of being different which is perhaps accentuated by the fact that the rest of the community tends to look down on them as 'rough and dirty' and to treat them as 'lower class,' while their income is unquestionably middle class."[101]

In the late 1950s and early 1960s, local black organizations protested and picketed construction sites to call attention to the problem, and the U.S. Civil Rights Commission and the House Committee on Education and Labor began to inquire into the system. The Nixon committee pressured contractors in Cleveland and Washington, DC, to allow blacks into the electrical trades, and AFL-CIO president George Meany threatened to revoke charters of locals in those cities and to recruit nonunion Negroes if the unions continued to resist. The Kennedy committee con-

98. Graham, *Civil Rights Era*, 51–59; Moreno, *From Direct Action to Affirmative Action*, 190–92.

99. F. Ray Marshall and Vernon M. Briggs Jr., *The Negro and Apprenticeship* (Baltimore, 1967), 63; President's Committee on Government Contract Compliance, "Hearings on Training," 10 Sep. 1952, p. 147, RG 9-001, Box 7, Meany Archives, Silver Spring.

100. Marshall, *The Negro Worker*, 74.

101. George Strauss and Sidney Ingerman, "Public Policy and Discrimination in Apprenticeship," *Hastings Law Journal* 16 (1965), 302.

tinued pressuring contractors to engage in preferential treatment in the selection of apprentices.[102]

The Department of Labor's Bureau of Apprenticeship and Training proposed forcing contractors to end nepotism and select apprentices on the basis of merit alone, or to retain nepotism along with a "system which gives preference for a significant number of positions to minority group applicants." Labor Secretary Willard W. Wirtz insisted that racial preferences were necessary only if nonmerit criteria were used, but union opposition forced him to withdraw the order until the end of the year, when he omitted the "significant number" phrasing. The effect of the wording was unclear but "obviously permits program sponsors to discriminate in favor of relatives and friends so long as they also discriminate in favor of enough Negroes to satisfy the Administrator of the Bureau of Apprenticeship and Training," an economic study concluded. It appeared likely that local unions would be able to manipulate the bureau and "objective standards" to maintain control of the system.[103]

STATE FAIR EMPLOYMENT EFFORTS

The states had perhaps the greatest potential to act against job discrimination. As early as 1920, Massachusetts had prohibited racial discrimination in public railway employment, and New York enacted a broader prohibition for public utilities in 1933. Individuals had to enforce these acts by civil suit, however, and they had no effect. Public utilities, as monopolies, could discriminate without cost, making them poor targets for weak gestures. Labor unions, which also began to acquire special legislative privileges from the states in the 1930s, could also be called on to meet public nondiscrimination standards. Pennsylvania's 1937 labor relations act did not assist unions that denied membership on the basis of race, creed, or color, which may have helped organizers reach out to blacks.[104] However, organized labor could be powerful enough to prevent such regulation or to weaken its enforcement. When the New York state legislature passed a similar bill in 1939, Gov-

102. Ibid., 305; Belz, *Equality Transformed,* 15.

103. Graham, *Civil Rights Era,* 114–16; Marshall and Briggs, *The Negro and Apprenticeship,* 198–200.

104. Arthur Earl Bonfield, "The Origins and Development of American Fair Employment Legislation," *Iowa Law Review* 52 (1967), 1057–58; Bernard E. Anderson, *The Negro in the Public Utilities Industry* (Philadelphia, 1970), 5–6, 68–73; George L. Schuyler, "Negro Workers Lead in Great Lakes Steel Drive," *Pittsburgh Courier,* 31 Jul. 1937 [DH VII: 58].

ernor Herbert Lehman vetoed it, saying that "fears had been expressed by many persons that approval of the bill 'would go far toward destroying the essential rights of organized labor.'"[105]

The war accelerated the movement for fair employment legislation, and New York enacted the first permanent fair employment law in March 1945. The law prohibited racial discrimination by employers and unions, and it established a commission to hear complaints, attempt conciliation, hold hearings, and ultimately issue judicially enforceable cease-and-desist orders. New Jersey enacted a similar law in 1945, and six other New England and far western states did so by 1949. Legislators modeled these commissions on the National Labor Relations Board, creating single-issue administrative agencies that would not have the legal impediments of civil or criminal court enforcement.[106]

Civil rights groups, who had been the most enthusiastic promoters of these laws, became their severest critics. The commissions were unwilling to consider industry-wide statistical evidence of discrimination, refused to apply the law retroactively, and emphasized conciliation rather than confrontation. The civil rights groups criticized the individual-complaint approach to the problem of job discrimination and also did not think that the commissions were eager enough to win remedies for individual complainants. In short, civil rights groups had been unable to "capture" the state fair employment commissions as organized labor had captured the NLRB. Yet since these laws were the most advanced in the nation and the model for fair employment bills in Congress, the groups usually muted their displeasure.[107]

Part of the moderation in criticism of the state FEPCs may also have been due to the recognition that they were fairly effective. On the eve of the Civil Rights Act of 1964, Herbert Hill unveiled a harsh study of the state commissions and thirty years later repeated that "Virtually every study of state FEP agencies concluded that

105. "Signs Bill Aimed at Discrimination," *New York Times*, 11 Jun. 1939, sec. I, p. 6; Note, "Legislative Attempts to Eliminate Racial and Religious Discrimination," *Columbia Law Review* 39 (1939), 986–1003; Bonfield, "Origins and Development of American Fair Employment Legislation," 1059. Robert F. Wagner Jr., was one of the assemblymen who voted against the law. Clayton Knowles, "Javits Says Rival Aids Segregation," *New York Times*, 30 Oct. 1956, p. 30.

106. Bonfield, "Origins and Development of American Fair Employment Legislation," 1068–93; Graham, *Civil Rights Era*, 19–22.

107. Moreno, *From Direct Action to Affirmative Action*, 116–25; Leon Mayhew, *Law and Equal Opportunity: A Study of the Massachusetts Commission Against Discrimination* (Cambridge, 1968), 287.

they operated on erroneous or inadequate assumptions, were unable to eliminate widespread patterns of job discrimination, and were generally ineffective." [108] This stance reflected the grander expectations of architects of affirmative action like Hill and Alfred W. Blumrosen. In fact, there have been few systematic studies of the state FEPCs. Both contemporary and historical accounts have been more mixed and moderate than Hill's.[109] The most recent economic study of the state FEPCs finds that the commissions begun in the 1940s were responsible for minority income gains that were not offset by higher unemployment. The commissions of the 1950s, facing a more difficult set of economic problems, were less effective.[110]

Most state fair employment laws applied to labor unions, and unions presented some of the most difficult cases that the commissions faced. Resistance was concentrated in craft unions, which discriminated for both racial and economic motives, often with the tacit agreement of management. "Largely because of these obstacles and complexities, the state and local FEPCs without exception have displayed a marked reluctance to take action against discriminatory unions," Paul Norgren observed.[111] Though most national union leaders were firm supporters of the FEPCs, locals continued to ignore national policies. As the wartime FEPC found, employers responded more readily than unions to the conciliatory approach and the threat of public exposure. The Railway Mail Association, a union that barred blacks, sued to overturn the New York civil rights law that preceded its fair employment act. Connecticut officials had to threaten an electrical workers local with jail sentences and fines before it accepted a black member.[112] But the New

108. Herbert Hill, "Twenty Years of State FEPCs: A Critical Analysis with Recommendations," *Buffalo Law Review* 14 (1965), 22–69; Hill, "Lichtenstein's Fictions," 88.

109. Moreno, *From Direct Action to Affirmative Action,* 125, 131; Norgren and Hill, *Toward Fair Employment,* 144.

110. William J. Collins, "The Labor Market Impact of State-Level Anti-Discrimination Laws, 1940–60," National Bureau of Economic Research Working Paper (2002), 31; Joseph B. Robison, "Comment," *Buffalo Law Review* 14 (1965), 121; Malcolm H. Liggett, "The Efficacy of State Fair Employment Practices Commissions," *Industrial and Labor Relations Review* 22 (1969), 567.

111. Jay Anders Higbee, *Development and Administration of the New York State Law against Discrimination* (University, AL, 1966), 104; Norgren and Hill, *Toward Fair Employment,* 136–38, 148; Paul H. Norgren, "Fair Employment Practice Laws—Experiences, Effects, Prospects," in Arthur M. Ross and Herbert Hill, eds., *Employment, Race, and Poverty* (New York, 1967), 550.

112. Merl E. Reed, *Seedtime for the Modern Civil Rights Movement: The President's Committee on Fair Employment Practice, 1941–46* (Baton Rouge, 1991), 46; Marshall, "The Negro and Organized Labor," 387–89; F. Ray Marshall and Vernon M. Briggs Jr., *The Negro and Apprenticeship* (Baltimore,

Jersey assistant commissioner of education, who supervised the state's fair employment law, told the CIO Committee to Abolish Discrimination that "we have had very pleasant experiences in dealing with most of the labor unions. There have been one or two of the unions affiliated with the AFL that had, in the beginning, resisted our recommendations concerning cases. However, the differences have been worked out and it has not been necessary to hold any public hearings regarding these unions."[113]

The most blatant discriminators were the AFL building trade unions, especially in their control of access to skilled jobs. A St. Louis Urban League report concluded that "organized labor unions, as a whole, did not keep pace with the improving attitude of management," and the national office reiterated the point, saying that union discrimination was intensified "because of the publicly pronounced policies of the AFL-CIO, often repeated and loudly proclaimed by its international officers and its friends and supporters."[114] Herbert Hill told the story of a Terre Haute carpenters local that refused to accept a skilled black applicant and subsequently picketed an independent job that he undertook, destroyed his work, and beat him until hospitalized. A bricklayers union in Wisconsin insisted on its right to deny membership to blacks despite the state's fair employment law, and the state supreme court agreed.[115]

Like the wartime FEPC, the state commissions were closely allied to organized labor. Even Charles Abrams, the chairman of the New York State Commission Against Discrimination, praised by civil rights groups and condemned by conservatives as a "zealot" on racial equality, took a guarded stance toward unions. In 1957, he told civil rights groups to stop making "vague accusations" against New

---

1967), 192; *Railway Mail Association v. Corsi,* 326 U.S. 88 (1945); *Wall Street Journal,* 16 Jul. 1952; *Business Week,* 10 Apr. 1954; *IBEW v. Commission on Civil Rights,* 140 Conn. 537 (1953); Norgren and Hill, *Toward Fair Employment,* 140.

113. Joseph L. Bustard to Peter Henle, 22 Nov. 1950, Box 1, RG 9-001, George Meany Memorial Archives, Silver Spring.

114. "Report Scores St. Louis Leaders," *New York Times,* 15 Feb. 1953, p. 34; Labor Relations Secretary Report for 1959 Annual Conference, Box 13, RG 9-001, George Meany Memorial Archives, Silver Spring.

115. Bruner, "The Negro Bids for Union Power," 208; "Wisconsin Upholds Negro Ban by Union," *New York Times,* 10 Apr. 1957, p. 65; "Negroes Lose Court Tilt for Union Membership," Associated Negro Press, 9 Apr. 1956 [CBP X: 256]; "Union's Ban on Negroes Upheld," *U.S. News and World Report,* 11 Oct. 1957, p. 127.

York building tradesmen and to come forward with evidence of discrimination.[116] The National Labor Relations Act also limited the ability of states to regulate labor relations. In 1962, the Colorado supreme court held that the state's antidiscrimination law interfered with federal power to regulate interstate commerce.[117]

POSTWAR ECONOMIC CHANGES

Significant economic changes by the mid-1950s altered the face of the civil rights and labor movements. While the industrialization and urbanization of the South helped give rise to the civil rights movement, the deindustrialization and suburbanization of the North posed problems that were beyond the power of traditional "civil rights" principles to solve. Few fair employment advocates realized it but, as one historian puts it, "just as attempts to provide blacks with a greater slice of the labor market pie began in earnest, the pie shrank."[118]

Black migration out of the South in the 1950s continued at nearly the same rate it had in the 1940s, even though industrial employment in the North was not increasing at a wartime rate. Auto employment had peaked in 1953. The recession of 1957 saw the first imported cars and the first time American steel imports exceeded exports. Over 2 million Americans left the nation's twelve largest cities in the 1940s; in the next decade 3.5 million whites left them and 4.5 million nonwhites entered them. While cities hosted two-thirds of the nation's production jobs in 1929, less than one-half of them were there by 1970.[119] The period immediately following the Korean War was among the best in American history in terms of relative racial employment and income statistics. It is probable that black migration, the most important factor in black economic progress, became less helpful by the mid-1950s,

116. Myrna Bain, "Organized Labor and the Negro," *National Review* 14 (1963), 455; Lester Velie, "Race Discrimination with a Union Label," *Readers Digest,* May 1959, pp. 66–71; "Union Leaders Vow State Fight on Bias," *New York Times,* 14 Jan. 1957, p. 1; George W. Brooks, "Comment," *Buffalo Law Review* 14 (1965), 125.

117. Michael I. Sovern, "The National Labor Relations Act and Racial Discrimination," *Columbia Law Review* 62 (1962), 590; *Colorado Anti-Discrimination Commission v. Continental Air Lines,* 149 Colo. 259 (1962). This decision was reversed by the U.S. Supreme Court, 372 U.S. 714 (1963).

118. Thomas J. Sugrue, *The Origins of the Urban Crisis: Race and Inequality in Postwar Detroit* (Princeton, 1996), 123.

119. Lichtenstein, *The Most Dangerous Man in Detroit,* 295; Edward C. Banfield, *The Unheavenly City Revisited* (Boston, 1974), 30, 116; Richard Polenberg, *One Nation Divisible: Class, Race, and Ethnicity in the United States since 1938* (New York, 1980), 150.

draining the South of its more productive workers and bringing them to areas of declining employment. As one economist put it, "the migrants were moving to the big city at the wrong point in history."[120]

A number of public policies promoted these economic changes. Government accelerated suburbanization by highway construction and tax policy; the Interstate Highway Act of 1956 began the largest public works project in human history. Urban redevelopment and "slum clearance" further weakened the labor market in cities. Urban planners of the postwar years continued the progressive campaign that made cities less hospitable to blue-collar employment. Zoning destroyed low-wage jobs in the cities and inhibited low-income migration to the suburbs. Antitrust policy and restrictions on investment banking retarded economic growth. Cold war economic policies built up foreign industries while neglecting America's.[121]

National labor policy also imposed a drag on employment. The power of organized labor reached its peak at the time of the AFL-CIO merger, with over a third of the American work force in unions. The increased labor costs that unions imposed eroded employment. Estimates in the early 1960s indicated that organized workers earned 10 to 15 percent more than comparably productive nonunion members, and the gap was increasing.[122] Unions and pro-union municipalities made unskilled jobs more remunerative, reducing the number of such jobs and making them attractive to white workers. Many of these white workers possessed education and skills beyond those needed for the jobs, and beyond those of black competitors.[123] Black workers did benefit to some extent from labor organization. A 1972 study estimated that the benefits of industrial unions more than cancelled

120. Moreno, *From Direct Action to Affirmative Action*, 138–39; Dewey, "Negro Employment in Southern Industry," 288–89; Thomas N. Maloney, "Wage Compression and Wage Inequality between Black and White Males in the United States, 1940–60," *Journal of Economic History* 54 (1994), 371; Timothy Bates, "Black Economic Well-Being since the 1950s," *Review of Black Political Economy* 12 (1984), 17.

121. Banfield, *The Unheavenly City Revisited*, 14–16; Joel Schwartz, *The New York Approach: Robert Moses, Urban Liberals, and Redevelopment of the Inner City* (Columbus, OH, 1993), 229–30, 254; Polenberg, *One Nation Divisible*, 130–32, 152–53; Sugrue, *Origins of the Urban Crisis;* Stein, *Running Steel,* 197–213.

122. James D. Gwartney and Richard L. Stroup, *Economics: Private and Public Choice,* 4th ed. (San Diego, 1987), 602–04; Richard Vedder and Lowell Gallaway, "The Economic Effects of Labor Unions Revisited," *Journal of Labor Research* 23 (2002), 105.

123. Banfield, *The Unheavenly City Revisited*, 107–11; Herbert R. Northrup, *The Negro in the Rubber Tire Industry* (Philadelphia, 1969), 20, 113; Gordon F. Bloom and F. Marion Fletcher, *The Negro in the Supermarket Industry* (Philadelphia, 1972), 138.

out the harm of craft unions and that unions overall improved the relative income of black workers by about 2 percent. But this did not take into account the increased unemployment that had resulted from labor organization and other labor policies since the New Deal.[124]

The black unemployment rate was consistently double the white rate after the mid-1950s. Even unions that made special efforts to be fair to black workers often ended up harming them. Blacks were able to break into the urban transport industry with the advent of unionization in the 1930s and 1940s. Powerful unions and public ownership made these jobs more desirable but also drove up costs. "This is the classic syndrome of the industry," one analyst observed. "To the extent that union power accelerates costs and reduces patronage and employment, it means fewer jobs in the industry for Negroes or whites."[125] Industrial unions benefited members but drove up costs for everyone else. The CIO did not attempt to create "one big union." Rather, it organized the "core" industries while those in the "periphery" remained unorganized—and most blacks continued to work in the periphery. Moreover, entry into the core industrial labor market would be harder because, with higher labor costs, employers reduced overall employment. Even if the entire national market were unionized, capital and employment would flow to lower-cost countries.[126]

In the mid-1950s, more Americans took jobs in the service sector of the economy than in the production industries, and such work required more skills and education. Technological innovations, spurred by higher costs for unskilled labor, also put a premium on "human capital." One of the chief problems that fair employment advocates faced by 1960 was the relative dearth of blacks with the requisite skills to compete in the dawning postindustrial economy. "There is little question that beginning in the early 1960s a shortage of qualified Negro employees began to develop," a historian observes. "Formed to deal with economically irrelevant forms of discrimination . . . the fair employment organizations suddenly found themselves confronted with economically relevant discrimination; i.e., that based on inability to perform the job."[127]

124. Orley Ashenfelter, "Racial Discrimination and Trade Unionism," *Journal of Political Economy* 80 (1972), 463; Norgren and Hill, *Toward Fair Employment,* 55; Rudy M. Fichtenbaum, "How Do Unions Affect Racial Wage Differentials?" in Patrick L. Mason, ed., *African Americans, Labor, and Society: Organizing for a New Agenda* (Detroit, 2001), 67–84.

125. Philip W. Jeffress, *The Negro in the Urban Transit Industry* (Philadelphia, 1970), 90.

126. Zieger, *The CIO,* 68, 305, 348.

127. Gelber, *Black Men and Businessmen,* 131.

Training and promotion posed the chief problems in employment discrimination by the late 1950s, and in these spheres unions had more influence than they had on hiring.[128] Walter Reuther continued to blame management hiring for employment discrimination, despite the influence that union seniority had on hiring in declining industries, the fact that auto managers had excluded blacks at the behest of white workers, and the control that skilled craft workers in the CIO unions exercised.[129] At the AFL-CIO's first convention, James B. Carey, head of the federation's civil rights committee, claimed that discriminatory patterns began "at the hiring gate, which in most instances is management's sole responsibility."[130] This analysis neglected the extent to which union influence over wages was tantamount to influence over hiring. By raising wages above their market value, unions decreased the demand for labor—the same effect as reducing the supply of labor.[131]

THE CIVIL RIGHTS ACT OF 1964

Congress finally enacted a national fair employment law as part of the Civil Rights Act of 1964. President Kennedy, feeling the pressure of black protest and southern white reaction in 1963, asked Congress for legislation to deal with the principal image of the civil rights movement, segregation in public accommodations. This was the priority of civil rights leaders as well, but George Meany fought for a fair employment title in the bill, over the objections of some in the executive council.[132] As he told a House committee in 1964, "We operate in a democratic way, and we cannot dictate even in a good cause. So in effect, we need a federal law to help us to do what we want to do—mop up those areas of discrimination which still per-

128. Milton R. Convitz, *A Century of Civil Rights* (New York, 1961), 216; "Nixon Cites Bias in Job Promotion," *New York Times,* 26 Oct. 1955, p. 19; Lawrence Stessin, "Labor's Color Line," *Forbes,* 15 Feb. 1955; "Drive on Bias Moves into Spotlight," *Business Week,* 29 Oct. 1955.

129. "Business Is Held Seeking Bias' End," *New York Times,* 16 Nov. 1951, p. 18; Lichtenstein, *The Most Dangerous Man in Detroit,* 375; Sugrue, *Origins of the Urban Crisis,* 102.

130. *Proceedings,* 1st Annual AFL-CIO Convention (Washington, 1955), 109–13 [DH VIII: 51].

131. Henry C. Simons, "Some Reflections on Syndicalism," *Journal of Political Economy* 52 (1944), 1–25.

132. Joseph L. Rauh Jr., "The Role of the Leadership Conference on Civil Rights in the Civil Rights Struggle of 1963–64," in Robert D. Loevy, ed., *The Civil Rights Act of 1964: The Passage of the Law That Ended Racial Segregation* (Albany, 1997), 52; Stein, *Running Steel,* 79–80; Goulden, *Meany,* 319; Jack Barbash, *Trade Unionism and Social Justice* (Madison, 1971), 12. Don Slaiman, head of the AFL-CIO Civil Rights Department, claimed that it had been his idea to add a fair employment section to the bill. Slaiman interview, 20 Dec. 1989, RG 9-001, George Meany Memorial Archives, Silver Spring.

sist in our own ranks." [133] Organized labor also played a key role in promoting the 1963 March on Washington that did so much to publicize the demand for a civil rights bill. Though the federation did not endorse the march, individual unions were free to do so, and unions contributed about half of the funds for it. A. Philip Randolph originally conceived a "Job Rights March and Mobilization," but other civil rights organizations turned it toward issues of social and legal, rather than political, equality, in what ended up a "March on Washington for Jobs and Freedom." [134] Kennedy did not ask for a fair employment title, requesting instead statutory authority for his executive antidiscrimination committee, but the House Judiciary Committee appended a fair employment section to the president's proposal.

The AFL-CIO had long been in favor of a national fair employment act; it supported Kennedy's proposal and the House Judiciary Committee's substitute. The national officers believed that the legislation would enable them to get recalcitrant local unions to comply with national policy. They also wanted it as a tool to get employers to stop discriminating. While unions everywhere in the country were already obligated to meet some kind of "fair employment" standard, employers outside of fair employment states were still free to discriminate. [135]

Southern segregationists insisted that the civil rights bill would force employers to grant preferential treatment to minorities and to maintain racial quotas in their work forces. Others argued that the bill's prohibition of union discrimination would destroy established seniority rights and allow blacks to take white jobs. These were not new criticisms; southerners had warned about the potential of racial quotas since the 1940s. Before 1963, labor and civil rights groups had consistently denied that nondiscrimination would require compensatory or preferential treatment for minorities. Most civil rights leaders continued to do so, but some, like James Farmer of the Congress of Racial Equality, had begun to advocate preferential treatment (although Farmer prudently abjured quotas when he testified

133. Quoted in Jonathan S. Leonard, "The Effect of Unions on the Employment of Blacks, Hispanics, and Women," *Industrial and Labor Relations Review* 39 (1985), 117.

134. Paula F. Pfeffer, "The Evolution of A. Philip Randolph and Bayard Rustin from Radicalism to Conservatism," in Peter Eisenstadt, ed., *Black Conservatism: Essays in Intellectual and Political History* (New York, 1999), 207.

135. Francis J. Vaas, "Title VII: Legislative History," *Boston College Industrial and Commercial Law Review* 7 (1966), 434; "Discussion of Satterfield Comments on Civil Rights Bill," c. 1964, LCCR Papers, Series E, Box 7; Stein, *Running Steel*, 110.

before the House Judiciary Committee). Similarly, AFL-CIO associate general counsel Thomas E. Harris denied that the bill would affect established union seniority rights. "The AFL-CIO cannot, however, accept the premise that some sort of superseniority ought to be established for those Negro workers who generally were discriminated against for so long," he said. "To do that would be unjust to the white workers who have been working there 15 or 20 years. We don't think that one form of injustice can be corrected or should be corrected by creating another." Also, Labor Secretary Willard W. Wirtz surmised that existing apprenticeship waiting lists based on previous discriminatory policies would be abolished. Like most fair employment advocates, union leaders argued that state fair employment practice commissions had never tampered with seniority or union privileges, and that the federal administrators would do likewise.[136]

In January 1964, Alabama senator Lister Hill led the attack on the bill's fair employment section (Title VII), which affected union security. Many considered Hill a southern liberal, a New Dealer elected to Hugo Black's seat when he was appointed to the Supreme Court. He was moderate on the race issue and a friend to organized labor, but his Republican challenger tried to use his civil rights position against him in their 1962 contest. Similar arguments were made by John C. Satterfield, former American Bar Association president and head of the "Coordinating Committee for Fundamental American Freedoms," a segregationist umbrella organization.[137]

The AFL-CIO legal department told its affiliates to ignore these charges. "Seniority rights already acquired would not be affected," it reassured them. "The AFL-CIO does not believe in righting ancient wrongs by perpetrating new ones. It does not believe that white workers who possess hard-earned seniority should be discriminated against in the future because Negroes were discriminated against in the past . . . [The Civil Rights Act] will take away nothing from the American worker which he has already acquired, and it will keep him from nothing to which he has a just claim."[138] Walter Reuther responded to Hill's charges in February. He

---

136. Graham, *Civil Rights Era*, 35, 100–21; "Equal Employment Opportunity," Hearings Before the General Subcommittee on Labor of the Committee on Education and Labor, House of Representatives, 81st Cong., 1st Sess. (Washington, DC, 1963), 83, 454; Hill, *Black Labor and the American Legal System*, 50.

137. Stein, *Running Steel*, 82; "Civil Rights Bill Destroys Union Seniority," Series E, Box 5, LCCR Papers.

138. "Comments on Senator Lister Hill's Criticism of Civil Rights Bill," 31 Jan. 1964, Series E, Box 7, LCCR Papers.

told Hill that neither the presidential committees nor wartime and state FEPCs had called for any kind of preferential treatment for minorities and that non-discrimination orders were all prospective, not retrospective. Reuther denied that union discrimination would be difficult to root out. "The time has long passed when responsible labor unions continue to exclude Negro workers from membership," he claimed, saying that employers were the ones responsible for discrimination.

> During the years when organized labor and particularly industrial unions won their strength and status in this country, the principal weapon of hostile employers was to divide the workers into embattled union and non-union factions . . . Today, antiunion employers seek the same results by a new division of the workers in which they would play off white against Negro to perpetuate fear . . . Throughout the South, and regretfully at times even in areas of the North and West as well, employers are playing the racial discrimination game to break the strength of labor and prevent organization. It is our primary hope that fair employment practices requirements will end the vicious game of divide-and-conquer.

The Justice Department similarly argued that the bill would have no effect on established seniority systems.[139]

As one historian has noted, "The AFL-CIO's interpretation was consistent with every judicial precedent . . . and also with every pronouncement of the bill's sponsors on the Senate floor. Lister Hill . . . appeared merely to be whistling Dixie."[140] Nevertheless, the Senate added an amendment (section 703[h]) to the bill stating that "it shall not be an unlawful employment practice for an employer to apply different standards of compensation, or different terms, conditions, or privileges of employment pursuant to a bona fide seniority or merit system." Republican senator John Tower of Texas sponsored the amendment, warning that the steps taken by the Labor Department apprenticeship program indicated that "racial balance" would be required by the act.[141] Herbert Hill, NAACP labor secretary, later claimed that "The AFL-CIO, as a condition of its support, insisted upon the inclusion of section 703(h) in Title VII, which they believed would protect the racial status quo

---

139. Walter Reuther to Lister Hill, 11 Feb. 1964, in *Congressional Record*, 8 Apr. 1964, pp. 7206–07; "Discussion of Satterfield Comments on Civil Rights Bill," Series E, Box 7, LCCR Papers; Albert Woll, "Labor Looks at Equal Rights in Employment," *Federal Bar Journal* 24 (1964), 99.

140. Graham, *Civil Rights Era*, 141.

141. John Tower, "FEPC—Some Practical Considerations," *Federal Bar Journal* 24 (1964), 89.

of seniority systems at least for a generation . . . This interpretation was the result of extensive negotiations between representatives of the AFL-CIO and sponsors of the legislation." [142] There is no evidence, however, that the federation did anything to promote this amendment, which most of the bill's sponsors regarded as redundant. [143] It would be up to the Equal Employment Opportunity Commission (EEOC), the enforcement agency created by Title VII, and the courts to implement congressional policy.

The question of established seniority systems that were the result of past discrimination arose in Congress with regard to A. Philip Randolph's all-black Brotherhood of Sleeping Car Porters. Defenders of AFL-CIO racial practices often accused Randolph of hypocrisy, since his own union was racially exclusive and had never bargained for a no-discrimination clause in its contracts with the Pullman Company. [144] Pennsylvania representative John Dent noted that the porters union had no explicit color bar but that its contract gave priority to laid-off porters in future Pullman hiring, a list that amounted to over five thousand, all black. When South Carolina representative Robert Ashmore argued that lawyers and judges would interpret the act to require racial balance, and thus destroy the rights of the laid-off porters, Rep. Charles Goodell of New York denied it. Numerous other congressional statements similarly reinforced the AFL-CIO position. [145]

Many civil rights activists who believed that the Civil Rights Act did not go far enough agreed with this interpretation. Carl Rachlin, the general counsel of CORE, contended that the seniority provision was among the act's weak points, "akin to asking the Negro to enter the 100-yard dash forty yards behind the starting line." "Seniority or merit systems are not covered by this title," he said. "Built-in discrimination practiced in prior years, whereby older employees with seniority cannot be affected, is protected." Some hoped that such systems could be altered if courts could be convinced that discriminatory results proved discriminatory intent. "Reading this section carefully, an argument may be made that past seniority,

142. Herbert Hill, "Black Workers, Organized Labor, and Title VII of the Civil Rights Act of 1964: Legislative History and Litigation Record," in Herbert Hill and James E. Jones Jr., eds., *Race in America: The Struggle for Equality* (Madison, 1993), 270.

143. Richard K. Berg, "Equal Employment Opportunity Under the Civil Rights Act of 1964," *Brooklyn Law Review* 31 (1964), 74.

144. Levey, "AFL-CIO Chiefs Score Randolph." Randolph responded that his union employed a white lawyer, accountant, and economist.

145. *Congressional Record* 110 (8 Feb. 1964), 2557–58.

built up on discriminatory practices of the past, may be the basis for a complaint with the Commission, since such seniority is not bona fide as required by the Act."[146] Law professor Michael Sovern was equally dubious that Title VII would do much to uproot union discrimination, believing that the National Labor Relations Act had more potential. The National Labor Relations Board decided that racial discrimination was an unfair labor practice the day after Congress passed the Civil Rights Act, but this did not indicate a shift in the board's basic attitude. It did not want to give the impression that it was a civil rights rather than a labor bureaucracy. Although many civil rights leaders wanted the NLRB to take a more active role, or to give the EEOC the powers that the board had, the federal courts proved to be the most effective antidiscrimination institution. Few liberals appreciated this fact, since courts historically had been hostile to unions, and the NLRB was the key liberal substitute for them.[147]

Yale law professor Ralph K. Winter cast doubt on the efficacy of the Civil Rights Act from a libertarian perspective. He noted that the political power of unions had delayed and impeded antidiscrimination efforts, rooted in the conflict of interest between union members and black competitors. An antibusiness bias caused liberals to exaggerate employer discrimination and discount the incentives that unions had to exclude blacks. They similarly overlooked the discrimination inherent in the seniority principle. Preferential treatment for minorities was likely to result from efforts to overcome "the racially biased exercise of monopoly power" that unions had engaged in.[148]

Winter was not alone in observing that fair employment laws counteracted liberal policies that had given power to labor unions and otherwise impeded black ability to compete in the marketplace. The Supreme Court had recognized this in its pragmatic invention of "fair representation" in the *Steele* case of 1944. Economist Harold Demsetz argued that all federal regulation before the 1960s harmed

---

146. Carl Rachlin, "Title VII: Limitations and Qualifications," *Boston College Industrial and Commercial Law Review* 7 (1966), 473–94; Rachlin, "The 1964 Civil Rights Law: A Hard Look," *Law in Transition Quarterly* 2 (1965), 82–83.

147. Michael Sovern, *Legal Restraints on Racial Discrimination in Employment* (New York, 1966), 73, 174, 191; Gould, *Black Workers in White Unions,* 40; Thomas O'Hanlon, "The Case against the Unions," *Fortune,* Jan. 1968, pp. 170–73, 188–90; Alfred W. Blumrosen, *Black Employment and the Law* (New Brunswick, 1971), 40.

148. Ralph K. Winter Jr., "Improving the Economic Status of Negroes through Laws against Discrimination: A Reply to Professor Sovern," *University of Chicago Law Review* 34 (1967), 838–44.

black Americans.[149] Law professor Owen Fiss, clerk to Justice Thurgood Marshall on the Second Circuit Court of Appeals when the Civil Rights Act was enacted, noted the irony "that the need for a fair employment law arises in part from the existence of other laws (such as minimum wage laws, laws protecting union hiring halls, laws limiting profit levels, and laws limiting entry) that impair the effectiveness of the market; by interfering with the market, these laws impair the capacity of the merit principle to protect itself. The need for the fair employment law, to the extent that it arises from statutes with a contrary effect, may simply reflect society's reluctance to abandon these other forms of government regulation—it wishes to have its cake and eat it too." [150]

Civil rights organizations would be surprised at how thoroughly the bureaucracy and courts broadened the Civil Rights Act. But this transformation also rekindled the conflict between organized labor and civil rights lobbies, dormant since the early 1960s while they had worked together to pass the act.

149. Harold Demsetz, "Minorities in the Market Place," *University of North Carolina Law Review* 43 (1965), 271–97; Stephen Plass, "Dualism and Overlooked Class Consciousness in American Labor Laws," *Houston Law Review* 37 (2000), 823–58.

150. Owen Fiss, "A Theory of Fair Employment Laws," *University of Chicago Law Review* 38 (1971), 251; Friedrich A. Hayek, *The Constitution of Liberty* (Chicago, 1960), 283.

7 / The Affirmative Action Dilemma, 1965–Present

Bureaucrats and judges rapidly transformed the Civil Rights Act from a simple command to end unequal treatment into a mandate for affirmative action to remedy the effects of past discrimination. This change—wrought in lawsuits by individuals and the Justice Department, the Equal Employment Opportunity Commission, and by Labor Department action under executive orders—bore particularly on labor unions. By the early 1970s, black-union relations were at their worst point since World War II. At the same time, economic changes devastated organized labor in the private sector, and Republican administrations after 1981 added to their decline. By the end of the century, union membership had fallen to the level of the beginning of the century, but a black-union alliance took deep root in the completely new area of public-sector employment. Affirmative action issues strained but did not break the black-union alliance. The New Deal had shifted problems of union discrimination from exclusion to promotion, but, once in the door, black organizations did not make the fundamentally antiunion protests that they had before the New Deal. Black strategy did shift back to the pro-employer stance of the pre-New Deal era. In this case the principal employer was the government—either directly or through government contractors that were subject to the Civil Rights Act.

THE PRESENT EFFECTS OF PAST DISCRIMINATION

The federal courts and bureaucracy began to revise the Civil Rights Act almost immediately after its enactment. This revision took place within the increasingly radical context of the late 1960s, as the civil rights campaign gave way to the "Black Power" movement, and ghetto riots flared through the summers of 1965–68. Black nationalists within organized labor engaged in their own revolts, forming several separatist "revolutionary union movements" within established unions like the United Auto Workers. The "Dodge Revolutionary Union Movement" was the first, begun by Black Power communists in 1968.[1] A. Philip Randolph, who had founded

---

1. James A. Geschwender, *Class, Race, and Worker Insurgency: The League of Revolutionary Black Workers* (Cambridge, 1977); Peter Henle, "Some Reflections on Organized Labor and the New Militants," *Monthly Labor Review* 92 (Jul. 1969), 20–25; William V. Deutermann Jr., "Steelworkers Debate Black Representation," *Monthly Labor Review* 91 (Nov. 1968), 16–17; Peter B. Levy, *The New Left and Labor in the 1960s* (Urbana, 1994), 64–83.

the Negro American Labor Council in 1960, resigned from it in 1966 as it was being taken over by radicals. He and Bayard Rustin attempted to defend the AFL-
CIO against Black Power attacks. They founded the A. Philip Randolph Institute
in 1964, with Rustin as its executive director, largely funded by and devoted to the
defense of the AFL-CIO.[2] "Generally speaking, these organizations had no com-
punctions about using the most violent, provocative language and excusing violence, including knifings and shootings, when committed by their members," observed law professor William Gould. "Sometimes they were paper organizations,
idolized by the New and Old Left newspapers, but simply mouthing radical slo-
gans and platitudes." For a time, these separatist movements posed a threat to the
bilateral labor-management scheme that had dominated American labor relations
since the New Deal, causing some observers to consider tri-lateral arbitration of
intra-union disputes.[3]

The unions and companies did respond to black demands. The auto makers
began to hire the "hard core unemployed" as well as to undertake government-
imposed affirmative action, which accelerated the decline of the industry.[4] The
UAW proposed that the auto companies adopt an "inverse seniority" plan where
white workers with the greatest seniority would be laid off first—at 95 percent of
regular pay.[5] The revolutionary unions proved ephemeral, disappearing by 1973.
The increasing disenchantment of the left with organized labor reached its peak in
these years. For the 60s radicals, the AFL-CIO was as much a part of "the establishment" as the corporations or the military.[6]

These developments strained, but did not break, the black-union alliance. The

2. Robert Zieger, *American Workers, American Unions, 1920–85* (Baltimore, 1986), 175; Paula F. Pfeffer, "The Evolution of A. Philip Randolph and Bayard Rustin from Radicalism to Conservatism," in Peter Eisenstadt, ed., *Black Conservatism: Essays in Intellectual and Political History* (New York, 1999), 216.

3. William B. Gould, *Black Workers in White Unions: Job Discrimination in the United States*
(Ithaca, NY, 1977), 277; "Generation Gap in Collective Bargaining," *Labor Relations Yearbook—1970*
(Washington, 1971), 54.

4. Raymond Wolters, *Right Turn: William Bradford Reynolds, the Reagan Administration, and Black
Civil Rights* (New Brunswick, 1996), 183; Geschwender, *Class, Race, and Worker Insurgency,* 168.

5. "How the Hard Core Can Survive Layoffs," *Business Week,* 29 Mar. 1969, p. 82; James E. Jones
Jr., "Cost-Sharing in Gaining Equal Employment Opportunity," *Monthly Labor Review* 99 (May 1976),
39; Sheldon Friedman et al., "Inverse Seniority as an Aid to Disadvantaged Groups," ibid., 36.

6. Gould, *Black Workers in White Unions,* 388–95; James A. Gross, *Broken Promise: The Subversion
of U.S. Labor Relations Policy, 1947–94* (Philadelphia, 1995), 191; Zieger, *American Workers,* 170; Thomas
Byrne Edsall, *The New Politics of Inequality* (New York, 1984), 49; Ronald Radosh, *Divided They Fell: The
Demise of the Democratic Party, 1964–96* (New York, 1996), 135, 140.

AFL-CIO expressed its support for "affirmative action" soon after the enactment of the Civil Rights Act, and endorsed President Johnson's 1965 address at Howard University, the clarion call for compensatory preferential treatment for blacks. George Meany claimed that organized labor looked forward to "aiding the Negro to move beyond opportunity to achievement" and advised unions to be ready to use the traditional union weapons of strike and boycott to compel employers to comply with the act.[7] In fact, unions would more often be the target of Black Power strikes and boycotts in the first decade of the act's implementation. In 1976, labor law professor James E. Jones asked, "What has collective bargaining contributed to the arena of equal employment opportunity? I would say the answer is, 'Most of the problems: Seniority, recall, transfer, and others.'"[8] Others noted the "anomalous and somewhat perilous position of organized labor with the enforcement of the statute that it helped to enact."[9] Institutions like the NAACP found themselves out of step with the militancy of new black organizations and hurried to catch up. Roy Wilkins told the AFL-CIO in 1967, "I want to state in the clearest possible terms that nothing—absolutely nothing—ever done by the NAACP is intended to be anti-labor, but it is pro-Negro. To the degree that our number of priorities are different, to that degree will there be some within organized labor who misunderstand, either honestly or otherwise, our activities on behalf of Negro wage-earners."[10] Bayard Rustin posed the question, "Which way will the blacks choose—to fight to eliminate segregation within the trade unions, or to become pawns in the conservatives' game of bust-the-unions?"[11]

The Equal Employment Opportunity Commission (EEOC) illustrated its extensive idea of nondiscrimination in its first important agreement with the Newport News Shipbuilding and Drydock Company. The company was the largest employer in Virginia and did not restrict blacks to the lowest occupational categories. It would not admit that it had discriminated but, largely for fear of bad publicity or losing government contracts, agreed to promote several blacks into supervisory positions and to retain an outside industrial-relations expert to consult

---

7. *Proceedings,* 6th Annual Convention, AFL-CIO, 2 vols. (Washington, 1965), II: 165; "AFL-CIO on FEP Title of Rights Act," *Labor Relations Yearbook—1965* (Washington, 1966), 274.

8. Jones, "Cost-Sharing."

9. Herbert Hammerman and Marvin Rogoff, "Unions and Title VII of the Civil Rights Act of 1964," *Monthly Labor Review* 99 (Apr. 1976), 34.

10. *Proceedings,* 7th Annual Convention, AFL-CIO, 2 vols. (Washington, 1967), I: 419 [DH VIII: 189].

11. Bayard Rustin, "The Blacks and the Unions," *Harper's,* May 1971 [SCCF 246]; Gould, *Black Workers in White Unions,* 16.

on further affirmative action. Since the company did not maintain a seniority system, this issue did not arise, but the union complained that the agreement provided for "reverse discrimination" and filed a protest with the EEOC. The agreement provoked the first strike in the company's history, a harbinger of conflict to come. The development of fair employment law lay in litigation, not conciliation.[12]

As part of its project to pursue retrospective application of the Civil Rights Act, the EEOC and Justice Department asked the AFL-CIO to consider revisions to seniority in the course of integrating job lines. "Union concepts of security and seniority were formulated in the period of struggle between company and union," said John Doar, the assistant attorney general for civil rights. "Now the struggle is between the Negroes and the unions . . . A basic conflict exists between labor union concepts and civil rights concepts. Something has to give."[13] In 1966, the executive director of the EEOC noted that it would be "resourceful . . . in seeking ways to give Negroes credit for plant-wide service," and an EEOC attorney noted, "In the context of past discriminatory practices, seniority clauses often become like those post–Civil War 'grandfather clauses' . . . This sort of thing demonstrates the 'present malicious effects of past practices of discrimination.'"[14] But William B. Gould, serving as consultant to the EEOC, claims that the union officials refused to revise seniority, with AFL-CIO civil rights department director Don Slaiman arguing that to do so would enable the opponents of the Civil Rights Act to say, "I told you so."[15] Employers also had no interest in crediting black workers with plant seniority as they merged segregated job lines. Seniority was "merely an arbitrary standard which allocates economic benefits on a preferential basis unrelated to qualifications or ability," Yale law professor Ralph Winter explained. Employers had long resisted it as "a preferential system unrelated to productivity."[16]

12. Paul Moreno, *From Direct Action to Affirmative Action: Fair Employment Law and Policy in America, 1933–72* (Baton Rouge, 1997), 233–34; Thomas O'Hanlon, "The Case against the Unions," *Fortune,* Jan. 1968, pp. 170–73, 188–90; Arthur Fletcher, *The Silent Sell-Out: Government Betrayal of Blacks to the Craft Unions* (New York, 1974), 51; "Now It's Whites Who Are Claiming Their Job Rights," *U.S. News and World Report,* 16 May 1966, p. 86.

13. O'Hanlon, "The Case against the Unions," 170.

14. "EEOC Analysis of Employment Patterns," *Labor Relations Yearbook—1966* (Washington, 1967), 357; "Problems of Compliance in Equal Job Opportunity," ibid., 234.

15. Gould, *Black Workers in White Unions,* 20.

16. Ralph K. Winter Jr., "Improving the Economic Status of Negroes through Laws against Discrimination: A Reply to Professor Sovern," *University of Chicago Law Review* 34 (1967), 817–55.

The relevant precedent appeared to be the 1959 *Whitfield* case, which abolished segregated job lines but did not give black workers any credit for past discrimination. Lawyers came to call this the "status quo," or "follow the white man," solution and urged the courts to move beyond it. The most radical alternative would be to allow blacks to displace incumbent whites, known as the "freedom now" position. Instead, the courts adopted an intermediate stance, known as the "rightful place" doctrine. The Philip Morris tobacco company allowed blacks to transfer out of formerly all-black departments but insisted that they start at the bottom of the new departmental seniority list—the "status quo" position. The federal district court ordered that they be given credit for time served in the previously segregated department. "Congress did not intend to require 'reverse discrimination,'" the Court held, but neither did it "intend to freeze an entire generation of Negro employees into discriminatory patterns that existed before the act."[17] Similar principles were applied in the southern paper industry. The judge who had handed down the *Whitfield* decision, John Minor Wisdom, now went beyond the "angels could do no more" position.

The integration of job lines in the tobacco and paper industries took place over the objections of local unions. When government pressure prompted the tobacco companies to integrate job lines, the Tobacco Workers International Union had to acquiesce, and blacks made more progress at the one significant nonunion firm of R. J. Reynolds. Paper mill owners had traditionally excluded black workers, or segregated them, at the behest of their white workers. Black rights depended on the goodwill of the employers. Without such patronage, white unions marginalized black workers.[18] The "rightful place" doctrine settled the conflict that employers faced between labor and civil rights laws. A lawyer who had counseled the United Steelworkers warned that "Employers and unions are headed for a back-pay bloodbath if they do not follow the seniority requirements judicially set under Title VII . . . It is madness for companies to function with anything less than plant-wide seniority."[19]

The revision of seniority systems comprised part of a larger effort by civil rights

17. Moreno, *From Direct Action to Affirmative Action*, 238–45.

18. Herbert R. Northrup, *The Negro in the Tobacco Industry* (Philadelphia, 1970), 31–39, 61. Cf. Ray Marshall, *The Negro Worker* (New York, 1967), 117; Herbert R. Northrup, *The Negro in the Paper Industry* (Philadelphia, 1969), 39; Timothy J. Minchin, *The Color of Work: The Struggle for Civil Rights in the Southern Paper Industry, 1945–80* (Chapel Hill, 2001), 19–27, 79.

19. "Federal and Local Bar Associations," *Labor Relations Yearbook—1974* (Washington, 1975), 99.

groups to expand what Congress had provided in the Civil Rights Act. The goal included shifting the traditional view of "equality" from individual rights, color-blindness, and equality of opportunity to one of group rights, color-consciousness, and equal outcomes. Thus, when union men like George Meany claimed that there were only "pockets" of discrimination left in organized labor, they were thinking of the older definition. As a technical matter, the project hinged on shifting the burden of proof from the plaintiff to the defendant, primarily by making "discrimination" a matter of effect rather than intent. For the most part, advocates had to resort to casuistry to overturn the plain meaning of the text of the act, or at best to argue that Congress did not understand what it was doing in 1964. The 1971 *Griggs* case, in which the Supreme Court read the new definition of discrimination into Title VII, did not involve union discrimination, but it provided the occasion for the court to ratify the doctrines that the EEOC and Justice Department had devised in union cases. To a large extent, affirmative action derived from union discrimination, a countervailing force compensating for the effects of earlier government regulations.[20]

One legal point that the reformers of the Civil Rights Act had in their favor—yet one that they did not develop in litigation—was that, unlike much employer discrimination before 1965, almost all union discrimination had been unlawful for two decades before the Civil Rights Act. As Arthur Fletcher, assistant secretary of labor, claimed, if fair representation had been enforced, no Civil Rights Act would have been necessary.[21] Indeed, civil rights lawyers were sensitive to the strain that seniority revision would place on the coalition of civil rights and labor organizations, and they attempted to relieve it by shifting burdens onto employers.

"It is a tragic irony that the success of the labor-liberal–civil rights coalition in passing the Civil Rights Act of 1964 laid a foundation for its own destruction," observed Alfred W. Blumrosen, the law professor and EEOC conciliator who was the chief architect of affirmative action. "But there is no doubt that the problems

20. Wolters, *Right Turn,* 157; Stephan and Abigail Thernstrom, *America in Black and White: One Nation, Indivisible* (New York, 1997), 429–31; Herbert Hill, "The AFL-CIO and the Black Worker: Twenty-Five Years after the Merger," *Journal of Intergroup Relations* 10 (1982), 36; Owen Fiss, "A Theory of Fair Employment Laws," *University of Chicago Law Review* 38 (1971), 251.

21. William B. Gould, "Employment Security, Seniority, and Race: The Role of Title VII of the Civil Rights Act of 1964," *Howard Law Journal* 13 (1967), 23; Alfred W. Blumrosen, "Seniority and Equal Employment Opportunity: A Glimmer of Hope," *Rutgers Law Review* 23 (1969), 273; Fletcher, *The Silent Sell-Out,* 26.

emerging under the statute, including the seniority problem, have contributed importantly to the breakdown of this coalition." To resolve this dilemma, Blumrosen proposed forcing employers to contribute to an "equal employment opportunity fund" that would provide cash compensation for black workers in lieu of seniority. The courts and government officials did not adopt this specific solution but pressed unions and employers to compromise. "During the debate in Congress, it was said that Title VII would not affect seniority systems—that is was not intended to remedy the present effects of past discrimination," an AFL-CIO lawyer commented in 1970. "No congressman . . . would have anticipated that the law would be applied as the courts have applied it." It was clear, however, that some form of compensatory treatment would be required, and "It is better to bargain it than to have it imposed."[22] The AFL-CIO's Department of Civil Rights director complained that the federation had supported Title VII while employers had not, so "those who had been discriminated against at the plant gate should be indemnified, but not at the expense of those already on the payroll who have achieved seniority." The NAACP did, however, push for suspension of seniority in layoff cases. In the long run, the Court was more lenient on union policies like seniority than it was on employer policies like testing.[23]

The Supreme Court accepted the idea of retroactive seniority in 1976, awarding seniority to blacks who had been discriminated against from the date of their rejected applications. Yet a year later, the Supreme Court reversed this interpretation of seniority revision. In 1977, the teamsters were able to defeat an attempt by the Justice Department to impose plant-wide seniority. The Court held that "the literal terms of section 703(h) and its legislative history showed that Congress considered the 'freezing' effect of desegregating seniority systems and protected them." Plaintiffs must prove discriminatory intent, not merely discriminatory effects. The U.S. Commission on Civil Rights saw the *Teamsters* decision as a barrier to equal employment opportunity and called for an amendment to Title VII to overturn it.

22. "Report of the 19th Annual Conference of Labor Mediation Agencies," *Labor Relations Yearbook—1970* (Washington, 1971), 135; *Report of the Proceedings of the 9th Constitutional Convention of the AFL-CIO,* 2 vols. (Washington, 1972), II: 213.

23. "Seminar on Corporate EEO Compliance Problems," *Labor Relations Yearbook—1975* (Washington, 1976), 159; "NAACP Adoption of Seniority Resolution," ibid., 197; Alfred W. Blumrosen, *Black Employment and the Law* (New Brunswick, 1971), 213; Blumrosen, *Modern Law: The Law Transmission System and Equal Employment Opportunity* (Madison, 1993), 207; Blumrosen, "Seniority and Equal Employment Opportunity," 307.

At the time, civil rights lawyers regarded the case as threatening the entire bureau-cratic and judicial revision of the Civil Rights Act, though it turned out to be an aberration. Seniority was "the only part of Title VII [that the Supreme Court] was inclined to interpret in accordance with the intent of Congress, and the only po-litical value it was willing to assert against the rule of racial preference," one histo-rian observes. By this point, however, most employers had already adopted trans-fer policies that did not put black employees at risk.[24]

The EEOC eventually engineered industry-wide alterations in labor relations systems, and these had a tremendous impact on unions. The EEOC followed the civil rights organizations in their effort to expand the definition of discrimination, rather than the unions, which sought to improve black economic prospects by economic restructuring along the lines of European "industrial democracy." The agency was effectively "captured" by the civil rights lobby. However, after the *Teamsters* decision endorsed the AFL-CIO's position on seniority, relations be-tween the federation and the commission, as well as between the federation and civil rights organizations, improved. The AFL-CIO continued to support affirma-tive action in hiring and most of the rest of the civil rights agenda. Separatist groups like the Coalition of Black Trade Unionists remained in operation but were largely reconciled with the union mainstream.[25]

By 1968, the steel industry faced more complaints about seniority and promo-tion than any other. After years of negotiations, the federal government sought plant-wide seniority for blacks only, and the steel companies were inclined to fa-vor this as well, but union resistance and the prospect of racial conflict among workers caused them to agree to plant seniority for all. The United Steelworkers

24. "1977 Report of the U.S. Civil Rights Commission," *Labor Relations Yearbook—1978* (Wash-ington, 1979), 339; Herman Belz, *Equality Transformed: A Quarter-Century of Affirmative Action* (New Brunswick, 1991), 62, 145, 212; Blumrosen, *Modern Law*, 205–07, 330; Norma M. Riccucci, *Women, Mi-norities, and Unions in the Public Sector* (Westport, 1990), 47–52; David L. Rose, "The State of the Union," *Vanderbilt Law Review* 42 (1989), 1146.

25. Judith Stein, *Running Steel, Running America: Race, Economic Policy, and the Decline of Liber-alism* (Chapel Hill, 1998), 101; Hugh Davis Graham, *The Civil Rights Era: Origins and Development of National Policy* (New York, 1990), 469; Wolters, *Right Turn*, 151; *Proceedings*, 11th Annual Convention, AFL-CIO (Washington, 1975), 215; "FMCS' Moffett on Decade of Détente," *Labor Relations Yearbook—1980* (Washington, 1981), 92; Richard Magat, "Foundation Connections to Black Workers and Labor Unions," in Samuel E. Myers, ed., *Civil Rights and Race Relations in the Post-Reagan-Bush Era* (West-port, 1997), 159.

and companies also implemented a 50 percent quota of blacks for admission to training programs for skilled jobs, and provided over $30 million in back pay for black workers—$3 million of which was paid by the union. The EEOC concluded similar sweeping settlements with AT&T and other companies in the mid-1970s, but the back-pay provision deterred other large consent decrees. The steel pact comprised a bundle of compromises—more than the steel companies wanted, less than the militant civil rights groups sought, with the United Steelworkers trying to balance the interests of its black and white members.[26]

Though the skilled training quota was the least controversial part of the decree, it led to one of the most important affirmative action cases of the decade. Brian Weber, a white employee of the Kaiser Aluminum Company in Gramercy, Louisiana, claimed that the company's 50 percent quota violated the nondiscrimination requirement of the Civil Rights Act of 1964. The Supreme Court upheld the plan. Most commentators agree that Justice William Brennan disingenuously rewrote Title VII to permit private employers to adopt "voluntary" preferences for blacks. The most significant aspect of the decision was that it insulated employers and unions against "reverse discrimination" suits by white workers like Brian Weber. Crucial to the settlement was that neither the steel companies nor the United Steelworkers admitted to ever having discriminated against blacks.[27] In legal terms, this amounted to *remedium absque injuria*: a remedy without injury.

The National Labor Relations Board did not play an active role in developing fair employment policy after the enactment of the Civil Rights Act, though civil rights activists had always hoped that it would. The chief advantage of the board as a forum was that it was faster and less expensive than litigation, and it could impose industry-wide orders more easily. But the board continued to regard itself as a union, rather than a civil rights, agency. Its associate general counsel called attention to "a philosophical conflict between the Taft-Hartley Act and Title VII" and acknowledged that the board was inclined to "protect its own turf" when the

26. O'Hanlon, "The Case against the Unions," 188; Gould, *Black Workers in White Unions*, 395; Bruce Nelson, *Divided We Stand: American Workers and the Struggle for Black Equality* (Princeton, 2001), 281; Stein, *Running Steel*, 171–85; Blumrosen, *Modern Law*, 200–204; Graham, *Civil Rights Era*, 252; Rose, "The State of the Union," 1145; "Steel Industry-EEOC Race and Sex Settlement," *Labor Relations Yearbook—1974*, p. 371.

27. *Report of the Proceedings of the 13th Constitutional Convention of the AFL-CIO*, 2 vols. (Washington, 1980), II: 291; *United Steelworkers v. Weber*, 443 U.S. 193 (1979); Belz, *Equality Transformed*, 158–73; National Steelworkers Rank and File Committee Report (c. 1979) [DH VIII: 32].

two clashed.[28] In 1969 a federal appeals court suggested that the NLRB would be forced to act against employer racial discrimination. The court held that a cotton processor's racial discrimination was an unfair labor practice in that "racial discrimination sets up an unjustified clash of interests between groups of workers which tends to reduce the likelihood and the effectiveness of their working in concert to achieve their legitimate goals under the act; and racial discrimination creates in its victims an apathy or docility which inhibits them from asserting their rights against the perpetrator of the discrimination."[29] The board rejected this application of the "divide-and-conquer" theory. Employer discrimination was just as likely to promote as to impede collective action, and the board would judge charges of discrimination on a case-by-case basis. The chairman of the NLRB warned that "if the board becomes a proper forum for all complaints of employer discrimination, I doubt whether the board can long survive as a viable institution, since there would be a real risk that it would be so inundated with cases that its procedures would bog down in a hopeless morass."[30] The DC Court of Appeals eventually upheld the NLRB's position. The long-established duty of fair representation that unions bore did not become a duty to pursue affirmative action. Thus when a Seattle police union sued against the city's racial hiring and promotion quotas, blacks sued the union for not representing their interests, but state courts upheld the union position. To some extent, the fair representation doctrine ceased to be a tool for minority antidiscrimination efforts and became a shield for whites against preferential treatment of minorities.[31]

THE PHILADELPHIA PLAN

The construction craft unions posed the greatest challenge to civil rights enforcement, and proved to be the sorest spot in union–civil rights relations. "Civil rights organizations and their allies have far more political power to break down our hiring practices and union security than the National Association of Manufacturers, the National Right to Work Committee, and all the big business tycoons and conservative senators and congressmen who ever existed," said the president of the

---

28. "Washington Conference on Title VII," *Labor Relations Yearbook—1974,* p. 93.

29. *UPWA v. NLRB,* 416 F. 2d 1126 (1969).

30. "Civil Rights Issues and the NLRB," *Labor Relations Yearbook—1974,* p. 117.

31. *USWA v. NLRB,* 504 F. 2d 271 (1974); Stephen A. Plass, "Arbitrating, Waiving and Deferring Title VII Claims," *Brooklyn Law Review* 58 (1992), 799; Riccucci, *Women, Minorities, and Unions,* 38; "Fair Representation," *Labor Relations Yearbook—1978,* p. 111.

plumbers union.[32] Even these most obviously discriminatory unions continued to deny responsibility for discrimination, attempting to shift the blame onto contractors. The EEOC and Justice Department pursued local unions, but Justice sued only two unions in the early years of enforcement. By 1969, federal courts had begun to impose racial quotas on recalcitrant craft unions.[33] The main thrust against union discrimination came from the Labor Department under executive orders for government contractors. While EEOC suits provided important doctrinal footing for affirmative action, the contracting program "comes very close to embodying, if it does not actually do so, two principles in the field of civil rights which have long been resisted—quotas and preferential treatment," said a study by the U.S. Commission on Civil Rights at the end of the decade.[34]

While the Eisenhower administration's committee first broached racial quotas, followed by the Kennedy committee's order that contractors take "affirmative action," the movement toward racial quotas began in earnest with President Johnson's Executive Order 11246 in 1965. The order moved the contract compliance program to the Department of Labor, under an Office of Federal Contract Compliance (OFCC). The new bureau's first high-profile case involved the Gateway Arch project in St. Louis, one of many sites of black protest at white construction trade exclusion. It persuaded one contractor to use the E. Smith Plumbing Company, a black firm associated with the Congress of Industrial Unions, an independent labor federation. Not one of the 1,200 AFL-CIO plumbers in the city was black. When E. Smith went to work, the white union men left the job. George Meany defended the plumbers of his home union when they took similar action. A federal court eventually enjoined the secondary boycott, and the OFCC realized it needed a more systematic approach.[35] The office soon established "area coordinators" for cities with evidence of particularly bad construction trades discrimination—Cleveland, Philadelphia, San Francisco, and St. Louis—and urged contractors there to adopt "affirmative action" plans. The vital step toward quotas was taken in Cleveland, when contractors agreed to adopt "manning tables," provid-

32. "Craft Unions Are Hurting," *New Republic,* 15 Jul. 1967, p. 9.

33. Marshall, *The Negro Worker,* 70; Nat Hentoff, *The New Equality* (New York, 1964), 101; Rose, "State of the Union," 1137; *Vogler v. McCarty,* 62 LC 9411 (1970).

34. Richard P. Nathan, *Jobs and Civil Rights: The Role of the Federal Government in Promoting Equal Opportunity in Employment and Training* (Washington, 1969), 96.

35. Robert J. Weiss, *"We Want Jobs": A History of Affirmative Action* (New York, 1997), 95; F. Ray Marshall and Vernon M. Briggs Jr., *The Negro and Apprenticeship* (Baltimore, 1967), 196; Hill, "The AFL-CIO and the Black Worker," 27.

ing specific numbers of blacks in particular trades. "It amounted to a contractor's promissory note that if he was awarded the job, he would hire x number of minority workers," a historian notes. "The logic of the numbers game pressed relentlessly toward such a quota requirement."[36]

The Labor Department soon backpedaled in the face of union opposition. Don Slaiman, head of the AFL-CIO civil rights department, opposed the system and urged instead that civil rights groups work with the unions to prepare young blacks to pass the necessary admissions tests. The OFCC policy "is disrupting what seemed to be permanent symbiosis between AFL unions and the Labor Department," the *New Republic* noted.[37] Labor Secretary Willard W. Wirtz told the Construction Trades Department in November 1967 that the Cleveland plan was exceptional and would not become general policy. When the government extended it to Philadelphia, it required only a "representative number" of minorities in each trade. The Government Accounting Office investigated the plan, and the Comptroller General concluded that the plan violated the rules of competitive bidding. The plans were shelved shortly after the November 1968 election.[38]

The Nixon administration quickly revived and extended what came to be called the "Philadelphia plan." Nixon's motives for strengthening the executive antidiscrimination program have occasioned much controversy. Observers often assume that Nixon began the Philadelphia plan but do not recall that the antidiscrimination committee that Nixon headed in the 1950s had adumbrated racial quotas. The standard union suspicion was that Nixon sought to drive a wedge between the civil rights and labor lobbies in the Democratic Party. The AFL-CIO declared in its 1969 convention that "Nixon administration officials are covering this retreat on civil rights enforcement [in education and voting rights] by trying to make a whipping boy of unions, especially those in the building trades . . . It is part of a calculated strategy of accommodating conservative elements in the South while, at the same time, trying to divide labor, minorities, and liberals who have been the backbone of the effort to achieve progress in the civil rights area."[39] Bayard Rustin similarly

36. Nathan, *Jobs and Civil Rights*, 108–09; Graham, *Civil Rights Era*, 287.

37. "Craft Unions Are Hurting."

38. Nathan, *Jobs and Civil Rights*, 96, 110, 196; Graham, *Civil Rights Era*, 290–94; Belz, *Equality Transformed*, 32–35.

39. *Proceedings*, 8th Annual Convention of the AFL-CIO, 2 vols. (Washington, 1969), I: 460–64, 472–73 [DH VIII: 41, 110]. At the same time, defenders of the quota system told unionists that the *repeal* of the quotas was a Nixonian effort to "divide and conquer." Vernon Jordan, address, 16th United Steelworkers of America Convention, 19 Sep. 1972 [DH VIII: 392].

claimed, "It is designed primarily to embarrass the unions and to organize public pressure against them. In simple truth, the plan is part and parcel of a general Republican attack on labor."[40]

Some historians and journalists have endorsed this standard "divide and conquer" refrain of unionists, but more comprehensive and detailed treatments have undermined it.[41] Nixon did not push any coherent race-based "southern strategy" and had favored race-specific remedies in the economic sphere for decades, but his personal and psychological character made it easy for his many fervent detractors to attribute conspiratorial motives to him.[42] As the associate solicitor for the Labor Department put it, "If this conspiracy exists, I haven't been made privy to it."[43] Moreover, the extension of these quotas to all contractors in 1970 belies a scheme to divide labor and black groups.

Unions faced the problem of insufficient numbers of qualified minority workers, one that employers had confronted since the 1950s. It was almost certainly the case by the late 1960s that the supply of qualified and interested blacks was not enough to produce a racially proportionate work force in the skilled trades—particularly when colleges and universities began to institute preferential admission policies for blacks.[44] But the blatant discrimination of the construction unions made most observers doubt the sincerity of their claims. As *Fortune* editor Charles E. Silberman put it, "The insistence that nothing but individual ability

40. Rustin, "The Blacks and the Unions"; Joseph C. Goulden, *Meany* (New York, 1972), 411–12; "'Philadelphia Plan' in Trouble," *U.S. News and World Report,* 6 Oct. 1969, p. 71.

41. Graham, *Civil Rights Era,* 325; John D. Skrentny, *The Ironies of Affirmative Action: Politics, Culture, and Justice in America* (Chicago, 1996), 181–82; Thomas B. and Mary D. Edsall, *Chain Reaction: The Impact of Race, Rights, and Taxes on American Politics* (New York, 1991), 87; Michael Lind, *The Next American Nation: The New Nationalism and the Fourth American Revolution* (New York, 1995), 182–84.

42. Judith Stein, "Affirmative Action and the Conservative Agenda: President Richard M. Nixon's Philadelphia Plan of 1969," in Glenn T. Eskew, ed., *Labor in the Modern South* (Athens, GA, 2001); Stein, *Running Steel,* 151; Belz, *Equality Transformed,* 39; Dean J. Kotlowski, *Nixon's Civil Rights: Politics, Principle, and Policy* (Cambridge, 2001), 8, 24, 30, 37, 98, 106; Kotlowski, "Richard Nixon and the Origins of Affirmative Action," *Historian* 60 (1998), 523–41.

43. *Labor Relations Yearbook—1971* (Washington, 1972), 273.

44. Gelber, *Black Men and Businessmen: The Growing Awareness of a Social Responsibility* (Port Washington, NY, 1974), 58, 130; Charles E. Silberman, *Crisis in Black and White* (New York, 1964), 70; Weiss, *"We Want Jobs,"* 193; Herbert R. Northrup, "Industry's Racial Employment Practices," in Arthur M. Ross and Herbert Hill, eds., *Employment, Race, and Poverty* (New York, 1967), 306. For the view that all concern about qualification was really a mask for discrimination, see Michelle Brattain, *The Politics of Whiteness: Race, Workers, and Culture in the Modern South* (Princeton, 2001), 243, 255.

shall count comes with particular lack of grace from trade unionists: the demand for special treatment is, after all, the very foundation on which the trade union movement was built, and the concept of group rather than individual rights is central to the unions' function." In addition, intellectuals and government officials had small regard for the skills or culture of construction workers and assumed that qualifications for such work were minimal.[45] The construction tradesmen faced the uphill task of defending old-fashioned discrimination (disparate treatment) when the courts and bureaucrats had adopted a new standard (disparate impact). Moreover, white unionists ever since Gompers had often dismissed black demands for equal treatment as demands for preferential treatment. In the long run the skilled trades unions were able to defend themselves and were subject to a diminished standard of civil rights enforcement.

In June 1969, the Labor Department issued a revised Philadelphia plan, which established a range of minority employment in several trades that bidders would promise to make a good faith effort to meet. Assistant Secretary of Labor Arthur Fletcher devised the new plan. Fletcher, a black businessman and politician, appeared to be a stalking horse in the Nixon effort to divide the labor and civil rights movements, but the "cheerleader for the Philadelphia Plan," though he often bitterly denounced union discrimination, was no such shill. He argued that union control of the job supply was a legitimate way to prevent employer "exploitation," and he told building contractors not to look on minorities as cheap labor. "Too often in history black people have been used as strike breakers, only to be put aside by management, and discriminated against by employers, when they had served the purpose of breaking the union . . . It is your responsibility to see that the civil rights movement is not perverted into an anti-labor, anti-worker movement."[46]

Fletcher's revised plan met the comptroller general's insistence that contract stipulations be made explicit prior to bidding. But the comptroller general now concluded that the racial goals violated the Civil Rights Act of 1964. Nixon's attorney general disputed this opinion, and the program continued. By the end of 1969, Congress was proposing to prohibit spending on any contract not approved by the comptroller general, but President Nixon cajoled the House of Representatives to reject the plan and got the Senate to accede to the House position. Contractors

45. O'Hanlon, "The Case against the Unions," 172; Stein, "Affirmative Action," 191–94; George Strauss and Sidney Ingerman, "Public Policy and Discrimination in Apprenticeship," *Hastings Law Journal* 16 (1965), 302; Silberman, *Crisis in Black and White*, 70, 216, 247.

46. "Non-Negotiable Goals of 'Philadelphia Plan,'" *Labor Relations Yearbook—1969* (Washington, 1970), 592; Stein, *Running Steel*, 152; Stein, "Affirmative Action"; Fletcher, *The Silent Sell-Out*, 90–95.

and the AFL-CIO construction unions sued to overturn the program, but federal courts upheld it. Early the next year, the Labor Department extended this affirmative action victory by applying Philadelphia plan numerical goals to all government contractors—perhaps half of all American workers were employed by a firm that held a federal contract and thus were encompassed by this program. The administration continued to press particularly hard on the construction unions, suspending the Davis-Bacon Act for a brief period in 1971.[47]

Remarkably, the construction unions that had been the source of the Philadelphia plan soon got themselves exempted from it. The Labor Department, responding to white union resistance that sometimes flared into violence, shifted from mandatory plans to voluntary "hometown plans." Nixon's quest for union support in the 1972 election led him to soften the Labor Department antidiscrimination program, and advisers who urged Nixon to exploit white resentment managed to oust Arthur Fletcher from his position as Assistant Secretary of Labor. Shortly after his reelection Nixon appointed Peter Brennan, head of the AFL-CIO Construction Trades Council, to be secretary of labor. Brennan had endeared himself to Nixon by leading a march of 100,000 "hard hats" in New York in support of the president's Vietnam policy.[48] "The fox was given the duty of guarding the chickens," said law professor and future NLRB chairman William B. Gould.[49] When New York City tried to impose more stringent affirmative action standards than the federal government required, Brennan threatened to withhold federal funds from any city that did so, and the construction unions got a federal court to overturn the city's plan. Labor economist F. Ray Marshall judged the Chicago hometown plan "a qualified success in many ways," a judgment for which he was attacked when Jimmy Carter appointed him secretary of labor.[50] Hometown plans were "designed to appease minority demands for construction employment while

47. Belz, *Equality Transformed*, 36–41; Graham, *Civil Rights Era*, 322–45; Fletcher, *The Silent Sell-Out*, 66; Rose, "The State of the Union," 1143; William Safire, *Before the Fall: An Inside View of the Pre-Watergate White House* (New York, 1975), 585; Stein, "Affirmative Action"; Stein, *Running Steel*, 151; *Report of the Proceedings of the 9th Constitutional Convention of the AFL-CIO*, II: 325.

48. Fletcher, *The Silent Sell-Out*, 70–74; Nicolas Laham, *The Reagan Presidency and the Politics of Race* (Westport, 1998), 20; Seymour M. Hersh, "Colson Is Accused of Improper Use of His Influence," *New York Times*, 1 Jul. 1973, p. 1; Safire, *Before the Fall*, 266, 585.

49. Kotlowski, *Nixon's Civil Rights*, 56, 112, 121; Fletcher, *The Silent Sell-Out*, 12; Gould, *Black Workers in White Unions*, 34.

50. Weiss, *"We Want Jobs,"* 215; Marshall and Briggs, *The Negro in Apprenticeship*, 225; Helen Dewar, "The New Labor Secretary: Not Exactly an 'Outsider,'" *Washington Post*, 20 Feb. 1977, p. F1.

minimizing outside incursion into traditional union prerogatives," one historian concludes. "As such, the plans often succeeded in disappointing both sides while satisfying neither."[51]

Richard Nixon never renounced the Philadelphia plan, which remained in effect in some cities (often at the behest of racially liberal mayors like John Lindsay in New York), but he never got any credit for it from the civil rights lobby.[52] Both parties supported affirmative action but denounced "quotas" in the 1972 campaign. The AFL-CIO remained neutral in the campaign, but black members formed a Coalition of Black Trade Unionists to support the Democrats. A. Philip Randolph and Bayard Rustin, who urged blacks to remain loyal to organized labor, were increasingly denounced as accommodationists—quondam militants were not militant enough for the Black Power movement.[53] The 1972 campaign was a clear sign of the primacy of political action to organized labor among black leaders. A century after the Liberal Republican revolt, black leaders seemed to warn, "The Democratic party is the deck; all else is the sea."

Hometown plans provided some relief for craft unions, but individual and government lawsuits continued, especially after the EEOC acquired power to initiate suits under 1972 amendments to the Civil Rights Act. The AFL-CIO had lobbied to have the OFCC transferred to the EEOC, but did better by gaining control of the Labor Department. The federation also failed to have union apprentice programs exempted from the broadened definition of discrimination that the EEOC had established in the *Griggs* case.[54]

The campaign against nepotistic discrimination in the skilled trades was as protracted as the Vietnam War that the unionists supported. The state of New York had begun to pressure Local 28 of the Sheet Metal Workers Union before the Civil Rights Act was passed. Eventually, a federal court ordered the union to meet a 29 percent minority quota and fined it $150,000 when it failed to do so. The union continued to resist and appeal, until in 1986—nearly twenty-five years after the campaign had begun—the U.S. Supreme Court upheld the quota, ruling that it

51. Weiss, "We Want Jobs," 139.

52. Kotlowski, *Nixon's Civil Rights*, 111, 117, 157.

53. Safire, *Before the Fall*, 571; Philip Shabecoff, "Black Unionists Form Coalition," *New York Times*, 3 Oct. 1972, p. 33; Stephen C. Schlesinger, "Black Caucus in the Unions," *The Nation* 218 (1974), 142–44 [DH VIII: 364, 370]; Paula F. Pfeffer, A. *Philip Randolph: Pioneer of the Civil Rights Movement* (Baton Rouge, 1990), 291–96.

54. Gould, *Black Workers in White Unions*, 47, 289.

was proper to impose remedies that benefit blacks who were not individual victims of discrimination, and to punish whites who were not individually guilty of discrimination, in such cases of "persistent and egregious discrimination."[55]

At the end of the decade, the Government Accounting Office reported that minorities had made few inroads into skilled construction jobs. The AFL-CIO Building and Construction Trades department dismissed the criticism of the unions, as "another in along series of GAO anti-union statements."[56] Three years later, the U.S. Commission on Civil Rights reported that a survey of twelve major unions showed little concern about employer discrimination or promotion of minorities into leadership posts.[57] But the commission had become an increasingly strident and partisan actor in the civil rights scene. At the same time, Herbert Hill, the scourge of the construction unions, now departed from the NAACP to an academic post, claimed that the federation had done nothing about discrimination since the 1955 merger. The AFL-CIO civil rights department director wearily replied, "He never says anything positive about the AFL-CIO."[58] A 1985 study of California found no negative effect of unionization on the employment of women and minorities, and a positive effect on the employment of black males. Indeed, "in California manufacturing unionization appears to act as a more powerful affirmative action program for black men than does the federal affirmative action program itself."[59] Whatever the extent of union discrimination, organized labor had a dwindling impact on construction employment. Where 84 percent of construction workers were union members in 1953, fewer than 20 percent were by the end of the century.[60] Such rapid deunionization in the private-sector economy was

55. *Local 28, Sheet Metal Workers v. EEOC*, 478 U.S. 421 (1986); Belz, *Equality Transformed*, 214–16; Robert R. Detlefsen, *Civil Rights under Reagan* (San Francisco, 1991), 94.

56. "Minority Progress in Skilled Construction Jobs," *Labor Relations Yearbook—1979* (Washington, 1980), 372.

57. "Failure of Unions to Meet EEO Goals," *Labor Relations Yearbook—1982* (Washington, 1983), 218.

58. Hill, "The AFL-CIO and the Black Worker"; William Serrin, "Study Finds Racial Bias in Union Movement," *New York Times*, 6 Jun. 1982, p. 28.

59. Jonathan S. Leonard, "The Effect of Unions on the Employment of Blacks, Hispanics, and Women," *Industrial and Labor Relations Review* 39 (1985), 123; Norman Hill, "Blacks and the Unions: Progress Made, Problems Ahead," *Dissent* 36 (1989), 496–500; Richard B. Freeman, *What Do Unions Do?* (New York, 1984), 29–30.

60. Seymour Martin Lipset and Ivan Katchanovski, "The Future of Private Sector Unions in the United States," in James T. Bennett and Bruce E. Kaufman, eds., *The Future of Private Sector Unionism*

the outstanding development in American labor relations in the last quarter of the twentieth century.

This burst of affirmative action activity took place on the eve of the collapse of private-sector organized labor. The 50 percent quota for admission to skilled training programs that Brian Weber sued against was suspended the year after it was instituted. The 1974 consent decree applied to 350,000 steel workers; only 135,000 remained in the industry when the decree was dissolved in 1988. Black steel employment in that period fell from 38,000 to 10,000. The major, "integrated" steel firms controlled virtually all of the domestic steel market in the late 1960s but only 60 percent by 1985, losing out to foreign and nonunion competition. Steel union membership fell from 1.3 million to 600,000 between 1978 and 1983. Some blacks were gaining a larger share of a rapidly shrinking pie: the percentage of electrician jobs in the industry held by blacks doubled while the number of black electricians was halved.[61]

The steel collapse dramatically illustrated the decline in basic manufacturing unionism across the United States and the entire industrialized world in the generation after the Civil Rights Act. The peak of organized labor's share of the U.S. work force was reached in 1953, and it declined every year afterward without a single exception. The absolute number of unionized workers rose until 1970 and then began to fall. A variety of factors contributed to the collapse of American industry: poor management; U.S. promotion of allied industrial recovery as part of its cold war strategy; irrational antitrust and banking policies; and the "new regulation" of the Johnson and Nixon period, including costly health, safety, and environmental regulations.[62]

Perhaps the most important factor was the advent of European and Japanese competition into American markets open since World War II. New Deal labor pol-

in the United States (Armonk, NY, 2002), 12; Armand J. Thieblot, "The Fall and Future of Unionism in Construction," ibid., 149.

61. Stein, Running Steel, 194; Blumrosen, Modern Law, 204; Edsall and Edsall, Chain Reaction, 198; Morgan O. Reynolds, Making America Poorer: The Cost of Labor Law (Washington, 1987), 167–73. The steel industry settlement did have some positive effect on black employment—Casey Ichniowski, "Have Angels Done More? The Steel Industry Consent Decree," Industrial and Labor Relations 36 (1983), 182–98.

62. Leo Troy, "Twilight for Organized Labor," Journal of Labor Research 22 (1991), 246; Troy, "Labor Confronts the End of Unionism," USA Today 123 (1995), 24–27; Stein, Running Steel, 197–213.

icy also pushed the decline, aggravated by the costs of affirmative action. Union workers did not begin to earn substantially more than nonunion workers until the New Deal. Steel workers earned 30 percent more than the average manufacturing employee in 1959, and 88 percent more in 1980. The autoworker premium also continued to rise while auto employment fell. Membership in the UAW fell from 1.5 million to 900,000 over the course of the 1978–82 recession; other unions followed—the machinists from 920,000 to 475,000, the clothing workers from 500,000 to 220,000. In general, the U.S. economy was coming out of its New Deal insulation of corporate and labor cartels and becoming more competitive. Relatively "progressive" unions contracted, and the most progressive of all, the United Packinghouse Workers, saw a decline in its black membership from nearly half to about a third by the time it merged with the Amalgamated Meat Cutters in 1968. Possibly the greatest crack in the house of organized labor was the United Mine Workers. Six hundred thousand strong at the end of World War II, the union was reduced to some 26,000 by the end of the century, buried in a shambles of corruption, violence, and scandal. The share of construction labor that was organized also declined, from 31 to 24 percent between 1980 and 1984. As the liberal economist Paul Samuelson put it, "The whole history of unionism has been . . . in determining how industries in decline are accelerated toward their extinction."[63]

At the same time that industrial unions and industrial employment faded, black men faced increased competition in the labor market from women and immigrants. After the Immigration Reform Act of 1965, 35 million immigrants entered the United States, and 26 million of them were eligible for racial preferences under the civil rights acts. Though economists differ on the economic effects of immigration on native labor, it is fairly clear that it depressed low-wage native employment and income levels. In addition, employers were able to meet racial quotas with immigrants rather than American blacks. Nevertheless, black organizations did not support immigration restriction strenuously, and by the end of the century they had come to oppose it.[64]

In one year, from the summer of 1979 to the summer of 1980, 670,000 jobs in

63. Richard Vedder and Lowell Gallaway, "The Economic Effects of Labor Unions Revisited," *Journal of Labor Research* 23 (2002), 105; Gould, *Black Workers in White Unions*, 401–02; Reynolds, *Making America Poorer*, 138, 147, 165, 170; Joseph E. Finley, *The Corrupt Kingdom: The Rise and Fall of the United Mine Workers* (New York, 1972); Leo Troy, "Twilight for Organized Labor," in Bennett and Kaufman, *The Future of Private Sector Unionism*, 66.

64. Hugh Davis Graham, *Collision Course: The Strange Convergence of Affirmative Action and Immigration Policy in America* (New York, 2002), 160, 174, 195.

auto and steel manufacturing vanished; this total would reach 1.2 million by 1982. During the depression, 3.7 million manufacturing jobs were shed, amounting to one out of seven manufacturing jobs in America. The U.S. economic decline of the late 1970s, combined with foreign policy disasters, ushered in a conservative Republican administration in 1980. Democrats could no longer label the Republicans the party of Hoover and depression when most voters blamed a union-dominated Democratic Party for the nation's economic problems.[65]

Early in his presidency, Ronald Reagan faced a dramatic confrontation with the air traffic controllers union. When Reagan successfully fired the striking public employees, it was widely believed to have altered the tone of labor-management relations in the private sector, contributing to further decline in unionism. As the National Labor Relations Board tilted toward Republican policy, AFL-CIO head Lane Kirkland went so far as to wonder whether organized labor would be better off without government protection.[66]

While unionism in the private sector shriveled, it grew rapidly in the public sector. Blacks played a decisive role in this transformation. Private-sector unions depended primarily on state power; public-sector unions depended entirely on it. Black political action was an important element in the growth of public employment and unionism within it. It can be said that blacks followed the AFL and CIO into syndicalism in the mid-twentieth century, but blacks led the AFL-CIO into American socialism in the late twentieth century. As the "private welfare state" built by the New Deal unions evaporated, unions turned increasingly to build the public welfare state. To this extent, unions as traditional labor organizations suffered by their political victories and became increasingly political institutions. Where the AFL-CIO spent 40 percent of members' dues on organizing activities in the 1950s, it spent under 4 percent by the 1990s.[67]

Organized labor overall became more public and more nonwhite. Government employment had grown rapidly since the New Deal, from 7 to 16 percent of total employment between 1940 and 1968. State and local employment rose 50 percent

65. Edsall and Edsall, *Chain Reaction*, 175, 198.

66. Charles W. Baird, "On the Right to Strike," in Hans F. Sennholz, ed., *American Unionism: Fallacies and Follies* (Irvington, NY, 1994), 57–64; Edsall and Edsall, *Chain Reaction*, 194; Reynolds, *Making America Poorer*, 126–31, 194.

67. James T. Bennett and Jason E. Taylor, "Labor Unions: Victims of Their Own Political Success?" in Bennett and Kaufman, *The Future of Private Sector Unionism*, 245; Leo Troy, "Twilight for Organized Labor," ibid., 60, 72; Edward E. Potter, "Labor's Love Lost?" ibid., 188

from 1950 to 1977. Only 18 percent of union members were public employees in 1968; nearly a third were by 1984. Blacks especially relied on public-sector employment, as both providers and recipients of government services. Blacks held 6 percent of government jobs in 1940, but this escalated to 14 percent of government employees in 1976. Historically, unions had shunned black workers; now blacks dominated unions. By 1980, 32 percent of nonwhite workers were organized, compared to 25 percent of white workers. While total union membership fell from 17 to 14 million, black membership increased from 2.4 to 2.5 million.[68]

Public employment organization got underway suddenly in the early 1960s. The National Labor Relations Act had exempted government employees, but by the late 1950s some state governments had begun to permit unionization. New York City mayor Robert F. Wagner Jr., the son of the National Labor Relation Act's author, allowed 100,000 municipal employees to join unions and bargain collectively in 1958. President John F. Kennedy took the decisive step in 1962 by signing an executive order allowing federal employees to do the same, adding to the momentum at the state and local level. Whereas there were fewer than a million government union members in 1960, by 1976 there were 6 million; and half of government workers were union members by 1980. The American Federation of State, County, and Municipal Employees (AFSCME) organized most government workers, though others joined the Service Employees International Union or the Teamsters. In 1984, 40 percent of AFSCME members were black. Union leaders, private and public, needed only to look at their members by the mid-1980s to become more aware of their dependence on minorities.[69]

The circumstances of public-employee unionism ensured that its racial issues

68. Edsall and Edsall, *Chain Reaction*, 212; Thernstrom and Thernstrom, *America in Black and White*, 188; Michael Goldfield, *The Decline of Organized Labor in the United States* (Chicago, 1987), 123; Michael H. Moskow et al., *Collective Bargaining in Public Employment* (New York, 1970); Walter W. Stafford and Lewis J. Carter III, "Black Manpower Priorities: Planning New Directions," *Crisis* 58 (1978) [DH VIII: 27]; William Darity Jr., and Samuel Myers Jr., *Persistent Disparity: Race and Economic Inequality in the United States Since 1945* (Cheltenham, UK, 1998), 52; "Economic Progress of Black Americans," *Labor Relations Yearbook—1976* (Washington, 1977), 407; Potter, "Labor's Love Lost," 195.

69. Moskow, *Collective Bargaining*, 38, 89, 135; Ken Auletta, *The Streets Were Paved with Gold* (New York, 1979), 45; Reynolds, *Making Us Poorer*, 179; Zieger, *American Workers*, 163–66; Dennis Bechara, "Unions and Government Employment," in Sennholz, *American Unionism*, 156–65; Morgan O. Reynolds, "Unions and Violence," in ibid., 78–86; James L. Stern, "A Look Ahead at Public Employee Unionism," *Annals of the American Academy of Political and Social Science* 473 (1984), 171–72; Blumrosen, *Modern Law*, 327–28.

would differ from that of the private sector. White racial prejudice had diminished greatly by the 1960s, making the psychological motive to discriminate weaker. As with the CIO unions in the 1930s, blacks already comprised a large part of the government work force by the 1960s, so it would not have been possible to exclude them. Above all, however, the economics of public-employee unions were different. Government employers had no "bottom line," and had not only monopoly control over the services that they provided but also had the ultimate power to gain their revenues by taxation. Therefore, they seldom resisted unionization. "Private employers oppose the unionization of their employees for competitive reasons, while most public employers often promote unionism for political reasons," one analyst noted. There were certainly limits to public-sector union growth—"tax revolts" and electoral pressure limited revenues, and there was some private-sector competition for government services, such as private schools. Strikes were also not effective public employee devices, even when illegal ones were tolerated. On the one hand, government employers lost no taxpayer revenue during strikes, and usually benefited from the drop in expenditures during them. On the other hand, increased welfare payments enabled strikers to strike for longer periods. Public reaction to public-sector strikes shifted against unions in the 1970s. "John Lindsay became a hero to the country—but a leper in New York—when he proposed that the National Guard be called in to break a 1968 sanitation strike," one journalist observed.[70]

Martin Luther King Jr. was assassinated while supporting an organizing drive among municipal sanitation workers in 1968, which showed the potential of interracial public sector unionism.[71] But the controversial demands of the Black Power movement posed serious problems in public employee unions as well. The most notable was the teachers strike in New York City later that year. The teachers union would by the end of the century become the largest and most powerful union in

70. Myron Lieberman, *Public-Sector Bargaining: A Policy Reappraisal* (Lexington, MA, 1980); Reynolds, "Unions and Violence"; Troy, "Twilight for Organized Labor," 252; Stern, "A Look Ahead," 165, 172, 174; J. Curtis Counts, speech to National Association of Manufacturers, 14 Jun. 1971, *Labor Relations Yearbook—1971*, p. 132; Auletta, *The Streets Were Paved with Gold*, 217. Public-sector unions were similarly more amenable to feminist demands for "equal pay for jobs of comparable worth." Riccucci, *Women, Minorities and Unions*, 157.

71. Robert E. Walsh, "The Question," in Walsh, ed., *Sorry . . . No Government Today: Unions vs. City Hall* (Boston, 1969), 2.

the country and, given the vital role of education in social mobility, perhaps the most important institution in the lives of young black Americans.

In the mid-1960s the New York City public school system had a majority of nonwhite students, while 90 percent of the teachers were white, primarily Jewish. The teachers union, the United Federation of Teachers (UFT), was the largest local union in the AFL-CIO. The chief demand of Black Power advocates was "community control," and they did not want union job security provisions to stand in their way. The movement degenerated into criminality and anti-Semitism: the principal of an experimental black middle school was indicted for conspiring to assassinate moderate civil rights leaders Roy Wilkins and Whitney Young, and leaders objected to the naming of a new Harlem middle school after Arthur Schomburg, on the assumption that the black bibliophile was a German Jew. Harassment and removal of white teachers in black schools provoked a strike in September 1968, in which Bayard Rustin, A. Philip Randolph's lieutenant, came to the aid of the union. Black militants regarded this as a sell-out, particularly when the A. Philip Randolph Institute moved into a building owned by the UFT. Substitute teacher strikebreakers were mostly white and a third were Jewish; they blamed the union for fomenting racial and religious opposition to community control and claimed that they were "proud to be scabs." The union won the strike but tarnished its image as a progressive union among left intellectuals and black leaders.[72]

The New York teachers strike could be seen as a throwback to the pre–New Deal era. White unionists vituperated employers, although now the employers were public rather than private. The Ford family was again embroiled in a racial strike, as the Ford Foundation had provided key grants to the community control advocates, and white teachers imagined that they were using blacks to break the power of their union. Some blacks eagerly embraced antiunionism but used Black Power or black victim rather than Atlanta Compromise ideology to do so. Others,

---

72. Diane Ravitch, *The Great School Wars: A History of the New York City Public Schools* (New York, 1988), 295–378; Jerald E. Podair, *The Strike That Changed New York: Blacks, Whites, and the Ocean Hill–Brownsville Crisis* (New Haven, 2002); Maurice R. Berube, ed., *Confrontation at Ocean Hill–Brownsville: The New York School Strikes of 1968* (New York, 1969); Melvin Urofsky, ed., *Why Teachers Strike: Teachers' Rights and Community Control* (New York, 1970); Paula F. Pfeffer, "The Evolution of A. Philip Randolph and Bayard Rustin from Radicalism to Conservatism," in Peter Eisenstadt, ed., *Black Conservatism: Essays in Intellectual and Political History* (New York, 1999), 219; Levy, *The New Left and Labor*, 78–83.

like A. Philip Randolph, called for interracial class solidarity. All parties accused one another of trying to "divide and conquer" in a situation that was much more complex than any of them would admit.

Albert Shanker, the leader of the New York teachers union, became the president of the national union, the American Federation of Teachers, in 1974. It continued to grow in numbers and political influence. After it endorsed Jimmy Carter in the 1976 primaries, Carter created the Department of Education—the AFT was called the only union with its own cabinet agency—which withstood Republican calls to abolish it in the next decade. Shanker's advice to Democratic presidential candidate Bill Clinton to denounce militant black rap singer Sister Souljah in 1992 was a key step in defining the future president as a moderate. When a Jewish magazine exposed the radical background of a black potential nominee for secretary of education, Jesse Jackson again complained of excessive Jewish influence in the government.[73]

On the whole, however, public employee unions promoted minority interests more than private-sector unions had, although not to the extent that their public image suggested. The National Education Association, the AFT's rival teacher union, imposed racial quotas for delegates to its conventions, a device that the Democratic Party adopted for its conventions in 1972. The AFL-CIO leadership, including Bayard Rustin, denounced this tactic. The association endorsed layoffs by racial quota rather than seniority, in opposition to almost every other union. The NEA also opposed the use of exams to determine teacher qualification. Testing was a point of contention in a number of public occupations, such as police and firefighting, that retained elements of "craft" status.[74]

The competition between the principles of job seniority and affirmative action presented another black-union problem in the 1970–80s. A widespread consensus among both big business and organized labor favored affirmative action in the 1980s, which prevented any serious effort to roll back racial preferences by the Rea-

73. Ravitch, *The Great School Wars*, 397; Ravitch, *The Troubled Crusade: American Education, 1945–80* (New York, 1983), 314; Radosh, *Divided They Fell*, 218–22.

74. Riccucci, *Women, Minorities, and Unions*, 3–4, 61; Stephen Arnberg, "The CIO Political Strategy in Historical Perspective," in Kevin Boyle, ed., *Organized Labor and American Politics, 1894–1994: The Labor-Liberal Alliance* (Albany, NY, 1998), 183; Schlesinger, "Black Caucus in the Unions"; William B. Gould, "Labor Relations and Race Relations," in Sam Zagoria, ed., *Public Workers and Public Unions* (Englewood Cliffs, NJ, 1972), 155; "NEA Blueprint for Education Reform," *Labor Relations Yearbook—1984* (Washington, 1985), 275.

gan administration. Indeed, Labor Secretary William Brock championed racial quotas in the administration and blunted the Justice Department's efforts to curtail affirmative action. But racial preferences in layoffs remained more controversial than in hiring. Unions persuaded the courts to limit quotas in this sphere. The only two cases in the decade in which the Supreme Court ruled against employment preferences involved seniority. The AFL-CIO applauded the Supreme Court for accepting its position on the principle.[75] One observer lamented, "The upshot is that women and minorities will systematically be the 'underclass' in the workplace."[76] Municipal unions could choose to bargain away the jobs of newly hired workers, who were more likely to be nonwhite.[77] One labor lawyer noted, "Union members are inevitably divided on affirmative action since the members' interest in racial or sex-based employment do not coincide."[78]

The conflict over affirmative action demonstrated the problem of racial allocation of union benefits that characterized nearly a century and a half of black-union relations. But for the most part the issue of union racial discrimination had been outgrown rather than solved. Certainly the problem was radically altered by the end of the twentieth century, if only because affirmative action involved preferences in favor of blacks rather than whites. Within the bounds of seniority and hometown plans, organized labor supported affirmative action, and the black-union alliance remained tight. When George Meany stepped down from the AFL-CIO in 1977, Benjamin Hooks of the NAACP praised him "for his uncompromising and fearless stand in defense of civil rights and social justice. History will record that hardly a significant advance has been made on the civil rights front without the active involvement of organized labor and the magnificent leadership of George Meany."[79] Similarly, when A. Philip Randolph, who in 1919 had de-

75. Laham, *The Reagan Presidency*, 22–30; Detlefsen, *Civil Rights under Reagan*, 151; Blumrosen, *Modern Law*, 269; Wolters, *Right Turn*, 251; Gary L. McDowell, "Affirmative Inaction," *Policy Review* 48 (1989), 32–37; Alfred H. Kelly, Winfred A. Harbison, and Herman Belz, *The American Constitution: Its Origins and Development*, 7th ed., 2 vols. (New York, 1991), II: 744; *Report of the Proceedings of the 16th Constitutional Convention of the AFL-CIO*, 2 vols. (Washington, 1986), II: 238; "Citizens' Commission on Civil Rights Report," *Labor Relations Yearbook—1984*, p. 369.

76. Riccucci, *Women, Minorities, and Unions*, 61.

77. Barry T. Hirsch and Edward J. Schumacher, "Private Sector Union Density and the Wage Premium," in Bennett and Kaufman, *The Future of Private Sector Unionism*, 120; Auletta, *The Streets Were Paved with Gold*, 217; Podair, *The Strike That Changed New York*, 194.

78. "More Discussion of *Stotts* Ruling," *Labor Relations Yearbook—1984*, p. 377.

79. *Proceedings*, 12th Annual Convention, AFL-CIO (Washington, 1977), 442–51 [DH VIII: 195].

nounced the AFL as the "most wicked machine for the propagation of race prejudices in the country," died in 1979, he was lauded by Meany's successor, Lane
Kirkland.[80]

But what were the benefits of this black-union alliance? The pragmatic turn of
black leaders to government employment in the 1960s did not pan out, as the
American economy became more competitive in the last two decades of the century. The NEA, the largest union in American history, and the one with the racial
policy most praised by civil rights groups, bestrode a dysfunctional public education system that probably did more harm to black employment prospects than any
other institution. On one side, left-wing academics hoped that a revitalized, militant labor movement would increase its attention to women and minorities and
push America toward true socialism. They were especially enthusiastic at the 1995
election of a new AFL-CIO leadership representing service and public-sector
unions composed of women and minorities. But little seemed to result from the
change.[81] The AFL-CIO dropped its historic opposition to large-scale immigration, and black organizations supported it, despite the fact that it undermined
black employment.[82] On the other side, a small set of conservative black academics counseled a return to classical liberal economics.[83] At the beginning of the
twenty-first century, there seems to be little likelihood of either twentieth-century
socialism or nineteenth-century liberalism as an alternative to the public union–
civil rights coalition that had been forged in the previous generation. This coalition, like the New Deal interest-group pluralist system of which it was a part, had
weathered the crisis of the 1960s.[84]

80. *AFL-CIO News,* 22 Mar. 1980 [DH VIII: 159]. In what may have been poorly chosen words, or
perhaps a reflection of an expansive sense of equality, Kirkland extolled Randolph's drive "to make certain that no person was better than any other."

81. Melvyn Dubofsky and Foster Rhea Dulles, *Labor in America: A History,* 6th ed. (Wheeling, IL,
1999), 402; Taylor E. Dark, *The Unions and the Democrats: An Enduring Alliance* (Ithaca, NY, 1999), 178;
Steven Fraser and Joshua B. Freeman, eds., *Audacious Democracy: Labor, Intellectuals, and the Social
Reconstruction of America* (Boston, 1997); Bennett and Kaufman, *The Future of Private Sector Unionism;* Herbert Hill, "Lichtenstein's Fictions Revisited: Race and the New Labor History," *New Politics* 7
(1999), 161.

82. Graham, *Collision Course,* 120, 187.

83. Edward Ashbee, "The Republican Party and the African-American Vote since 1964," in Eisen-
stadt, *Black Conservatism,* 239–43; Walter Williams, *The State against Blacks* (New York, 1982); Thomas
Sowell, *Markets and Minorities* (New York, 1981); Thomas D. Boston, *Race, Class, and Conservatism*
(Boston, 1988).

84. Kelly, Harbison, and Belz, *The American Constitution,* II: 651.

Conclusion

Historians have been chasing their tails about race and class for decades. A half century ago, Richard Hofstadter, discussing ethnic and class consciousness among immigrants, wrote, "Of course one reason why the immigrant held so fast to his ethnic loyalties was that he could not develop any class loyalties because he was excluded by the unions."[1] In other words, the reason people are race conscious is that they cannot become class conscious because people are race conscious. What this study shows is more straightforward: white unionists found that race was a convenient basis on which to do what unions do—control the labor supply.[2]

Throughout this history, black workers paid attention to political developments among whites and acted accordingly, adjusting their responses to shifts in the political economy. The American political economy went through four phases after the Civil War: a liberal or laissez-faire period through the 1890s; a progressive period until the Great Depression; the New Deal period until the 1960s; and a postindustrial phase since then. Organized labor was shaping its identity in the first, dominated by the AFL in the second, augmented by the CIO in the third, and eclipsed by public-sector unionism in the last. Black Americans' attitude toward organized labor varied in response to these regime changes.

The seeds of black-union conflict were sown in the antebellum period. White worker organization attempted to control and exclude free black competition and often opposed emancipation because it would increase labor competition. Abolitionists, by contrast, opposed labor organization due to the same liberal individualism that led them to call for emancipation. It is not surprising that black Americans remained loyal to the liberal principles that promoted abolition and opposed a largely hostile white labor movement.

The overwhelming factors determining the interaction of black Americans and organized labor were the legal and constitutional principles of the United States. In the late nineteenth century, the United States was overwhelmingly hostile to the tactics that unions used to make their demands. Even perfectly harmonious black-

---

1. Richard Hofstadter, *The Age of Reform: From Bryan to FDR* (New York, 1955), 216.
2. Jennifer Roback, "Racism as Rent-Seeking," *Economic Inquiry* 27 (1989), 661–81.

union relations would not have altered the development of American unionism. As it was, blacks fought their way—sometimes literally—into the industrial work force over white hostility. This conflict certainly intensified racial animus in the short term, but eventually the determination and ability of black workers impressed both white employers and white workers. Even in the AFL they won a measure of recognition and concessions, a reflection of the way in which many blacks made the best that they could of segregation.[3]

When the New Deal revolutionized American labor relations by promoting industrial unionism, it forced the CIO to organize black workers. Black resistance, which was considerable, could not have prevented the vast increase in unionization that took place in the 1930s and 1940s. So blacks and unions recognized the mutual advantage of cooperation and worked together. This does not mean that union discrimination ended. While the CIO and AFL became more responsive to black interests, discrimination persisted once blacks were inside the unions. As a result, federal courts began to devise doctrines to protect the rights of blacks as a minority group within the system of majority-rule unionism.

The federal government did not become serious about pressuring employers and unions to give black workers equal—or preferential—treatment in the labor market until the 1960s. At that point, black organizations returned to their pro-employer position of the pre–New Deal period. At the same time that race-conscious government programs were sowing animosity between blacks and organized labor, and while traditional, blue-collar industrial jobs were disappearing, black workers became an important part of the new work force of the postindustrial economy, in the newly organized public sector.

In 1962, Milton Friedman observed that minority groups should have the greatest interest in limiting the power of the state, since they had suffered the most from majority tyranny, but black Americans had come to depend on the power of the central government. He noted "one of the paradoxes of experience is that, in spite of the historical evidence, it is precisely the minority groups that have frequently furnished the most vocal and numerous advocates of fundamental alterations in a capitalist society." It may well be that "As a general rule, any minority that counts on specific majority action to defend its interests is short-sighted in the extreme."[4]

3. Joe William Trotter Jr., *Coal, Class, and Color: Blacks in Southern West Virginia, 1915–32* (Urbana, 1990), 50.

4. Milton Friedman, *Capitalism and Freedom* (Chicago, 1962), 108–09, 114.

But it took a long time for black Americans to embrace this idea, and they have never embraced it fully. As one adviser to black leaders put it, "One of the most important qualities of effective minority group leadership is opportunism. This ability to take advantage of opportunities as they present themselves, properly used, can oftentimes compensate for numerical or material weakness. And minorities have a right to expect such opportunism in intelligent leaders."[5] Individual black workers, black labor organizations, and black leaders displayed a wide range of behavior, taking advantage of opportunities to compete and protesting to escape the confines of coercion.

Most historians have argued that the antagonism between blacks and unions was due to employer manipulation of racial animus, or to the failure of the labor movement to hew to the left. They lament the failure of the Knights of Labor or Industrial Workers of the World, though neither of these organizations established much of a record in union organization in general or with regard to blacks in particular. Even harder to believe is the argument that the purge of the communists from the CIO in the early cold war years eviscerated union egalitarianism. The contention that anyone would have been better off had the Stalinists prevailed is perverse, to say the least. Finally, more plausible is the idea that the socialism of public-sector unionism and affirmative action, which characterizes today's labor movement, demonstrates the benefits of statism for blacks. However, these government interventions really correct earlier antiblack government interventions.

Socialist accounts of the black-union conflict fail for the same reason that socialist economies fail: they try to fit the almost infinite number of individuals and their acts into an artificial category such as race or class. Even libertarian analysts concede that a stricter adherence to free market principles may not have improved black economic fortunes, but certainly the market provides a better model for historical analysis in that it is more open to the variety of individual experience, particularly the penchant for individuals and groups to use fictions like race and class to advance their own particular interests.[6] Labor unions in American history have attempted to control and limit individual competition, but they could only do so in a limited fashion. Thus the lack of "solidarity" among "the working class" is not to be wondered at. Why should boilermakers want to organize tailors any more

---

5. A. J. Allen, "Selling Out the Workers," *Crisis* 45 (1938), 80 [DH VII: 18].

6. David Bernstein, *Only One Place of Redress: African Americans, Labor Regulations, and the Courts from Reconstruction to the New Deal* (Durham, 2001), 113.

than steel makers want to organize their suppliers or customers? If everybody is organized, then nobody gains any advantage from organization. Most of us want socialism for ourselves and competition for everyone else.[7] The carpenters or enginemen did well by leaving the rest of the work force unorganized—organizing the rest would only raise prices for themselves as consumers. Thus, the CIO was happy to create a private welfare state for its members. And, in general, white unionists did well by excluding or segregating blacks.

7. Plato, *Republic*, book I; Adam Smith, *An Inquiry into the Nature and Causes of the Wealth of Nations*, 2 vols. (Indianapolis, 1981 [1776]), I: 145.

Appendix

"Divide and Conquer": The Folklore of Socialism

Often asserted but almost never documented, the "divide-and-conquer" thesis holds that capitalism produces and intensifies ethnic and racial divisions among workers in order to prevent them from developing "class consciousness."[1] It enables owners to lower wages for all workers; the lower earnings of minority workers are known as "superexploitation" and amount to "superprofits" for owners. The term evokes war and diplomacy, a policy adopted among enemies, assumes the class-conflict description of economic relations, and depicts employers with the imperial and hegemonic powers of ancient Rome or nineteenth-century Britain. American labor union leaders and labor historians have often cited this as the reason for union problems with black workers, and the socialist and communist unionists invoked it most often. Concrete examples of employer use of "divide and conquer" tactics are rarely given, however. Most often, *any* kind of employer resistance to unionization is interpreted as an attempt to divide and conquer the working class. The terms and definitions used in the argument are very loose, and historical examples tend to weaken or disappear when scrutinized.[2]

In 1932 W. E. B. Du Bois told the intellectual historian Merle Curti that William Baldwin, an industrialist supporter of Booker T. Washington, "openly stated that his plan was to train in the South two sets of workers, equally skilled, black and white, who could be used to offset each other and break the power of the trade

1. Joel Kaplan, "The Divide and Conquer Hypothesis: An Analysis of Internal Labor Markets and Racial Inequality of Men in the United States" (Ph.D. diss., American University, 1985) is a good overview of the various theories. For expositions of the theory, see Richard Edwards, *Contested Terrain: The Transformation of the Workplace in the Twentieth Century* (New York, 1979), 177–96; Robert Asher and Charles Stephenson, eds., *Labor Divided: Race and Ethnicity in U.S. Labor Struggles* (Albany, NY, 1990). The general idea is ancient and widespread: Plato, *Laws*, 777c–d; Aristotle, *Politics*, 1330a; Sun Tzu, *The Art of War* (Boston, 1991), 92.

2. A good critique is Steven Shulman, "Racism and the Making of the American Working Class," *International Journal of Politics, Culture, and Society* 2 (1989), 361–66. See also Patrick L. Mason, "The Divide-and-Conquer and Employer/Employee Models of Discrimination: Neoclassical Competition as a Familial Defect," *Review of Black Political Economy* 20 (1992), 73–89.

unions." Curti asked for evidence for this claim, and Du Bois replied, "I do not think you will find any printed reference to Baldwin's remark." Du Bois averred that Baldwin had said it to him personally, that he had told Baldwin's biographer about it, but that the biographer did not use it. Du Bois was never consistent in his Marxism, and had a difficult time throughout his life believing the communist argument that class conflict produced racism. He was also often an unreliable historical source.[3]

More concrete evidence is found in a letter to Booker T. Washington in 1900, where Baldwin wrote, "labor unionism will grow and increase not only in the North but in the South . . . [N]othing can stop it. It is in the nature of things . . . There is a clash between the present labor unions and the Negroes . . . [O]rganized labor will raise the wages beyond a reasonable point, and then the battle will be fought, and the negro will be put in at a less wage, and the labor union will either have to come down in wages, or negro labor will be employed. The last analysis is the employment of the negro in the various arts and trades of the South, but this will not be a clearly defined issue until your competition in the markets of the world will force you to compete with cheap labor in other countries." This sounds more consistent with the biographical character of Baldwin, a "progressive" and pro-union businessman.[4] As similar as it may sound to Du Bois's comment, it differs fundamentally. Baldwin's is a neat statement of the "split labor market" theory, which is in fact very similar to the neoclassical position.[5] Capitalists do not foment racial antagonism. Rather, individual and racial competition in the labor market integrates the work force and erodes discrimination.

Most often, the divide-and-conquer argument results from axiomatic, dogmatic assumption. Thomas Sugrue, for example, says that Detroit "auto employers had most frequently used black labor as part of a *classic* divide-and-conquer strategy in the workplace: in times of industrial unrest, the auto companies hired blacks as strikebreakers."[6] No evidence or authority is cited for this claim. In fact,

3. Correspondence between Curti and Du Bois, 5–14 Dec. 1932 [DuBP XXXVI: 1046]; "Comments on My Life," *Freedomways* 5 (1965), 128; David Levering Lewis, *W. E. B. Du Bois: Biography of a Race, 1868–1919* (New York, 1993), 540; Raymond Wolters, *Du Bois and His Rivals* (Columbia, MO, 2002), 213.

4. Eric Anderson and Alfred A. Moss Jr., *Dangerous Donations: Northern Philanthropy and Southern Black Education, 1902–30* (Columbia, MO, 1999), 63; "William Baldwin," ANB.

5. Michael L. Wachter, "Primary and Secondary Labor Markets: A Critique of the Dual Approach," *Brookings Papers on Economic Activity* 3 (1974), 637–80.

6. Thomas J. Sugrue, *The Origins of the Urban Crisis: Race and Inequality in Postwar Detroit* (Princeton, 1996), 26. Emphasis added.

the auto industry was one in which blacks did not enter as strikebreakers. There was little union activity and almost no strikes in the industry before the Wagner Act, and "Negroes were not, therefore, introduced into the industry under strike conditions."[7] Ford recruited workers to prevent UAW organization in 1937, but this was "in contrast to the policy of management in the previous auto strikes" and included both black and white workers.[8] Sugrue continues, "The pattern broke down in the early 1940s, when the UAW forged an alliance with black churches and reform organizations." In fact, it was only in the 1939–41 period, in the Chrysler strike of 1939 and Ford strike of 1941, that what might be regarded as substantial charges of divide-and-conquer tactics began to be made. Sugrue's first resort to the divide-and-conquer thesis is surprising for a work that aims "to complicate the conventional narratives of post–World War II American history" and which rebukes "monocausal explanations of racial discrimination."[9]

The divide-and-conquer tactic is so malleable that it can both decrease and increase discrimination. On the one hand, Earl Lewis argues that no racial group predominated in the Appalachian coal fields, so operators employed a variety of ethnic groups, and this "enabled them to divide and conquer by offering the carrot of equal opportunity to all miners without regard to race or color or nationality."[10] Far from "pitting one race against another," "operators integrated the races more or less indiscriminately and, through equal opportunity and equal pay, attempted to mute irrational racial animosities which might hinder production and profits."[11] On the other hand, the racial tactics of Alabama coal operators are the clearest evidence of divide-and-conquer that anyone has provided, but the attempt to see the same process at work everywhere requires dogmatic faith and elastic ev-

7. Herbert R. Northrup, *The Negro in the Automobile Industry* (Philadelphia, 1968), 8.

8. Lloyd H. Bailer, "The Automobile Unions and Negro Labor," *Political Science Quarterly* 59 (1944), 552; Paul Norgren et al., "Negro Labor and Its Problems" (unpublished ms. for the Carnegie-Myrdal Study, 1940), 532–35.

9. Sugrue, *Origins of the Urban Crisis*, 6, 284.

10. *Black Coal Miners in America: Race, Class, and Community Conflict, 1780–1980* (Lexington, KY, 1987), 121. As one economic historian put it, "When social critics accused southern employers of using the race issue to divide and subjugate the working class, we can translate this into the statement that both were paid the going wage in the regional market." Gavin Wright, "The Strange Career of the New Southern Economic History," *Reviews in American History* 10 (1982), 176.

11. Lewis, *Black Coal Miners*, 146. Joe William Trotter Jr., also sees the black experience in West Virginia as "confirmation of conventional Marxist interpretations"; *Coal, Class, and Color: Blacks in Southern West Virginia, 1915–32* (Urbana, 1990), 265.

idence.[12] What one economic historian has said about West Virginia coal can be extended: "The black experience in different regions can be explained just as easily using standard labor economics and emphasizing the tightness or looseness of labor markets and the extent of unionization."[13]

Rick Halpern provides the most explicit example of employer divide-and-conquer tactics. He cites Philip Armour, "candidly explaining to his biographers that eastern European immigrants helped forestall unionism 'by displacing experienced and perhaps disillusioned employees . . . who might have been contaminated by contacts with union organizers.' Moreover, he admitted pursuing policies intended to 'keep the races and nationalities apart after working hours, and to foment suspicion, rivalry, and even enmity among such groups.'"[14] In fact, Armour admitted no such thing, candidly or otherwise. Halpern's source, Armour biographers Harper Leech and John Charles Carroll, wrote in 1938: "It was the policy of the 'labor relations men,' although they had no such high-sounding titles in those days, to keep the races and nationalities apart after working hours, and to foment suspicion, rivalry and even enmity among such groups. The packer did it. Everybody did it. The direct responsibility of Philip D. Armour, Gustavus F. Swift, Andrew Carnegie, and men like them is impossible to estimate. They did not have to direct it. All they had to do was to wink at it."[15] Armour made no confessions to these biographers, who admit that there is no evidence for their claim. "Armour lived before the days of organized business publicity," they explain. "His generation believed in reticence rather than records." Indeed, Leech and Carroll use as an epigram to their appendix an Armour apothegm: "Intuitive knowledge is one of Nature's most princely gifts."[16]

Interestingly, both Halpern and Armour's biographers admit that simple economic forces were at work. "Market forces undoubtedly played a role in this pro-

---

12. Daniel Letwin, *The Challenge of Interracial Unionism: Alabama Coal Miners, 1878–1921* (Chapel Hill, 1998).

13. Price Van Meter Fishback, *Soft Coal, Hard Choices: The Economic Welfare of Bituminous Coal Miners, 1890–1930* (New York, 1992), 171.

14. *Down on the Killing Floor* (Urbana, 1997), 24. Even Upton Sinclair did not go this far. Though he pressed his dime-novelist freedom to accuse the packers of every imaginable crime, he attributed the claim that "old man Durham [presumably Armour] himself was responsible for these immigrations" to the hearsay of morbid Grandmother Majauszkiene. *The Jungle* (New York, 1990 [1905]), 70.

15. Harper Leech and John Charles Carroll, *Armour and His Times* (New York, 1938), 232.

16. Ibid., vii, 359.

cess by facilitating the packers' access to an abundant supply of cheap labor," Halpern writes, later noting that "Of course it was more than the workings of the free market that threw white and black labor in competition with each other."[17] Leech and Carroll similarly admit, "In part these migrations were natural outflows from a crowded continent to a new land."[18] But an unsubstantiated canard overshadows this simple explanation.

The Interchurch World Movement's *Report on the Steel Strike* is another favorite source for divide-and-conquer stories.[19] The *Report* itself was a controversial one, seen by many as union propaganda.[20] Historians have exaggerated or distorted its claims. Bruce Nelson recently wrote that "the Interchurch World Movement expressed the fear that the steel companies were 'deliberately attempting to turn the Negroes into a race of strikebreakers, with whom to hold the white workers in check.'"[21] His quotation, however, is not from the Interchurch World Movement itself but from William Z. Foster's account of the strike. Foster was a syndicalist-turning-communist, halfway on his journey from Bryan to Stalin.[22]

Robert K. Murray notes, "The steel companies purposely aroused racial hatred and prejudice by instructing their agents 'to stir up as much bad feeling as you possibly can,' and by using Negro strikebreakers against white pickets," quoting the Interchurch World Movement report.[23] In fact, while the ICW condemned the use of detective or "labor spy" companies, it did not show any instruction from the

---

17. *Down on the Killing Floor*, 24, 39.

18. *Armour and His Times*, 231.

19. Commission of Inquiry, Interchurch World Movement, *Report on the Steel Strike of 1919* (New York, 1920).

20. Marshall Olds, *Analysis of the Interchurch World Movement Report on the Steel Strike* (New York, 1923); Ernest W. Young, *Comments on the Interchurch Report on the Steel Strike of 1919* (Boston, 1922); E. Victor Bigelow, *Mistakes of the Interchurch Steel Report* (n. p., c. 1920). David Brody notes that the report "has evident deficiencies, particularly in its discussion of wages and hours . . . Used carefully, however, the *Report* and the later volume, *Public Opinion and the Steel Strike*, provide a wealth of information on the strike." *Steelworkers in America: The Nonunion Era* (Cambridge, 1960), 272.

21. *Divided We Stand: American Workers and the Struggle for Black Equality* (Princeton, 2001), 166.

22. (New York, 1920). Actually, Nelson cites Horace R. Cayton and George S. Mitchell, *Black Workers and the New Unions* (Chapel Hill, 1939), p. 80, which clearly identifies Foster as the one making the statement. However, Cayton and Mitchell misidentify the source as the ICWM *Report* in their footnote. In preceding notes, Nelson quotes the *Report* directly.

23. "Communism and the Great Steel Strike of 1919," *Mississippi Valley Historical Review* 38 (1951), 457.

steel companies to their detective agents. The ICW noted, "Nor was it the custom of certain strike-breaking concerns to wait for 'labor trouble.' The sub-report details, from affidavits of former operatives, how certain concerns provoked strikes in peaceful shops in the past to create 'business.'" This could hardly be the goal of the principals, the steel companies, as the ICW continues. "Some steel companies placed implicit confidence in the reports and advice of these strike-breaking spy-corporations. Other companies were skeptical and dissatisfied but puzzled about what else to do." In the case cited by Murray, blacks were not involved at all. The detective company instructed its operative "to stir up as much bad feeling as you possibly can between the Serbians and Italians," playing upon the postwar diplomatic dispute over Trieste/Fiume—a controversy on which black Americans would make no impression.[24] Here again, the very act of using blacks to break a strike was regarded as a divide-and-conquer tactic.[25]

The *ur*-source of the divide-and-conquer argument was John R. Commons. It is quite remarkable that Commons would try to blame employers for fomenting racial friction when the labor movement, and Commons in particular, had such clearer motives and evinced so much more obvious racial animus. In 1935, he described antiunion sentiment as "a reaction towards Fascism and Nazism," and recounted that he had "learned, in 1904, one of the methods of this emerging Fascism in preventing the organization of labor. In Chicago there were eight or ten of these great firms, each with several thousand employees. I visited the employment office of Swift and Company. I saw, seated on benches around the office, a sturdy group of blond-haired Nordics. I asked the employment agent, How comes it you are employing only Swedes? He answered, Well, you see, it is only for this week. Last week we employed Slovaks. We change about among different nation-

24. Interchurch World Movement, *Report on the Steel Strike of 1919*, 229–31. Professional strike-breaking firms could also work with *unions* to foster industrial strife, thus increasing business. Unions also used gangland connections against employers and other unions. "Strikebreaking," *Fortune* 11 (1935), 56; Steven Fraser, *Labor Will Rule: Sidney Hillman and the Rise of American Labor* (Ithaca, NY, 1991), 178, 243–52.

25. Charles A. Gulick, *Labor Policy of the United States Steel Corporation* (New York, 1924), 111–30. A recent analysis of the postwar strikes by sociologist Cliff Brown, using "event structure analysis," found "divide-and-conquer" in meatpacking but not in steel. "The Role of Employers in Split Labor Markets: An Event-Structure Analysis of Racial Conflict and AFL Organizing, 1917–19," *Social Forces* 79 (2000), 653–81. See also Brown's *Racial Conflict and Violence in the Labor Market: Roots in the 1919 Steel Strike* (New York, 1998), 79, which this article appears to revise.

alities and languages. It prevents them from getting together. We have the thing systematized."[26]

Employers sometimes effected division by packing different national groups close together. "Garment manufacturers deliberately seated Yiddish-speaking women next to Italian speakers in some New York shirtwaist factories as a way of preventing workers' alliances."[27] Commons claimed that "almost the only device and symptom of originality displayed by American employers in disciplining their labor force has been that of playing once race against another. They have, as a rule, been weak in methods of conciliation and feelings of considerations for their employees, as well as the means of safeguarding life and health, but they have been strong with the weapon 'divide and conquer.'"[28]

Selig Perlman wrote in Commons's four-volume *History of Labor in the United States,* "The anti-Chinese agitation in California, culminating as it did in the Exclusion Law of 1882, was doubtless the most important single factor in the history of American labor, for without it the entire country might have been overrun by Mongolian labor, and the labor movement might have become a conflict of races instead of one of classes."[29] Earlier, Commons noted, "The Jew occupies a unique position in the clothing trade. His physical strength does not fit him for manual labor. His instincts lead him to speculation and trade. His individualism unsuits him for the life of a wage-earner, and especially for the discipline of a labor organization."[30]

Commons attributed black inferiority to the equatorial African environment, which had produced "a race indolent, improvident, and contented. Seventy-five percent of the deaths are said to be executions for supposed witchcraft, which has killed more men and women than the slave trade."[31] It would not be excessively

26. *History of Labor in the United States,* 4 vols. (New York, 1918–1935), III: xv.

27. Matthew Frye Jacobson, *Barbarian Virtues: The United States Encounters Foreign Peoples at Home and Abroad, 1876–1917* (New York, 2000), 69. A simpler explanation might be that the supervisors were attempting to keep the workers' attention focused on the work at hand, rather than chatting. Halpern similarly claims that the packers' policy in the 1920s of diffusing blacks throughout their plants, at higher skill levels, "was both an attempt to diffuse ethnic solidarity among skilled workers and a conscious effort to sow seeds of racial discord." *Down on the Killing Floor,* 79. No evidence is cited for this claim.

28. *Races and Immigrants in America* (New York, 1907), 150.

29. *History of Labor in the United States,* II: 252.

30. *Trade Unionism and Labor Problems* (Boston, 1905), 329.

31. John R. Commons, *Races and Immigrants in America* (New York, 1907), 39.

presentist to expect that Commons might have asked what the death rate among a *less* contented people would have been. He went on to explain that the Reconstruction experiment had collapsed due to the "nature of the race at that state of its development." While "other races of immigrants, by contact with our institutions, have been civilized—the Negro has been only domesticated."[32] Yet Commons claimed that in its treatment of blacks, as opposed to its treatment of the Chinese and immigrants, organized labor had displayed its "most humane fraternity."[33]

One slippery version of the divide-and-conquer thesis is often used to explain the origins of segregation in the 1890s. By this account, the Populists mounted an interracial class-based challenge to the Democrats who, in response, "played the race card" to divide the coalition. This interpretation is usually associated with C. Vann Woodward, whose 1938 biography of Tom Watson depicted an interracial Dr. Jekyll who was turned into a racist Mr. Hyde by the machinations of the Bourbons.[34] Recent works continue to purvey this argument.[35] But Woodward made contradictory claims in *The Origins of the New South,* indicating that blacks did not respond much to Populist appeals and that the Populist constituency was the principal force for segregation and disfranchisement. While the conservative Bourbons were in power, "the racial code was considerably less severe than it later became." Before the Populist insurgency, "concessions to the harsher code and developing phobias of the hillbillies of the white counties had to be made . . . It is one of the paradoxes of southern history that political democracy for the white man and ra-

32. Ibid., 41.

33. *History of Labor in the United States,* I: 10.

34. Herbert Aptheker made a similar, more strictly Marxist, account in "American Imperialism and White Chauvinism," *Jewish Life* 4 (1950), 21–23. Woodward was close to communism in the 1930s and very impressed by Du Bois's Marxist account in *Black Reconstruction.* Michael O'Brien, "C. Vann Woodward and the Burden of Southern Liberalism," *American Historical Review* 78 (1973), 593; John David Smith, *When Did Southern Segregation Begin?* (New York, 2002), 28–29. Like Woodward, Du Bois was never able to hew to the straight divide-and-conquer line. Lewis, *W. E. B. Du Bois : Biography of a Race,* 419; Lewis, *W. E. B. Du Bois: The Fight for Equality and the American Century, 1919–1963* (New York, 2000), 195, 250, 264, 308.

35. Brian Kelly, "Labor, Race, and the Search for a Central Theme in the History of the Jim Crow South," *Irish Journal of American Studies* 10 (2003), 55–74; Alex Lichtenstein, "Racial Conflict and Racial Solidarity in the Alabama Coal Strike of 1894: New Evidence for the Hill-Gutman Debate," *Labor History* 36 (1995), 63–76; Mark Bauerlein, *Negrophobia: A Race Riot in Atlanta, 1906* (San Francisco, 2001), 15–19; Michael Lind, *The Next American Nation: The New Nationalism and the Fourth American Revolution* (New York, 1995), 184.

cial discrimination for the black were often products of the same dynamics . . . The barriers of racial discrimination mounted in direct ratio with the tide of political democracy among whites. In fact, an increase of Jim Crow laws upon the statute books of a state is almost an accurate index of the decline of the reactionary regimes of the Redeemers and triumph of white democratic movements."

On the labor movement in particular, he noted that strikes for white job control "testify to white labor's determination to draw a color line of its own. It is clear that in its effort to relegate to the Negro the less desirable, unskilled jobs, and to exclude him entirely from some industries, white labor did not always have the cooperation of white employers."[36] A few years later, Woodward returned to the Tom Watson line.

> The tactics by which the conservatives crushed the Populist revolt completely undermined their moral position on race policy, for their methods had made a mockery of the plea for moderation and fair play. The Populist experiment in interracial harmony, precarious at best and handicapped from the start by suspicion and prejudice, was another casualty of the political crisis of the 90s. While the movement was at the peak of zeal the two races had surprised each other and astonished their opponents by the harmony they achieved and the good will with which they cooperated. When it became apparent that their opponents would stop at nothing to divide them, however, and would steal the Negroes' votes anyway, the bi-racial partnership began to dissolve in frustration and bitterness.[37]

It is perhaps too much to say that "Woodward's argument is wrong in all its major parts," but certainly the New South story is more complicated than *Tom Watson* and *The Strange Career of Jim Crow* allow.[38] Both these works were written with an unusual degree of "presentism," reflecting Woodward's long search for a "usable past" that included a legacy of southern racial liberalism.[39] In 1938, he

36. C. Vann Woodward, *Origins of the New South, 1877–1913* (Baton Rouge, 1951), 210–11, 222.

37. C. Vann Woodward, *The Strange Career of Jim Crow*, 3d. ed. (New York, 1974 [1955]), 80.

38. David Hackett Fischer, *Historians' Fallacies: Toward a Logic of Historical Thought* (New York, 1970), 148; James T. Moore, "The Historical Context for 'Redeemers Reconsidered,'" in John B. Boles and Bethany L. Johnson, eds., *Origins of the New South Fifty Years Later: The Continuing Influence of a Historical Classic* (Baton Rouge, 2003), 142.

39. David M. Potter, "C. Vann Woodward and the Uses of History," in Don E. Fehrenbacher, ed., *History and American Society: Essays of David M. Potter* (New York, 1973), 135–79.

hoped that the CIO represented an interracial working-class alliance and, in 1955, hoped that southerners would see that segregation was a relatively recent invention. The books did not account for the disfranchisement, lynchings, and segregation that preceded the rise, let alone the defeat, of Populism. Woodward exaggerated Populist appeals to blacks and ignored Democratic appeals, to which blacks often responded. As one critic concluded, "Many black voters, who apparently grasped the fact that they had little or nothing to gain from the reformers, voted conservative as the lesser of two evils. It would be absurd to paint the conservatives in glowing colors since they believed as passionately in white supremacy, but it is important to note that they were also inclined to accept the status quo and to doubt any urgent need for new repressive measures."[40] In his memoir, Woodward conceded that "Populist gains in interracial cooperation were limited and . . . their significance is easily exaggerated."[41]

Woodward did not consider that economic liberalism was behind the social liberalism that he sought. Sharing the anticapitalist biases of most historians, he simply could not entertain the possibility that capitalism was a force of progress rather than reaction. He mistook the *reaction* to industrialization for the effect of industrialization itself.[42] Edward Ayers has explained the process more accurately. The modernizing forces of industrialization and urbanization disoriented the South, throwing blacks and whites together in cities and workplaces, undermining the racial order. Segregation represented the imposition of the old racial order in a new, urban, and industrial environment. Capitalists did not seek it, and often resisted it, but accepted it as the price that they had to pay to do business in the South.[43] It seems closer to the truth to say that segregation and disfranchisement were demands of the Populists and their successors, rather than devices used

40. Charles Crowe, "Tom Watson, Populists, and Blacks Reconsidered," *Journal of Negro History* 55 (1970), 114; Charles L. Flynn Jr., *White Land, Black Labor: Caste and Class in Late-Nineteenth-Century Georgia* (Baton Rouge, 1983), 3–4, 30, 54, 113, 152.

41. C. Vann Woodward, *Thinking Back: The Perils of Writing History* (Baton Rouge, 1986), 36. Woodward seems to have largely dropped the divide-and-conquer argument in *American Counterpoint: Slavery and Racism in the North-South Dialogue* (Boston, 1971), 220, 254–59, though a vestige remains at 223.

42. C. Vann Woodward, "New South Fraud Is Papered by Old South Myth," *Washington Post*, 9 Jul. 1961, p. E3.

43. Edward L. Ayers, *The Promise of the New South: Life after Reconstruction* (New York, 1992), 140–45; Smith, *When Did Southern Segregation Begin?* 34; John W. Cell, *The Highest Stage of White Supremacy: The Origins of Segregation in South Africa and the American South* (New York, 1982), 169–70.

to defeat them. As one recent observer puts it, "the racism so clearly evident after 1900 was there all along, . . . 'an organic part of progressive reformism.'"[44]

Most recently, the divide-and-conquer theory has explained the electoral strategy of the Republican Party since the 1960s. It was part of Nixon's "southern strategy" to appeal to southern whites by obstructing desegregation and the administration's imposition of racial quotas on white construction unions was a gambit to sow discord between civil rights and labor organizations.[45] More recent and comprehensive treatments have rendered this interpretation untenable. Judith Stein points out that Nixon's chief concern regarding construction unions was to control wage inflation. Labor Secretary George Shultz, a University of Chicago economist, was particularly eager to curb inflationary union wage pressure.[46] Herman Belz concluded that the administration's motives were mixed, "all tactics, and no strategy . . . The political motives behind the Philadelphia Plan, however, though characteristically vigorous and shrewd in the Nixon manner, should not be seen as producing unintended long-range consequences, but rather as reinforcing Nixon's genuine tendency to support preferential treatment."[47] Dean Kotlowski, in the most recent treatment of Nixon's civil rights policy, notes that "To be sure, Nixon was cunning and capable of such Machiavellian thinking" but that this was not his principal motive. Indeed, Kotlowski concludes that it is "hard to believe the White House consistently pursued a southern strategy" at all.[48] Similarly, far from exploiting white resentment against affirmative action for political gain, political considerations caused the Reagan administration to retreat from reforming affirmative action.[49]

44. Robert C. McMath Jr., "C. Vann Woodward and the Burden of Southern Populism," *Journal of Southern History* 67 (2001), 765–66.

45. Lind, *The Next American Nation*, 141, 172–84; Michael Goldfield, *The Color of Politics: Race, Class, and the Mainsprings of American Politics* (New York, 1997), 109, 312. A subtler version of the theory is Thomas B. and Mary D. Edsall, *Chain Reaction: The Impact of Race, Rights, and Taxes on American Politics* (New York, 1991).

46. Judith Stein, "Affirmative Action and the Conservative Agenda: President Richard M. Nixon's Philadelphia Plan of 1969," in Glenn T. Eskew, ed., *Labor in the Modern South* (Athens, GA, 2001); Stein, *Running Steel*, 151.

47. Belz, *Equality Transformed*, 39.

48. Dean J. Kotlowski, *Nixon's Civil Rights: Politics, Principle, and Policy* (Cambridge, 2001), 8, 24, 30, 37, 98, 106; Kotlowski, "Richard Nixon and the Origins of Affirmative Action," *Historian* 60 (1998), 523–41.

49. Nicolas Laham, *The Reagan Presidency and the Politics of Civil Rights: In Pursuit of Colorblind Justice and Limited Government* (Westport, 1998).

Efficient markets are not always pretty, often demonstrating the "creative destruction" aspect of capitalism. The hard bargain accepted by the "twentieth man," desperate as it might seem to more comfortable earlier arrivals, represented opportunity nevertheless. What migrant would have come to America if the sentiments of well-established natives about his passage and settlement had controlled the decision? In a sense, capitalism pits everyone against everyone, in a voluntary, law-bound way. Here as elsewhere, anticapitalist fables and folklore have obscured the way in which free markets have liberated and humanized our condition.[50] Economic freedom calls forth effort, opens opportunities, and enables people to develop and display their talents and to be rewarded accordingly. But freedom and equal opportunity produce unequal results. To condemn this kind of competition is to condemn freedom.

Class-conflict analyses conflate competition and conflict. The divide-and-conquer delusion helps to mask several other themes in the folklore of socialism—the myth of labor's inequality of bargaining power, the myth that violence was more often used against than by unions, and the myth that labor conflict is between labor and capital rather than among workers.[51] What appear to be divide-and-conquer machinations are usually the result of simple economic competition. Indeed, such tactics may have been more common and more effective when used by labor unions than they were by employers, and the behavior of both was driven ultimately by the most frequently overlooked actor, the consumer.[52]

Karl Marx understood that capitalism undermined racial division. "All fixed, fast, frozen relations, with their train of ancient and venerable prejudices and opinions, are swept away," he wrote in the *Communist Manifesto*. "National one-sidedness and narrow-mindedness become more and more impossible . . . National differences and antagonism between peoples are daily more and more vanishing, owing to the development of the bourgeoisie, to freedom of conscience, to

50. Thomas L. Haskell, "Capitalism and the Origins of the Humanitarian Sensibility, Part 2," *American Historical Review* 90 (1985), 549–50.

51. Friedrich A. Hayek, *The Constitution of Liberty* (Chicago, 1960), 273–74; Morgan O. Reynolds, *Power and Privilege: Labor Unions in America* (New York, 1984); Reynolds, "The Myth of Labor's Inequality of Bargaining Power," *Journal of Labor Research* 12 (1991), 167–83; Arnold J. Thieblot Jr., and Thomas R. Haggard, *Union Violence: The Record and the Response by Courts, Legislatures, and the NLRB* (Philadelphia, 1983).

52. Clarence E. Bonnett, *History of Employers' Associations in the United States* (New York, 1956), 76, 82, 237, 365, 380, 441, 443, 449, 485.

the world market, to uniformity in the mode of production, and in the conditions of life corresponding thereto." [53] Marx expected this process would continue as it created a working class united in misery that overthrew the capitalist order. When Marx's prophecy failed to pan out, the divide-and-conquer corollary provided an escape, but the earlier part of Marxist thinking, crediting the universalizing force of capitalism, was the better prophecy. To some extent, black Americans used this force, what Shakespeare called "the bias of the world," to undermine racial bias in the labor market. [54]

53. "The Communist Manifesto," Eugene Kamenka, ed., *The Portable Karl Marx* (New York, 1983), 207–08, 217.

54. *King John,* II.ii.

Bibliographical Essay

A topical index to labor publications is Lloyd George Reynolds and Charles C. Killingsworth, *Trade Union Publications: The Official Journals, Convention Proceedings, and Constitutions of International Unions and Federations, 1850–1941* (Baltimore, 1944). Evelyn Brooks Higginbotham et al., eds., *The Harvard Guide to African-American History* (Cambridge, 2001), is an excellent compendium of primary and secondary sources in black history. Useful bibliographies of secondary sources include Joseph Wilson, ed., *Black Labor in America, 1865–1983: A Selected Annotated Bibliography* (Westport, 1986), and Maurice F. Neufeld, *American Working Class History: A Representative Bibliography* (New York, 1983). James Gilbert Cassedy, "African Americans and the American Labor Movement," *Prologue* 29 (1997), provides an overview of records relating to blacks and labor in the National Archives.

Many published document collections deal with black workers and the labor movement. Philip S. Foner and Ronald L. Lewis, eds., *The Black Worker: A Documentary History from Colonial Times to the Present,* 8 vols. (Philadelphia, 1978–84), is an indispensable source. Though it is sometimes carelessly edited and gives too much emphasis to the radical left, it contains over two thousand documents and is particularly useful on the black press in the nineteenth century. Black newspaper clippings are collected in the Claude A. Barnett Papers, 198 reels (Frederick, MD, 1984); the microfiche Schomburg Center Clipping File (New York, 1974); and the microfiche Hampton University Newspaper Clipping File. The papers of the NAACP are available on microfilm; the papers of the National Urban League remain in the Library of Congress. The Urban League's journal, *Opportunity*, has been indexed from 1923 to 1949: Ethel M. Ellis, comp., *Opportunity: Journal of Negro Life* (New York, 1971). Two good collections of primary sources on microfilm are James R. Grossman, ed., *Black Workers in the Era of the Great Migration* (25 reels), and John B. Kirby, ed., *New Deal Agencies and Black America in the 1930s* (25 reels). Two multivolume federal studies, U.S. Industrial Commission, *Reports,* 19 vols. (Washington, 1900–02) and U.S. Immigration Commission, *Reports,*

42 vols. (Washington, 1911), contain useful material on ethnic and racial factors in industry. The U.S. Department of Labor's *Monthly Labor Review,* published monthly since 1918, contains many useful statistical snapshots and analyses over the century. The *Labor Relations Yearbook* was a digest of labor-related events and articles published from 1965 to 1984 by the Bureau of National Affairs.

GENERAL LABOR HISTORY

One of the founding works in labor history, John R. Commons et al., eds., *History of Labor in the United States,* 4 vols. (New York, 1918–35), still contains valuable material. Foster Rhea Dulles and Melvyn Dubofsky, *Labor in America: A History,* 6th ed. (Wheeling, IL, 1999), is the latest edition of a serviceable text. Robert H. Zieger, *American Workers, American Unions, 1920–85* (Baltimore, 1986), is a brief recent work. Jack Barbash, *The Practice of Unionism* (New York, 1956), is an older general treatment. Gerald Grob, *Workers and Utopia: A Study of Ideological Conflict in the American Labor Movement, 1865–1900* (Evanston, IL, 1961), is a brilliant treatment of the often bewildering variety of labor activity in the late nineteenth century, as is William Dick, *Labor and Socialism in America: The Gompers Era* (Port Washington, 1972). Howard Dickman, *Industrial Democracy in America: Ideological Origins of National Labor Relations Policy* (La Salle, IL, 1987), is a much-needed market-based analysis of the philosophy of American unionism.

Discussions of the Knights of Labor include Leon Fink, *Workingmen's Democracy: The Knights of Labor and American Politics* (Urbana, 1983); Jason Kaufman, "The Rise and Fall of a Nation of Joiners: The Knights of Labor Revisited," *Journal of Interdisciplinary History* 31 (2001); and Robert Weir, *Beyond Labor's Veil: The Culture of the Knights of Labor* (University Park, PA, 1996). Gwendolyn Mink addresses broader union-ethnic problems in *Old Labor and New Immigrants in American Political Development: Union, Party, and State, 1875–1920* (Ithaca, NY, 1986). The standard history of the IWW is Melvyn Dubofsky, *We Shall Be All: A History of the Industrial Workers of the World,* 2d ed. (Urbana, 1988).

Many have called for an up-to-date history of the American Federation of Labor. In the meantime we have Philip Taft, *Organized Labor in American History* (New York, 1964). Joseph A. McCartin, *Labor's Great War: The Struggle for Industrial Democracy and the Origins of Modern American Labor Relations, 1912–21* (Chapel Hill, 1997), is a good recent look at wartime labor policy. The 1920s are treated in Robert H. Zieger, *Republicans and Labor, 1919–29* (Lexington, KY, 1969), and Ruth Ann O'Brien, *Workers' Paradox: The Republican Origins of New Deal Labor Policy, 1886–1935* (Chapel Hill, 1998).

Robert H. Zieger, *The CIO: 1935–55* (Chapel Hill, 1995), is a comprehensive account of the industrial union federation. Jerold Auerbach, *Labor and Liberty: The La Follette Committee and the New Deal* (Indianapolis, 1966), explains an important episode in the pro-union turn of federal labor policy. The post–World War Two effort to extend unionism in the South is the subject of Barbara S. Griffith, *The Crisis of American Labor: Operation Dixie and the Defeat of the CIO* (Philadelphia, 1988).

Collections of essays include Robert Zieger, ed., *Organized Labor in the Twentieth Century South* (Knoxville, 1991); Gary M. Fink and Merl E. Reed, eds., *Essays in Southern Labor History: Selected Papers, Southern Labor History Conference, 1976* (Westport, 1977); Steven Rosswurm, ed., *The CIO's Left-Led Unions* (New Brunswick, 1992); Robert Asher and Charles Stephenson, eds., *Labor Divided: Race and Ethnicity in U.S. Labor Struggles, 1835–1960* (Albany, NY, 1990); Glenn T. Eskew, ed., *Labor in the Modern South* (Athens, GA, 2001); and James T. Bennett and Bruce E. Kaufman, eds., *The Future of Private Sector Unionism in the United States* (Armonk, NY, 2002).

ECONOMICS, LABOR, AND RACE

Among the first economists to recognize the racial impact of labor organization was W. H. Hutt, who taught in South Africa from 1928 to 1965 and criticized the role that white trade unions played in apartheid. See *The Economics of the Colour Bar* (London, 1964), and Charles W. Baird, "Equality for the Labor Market: An Appreciation of W. H. Hutt," *Journal of Labor Research* 18 (1997). Jennifer Roback deals with the economics of discrimination in "The Political Economy of Segregation: The Case of Segregated Streetcars," *Journal of Economic History* 46 (1986), and "Southern Labor in the Jim Crow Era: Exploitative or Competitive?" *University of Chicago Law Review* 51 (1984). The title of Richard Epstein's work, *Forbidden Grounds: The Case against Employment Discrimination Laws* (Cambridge, 1992), speaks for itself. Steven Shulman and William Darity, eds., *The Question of Discrimination: Racial Inequality in the U.S. Labor Market* (Middletown, CT, 1989), contains fine essays from multiple perspectives. James P. Smith, "Race and Human Capital," *American Economic Review* 74 (1984), was a seminal study of black economic progress. See also Thomas N. Maloney, "Wage Compression and Wage Inequality between Black and White Males in the United States, 1940–60," *Journal of Economic History* 54 (1994), and Timothy Bates, "Black Economic Well-Being since the 1950s," *Review of Black Political Economy* 12 (1984).

Many new works have emphasized the economic and business aspects of the civil rights movement. Gavin Wright provides an excellent overview in "The Economics of Civil Rights," an unpublished paper prepared for the Citadel Conference on the Civil Rights Movement in South Carolina, 5–8 March 2003. Steven M. Gelber, *Black Men and Businessmen: The Growing Awareness of a Social Responsibility* (Port Washington, 1974), is a much-neglected treatment of business and race. James C. Cobb, *Industrialization and Southern Society, 1877–1984* (Lexington, KY, 1984), deals with labor and race issues in the South. See also Cobb, *The Selling of the South: The Southern Crusade for Industrial Development, 1936–90,* 2d ed. (Urbana, 1993). The relationship of economics and segregation is treated in J. Milton Yinger and George E. Simpson, "Can Segregation Survive in an Industrial Society?" *Antioch Review* 28 (1958). The question was taken up by William H. Nicholls, *Southern Tradition and Regional Progress* (Westport, 1976 [1960]) and "Southern Tradition and Regional Economic Progress," *Southern Economic Journal* 26 (1960). Guy Hunter, ed., *Industrialisation and Race Relations: A Symposium* (New York, 1965), presents a variety of views on the subject. Many excellent essays treating business and the civil rights movement can be found in Elizabeth Jacoway and David R. Colburn, eds., *Southern Businessmen and Desegregation* (Baton Rouge, 1982). Robert E. Weems Jr., *Desegregating the Dollar: African American Consumerism in the Twentieth Century* (New York, 1998), treats the importance of the growing "black market."

On fair employment laws, Ralph K. Winter Jr., "Improving the Economic Status of Negroes through Laws against Discrimination: A Reply to Professor Sovern," *University of Chicago Law Review* 34 (1967), provides an incisive analysis of the Civil Rights Act of 1964. See also Harold Demsetz, "Minorities in the Market Place," *University of North Carolina Law Review* 43 (1965), and the acute "A Theory of Fair Employment Laws," *University of Chicago Law Review* 38 (1971), by Owen Fiss.

A good introduction to the law-and-economics view of unions as cartels is Richard A. Posner, "Some Economics of Labor Law," *University of Chicago Law Review* 51 (1984). Morgan O. Reynolds, *Power and Privilege: Labor Unions in America* (New York, 1984), is an incisive critique of organized labor. A defense of the economic role of unions is Richard B. Freeman, *What Do Unions Do?* (New York,

1984). Selig Perlman, "The Basic Philosophy of the American Labor Movement," *Annals of the American Academy of Political and Social Science* 274 (1951), and *A Theory of the Labor Movement* (New York, 1928) are dated but contain valuable assessments. Richard Vedder and Lowell Gallaway, "The Economic Effects of Labor Unions Revisited," *Journal of Labor Research* 23 (2002), is a good, recent public-choice interpretation.

Gavin Wright, *Old South, New South: Revolutions in the Southern Economy since the Civil War* (New York, 1986), is extremely valuable. Herman Feldman, *Racial Factors in American Industry* (New York, 1931), was among the first studies of its kind. American Management Association, *The Negro in Industry* (New York, 1923), is another early account. Thomas N. Maloney, "Personnel Policy and Racial Inequality in the Pre–World War II North," *Journal of Interdisciplinary History* 30 (1999), discusses the origins of bureaucratic barriers to racial advancement; see also his "Degrees of Inequality: The Advance of Black Male Workers in the Northern Meat Packing and Steel Industries before World War II," *Social Science History* 19 (1995). William A. Sundstrom, "Last Hired, First Fired? Unemployment and Urban Black Workers during the Great Depression," *Journal of Economic History* 52 (1992), deals with the 1930s.

SPECIFIC INDUSTRY AND LOCAL STUDIES

With a grant from the Ford Foundation, the Wharton School of the University of Pennsylvania published a thirty-one-volume "Racial Policies of American Industry Series" between 1968 and 1974, that covers every major industry (autos, steel, meatpacking, petroleum, textiles), as well as many minor ones. Herbert Northrup directed the series and wrote several of the volumes. This is supplemented by the eight-volume "Studies in Negro Employment" series, the most important of which is Herbert Northrup et al., *Negro Employment in Basic Industry: A Study of Racial Policies in Six Industries (Automobile, Aerospace, Steel, Rubber Tire, Petroleum, and Chemicals)* (Philadelphia, 1970). For a fascinating retrospect on Northrup's career, see Bruce E. Kaufman, "An Interview with Herbert R. Northrup," *Journal of Labor Research* 19 (1998).

Coal mining has gotten an inordinate amount of attention, particularly from those who depict black-union relations in a favorable light. Price Van Meter Fishback, *Soft Coal, Hard Choices: The Economic Welfare of Bituminous Coal Miners, 1890–1930* (New York, 1992), is unique in its attention to labor economics and cuts through the plethora of myths about the industry. Herbert Gutman's essay, "The

Negro and the United Mine Workers of America: The Career and Letters of Richard L. Davis and Something of Their Meaning, 1890–1900," in Jacobson, ed., *The Negro and the American Labor Movement*, was a groundbreaking interpretation. See also his "Reconstruction in Ohio: Negroes in the Hocking Valley Coal Mines in 1873 and 1874," *Labor History* 3 (1962). Brian Kelly, *Race, Class, and Power in the Alabama Coalfields, 1908–21* (Urbana, 2001), follows Gutman, while Daniel Letwin, *The Challenge of Interracial Unionism: Alabama Coal Miners, 1878–1921* (Chapel Hill, 1998), offers a more balanced interpretation. Other accounts include Ronald L. Lewis, *Black Coal Miners in America: Race, Class, and Community Conflict, 1780–1980* (Lexington, KY, 1987); Joe William Trotter Jr., *Coal, Class, and Color: Blacks in Southern West Virginia, 1915–32* (Urbana, 1990); Richard A. Straw, "The Collapse of Biracial Unionism: The Alabama Coal Strike of 1908," *Alabama Historical Quarterly* 37 (1975); Earl Lewis, "Job Control and Race Relations in the Coal Fields, 1870–1920," *Journal of Ethnic Studies* 12 (1985), and "From Peasant to Proletarian: The Migration of Southern Blacks to the Central Appalachian Coal Fields," *Journal of Southern History* 55 (1989); David Corbin, *Life, Work, and Rebellion in the Coal Fields: The Southern West Virginia Miners, 1880–1922* (Urbana, 1981); and Kenneth R. Bailey, "A Judicious Mixture: Negroes and Immigrants in the West Virginia Mines, 1880–1920," *West Virginia History* 34 (1973). The Illinois coal conflict of 1898 is treated in John H. Keiser, "Black Strikebreakers and Racism in Illinois, 1865–1900," *Journal of the Illinois State Historical Society* 65 (1972).

On steel, see David Brody, *Steelworkers in America: The Nonunion Era* (Cambridge, MA, 1960), and Dennis C. Dickerson, *Out of the Crucible: Black Steelworkers in Western Pennsylvania, 1875–1980* (Albany, NY, 1986). Henry M. McKiven Jr., *Iron and Steel: Class, Race, and Community in Birmingham, Alabama, 1875–1920* (Chapel Hill, 1995), emphasizes black independence and the reasons for black hostility to organized labor. This contrasts with Paul Worthman, "Black Workers and Labor Unions in Birmingham, Alabama, 1897–1904," in Cantor, ed., *Black Labor in America*, and is reinforced by Robert Norrell, "Caste in Steel: Jim Crow Careers in Birmingham, Alabama," *Journal of American History* 73 (1986). Still valuable is Herbert R. Northrup, "The Negro and Unionism in the Birmingham, Alabama, Iron and Steel Industry," *Southern Economic Journal* 10 (1943). Bruce Nelson, *Divided We Stand: American Workers and the Struggle for Black Equality* (Princeton, 2001), concerns steel and longshore labor. Judith Stein, *Running Steel, Running America: Race, Economic Policy, and the Decline of Liberalism* (Chapel Hill, 1998), is a thoughtful treatment of American industrial and race policy.

In the automobile industry, Lloyd Bailer did pioneering work. His unpublished dissertation, "The Negro in the Automobile Industry" (University of Michigan, 1943), was the source of many subsequent accounts. Bailer published "The Negro Automobile Worker," *Journal of Political Economy* 51 (1943), and "The Automobile Unions and Negro Labor," *Political Science Quarterly* 59 (1944). Thomas N. Maloney and Warren C. Whatley, "Making the Effort: The Contours of Racial Discrimination in Detroit's Labor Markets, 1920–40," *Journal of Economic History* 55 (1995), is an intriguing recent treatment. See also Warren C. Whatley and Gavin Wright, "Getting Started in the Auto Industry: Black Workers at the Ford Motor Company, 1918–47," *Cliometrics Society Newsletter* 5 (1990). August Meier and Elliott M. Rudwick, *Black Detroit and the Rise of the UAW* (New York, 1979), is the best-known work in this area. Other pieces include Joyce Shaw Peterson, "Black Automobile Workers in Detroit, 1910–30," *Journal of Negro History* 64 (1979), and John Brueggemann, "The Power and Collapse of Paternalism: The Ford Motor Company and Black Workers, 1937–41," *Social Problems* 47 (2000).

Longshoremen are the subject of Eric Arnesen, *Waterfront Workers of New Orleans: Race, Class, and Politics, 1863–1923* (Urbana, 1994), describing black-union accommodation in a southern city, and Herbert Northrup, "The New Orleans Longshoremen," *Political Science Quarterly* 57 (1947).

Eric Arnesen provides detailed and balanced work on railroad labor in "'Like Banquo's Ghost, It Will Not Down': The Race Question and the American Railroad Brotherhoods, 1880–1920," *American Historical Review* 99 (1994), and *Brotherhoods of Color: Black Railroad Workers and the Struggle for Equality* (Cambridge, 2001). David E. Bernstein, "Racism, Railroad Unions, and Labor Regulations," *Independent Review* 5 (2000), applies a public choice interpretation. Accounts of the Georgia Railroad that blame the railroad are John Michael Matthews, "The Georgia 'Race Strike' of 1909," *Journal of Southern History* 40 (1974), and Hugh B. Hammett, "Labor and Race: The Georgia Railroad Strike of 1909," *Labor History* 16 (1975).

Meatpacking has also received a great deal of attention. Alma Herbst's pioneering work, *The Negro in the Slaughtering and Meat-Packing Industry in Chicago* (New York, 1932), is still frequently drawn upon. More recent accounts include James R. Barrett, *Work and Community in the Jungle: Chicago's Packinghouse Workers, 1894–1922* (Urbana, 1987); Paul Street, "The Logic and Limits of 'Plant Loyalty': Black Workers, White Labor, and Corporate Racial Paternalism in Chicago's Stockyards, 1916–40," *Journal of Social History* 29 (1996); Rick Halpern, *Down on the Killing Floor: Black and White Workers in Chicago's Packinghouses, 1904–54* (Urbana, 1997); and Roger Horowitz, *"Negro and White, Unite and Fight!" A Social History of Industrial Unionism in Meatpacking, 1930–90* (Urbana, 1997).

On the segregation and reintegration of baseball, see David W. Zang, *Fleet Walker's Divided Heart: The Life of Baseball's First Black Major Leaguer* (Lincoln, NE, 1995); Jerry Malloy, ed., *Sol White's History of Colored Base Ball, with Other Documents on the Early Black Game, 1886–1936* (Lincoln, NE, 1995); Robert Peterson, *Only the Ball Was White: A History of Legendary Black Players and All-Black Professional Teams before Black Men Played in the Major Leagues* (New York, 1984); Mark Ribowsky, *A Complete History of the Negro Leagues* (New York, 1995); Dick Clark and Larry Lester, eds., *The Negro Leagues Book* (Cleveland, 1994); and Robert F. Burk, *Never Just a Game: Players, Owners, and American Baseball to 1920* (Chapel Hill, 1994), and *Much More Than a Game: Players, Owners, and American Baseball since 1921* (Chapel Hill, 2001). The Jackie Robinson story is told in Jules Tygiel, *Baseball's Great Experiment: Jackie Robinson and His Legacy* (New York, 1983). Also useful is Dan W. Dodson, "The Integration of Negroes in Baseball," *Journal of Educational Sociology* 28 (1954).

Other industries are explored in Kenneth W. Porter, "Negro Labor in the Western Cattle Industry, 1866–1900," in Cantor, ed., *Black Labor in America;* Herbert R. Northrup, "The Tobacco Workers International Union," *Quarterly Journal of Economics* 56 (1942); and Ray Marshall, "Some Factors Influencing the Upgrading of Negroes in the Southern Petroleum Refining Industry," *Social Forces* 42 (1963).

The Civil War–Reconstruction period is explored in Peter Rachleff, *Black Labor in Richmond, 1865–90* (Urbana, 1984), and William C. Hine, "Black Organized Labor in Reconstruction Charleston," *Labor History* 25 (1984). Jerrell H. Shofner has written several studies of this period in Florida: "Militant Negro Laborers in Reconstruction Florida," *Journal of Southern History* 39 (1973); "Negro Laborers and the Forest Industries in Reconstruction Florida," *Journal of Forest History* 19 (1975); and "The Labor League of Jacksonville: A Negro Union and White Strikebreakers," *Florida Historical Quarterly* 50 (1972). On conflict in the Louisiana sugar fields, see three articles in *Agricultural History* 72 (1998): Louis Ferleger, "The Problem of 'Labor' in the Post-Reconstruction Sugar Industry"; John C. Rodrigue, "'The Great Law of Demand and Supply': The Contest over Wages in Louisiana's Sugar Region, 1870–80"; and Joseph P. Reidy, "Mules and Machines and Men: Field Labor on Louisiana Sugar Plantations, 1887–1915," in addition to Jeffrey Gould, "Sugar War," *Southern Exposure* 12 (1984). David Gerber, *Black Ohio and the Color Line, 1860–1915* (Urbana, 1976), is an outstanding study of a northern state. John E. Bodnar, "The Impact of the 'New Immigration' on the Black Worker: Steelton, Pennsylvania, 1880–1920," *Labor History* 17 (1976), is a good local study. Ernest Obadele-Starks, *Black Unionism in the Industrial South* (College Station, TX, 2000), focuses on the southwest. On Detroit, see Thomas J. Sugrue, *The Origins of the Urban Crisis: Race and Inequality in Postwar Detroit* (Princeton, 1996). The decline of several postwar cities is treated in Fred Siegel, *The Future Once Happened Here: New York, D.C., L.A., and the Fate of America's Big Cities* (New York, 1997). Journalist Ken Auletta traces the crisis of New York City in *The Streets Were Paved with Gold* (New York, 1979). See also Charles R. Morris, *The Cost of Good Intentions: New York City and the Liberal Experiment, 1960–75* (New York, 1980), and Jim Sleeper, *The Closest of Strangers: Liberalism and the Politics of Race in New York* (New York, 1990).

Labor competition and race riots are the subject of Elliott Rudwick, *Race Riot at East St. Louis: July 2, 1917* (Carbondale, 1964). In Chicago, see the classic study by the Chicago Commission on Race Relations, *The Negro in Chicago: A Study of Race Relations and a Race Riot* (Chicago, 1922). William H. Tuttle, *Race Riot: Chicago in the Red Summer of 1919* (Urbana, 1996 [1970]); James R. Grossman, *Land of Hope: Chicago, Black Southerners, and the Great Migration* (Chicago, 1989); and David Brody, *Labor in Crisis: The Steel Strike of 1919,* rev. ed. (Urbana, 1987), also concern Chicago. William Z. Foster discusses the black role in the 1919 steel strike in *The Great Steel Strike and Its Lessons* (New York, 1920). Depression-era Chicago and ethnic politics are the subjects of Lizabeth Cohen, *Making a New Deal: Industrial Workers in Chicago, 1919–39* (New York, 1990).

IDEAS, BIOGRAPHIES, AUTOBIOGRAPHIES

John A. Garraty et al., eds., *American National Biography,* 24 vols. (New York, 1999), with electronic updates, is indispensable. Rayford W. Logan and Michael R. Winston, eds., *Dictionary of American Negro Biography* (New York, 1982), and Melvyn Dubofsky and Warren Van Tine, eds., *Labor Leaders in America* (Urbana, 1986), are also useful.

Peter Eisenstadt, ed., *Black Conservatism: Essays in Intellectual and Political History* (New York, 1999), contains many thoughtful pieces. Roi Ottley, *The Lonely Warrior: The Life and Times of Robert S. Abbott* (Chicago, 1955), deals with the influential editor of the Chicago *Defender.* The views of the often-neglected conservative Kelly Miller can be found in his collection of essays, *The Everlasting Stain*

(Washington, 1924). The iconoclastic George S. Schuyler tells his story in *Black and Conservative: The Autobiography of George S. Schuyler* (New Rochelle, NY, 1966). Clarence E. Walker, *Deromanticizing Black History: Critical Essays and Reappraisals* (Knoxville, 1991), is incisive and provocative.

Robert L. Factor, *The Black Response to America: Men, Ideals, and Organizations from Frederick Douglass to the NAACP* (Reading, MA, 1970), contains a discussion of Douglass's economic ideas. William S. McFeely, *Frederick Douglass* (New York, 1990), is a good overall biography. For Douglass's works, see John W. Blassingame, et al., eds., *The Frederick Douglass Papers*, 5 vols. (New Haven, 1979), and Philip S. Foner, ed., *The Life and Writings of Frederick Douglass*, 4 vols. (New York, 1950–75).

James P. Grossman, *William Sylvis, Pioneer of American Labor: A Study in the Labor Movement during the Era of the Civil War* (New York, 1965), describes the life of the founder of the National Labor Union. A collection of Sylvis's writings can be found in James C. Sylvis, ed., *The Life, Speeches, Labors and Essays of William H. Sylvis* (Philadelphia, 1968 [1872]). The patron of the Knights of Labor tells his story in Terence Powderly, *Thirty Years of Labor, 1859–89* (New York, 1967 [1890]). Powderly's racial views are treated in Sr. William Marie Turnbach, "The Attitudes of Terence V. Powderly toward Minority Groups, 1879–93" (M.A. thesis, Catholic University of America, 1956).

Louis Harlan's critical two-volume biography, *Booker T. Washington: The Making of a Black Leader, 1856–1901* (New York, 1972) and *Booker T. Washington: The Wizard of Tuskegee, 1901–15* (New York, 1983), remains the standard work. Harlan compiled an edition of Washington's papers, *The Booker T. Washington Papers*, 14 vols. (Urbana, 1972–89). Harlan focuses on Washington's business vision in "Booker T. Washington and the National Negro Business League," in William G. Shade and Roy C. Herrenkohl, eds., *Seven on Black: Reflections on the Negro Experience in America* (Philadelphia, 1969). This can be supplemented by the more detailed work of John H. Burrows, *The Necessity of Myth: A History of the National Negro Business League, 1900–45* (Auburn, AL, 1988). The papers of the NNBL are available on microfilm: Kenneth M. Hamilton and Robert Lester, eds., *Records of the National Negro Business League*, 14 reels (Bethesda, MD, 1994). Kevern Verney, *The Art of the Possible: Booker T. Washington and Black Leadership in United States, 1881–1925* (London, 2001); John Sibley Butler, "Why Booker T. Washington Was Right: A Reconsideration of the Economics of Race," in Thomas D. Boston, ed., *A Different Vision: African-American Economic Thought*, 2 vols. (New York, 1997); W. D. Wright, *Critical Reflections on Black History* (Westport, 2002); and Elizabeth

Wright, "Booker T. Washington," *American Enterprise* 6 (1995), offer recent revisions appreciative of Washington's thought. Emma Lou Thornbrough, ed., *Booker T. Washington* (Englewood Cliffs, NJ, 1969), contains selected writings. Washington's most important statement on unions came near the end of his life in "The Negro and the Labor Unions," *Atlantic Monthly* 111 (1913). Judith Stein provides a Marxist argument in "'Of Mr. Booker T. Washington and Others': The Political Economy of Racism in the United States," *Science and Society* 38 (1974–75). Alfred A. Moss Jr., tells the story of the organization that led the shift away from Washington in *The American Negro Academy: Voice of the Talented Tenth* (Baton Rouge, 1981). Alexander Crummell is dealt with in Gregory U. Rigsby, *Alexander Crummell: Pioneer in Nineteenth-Century Pan-African Thought* (New York, 1987). T. Thomas Fortune's thought in the 1880s is expressed in *Black and White: Land, Labor, and Politics in the South* (New York, 1968 [1884]), and his life is recounted in Emma Lou Thornbrough, *T. Thomas Fortune: Militant Journalist* (Chicago, 1972).

The work of W. E. B. Du Bois is vital to the study of black economic life and thought. David Levering Lewis's two-volume biography, *W. E. B. Du Bois: Biography of a Race, 1868–1919* (New York, 1993), and *W. E. B. Du Bois: The Fight for Equality and the American Century, 1919–63* (New York, 2000), is comprehensive, though he often shares his subject's passionate, activist voice. Raymond Wolters, *Du Bois and His Rivals* (Columbia, MO, 2002), is a brief, nuanced, and persuasive companion. Du Bois's papers are available on 89 reels of microfilm (Sanford, NC, 1980–81). Among his most important economic and sociological studies are *The Philadelphia Negro* (Atlanta, 1899); *The Negro in Business* (Atlanta, 1899); *The Negro Artisan* (Atlanta, 1902); and *The Negro American Artisan* (Atlanta, 1912). Several of his Atlanta University studies were compiled and reprinted by the Arno Press in *Publications* (New York, 1968). Several collections of Du Bois's published and unpublished works include Julius Lester, ed., *The Seventh Son: The Thought and Writings of W. E. B. Du Bois,* 2 vols. (New York, 1971); Herbert Aptheker, ed., *Newspaper Columns by W. E. B. Du Bois,* 2 vols. (White Plains, NY, 1986); *The Correspondence of W. E. B. Du Bois,* 3 vols. (Amherst, 1973–78); Nathan Huggins, ed., *Du Bois: Writings* (New York, 1986). A useful introduction to Du Bois's early thought is Thomas D. Boston, "W. E. B. Du Bois and the Historical School of Economics," *American Economic Review* 81 (1991).

James B. Stewart, "The Rise and Fall of Negro Economics: The Economic Thought of George Edmund Haynes," *American Economic Review* 81 (1991), focuses on the Urban League pioneer. Nancy J. Weiss, *The National Urban League,*

1910–40 (New York, 1974), is the best account of the organization's early years. Robert C. Weaver's reflections on public policy and black labor are available in *Negro Labor: A National Problem* (New York, 1946). See also Cecilia A. Conrad and George Sherer, "From the New Deal to the Great Society: The Economic Activism of Robert C. Weaver," in Boston, *A Different Vision.*

Studies of Marcus Garvey include Edmund David Cronon, *Black Moses: The Story of Marcus Garvey and the Universal Negro Improvement Association* (Madison, 1955), and Tony Martin, *Race First: The Ideological and Organizational Struggles of Marcus Garvey and the Universal Negro Improvement Association* (Westport, 1976). A selection of Garvey's works is contained in Amy Jacques-Garvey, ed., *Philosophy and Opinions of Marcus Garvey,* 2 vols. (New York, 1968–69 [1923–35]). Some of Garvey's papers are collected in Robert A. Hill, ed., *The Marcus Garvey and Universal Negro Improvement Papers,* 9 vols. (Berkeley, CA, 1983–95).

A. Philip Randolph, the most important figure in bringing blacks into the labor movement, is the subject of William H. Harris, *Keeping the Faith: A. Philip Randolph, Milton P. Webster, and the Brotherhood of Sleeping Car Porters, 1925–37* (Urbana, 1977); Paula Pfeffer, *A. Philip Randolph, Pioneer of the Civil Rights Movement* (Baton Rouge, 1990); and Pfeffer, "The Evolution of A. Philip Randolph and Bayard Rustin from Radicalism to Conservatism" in Peter Eisenstadt, ed., *Black Conservatism: Essays in Intellectual and Political History* (New York, 1999). Walter White tells his story in *A Man Called White: The Autobiography of Walter White* (New York, 1948). Kenneth R. Janken, *White: The Biography of Walter White, Mr. NAACP* (New York, 2003), is a recent work.

America's premier socialist is portrayed in Nick Salvatore, *Eugene V. Debs: Citizen and Socialist* (Urbana, 1982). His writings can be consulted in J. Robert Constantine, ed., *Letters of Eugene V. Debs,* 3 vols. (Urbana, 1990). For the Socialist Party, see R. Laurence Moore, "Flawed Fraternity: American Socialist Response to the Negro, 1901–12," *The Historian* 32 (1969), and Ira Kipnis, *The American Socialist Movement, 1897–1912* (New York, 1952). Philip S. Foner treats the Wobblies in "The IWW and the Black Worker," *Journal of Negro History* 55 (1970). Keith P. Griffler, *What Price Alliance? Black Radicals Confront White Labor, 1918–38* (New York, 1995), recounts the early history of black labor and the Left. Economist William Darity Jr., has done extensive work on economist Abram L. Harris. *Race, Radicalism, and Reform: Selected Papers, Abram L. Harris* (New Brunswick, 1989), contains some of Harris's work. A good interpretation is William Darity Jr. and Julian

Ellison, "Abram Harris Jr.: The Economics of Race and Social Reform," *History of Political Economy* 22 (1990).

An excellent review of the literature on American communism is John Earl Haynes, "The Cold War Debate Continues: A Traditionalist View of Historical Writing on Domestic Communism and Anti-Communism," *Cold War Studies* 2 (2000). As Haynes points out, defenders of American communism have done numerous local studies that depict "little more than a 'conspiracy' of well-meaning liberals to raise the minimum wage and secure social justice for Negroes," a genre which has produced a history of "communists-without-communism." Robert Korstad and Nelson Lichtenstein, "Opportunities Found and Lost: Labor, Radicals, and the Early Civil Rights Movement," *Journal of American History* 75 (1988), and Michael Goldfield, "Race and the CIO: The Possibilities for Racial Egalitarianism during the 1930s and 1940," *International Labor and Working Class History* 44 (1993), reflect this pose. Better, traditional works include Wilson Record, *The Negro and the Communist Party* (Chapel Hill, 1951), and *Race and Radicalism: The NAACP and the Communist Party in Conflict* (Ithaca, 1964); William A. Nolan, *Communism* versus *the Negro* (Chicago, 1951); Harvey Klehr and William Thompson, "Self-Determination in the Black Belt: Origins of a Communist Policy," *Labor History* 30 (1989); and John W. Van Zanten, "Communist Theory and the American Negro Question," *Review of Politics* 29 (1967). August Meier and Elliott Rudwick, "Communist Unions and the Black Community: The Case of the Transport Workers Union, 1934–44," *Labor History* 23 (1982), is a good treatment of a party union during the depression and World War II period, as is Donald T. Critchlow, "Communist Unions and Racism," *Labor History* 17 (1976). Gerald Zahavi, "Passionate Commitments: Race, Sex, and Communism at Schenectady General Electric, 1932–54," *Journal of American History* 83 (1996), is another local study.

Stuart Kaufman, *Samuel Gompers and the Origins of the American Federation of Labor, 1848–96* (Westport, 1973), is an insightful biography. Ten volumes of the Gompers papers have appeared to date, edited by the late Stuart Kaufman and his successors, and published by the University of Illinois Press. Craig Phelan, *William Green: Biography of a Labor Leader* (Albany, NY, 1989), treats this usually overlooked figure. John L. Lewis, CIO founder, is well covered in Robert H. Zieger's brief work, *John L. Lewis: Labor Leader* (Boston, 1988). For a fuller account, see Melvyn Dubofsky, *John L. Lewis: A Biography,* abridged ed. (Urbana, 1986). The UAW's leader is given sympathetic but critical treatment in Nelson Lichtenstein,

The Most Dangerous Man in Detroit: Walter Reuther and the Fate of American Labor (New York, 1995). Steven Fraser, *Labor Will Rule: Sidney Hillman and the Rise of American Labor* (Ithaca, NY, 1991), treats another CIO founder. Robert D. Reynolds Jr., "A Career at Labor Headquarters: The Papers of Boris Shishkin," *Labor's Heritage* 1 (1989), is a brief account of the AFL's civil rights man. Joseph C. Goulden, *Meany* (New York, 1972), is a serviceable journalistic account.

LEGAL-CONSTITUTIONAL AND STATE POLICY STUDIES

Alfred H. Kelly, Winfred A. Harbison, and Herman Belz, *The American Constitution: Its Origin and Development*, 7th ed., 2 vols. (New York, 1991), is the standard work in the field. Bernard H. Siegan, *Economic Liberties and the Constitution* (Chicago, 1980), gives a libertarian interpretation of the fundamental law.

Free labor principles are discussed in William E. Forbath, "The Ambiguities of Free Labor: Labor and the Law in the Gilded Age," *Wisconsin Law Review* (1985); Eric Foner, *Politics and Ideology in the Age of the Civil War* (New York, 1980); Robert J. Steinfeld, *The Invention of Free Labor: The Employment Relation in English and American Law and Culture, 1350–1870* (Chapel Hill, 1991); and Christopher L. Tomlins, *The State and the Unions: Labor Relations, Law, and the Organized Labor Movement in America, 1880–1960* (Cambridge, 1985). Sylvester Petro, "Injunctions and Labor Disputes, 1880–1932," *Wake Forest Law Review* 14 (1978), revises the orthodox view about the labor injunction handed down in Felix Frankfurter and Nathan Greene, *The Labor Injunction* (New York, 1930). Daniel Ernst, "The Yellow-Dog Contract and Liberal Reform, 1917–32," *Labor History* 30 (1989), also treats this antiunion device. Morgan O. Reynolds, "An Economic Analysis of the Norris–LaGuardia Act, the Wagner Act, and the Labor Representation Industry," *Journal of Libertarian Studies* 6 (1982), contains valuable insights. George I. Lovell, *Legislative Deferrals: Statutory Ambiguity, Judicial Power, and American Democracy* (Cambridge, 2002), provides a close reading and revisionist interpretation of four landmark labor laws from 1898 to 1935. David Bernstein, *Only One Place of Redress: African Americans, Labor Regulations, and the Courts from Reconstruction to the New Deal* (Durham, 2001), is a unique law-and-economics interpretation drawn from several of the author's law review articles. Armand Thieblot Jr., *The Davis-Bacon Act* (Philadelphia, 1975), discusses one of these acts in detail.

Republican policy in the Civil War and Reconstruction period is treated in Earl Maltz, *Civil Rights, the Constitution, and Congress, 1863–69* (Lawrence, KS, 1990); Maltz, "Reconstruction without Revolution: Republican Civil Rights Theory in the

Era of the Fourteenth Amendment," *Houston Law Review* 24 (1987); and Herman Belz, *A New Birth of Freedom: The Republican Party and Freedmen's Rights, 1861–66* (Westport, 1976). Michael Les Benedict gives a balanced treatment of the problem of Reconstruction in "The Problem of Constitutionalism and Constitutional Liberty in the Reconstruction South," in Kermit Hall and James W. Ely, eds., *An Uncertain Tradition: Constitutionalism and the History of the South* (Athens, GA, 1989).

The dusk of Reconstruction and the position of the Liberal Republicans is examined in John G. Sproat, *"The Best Men": Liberal Reformers in the Gilded Age* (Chicago, 1968), a splenetic assault on the liberals. Fairer treatments can be found in David M. Tucker, *Mugwumps: Public Moralists of the Gilded Age* (Columbia, MO, 1998); William H. Ahern, "Laissez-Faire versus Equal Rights: Liberal Republican and the Negro, 1861–77" (Ph. D. diss., Northwestern University, 1968); and Earle Dudley Ross, *The Liberal Republican Movement* (New York, 1971 [1919]). The older literature is surveyed in Richard Allan Gerber, "The Liberal Republicans of 1872 in Historiographical Perspective," *Journal of American History* 62 (1975).

A good overview of the development of American statism is Robert Higgs, *Crisis and Leviathan: Critical Episodes in the Growth of American Government* (New York, 1987). Race in the Progressive era is the subject of David W. Southern, *The Malignant Heritage: Yankee Progressives and the Negro Question, 1901–14* (Chicago, 1968). The racial impact of the La Follette Seamen's Act can be seen in Jerold S. Auerbach, "Progressives at Sea: The La Follette Act of 1915," *Labor History* 2 (1961). For works on black labor in World War I, see Joseph A. McCartin, "Abortive Reconstruction: Federal War Labor Policies, Union Organization, and the Politics of Race, 1917–20," *Journal of Policy History* 9 (1997); Jane Lang and Harry N. Scheiber, "The Wilson Administration and the Wartime Mobilization of Black Americans, 1917–18," *Labor History* 10 (1969); and Henry P. Guzda, "Social Experiment of the Labor Department: The Division of Negro Economics," *The Public Historian* 4 (1982), and "Labor Department's First Program to Assist Black Workers," *Monthly Labor Review* 105 (June 1982).

The NAACP and AFL campaign against Judge John J. Parker's appointment to the Supreme Court is the subject of Richard L. Watson Jr., "The Defeat of Judge Parker: A Study in Pressure Groups and Politics," *Mississippi Valley Historical Review* 50 (1963), and Kenneth W. Goings, *The NAACP Comes of Age: The Defeat of Judge John J. Parker* (Bloomington, IN, 1990).

Irving Bernstein, *The New Deal Collective Bargaining Policy* (Berkeley, 1950), is an early and still standard work on New Deal policy. Jim F. Couch and William F.

Shugart, *The Political Economy of the New Deal* (Cheltenham, UK, 1998), and Gene Smiley, *Rethinking the Great Depression* (Chicago, 2002), are recent works on the New Deal from a libertarian perspective. James A. Gross, *The Making of the National Labor Relations Board: A Study in Economics, Politics, and the Law* (Albany, NY, 1974), is more pro-CIO. David Plotke, "The Wagner Act, Again: Politics and Labor, 1935–37," *Studies in American Political Development* 3 (1989), is a valuable analysis of the landmark labor act. Other useful treatments include John A. Wettergreen, "The Regulatory Policy of the New Deal," in Robert Eden, ed., *The New Deal Legacy: Critique and Reappraisal* (Westport, 1989), and Daniel Nelson, "The Other New Deal and Labor: The Regulatory State and the Unions, 1933–40," *Journal of Policy History* 13 (2001). James A. Gross, *Broken Promise: The Subversion of U.S. Labor Relations Policy, 1947–94* (Philadelphia, 1995), argues that the ambitious pro-union goals of national labor legislation were betrayed by later administrators.

Many books discuss the New Deal and black Americans. The best are Raymond Wolters, *Negroes and the Great Depression: The Problem of Economic Recovery* (Westport, 1970), and John B. Kirby, *Black American in the Roosevelt Era: Liberalism and Race* (Knoxville, 1980). See also Harvard Sitkoff, *A New Deal for Blacks: The Emergence of Civil Rights as a National Issue* (New York, 1978); Donna Cooper Hamilton, "The NAACP and New Deal Reform Legislation: A Dual Agenda," *Social Service Review* 68 (1994); and Paul Moreno, "An Ambivalent Legacy: Black Americans and the New Deal Political Economy," *Independent Review* 6 (2002). Race-conscious New Deal policies are treated in Mark W. Kruman, "Quotas for Blacks: The PWA and the Black Construction Worker," *Labor History* 16 (1975); August Meier and Elliott Rudwick, "The Origins of Nonviolent Direct Action," in Meier and Rudwick, eds., *Along the Color Line* (Urbana, 1976); and Paul Moreno, "Racial Proportionalism and the Origins of Employment Discrimination Policy, 1933–50," *Journal of Policy History* 8 (1996).

The authoritative treatment of the Fair Employment Practice Committee is Merl E. Reed, *Seedtime for the Modern Civil Rights Movement: The President's Committee on Fair Employment Practice, 1941–46* (Baton Rouge, 1991). Still useful are the older works, Herbert Garfinkel, *When Negroes March: The March on Washington Movement in the Organizational Politics for FEPC* (New York, 1958); Louis Ruchames, *Race, Jobs, and Politics: The Story of FEPC* (New York, 1952); and Louis C. Kesselman, *The Social Politics of FEPC: A Study in Reform Pressure Movements* (Chapel Hill, 1948). James A. Neuchterlein, "The Politics of Civil Rights: The FEPC, 1941–46," *Prologue* 10 (1978), 685–97, is a useful introduction. Recent works that cast a more favorable light on the commission's accomplishments are Andrew E. Kersten, *Race, Jobs, and the War: The FEPC in the Midwest, 1941–46* (Urbana, 2000), and William J. Collins, "Race, Roosevelt, and Wartime Production: Fair Employment in World War II Labor Markets," *American Economic Review* 91 (2001). The commission's *First Report* (Washington, 1945) and *Final Report* (Washington, 1947) are important sources, along with FEPC chairman Malcolm Ross's memoir, *All Manner of Men* (New York, 1948). Some of the records of the FEPC are reproduced in Bruce I. Friend, and Charles Zaid, eds., *Selected Documents from Records of the Committee on Fair Employment Practice,* 213 reels (Glen Rock, NJ, 1970).

The National Labor Relations Board is treated in Michael Jordan, "The NLRB Racial Discrimination Decisions, 1935–41: The Empiric Process of Administration and the Inner Eye of Racism," *Connecticut Law Review* 24 (1991); Michael I. Sovern, "The National Labor Relations Act and Racial Discrimination," *Columbia Law Review* 62 (1962); Daniel H. Pollitt, "The NLRB and Race Hate Propaganda in Union Organization Drives," *Stanford Law Review* 17 (1965); and John E. Drotning, "Race Propaganda: The NLRB's Impact on Employer Subtlety and the Effect of This Propaganda on Voting," *Labor Law Journal* (1967).

Presidential histories focusing on civil rights include William C. Berman, *The Politics of Civil Rights in the Truman Administration* (Columbus, 1970); Donald R. McCoy and Richard T. Ruetten, *Quest and Response: Minority Rights and the Truman Administration* (Lawrence, KS, 1973); Robert F. Burk, *The Eisenhower Administration and Black Civil Rights* (Knoxville, 1984); and Carl M. Brauer, *John F. Kennedy and the Second Reconstruction* (New York, 1977). Hugh Davis Graham, *The Civil Rights Era: Origins and Development of National Policy, 1960–72* (New York, 1990), is an outstanding work that covers several administrations. Dean J. Kotlowski, *Nixon's Civil Rights: Politics, Principle, and Policy* (Cambridge, 2001), is notable for the credit it gives Nixon on civil rights issues. Arthur Fletcher provides a memoir of the Nixon effort in *The Silent Sell-Out: Government Betrayal of Blacks to the Craft Unions* (New York, 1973). Longtime NAACP labor secretary Herbert Hill treats many issues of labor discrimination in *Black Labor and the American Legal System: Race, Work, and the Law* (Washington, 1977).

Jack Greenberg, *Race Relations and American Law* (New York, 1959), is a comprehensive treatment of legal aspects of the civil rights period. In the sphere of employment, see Michael Sovern, *Legal Restraints on Racial Discrimination in Employment* (New York, 1966). On state fair employment efforts, see Arthur Earl Bonfield, "The Origins and Development of American Fair Employment Legislation," *Iowa Law Review* 52 (1967); Leon Mayhew, *Law and Equal Opportunity: A Study of the Massachusetts Commission Against Discrimination* (Cambridge, 1968); and Jay Anders Higbee, *Development and Administration of the New York State Law Against Discrimination* (University, AL, 1966). On the effect of the FEPCs, Herbert Hill, "Twenty Years of State FEPCs: A Critical Analysis with Recommendations," *Buffalo Law Review* 14 (1965), is the principal critical treatment; this issue of the *Buffalo Law Review* contains a symposium on the FEPCs. See also Malcolm H. Liggett, "The Efficacy of State Fair Employment Practices Commissions," *Industrial and Labor Relations Review* 22 (1969). More recent works include Paul Moreno, *From Direct Action to Affirmative Action: Fair Employment Law and Policy in America, 1932–72* (Baton Rouge, 1997), and William J. Collins, "The Labor Market Impact of State-Level Anti-Discrimination Laws, 1940–60," National Bureau of Economic Research Working Paper (2002).

Several recent works have examined the effect of the cold war on the civil rights movement; among them are Mary L. Dudziak, *Cold War Civil Rights: Race and the Image of American Democracy* (Princeton, 2000), 11–12; Azza Salama Layton, *International Politics and Civil Rights Policies in the United States, 1941–60* (New York, 2000); and Thomas Borstelmann, *The Cold War and the Color Line: American Race Relations in the Global Arena* (Cambridge, 2001). A recent view to the contrary, arguing that the cold war undermined civil rights progress, is Jacquelyn Dowd Hall, "The Long Civil Rights Movement and the Political Uses of the Past," *Journal of American History* 91 (2005).

Thomas B. and Mary D. Edsall, *Chain Reaction: The Impact of Race, Rights, and Taxes on American Politics* (New York, 1991), is a popular account of reaction to 1960s civil rights and liberalism. Ronald Radosh, *Divided They Fell: The Demise of the Democratic Party, 1964–96* (New York, 1996), is an updated, more balanced account. On affirmative action, Herman Belz, *Equality Transformed: A Quarter-Century of Affirmative Action* (New Brunswick, 1991), is deeply researched and critical. Robert J. Weiss, *"We Want Jobs": A History of Affirmative Action* (New York, 1997), is more sympathetic, as is the work by sociologist John D. Skrentny, *The Ironies of Affirmative Action: Politics, Culture, and Justice in America* (Chicago, 1996). Hugh Davis Graham explores further ironies in *Collision Course: The Strange Convergence of Affirmative Action and Immigration Policy in America* (New York, 2002).

Histories of civil rights policy in the Reagan years include Raymond Wolters,

Right Turn: William Bradford Reynolds, the Reagan Administration, and Black Civil Rights (New Brunswick, 1996); Nicolas Laham, *The Reagan Presidency and the Politics of Race* (Westport, 1998); Robert R. Detlefsen, *Civil Rights under Reagan* (San Francisco, 1991); and Norman C. Amaker, *Civil Rights and the Reagan Administration* (Washington, 1988). Gary L. McDowell, "Affirmative Inaction," *Policy Review* 48 (1989), tells the story of the administration's failure to end affirmative action by executive order.

BLACKS AND THE LABOR MOVEMENT—OVERVIEWS

Charles H. Wesley, *Negro Labor in the United States: A Study in American Economic History* (New York, 1927), and Lorenzo Greene and Carter G. Woodson, *The Negro Wage Earner* (New York, 1930), were pioneer works that are still valuable, especially as representatives of an older black faith in competition. Sterling D. Spero and Abram L. Harris's classic, *The Black Worker: The Negro and the Labor Movement* (New York, 1930), is comprehensive, detailed, and fair. Horace R. Cayton and George S. Mitchell, *Black Workers and the New Unions* (Chapel Hill, 1939), treats the communist and early CIO organizing drive in a sympathetic light. Herbert Northrup, *Organized Labor and the Negro* (New York, 1944), carries the story through the wartime FEPC years and was part of the Carnegie-Myrdal study that became *An American Dilemma* (New York, 1944). Two additional Northrup summaries are "Industry's Racial Employment Practices," in Arthur M. Ross and Herbert Hill, eds., *Employment, Race, and Poverty* (New York, 1967), and "Race Discrimination in Unions," *American Mercury* (July 1945).

Paul Norgren, "Negro Labor and Its Problems: A Research Memorandum," the principal source for the labor sections of *An American Dilemma,* is available on microfilm. It contains work by Lloyd Bailer and Herbert Northrup and discusses some industries not previously or subsequently treated. Robert C. Weaver, *Negro Labor: A National Problem* (New York, 1946), deals with many important aspects of black labor in the New Deal and war years. In addition to Weaver's articles in *Opportunity* and *Crisis,* see "Recent Events in Negro-Union Relationships," *Journal of Political Economy* 52 (1944), and "Negro Labor since 1929," *Journal of Negro History* 35 (1950).

Ray Marshall's work was the most important in the next generation. His many works include "Union Racial Problems in the South," *Industrial Relations* 1 (1962); "The Negro and Organized Labor," *Journal of Negro Education* 32 (1963); "Industrialization and Race Relations in the Southern United States," in Hunter, ed., *In-*

dustrialisation and Race Relations; "Equal Employment Opportunities: Problems and Prospects," *Labor Law Journal* 16 (1965); *Organized Labor and the Negro* (New York, 1965); *Labor in the South* (Cambridge, 1967); and *The Negro Worker* (New York, 1967). Herman D. Bloch also provided several useful overviews in these years. See "Labor and the Negro, 1866–1910," *Journal of Negro History* 50 (1965), and "Craft Unions and the Negro in Historical Perspective," *Journal of Negro History* 43 (1958).

More recent syntheses include William H. Harris, *The Harder We Run: Black Workers since the Civil War* (New York, 1982), and Philip S. Foner, *Organized Labor and the Black Worker,* 2d ed. (New York, 1981). Three useful essay collections are Jacobson, *The Negro and the American Labor Movement,* and Cantor, *Black Labor in America,* which contains articles from a volume of *Labor History* devoted to race relations; and John H. Bracey, August Meier, and Elliott Rudwick, eds., *Black Workers and Organized Labor* (Belmont, CA, 1971).

Warren C. Whatley provides a balanced account of black strikebreaking in "African-American Strikebreaking from the Civil War to the New Deal," *Social Science History* 17 (1993). Labor conflict and violence is also treated in Susan Olzak, "Labor Unrest, Immigration, and Ethnic Conflict in Urban America, 1880–1914," *American Journal of Sociology* 94 (1989), 1303–33. Stephen H. Norwood, *Strikebreaking and Intimidation: Mercenaries and Masculinity in Twentieth-Century America* (Chapel Hill, 2002), includes a chapter on blacks that gives a gender or cultural studies spin.

BLACK WORKERS AND THE LABOR MOVEMENT
THROUGH RECONSTRUCTION

Abolitionist attitudes are treated in Jonathan A. Glickstein, "Poverty Is Not Slavery: American Abolitionists and the Competitive Labor Market," in Lewis Perry and Michael Fellman, eds., *Antislavery Reconsidered: New Perspectives on the Abolitionists* (Baton Rouge, 1979); Bernard Mandel, *Labor, Free and Slave: Workingmen and the Anti-Slavery Movement in the United States* (New York, 1955); Joseph G. Rayback, "The American Workingman and the Antislavery Crusade," *Journal of Economic History* 3 (1943); Williston H. Lofton, "Abolition and Labor," *Journal of Negro History* 33 (1948); and Marcus Cunliffe, *Chattel Slavery and Wage Slavery: The Anglo-American Context, 1830–60* (Athens, GA, 1979). Philip S. Foner and Herbert Shapiro, eds., *Northern Labor and Antislavery: A Documentary History*

(Westport, 1994), emphasizes the sympathy of labor leaders for abolitionism, and contains many useful documents on both sides of the issue. The problems of unions and black workers are treated in Williston H. Lofton, "Northern Labor and the Negro during the Civil War," *Journal of Negro History* 34 (1949), and M. Ray Della Jr., "The Problems of Negro Labor in the 1850s," *Maryland Historical Magazine* 66 (1971). Albon P. Man Jr., "Labor Competition and the New York Draft Riots of 1863," *Journal of Negro History* 36 (1951), discusses the labor aspect of the most deadly racial clash in American history.

Sumner E. Matison, "The Labor Movement and the Negro during Reconstruction," *Journal of Negro History* 33 (1948), continues the story after the war. Bettye C. Thomas, "A Nineteenth-Century Black-Operated Shipyard, 1866–84," *Journal of Negro History* 59 (1974), discusses the enterprise begun by Isaac Myers. Herman D. Bloch, "The New York City Negro and Occupational Eviction, 1860–1910," *International Review of Social History* 5 (1960), recounts the fortunes of the black worker in the North.

BLACKS AND LABOR BEFORE WORLD WAR I

The broad context of southern development is treated in a progressive vein in C. Vann Woodward, *Origins of the New South, 1877–1913* (Baton Rouge, 1951), and has been updated in Edward Ayers, *The Promise of the New South: Life after Reconstruction* (New York, 1992).

Robert Higgs, *Competition and Coercion: Blacks in the American Economy, 1865–1914* (Cambridge, 1977), provides a clear and balanced overview of black economic progress from the public choice perspective. Also useful are Jay Mandle, *Not Slave, Not Free: The African-American Economic Experience since the Civil War* (Durham, 1992), and Gerald D. Jaynes, *Branches Without Roots: Genesis of the Black Working Class in the American South, 1862–82* (New York, 1986). William Cohen, *At Freedom's Edge: Black Mobility and the Southern White Quest for Racial Control, 1861–1915* (Baton Rouge, 1991), is an excellent treatment of the extent and limits of black physical mobility.

The revival of interest in the oft-neglected matter of black business and entrepreneurship is displayed in Robert C. Kenzer, *Enterprising Southerners: Black Economic Success in North Carolina, 1865–1915* (Charlottesville, 1997), and "The Black Businessman in the Postwar South: North Carolina, 1865–80," *Business History Review* 63 (1989); John Sibley Butler, *Entrepreneurship and Self-Help among Black*

Americans: A Reconsideration of Race and Economics (Albany, NY, 1991); and Margaret Levenstein, "African American Entrepreneurship: The View from the 1910 Census," *Business and Economic History* 24 (1995).

Black involvement in the Knights of Labor is covered in Melton A. McLaurin, *The Knights of Labor in the South* (Westport, 1978); Sidney Kessler, "The Organization of Negroes in the Knights of Labor," *Journal of Negro History* 37 (1952), a condensed version of his 1950 M.A. thesis at Columbia University; Kenneth Kann, "The Knights of Labor and the Southern Black Worker," *Labor History* 18 (1977); and Claudia Miner, "The 1886 Convention of the Knights of Labor," *Phylon* 44 (1983). Bernard Mandel, "Samuel Gompers and the Negro Workers, 1886–1914," *Journal of Negro History* 40 (1955), makes no apology for the AFL founder.

BLACKS AND UNIONS IN THE TWENTIETH CENTURY

The Great Migration to the urban North is explored in U.S. Department of Labor, Division of Negro Economics, *Negro Migration in 1916–17* (New York, 1969 [1919]), and Alferdteen Harrison, ed., *Black Exodus: The Great Migration from the American South* (Jackson, MS, 1991). William J. Collins, "When the Tide Turned: Immigration and the Delay of the Great Black Migration," *Journal of Economic History* 57 (1997), provides a valuable new interpretation of the timing of the movement. Cliff Brown, "The Role of Employers in Split Labor Markets: An Event-Structure Analysis of Racial Conflict and AFL Organizing, 1917–19," *Social Forces* 79 (2000), looks at black entry into steel and meatpacking during World War I. Ira De A. Reid, *Negro Membership in American Labor Unions* (New York, 1969 [1930]), is the standard National Urban League report on the eve of the depression. A symposium on race and the CIO, focusing on the role of communist unions, can be found in *International Labor and Working Class History* 44 (1993) and 46 (1994).

Postwar analyses include Scott Greer, *Last Man In: Racial Access to Union Power* (Glencoe, IL, 1959), and Lloyd H. Bailer, "Organized Labor and Racial Minorities," *Annals of the American Academy of Political and Social Science* 274 (1951). For the problem of race and nepotism, see George Strauss and Sidney Ingerman, "Public Policy and Discrimination in Apprenticeship," *Hastings Law Journal* 16 (1965), and F. Ray Marshall and Vernon M. Briggs Jr., *The Negro and Apprenticeship* (Baltimore, 1967),

Alan Draper, *Conflict of Interest: Organized Labor and the Civil Rights Movement, 1954–68* (Ithaca, 1994), explores the civil rights movement. William J. Gould, *Black Workers in White Unions: Job Discrimination in the United States* (Ithaca,

1977), is strong in the postwar period. James A. Geschwender, *Class, Race, and Worker Insurgency: The League of Revolutionary Black Workers* (Cambridge, 1977), and Peter Henle, "Some Reflections on Organized Labor and the New Militants," *Monthly Labor Review* 92 (1969), discuss the Black Power movement within organized labor. Bayard Rustin delivered an exhortation for black-union teamwork in "The Blacks and the Unions," *Harper's,* May 1971.

Orley Ashenfelter, "Racial Discrimination and Trade Unionism," *Journal of Political Economy* 80 (1972), considers the racial-economic effects of labor organization. On the impact of civil rights laws and affirmative action policies, see Herbert Hammerman and Marvin Rogoff, "Unions and Title VII of the Civil Rights Act of 1964," *Monthly Labor Review* 99 (April 1976). Herbert Hill continued his attack on union discrimination in "The AFL-CIO and the Black Worker: Twenty-Five Years after the Merger," *Journal of Intergroup Relations* 10 (1982). Alfred W. Blumrosen, the chief architect of affirmative action in the EEOC, wrote many articles on the development, collected in *Black Employment and the Law* (New Brunswick, 1971). A later analysis is in Blumrosen, *Modern Law: The Law Transmission System and Equal Employment Opportunity* (Madison, 1993).

On pubic-sector unionism, see Sam Zagoria, ed., *Public Workers and Public Unions* (Englewood Cliffs, NJ, 1972); Michael H. Moskow et al., *Collective Bargaining in Public Employment* (New York, 1970); and Norma M. Riccucci, *Women, Minorities, and Unions in the Public Sector* (Westport, 1990). On the controversial New York City teachers strike of 1968, see Diane Ravitch, *The Great School Wars: A History of the New York City Public Schools* (New York, 1988); Jerald E. Podair, *The Strike That Changed New York: Blacks, Whites, and the Ocean Hill–Brownsville Crisis* (New Haven, 2002); Maurice R. Berube, ed., *Confrontation at Ocean Hill–Brownsville: The New York School Strikes of 1968* (New York, 1969); and Melvin Urofsky, ed., *Why Teachers Strike: Teachers' Rights and Community Control* (New York, 1970).

Index